New St. Joseph

Handbook for Proclaimers of the Word

LITURGICAL YEAR B

2018

By
Rev. Jude Winkler, OFM Conv.

**WITH THE "NEW AMERICAN BIBLE" TEXT
FROM THE REVISED SUNDAY LECTIONARY**

C.B.   P.C.

CATHOLIC BOOK PUBLISHING CORP.
New Jersey

ACKNOWLEDGMENTS

The Scriptural Readings and Responsorial Psalms are taken from the *Lectionary for Mass* © 2001, 1998, 1997, 1986, 1970 by Confraternity of Christian Doctrine, Inc., Washington, DC. All rights reserved. No part of this work may be reproduced or transmitted in any form or by any means, electronic or mechanical, including photocopying, recording, or by any information storage and retrieval system, without permission in writing from the copyright owner.

The English translation of some Psalm Responses, some Alleluia Verses and Gospel Verses, the Lenten Gospel Acclamations, and the Conclusions to the Readings from *Lectionary for Mass* © 1969, 1981, 1997, International Commission on English in the Liturgy Corporation. All rights reserved.

The poetic English translations of the Sequences of the Roman Missal are taken from *The Roman Missal* approved by the National Conference of Catholic Bishops of the United States © 1964 by the National Catholic Welfare Conference, Inc. All rights reserved.

(T-85)

ISBN 978-0-89942-086-8

© 2017 by Catholic Book Publishing Corp., N.J.
Printed in the U.S.A.
www.catholicbookpublishing.com

CONTENTS

CONTENTS

INTRODUCTION

THE WORD OF GOD

"The word of God is living and effective, sharper than any two-edged sword, penetrating even between soul and spirit, joints and marrow, and able to discern reflections and thoughts of the heart" (Hebrews 4:12).

With these words, the author of the Letter to the Hebrews speaks of the power of the word of God. It has a profound effect both upon creation and within our hearts. It was by the word that God created the heavens and the earth. The word is effective, for in Hebrew theology the word makes present and real the things that it proclaims. Thus, God speaks, and those things come into existence. God even shares the power of the word with us, for he commands Adam to name the animals he had created. By naming the animals, Adam is given dominion over all of creation.

The word is the communication of God's will. He reveals his word to the prophets who then proclaim it to the people of Israel. He gives his law that teaches them how to walk in God's ways. (Remember, the Ten Commandments are also called the "decalogue," which means the "ten words.") He sends wisdom to reveal his mysteries to his beloved chosen people. Wisdom instructs the foolish and brings them to the path of righteousness.

In the New Testament, we hear that the word of God is Jesus, the Son of God. The word of God existed in the beginning. It was communicated to God's people, Israel, throughout their history. Then, in the fullness of time, it was made flesh and dwelt among us.

Jesus proclaimed the word of God in word and deed to those who would listen and change their hearts. He promised the gift of the Holy Spirit so that the community could remember what he had done and understand what it all meant.

As the community of believers grew and matured, it realized that it needed to preserve their words about Jesus. Members of the community wrote letters, gospels, collections of stories, and even prophetic revelations so that they would know the life and teaching of Jesus and also what those things meant for their daily lives.

MINISTERS OF THE WORD

The Church affirmed that this word (the New Testament) and the word of revelation known as the Hebrew Scriptures (the Old Testament) were inspired by the Holy Spirit. She entrusted that word to the community. Some in the community were called to copy and preserve the word, others to study it, others to proclaim it liturgically, others to preach on how to apply it to their lives, etc.

As lectors, you share in the tradition of proclaiming the word to the community. This is not a responsibility to be taken lightly. God has called you to this mission. The Spirit has given you the gift of being able to present the word to the community and, even more important, the gift of being able to discern its meaning for yourself.

GIFT OF THE SPIRIT

Saint Paul speaks about how the Spirit gives these gifts to members of the community. These gifts are called charisms. Everyone has received gifts from the Lord that were given for the good of that community. Not all the gifts are the same. Not everyone has received the same gift. This is important, for it means that we need everyone and their gifts to make the community complete. If we do not allow certain members of the community to share their gifts, we will be subtly rejecting the gifts that the Spirit of God has given to us, and we will be lacking something of what we need to grow in the Spirit.

Your call to be a lector in the community is not your own choice, nor is it the choice of the pastor or committee that invited you to read at Mass. Rather, it is the Spirit who has called you. The Holy Spirit worked in and through various means (the pastor, the committee, the hunger in your own heart that made you volunteer for service, etc.) to bring you to this ministry.

Now, you must discern how to respond in the best manner possible to that call. It is not enough to say that if the Spirit called you, the Spirit will provide what is needed. As with all gifts of the Spirit, we must work to perform our ministry well. We are, as Saint Paul says in the First Letter to the Thessalonians, God's coworkers. While this is God's work, he has entrusted it to us. It has been said that we must do everything as if it depended upon us, realizing that it all depends upon the Lord.

This preparation involves working on the technique of presentation, but also working on our own hearts so that the things that we proclaim might be proclaimed with a profound faith.

PREPARING THE READING

A first logical step in preparing for this service is to read and reread the text that we are going to proclaim. It is not enough to show up in the sacristy a few minutes before the Mass and read over the text once or twice. Preferably, we should have read it early in the week and often during the week.

This text should be read aloud. It might seem a bit embarrassing to read it out loud to ourselves, but it is essential. There are words and phrases that might appear to present no difficulty when we are reading them silently but that end up being much more difficult when we read them out loud.

We must check out the pronunciation of difficult words (especially unusual names). A Pronunciation Guide will be found on pages 399-409 to help you in this task.

If you do not know the meaning of certain words, it is always advisable to do a bit of research in a dictionary or some other source book.

Some of the liturgical texts that you will read are rather short and difficult to understand if you do not know their context. Thus, it might be a good idea to go to the Bible and read at least the entire chapter in which your reading occurs.

A good amount of information has been provided in this handbook so that you might understand better what you are reading (both alongside of the readings and in the appendices at the end of the handbook). If those are not enough, you could check in your parish library or with your liturgy committee or lector coordinator for recommendations for other resources. It might even be a good project to study at least one book of the Bible each year as part of your study preparations for your ministry. Adult education classes are also a good aid to one's own personal growth.

PHYSICAL CONSIDERATIONS

There are also a number of physical considerations in your presentations.

Know when you are supposed to read. Check the schedule and be responsible in either being there when you are assigned or in arranging for a substitute when you cannot be present. (Each parish has a different way of arranging for substitute readers.)

Dress appropriately. You should be drawing attention to the word of God and not to yourself. You should dress in a simple and yet respectful manner, which shows that you recognize the dignity of what you are doing.

Walk to the lectern with a dignified, deliberate pace. Do not run. Do not walk so slowly that people feel uncomfortable. In theory, only one thing should be happening in the liturgy at a time. Thus, the lector should approach the lectern after the Collect and not during it (unless you have been instructed by the coordinator of lectors to do otherwise).

Know which year you are reading. If your Sunday Lectionary has A, B, and C readings or your Weekday Lectionary has year I and II readings, you should know which year it is.

Know your microphone system. Each system is different. Each microphone has an optimal distance and direction from which you should read. Some systems have cut-offs that will block the sound if you are too loud. Others are temperamental. Before you ever read for Mass, make sure that you have tried out the system. This should be done at a time when it will not disturb people who are trying to pray in church, e.g., immediately before Mass.

Read questions as questions. Read phrases that end with exclamation points with emphasis. Know the mood of the reading. If the author is being dramatic, the reading should have a bit of drama. Try not to be monotonous in your reading.

Be careful with certain sounds when you read. The letters "S" and "P" can be picked up by the sound system as a hissing or an explosive sound.

Do not make gestures that render you the center of attention. Your hands, in fact, should be placed where they will not distract. If you are nervous, you might hold on to the sides of the lectern.

Read from the Lectionary. There is a certain dignity to that which you are doing. You should not be reading from a missalette or from this handbook. If you have prepared the reading from one of these other sources, check out where the reading is on the page of the Lectionary so that you will not have to search for it when you stand up to read.

Do not read too quickly or too slowly. Make sure you pause when you reach the end of a phrase. (This is much easier now that the Lectionary has divided the reading into sense lines.) Read slowly enough that you communicate the dignity of the occasion, without becoming overly dramatic. If the reading is a hymn, read it as such (i.e., poetry is always read in a more dramatic manner than simple narratives).

Try to look up during the reading. When you first start reading, this might be both difficult and a bit artificial, but it is always good to keep eye contact with the audience.

Know whether you will be reading the Responsorial Psalm or whether it will be sung. It is not a good idea to arrive at the psalm and then glance at the organist with a quizzical look on your face.

A few people have the habit of memorizing the reading and then proclaiming it without reading it. While that is admirable from a certain point of view, it is also very distracting. People almost always are more attentive to the reader's remarkable memory than to what is actually being proclaimed.

If you make a mistake, do not become nervous or feel anxious. If you judge it appropriate, simply reread the phrase correctly. If needed, you could make a comment that lets the community know that you have made a mistake (e.g., "I'm sorry, I started the wrong reading").

This ministry is so important to the faith life of the community that it is essential for its ministers to have a sense of humility. Ask for your friends or family members to give you an occasional honest critique on your reading style. If you are not reading well, admit it and seek help. If, after having sought help, you still cannot read well, it is important to be humble enough to admit it and suggest to your community that it might be better for you to serve it in some other ministry.

GOD'S WORD AND OUR HEARTS

Having spoken about a number of the physical considerations in reading for the liturgy, we now must speak about some of the questions of the Spirit.

We have to allow God's word to speak to us. If we are not listening to God's word at the deepest part of our heart, then those who are listening to us will perceive that we are reading and not proclaiming. They will understand without our ever saying it that we really do not believe what we are proclaiming.

This means that we must pray God's word. We have to ask ourselves what this word means for us today. We have to allow the Spirit of God to make it real and alive. Just as the Spirit inspired the sacred authors to write these texts in the first place, so now that same Spirit breathes into our hearts so that we can make the word of God alive again for ourselves and our community.

We have to place our own experiences in the context of the word. It is a wonderful thing if we find ourselves asking, "What does God's word say to me in these circumstances?" God's word is not a history book about things long since dead, it is a presentation of salvation history that is still alive and vitally important today.

Every reading and every Gospel should in some way call us to conversion. If, after preparing the readings for a Sunday, you cannot say that the readings are calling you to change even one thing in your life, you have probably missed the point. It is not a bad idea to ask what you would preach about the reading if you had the opportunity. (Some parishes, in fact, have preparation meetings in which parishioners suggest to the preachers what might be said that weekend.)

Become that which you read. Your actions on a daily basis will proclaim loud and clear whether what you are proclaiming on Sunday are "just words" or whether they are words that are like a two-edged sword. People do look at what you are doing outside of the church, and they are either edified or scandalized by whether you are living the word of God or in some way denying it.

Finally, if possible, arrive in church well before the beginning of the Mass so that you can pray to the Spirit to guide you in your ministry that day.

May God bless you in your ministry.

Shalom,

Fr. Jude Winkler, OFM Conv.

A LECTOR'S PRAYER

EVERLASTING Father,
in the beginning your Word brought forth life
and called us into being.

In the fullness of time,
Jesus, your Son, the Word became flesh.

In the synagogue at Nazareth
and on the hills of Galilee,
he taught the good news of salvation,
the Gospel of life and of truth.

In an act of everlasting love
he opened his arms on the cross
and by his death destroyed all death,
leading us to everlasting life.

Lord, open my lips,
that my mouth may declare your praise.
Open my heart,
that I may proclaim the Word made flesh.
Strengthen my mind,
that I may live the holy words I speak.

For your Word is all holy and all true
and lives in glory with you and the Holy Spirit,
one God, forever and ever. Amen.

December 3, 2017

FIRST SUNDAY OF ADVENT

Lect.
No. 2

FIRST READING:
Isaiah 63:16b–17, 19b; 64:2–7

This passage is taken from the third part of the Book of the Prophet Isaiah. Unlike the second part, which was written by Deutero-Isaiah (chs. 40—55) and emphasized the overwhelming mercy of the LORD, this section was written by an individual or group after the end of the exile (c. 539 B.C.), and it emphasizes the necessity for conversion. Israel cannot hope to experience the restoration promised in Deutero-Isaiah until it converts its ways.

Yet, even that is impossible if God does not intervene in a miraculous way in order to give Israel the strength to change its ways. Left on our own, we will never find the strength and courage to choose the good and reject evil. We desperately need the grace of God to use this Advent as a season of conversion.

This author (as well as we ourselves) trusts that God will provide this grace, for God is a loving parent who would never abandon his beloved children.

God is also a potter who carefully shapes our hearts to respond to his call.

A reading from the Book of the Prophet Isaiah

You, LORD, are our father,
our redeemer you are named forever.
Why do you let us wander, O LORD, from your ways,
and harden our hearts so that we fear you not?
Return for the sake of your servants,
the tribes of your heritage.
Oh, that you would rend the heavens and come down,
with the mountains quaking before you,
while you wrought awesome deeds we could not hope for,
such as they had not heard of from of old.
No ear has ever heard, no eye ever seen, any God but you
doing such deeds for those who wait for him.
Would that you might meet us doing right,
that we were mindful of you in our ways!
Behold, you are angry, and we are sinful;
all of us have become like unclean people,
all our good deeds are like polluted rags;
we have all withered like leaves,
and our guilt carries us away like the wind.
There is none who calls upon your name,
who rouses himself to cling to you;
for you have hidden your face from us
and have delivered us up to our guilt.
Yet, O LORD, you are our father;
we are the clay and you the potter:
we are all the work of your hands.

The word of the Lord.

| Lect.
No. 2 | **RESPONSORIAL PSALM: Ps 80:2-3, 15-16, 18-19 (℟.: 4)** |

This psalm continues the theme found in the First Reading. God is omnipotent, the LORD of Israel and king of the heavens and the earth. He sits upon the cherubim (a reference to the angels found on the Ark of the Covenant). Yet God is also a loving shepherd who cares for his flock with gentle concern.

Because of this, we trust that God both can and will intervene on our behalf. God will not abandon us to the prison that we have made for ourselves with our sinful choices. God loves us so much that he will not merely watch from the heavens as we destroy everything that is good and precious in our lives. Rather, God will intervene in a powerful way to teach us his ways.

This is exactly what we are celebrating throughout Advent: the fact that God offers us new life both through the birth of his Son in Bethlehem and through the sacraments that continue Jesus' presence in our lives.

℟. **Lord, make us turn to you; let us see your face and we shall be saved.**

O shepherd of Israel, hearken,
  from your throne upon the cherubim, shine forth.
Rouse your power,
  and come to save us.

℟. **Lord, make us turn to you; let us see your face and we shall be saved.**

Once again, O LORD of hosts,
  look down from heaven, and see;
take care of this vine,
  and protect what your right hand has planted,
  the son of man whom you yourself made strong.

℟. **Lord, make us turn to you; let us see your face and we shall be saved.**

May your help be with the man of your right hand,
  with the son of man whom you yourself made strong.
Then we will no more withdraw from you;
  give us new life, and we will call upon your name.

℟. **Lord, make us turn to you; let us see your face and we shall be saved.**

PASTORAL REFLECTIONS

When we pray the Responsorial Psalm, we are continuing a long tradition (almost 3,000 years old). In a mystical way, we can sense the communion of saints (living and deceased) who join us in worship in this liturgy. It is as if the divisions of space and time are overcome in this great act of praise.

Lect.
No. 2

SECOND READING: 1 Corinthians 1:3-9

The Second Reading speaks of the second coming. The First Sunday of Advent emphasizes Jesus' return in glory at the end of time and not his coming in his birth at Bethlehem. This continues a theme developed over the past couple of Sundays concerning how we must convert our lives in order to be ready for the Day of the LORD (whether it be the end of the world or our own death).

We might also observe the importance of Jesus the Christ in the greeting of the First Letter to the Corinthians. This community had overemphasized the importance of the Holy Spirit in their spiritual lives. In order to balance their theology, Saint Paul speaks of how Christ must be the center of our lives and our love. He is the one who makes our lives and our hearts complete.

A reading from the first Letter of Saint Paul to the Corinthians

Brothers and sisters:
Grace to you and peace from God our Father
and the Lord Jesus Christ.

I give thanks to my God always on your account
   for the grace of God bestowed on you in Christ Jesus,
   that in him you were enriched in every way,
   with all discourse and all knowledge,
   as the testimony to Christ was confirmed among you,
   so that you are not lacking in any spiritual gift
   as you wait for the revelation of our Lord Jesus Christ.
He will keep you firm to the end,
   irreproachable on the day of our Lord Jesus Christ.
God is faithful,
   and by him you were called to fellowship with his Son, Jesus Christ our Lord.

The word of the Lord.

Lect.
No. 2

ALLELUIA: Psalm 85:8

The Alleluia Verse continues the call for an intervention so that we might experience God's love in our lives. This is the meaning of salvation: to live in God's love.

℟. **Alleluia, alleluia.**

Show us, Lord, your love;
and grant us your salvation.

℟. **Alleluia, alleluia.**

Lect. No. 2

GOSPEL: Mark 13:33-37

In the earliest days of the Church, Christians believed that Jesus was going to return in glory within a very short while. As time passed, they came to realize that it might be quite some time before Jesus did come. Thus, they began to speak about the second coming as something that would happen as unexpectedly as the arrival of a thief in the night.

We do not know how long we are going to live. This does not mean that we should live in terror, but rather that we should live with the proper perspective. We must live each day as something precious, for there might not be another day.

We must live today as if it were our first day, last day, and only day.

A reading from the holy Gospel according to Mark

Jesus said to his disciples:
"Be watchful! Be alert!
You do not know when the time will come.
It is like a man traveling abroad.
He leaves home and places his servants in charge,
    each with his own work,
    and orders the gatekeeper to be on the watch.
Watch, therefore;
    you do not know when the lord of the house is
        coming,
    whether in the evening, or at midnight,
    or at cockcrow, or in the morning.
May he not come suddenly and find you sleeping.
What I say to you, I say to all: 'Watch!'"

The Gospel of the Lord.

PASTORAL REFLECTIONS

Advent is a season of expectation (waiting and preparing for the celebration of the birth of Jesus and also for his return in glory). It is a period to convert our hearts and also to live in hope (as we wait for that which has not yet arrived).

This is why it is important not to anticipate our celebration of Christmas. If we begin listening to Christmas carols and putting up our Christmas decorations right after Thanksgiving, then when Christmas finally arrives, we will greet it with a sense of relief that we can finally get it over with (for the preparations had dragged on for a month already). If we wait a little longer with our Christmas preparations (and possibly simplify them a bit), then we will have the energy to truly celebrate Christmas and its octave the way that they should be celebrated.

December 8, 2017

THE IMMACULATE CONCEPTION OF THE BLESSED VIRGIN MARY

Lect. No. 689 **FIRST READING: Genesis 3:9-15, 20**

On this feast of the Immaculate Conception, we read about the entrance of sin into the world and the punishment that we received because of it.

The first effect of sin is alienation: from God, from each other, and even from nature.

Before they sinned, Adam and Eve were naked, but they felt no shame. They had been living in a state of pure innocence. After their sin they felt only shame. They hid themselves and ran away from God, the one who loved them most. They blamed each other and even the snake for their fall.

God punished the man, the woman, and the snake. The man's punishment, which we do not hear in this passage, was to work hard for a living but never to receive a just recompense. The woman suffers childbirth pains. The snake loses its legs and crawls on its belly.

We also hear that the woman and her offspring will live in perpetual enmity with the serpent and his offspring. Satan would torment humanity, but Jesus,

A reading from the Book of Genesis

After the man, Adam, had eaten of the tree,
the LORD God called to the man and asked him,
"Where are you?"
He answered, "I heard you in the garden;
but I was afraid, because I was naked,
so I hid myself."
Then he asked, "Who told you that you were naked?
You have eaten, then,
from the tree of which I had forbidden you to eat!"
The man replied, "The woman whom you put here
with me—
she gave me fruit from the tree, and so I ate it."
The LORD God then asked the woman,
"Why did you do such a thing?"
The woman answered, "The serpent tricked me into
it, so I ate it."

Then the LORD God said to the serpent:
"Because you have done this, you shall be banned
from all the animals
and from all the wild creatures;
on your belly shall you crawl,
and dirt shall you eat
all the days of your life.
I will put enmity between you and the woman,
and between your offspring and hers;
he will strike at your head,
while you strike at his heel."

born of an immaculate mother, would deliver us from our slavery to sin.

The man called his wife Eve,
   because she became the mother of all the living.

The word of the Lord.

Lect. No. 689

RESPONSORIAL PSALM: Ps 98:1, 2-3ab, 3cd-4 (℟.: 1a)

As we meditate upon the meaning of this feast, that God prepared the Blessed Virgin Mary in a miraculous way to be the mother of his Son, we are filled with gratitude and wonder. We break into song to celebrate God's goodness.

"The LORD has made his salvation known." There are two understandings of salvation in the New Testament. In Saint Paul's writings, we will be saved during the final judgment at the end of time. Jesus will intercede for us so that we might obtain the fullness of God's mercy.

According to Saint Luke, salvation is something that we already experience here upon the earth. Jesus has come into our lives with great signs of mercy and love. We already experience that here and now. Our lives have meaning because Jesus is a part of them.

℟. **Sing to the Lord a new song, for he has done marvelous deeds.**

Sing to the LORD a new song,
   for he has done wondrous deeds;
His right hand has won victory for him,
   his holy arm.

℟. **Sing to the Lord a new song, for he has done marvelous deeds.**

The LORD has made his salvation known:
   in the sight of the nations he has revealed his justice.
He has remembered his kindness and his faithfulness
   toward the house of Israel.

℟. **Sing to the Lord a new song, for he has done marvelous deeds.**

All the ends of the earth have seen
   the salvation by our God.
Sing joyfully to the LORD, all you lands;
   break into song; sing praise.

℟. **Sing to the Lord a new song, for he has done marvelous deeds.**

Lect. No. 689

SECOND READING: Ephesians 1:3-6, 11-12

This reading is a hymn of praise to celebrate the fact that we were chosen by our Lord for salvation before the foundation of the world. This is the proper idea of predestination, that God has always called us to participate in his life.

A reading from the Letter of Saint Paul
to the Ephesians

Brothers and sisters:
Blessed be the God and Father of our Lord Jesus
   Christ,
who has blessed us in Christ

Predestination does not mean that we must do something; it means that we have the freedom to do it. We always have the possibility of saying no, but why would we want to?

The extent of God's favor is expressed in the fact that we have been adopted as God's children. We have become his chosen ones, his beloved.

It is Jesus who, through his death and resurrection, made all of this possible. He is our brother, and God is our "Abba," Father.

Our only possible response to this miracle is gratitude and praise. We live to praise the Lord.

with every spiritual blessing in the heavens,
as he chose us in him, before the foundation of
   the world,
to be holy and without blemish before him.
In love he destined us for adoption to himself
   through Jesus Christ,
in accord with the favor of his will,
for the praise of the glory of his grace
that he granted us in the beloved.

In him we were also chosen,
   destined in accord with the purpose of the One
   who accomplishes all things according to the in-
      tention of his will,
   so that we might exist for the praise of his glory,
   we who first hoped in Christ.

The word of the Lord.

Lect.
No. 689

We honor Mary with the words the archangel Gabriel used when he came to give her the glorious message that she was to be the Mother of God and blessed among all women.

ALLELUIA: cf. Luke 1:28

℟. **Alleluia, alleluia.**

Hail, Mary, full of grace, the Lord is with you;
blessed are you among women.

℟. **Alleluia, alleluia.**

Lect.
No. 689

The Annunciation is patterned after many of the annunciation stories found in the Old Testament. It is also a loose parallel to the annunciation of John the Baptist. While John's birth is great, that of Jesus is even greater. John's mother and father were elderly; Jesus' mother was a virgin.

GOSPEL: Luke 1:26-38

A reading from the holy Gospel according to Luke

The angel Gabriel was sent from God
   to a town of Galilee called Nazareth,
   to a virgin betrothed to a man named Joseph,
   of the house of David,
   and the virgin's name was Mary.
And coming to her, he said,
   "Hail, full of grace! The Lord is with you."

The archangel Gabriel greets Mary by stating, "Hail, full of grace!" This greeting is actually an important scriptural proof for the dogma of the Immaculate Conception.

The phrase, "full of grace" is in the perfect tense in the original Greek version of this gospel. The perfect was used for things that began in the past and were still true in the present, such as saying that the flowers bloomed yesterday and were still in bloom today.

Mary was already full of grace even before the angel arrived. She had been protected from the effects of the original sin.

This is why Mary could respond with so much generosity to the invitation of the Lord. Those of us who have been wounded by sin tend to be selfish. Mary, on the other hand, was able to think in terms of service and vulnerability. She pronounced herself the handmaid of the Lord.

The birth came about through the intervention of the Holy Spirit who overshadowed her, even as the cloud had overshadowed the Ark of the Covenant in the Old Testament.

But she was greatly troubled at what was said
and pondered what sort of greeting this might be.
Then the angel said to her,
"Do not be afraid, Mary,
for you have found favor with God.
Behold, you will conceive in your womb and bear a son,
and you shall name him Jesus.
He will be great and will be called Son of the Most High,
and the Lord God will give him the throne of David his father,
and he will rule over the house of Jacob forever,
and of his Kingdom there will be no end."
But Mary said to the angel,
"How can this be,
since I have no relations with a man?"
And the angel said to her in reply,
"The Holy Spirit will come upon you,
and the power of the Most High will overshadow you.
Therefore the child to be born
will be called holy, the Son of God.
And behold, Elizabeth, your relative,
has also conceived a son in her old age,
and this is the sixth month for her who was called barren;
for nothing will be impossible for God."
Mary said, "Behold, I am the handmaid of the Lord.
May it be done to me according to your word."
Then the angel departed from her.

The Gospel of the Lord.

PASTORAL REFLECTIONS

In an era that speaks about the long-term effects of dysfunctionality, it is a tremendous consolation to have a mother who can love us with a totally unconditional love.

December 10, 2017

SECOND SUNDAY OF ADVENT

Lect. No. 5 | **FIRST READING: Isaiah 40:1-5, 9-11**

This passage is the beginning of the section of the Book of the Prophet Isaiah that we call Deutero-Isaiah. It was written by an anonymous author as a book of consolation for the people of Israel who were living in exile in Babylon. They had been defeated by the armies of Babylon in 587 B.C.

Jerusalem had been destroyed and the elite of Israel had been carried off into exile. They began to wonder whether God was less powerful than the gods of Babylon. (After all, Babylon's army had defeated the army of the chosen people.) They even wondered whether God was so angry at them that he would never forgive them.

The very first words of this prophecy respond to these concerns. Israel will be consoled and comforted. She had more than paid the debt for her sins. God only wanted to heal her and restore her to the promised land. He would treat her with great gentleness, like a shepherd treats his sheep.

This gives us an insight into the meaning of Advent, for it is a time of penance and conversion that will lead us to great joy.

A reading from the Book of the Prophet Isaiah

Comfort, give comfort to my people,
  says your God.
Speak tenderly to Jerusalem, and proclaim to her
  that her service is at an end,
  her guilt is expiated;
indeed, she has received from the hand of the
  LORD
  double for all her sins.

    A voice cries out:
In the desert prepare the way of the LORD!
  Make straight in the wasteland a highway for
  our God!
Every valley shall be filled in,
  every mountain and hill shall be made low;
the rugged land shall be made a plain,
  the rough country, a broad valley.
Then the glory of the LORD shall be revealed,
  and all people shall see it together;
  for the mouth of the LORD has spoken.

Go up onto a high mountain,
  Zion, herald of glad tidings;
cry out at the top of your voice,
  Jerusalem, herald of good news!
Fear not to cry out
  and say to the cities of Judah:
  Here is your God!
Here comes with power
  the Lord GOD,
  who rules by his strong arm;

Sin leads to loneliness and alienation; conversion leads to joy. When we turn away from selfishness, we find true freedom, which is the freedom to love. Furthermore, we will learn the meaning of true generosity.

here is his reward with him,
  his recompense before him.
Like a shepherd he feeds his flock;
  in his arms he gathers the lambs,
carrying them in his bosom,
  and leading the ewes with care.

The word of the Lord.

Lect.
No. 5

RESPONSORIAL PSALM: Ps 85:9-10, 11-12, 13-14 (℟.: 8)

This psalm celebrates the peace that the Lord will shower upon the earth. The Hebrew concept of peace (Shalom) is much greater than the simple absence of war. It is a peace that encompasses body and soul and transforms the world around us.

This is why Isaiah spoke of the lion lying down with the lamb, for even the divisions of nature would be healed. This is the meaning of salvation.

The only way that this peace can dawn upon the earth is through the practice of justice and righteousness. We learn the meaning of justice from God.

We hear in the Letter to the Romans that God redefines the concept of justice. It is no longer giving each person what that person deserves, but rather giving each person unlimited mercy and love.

℟. **Lord, let us see your kindness, and grant us your salvation.**

I will hear what God proclaims;
  the LORD—for he proclaims peace to his people.
Near indeed is his salvation to those who fear him,
  glory dwelling in our land.

℟. **Lord, let us see your kindness, and grant us your salvation.**

Kindness and truth shall meet;
  justice and peace shall kiss.
Truth shall spring out of the earth,
  and justice shall look down from heaven.

℟. **Lord, let us see your kindness, and grant us your salvation.**

The LORD himself will give his benefits;
  our land shall yield its increase.
Justice shall walk before him,
  and prepare the way of his steps.

℟. **Lord, let us see your kindness, and grant us your salvation.**

Lect. No. 5

SECOND READING: 2 Peter 3:8-14

The Second Letter of Saint Peter addresses the question of why Jesus had not yet returned in glory by the time that this letter was written.

In the early Church, Christians believed that Jesus would return in glory within a very short time. Saint Paul even recommended that the Corinthians not get married so that they could dedicate themselves to the ways of the Lord Jesus in the few days that remained before the return of the Lord.

Time went by, and still Jesus did not arrive. Some Christians began to ask whether Jesus ever would return. Was something wrong?

In this letter we hear that the Lord will return at the end of time, and that his delay is not due to his forgetting his promises. Rather, God is giving us extra time for conversion. Jesus wants to give us all the opportunity to turn our lives around and dedicate ourselves to the ways of the Lord. He wants our salvation and not our destruction.

We should use that time carefully in order to be ready when the end (whether our end or the end of the world) does come.

A reading from the second Letter of Saint Peter

Do not ignore this one fact, beloved,
that with the Lord one day is like a thousand years
and a thousand years like one day.
The Lord does not delay his promise, as some regard "delay,"
but he is patient with you,
not wishing that any should perish
but that all should come to repentance.
But the day of the Lord will come like a thief,
and then the heavens will pass away with a mighty roar
and the elements will be dissolved by fire,
and the earth and everything done on it will be found out.

Since everything is to be dissolved in this way,
what sort of persons ought you to be,
conducting yourselves in holiness and devotion,
waiting for and hastening the coming of the day of God,
because of which the heavens will be dissolved in flames
and the elements melted by fire.
But according to his promise
we await new heavens and a new earth
in which righteousness dwells.
Therefore, beloved, since you await these things,
be eager to be found without spot or blemish before him, at peace.

The word of the Lord.

Lect.
No. 5

Advent is a special time of conversion when we make straight the ways of the Lord. We are given the opportunity to remove every hindrance that prevents us from experiencing God's salvation.

Lect.
No. 5

The beginning of the Gospel of Mark speaks of John the Baptist as a new Elijah who would prepare the way of the Lord and make straight the paths before him. He would preach conversion to the people of Israel so that they would be able to open their hearts to Jesus when he arrived.

John practiced a baptism of conversion that cleansed the people of their sins. This might have been a practice that John learned in Qumran, a community of celibate monks near the Dead Sea that was awaiting the Day of the Lord. They performed ceremonial ablutions to purify themselves from their sins.

Yet, while John practiced this type of baptism, he also pointed to another type of Baptism. This new Baptism not only washed us free of our sins but also gave us the gift of the Holy Spirit.

It is the Holy Spirit who makes us children of God, heirs to the Kingdom of God, and brothers and sisters of Jesus. This is the meaning of our Christian Baptism.

ALLELUIA: Luke 3:4, 6

℟. **Alleluia, alleluia.**

Prepare the way of the Lord, make straight his paths:
all flesh shall see the salvation of God.

℟. **Alleluia, alleluia.**

GOSPEL: Mark 1:1-8

A reading from the holy Gospel according to Mark

The beginning of the gospel of Jesus Christ the Son of God.

As it is written in Isaiah the prophet:
Behold, I am sending my messenger ahead of you;
he will prepare your way.
A voice of one crying out in the desert:
"Prepare the way of the Lord,
make straight his paths."
John the Baptist appeared in the desert
proclaiming a baptism of repentance for the forgiveness of sins.
People of the whole Judean countryside
and all the inhabitants of Jerusalem
were going out to him
and were being baptized by him in the Jordan River
as they acknowledged their sins.
John was clothed in camel's hair,
with a leather belt around his waist.
He fed on locusts and wild honey.
And this is what he proclaimed:
"One mightier than I is coming after me.
I am not worthy to stoop and loosen the thongs of his sandals.
I have baptized you with water;
he will baptize you with the Holy Spirit."

The Gospel of the Lord.

December 17, 2017
THIRD SUNDAY OF ADVENT

| Lect. No. 8 | **FIRST READING: Isaiah 61:1-2a, 10-11** |

This reading is taken from the third part of the Book of the Prophet Isaiah. It was written after Israel's return from exile in Babylon.

It is filled with the hope of a fulfillment of the joy that the LORD had promised through the mouth of Deutero-Isaiah, the prophet who promised a time of restoration to Israel during the exile in Babylon (587-539 B.C.).

This passage speaks of the Spirit of God being upon the Messiah. It was through the Spirit that the land would be restored. There would be a year of favor (which is an allusion to the Jubilee Year tradition when all debts would be forgiven in Israel and those in distress would receive a time of consolation).

A reading from the Book of the Prophet Isaiah

The spirit of the Lord GOD is upon me,
because the LORD has anointed me;
he has sent me to bring glad tidings to the poor,
    to heal the brokenhearted,
to proclaim liberty to the captives
    and release to the prisoners,
to announce a year of favor from the LORD
    and a day of vindication by our God.

I rejoice heartily in the LORD,
    in my God is the joy of my soul;
for he has clothed me with a robe of salvation
    and wrapped me in a mantle of justice,
like a bridegroom adorned with a diadem,
    like a bride bedecked with her jewels.
As the earth brings forth its plants,
    and a garden makes its growth spring up,
so will the Lord GOD make justice and praise
    spring up before all the nations.

The word of the Lord.

| Lect. No. 8 | **RESPONSORIAL PSALM: Luke 1:46-48, 49-50, 53-54 (℟.: Is 61:10b)** |

The First Reading spoke of a time of restoration when the Spirit of the LORD would shower justice upon the earth. This hymn, Mary's canticle, celebrates this time of favor when the LORD would raise up the lowly and bring down the mighty.

℟. **My soul rejoices in my God.**

My soul proclaims the greatness of the Lord;
    my spirit rejoices in God my Savior,
for he has looked upon his lowly servant.
    From this day all generations will call me blessed:

℟. **My soul rejoices in my God.**

The birth of Jesus brings about a time of peace and restoration upon the earth and in our hearts.

God reaches out to those who were lost and confused. We had lost our way through sin. We had squandered our inheritance, the love of God, and found ourselves alienated and helpless. Jesus brings us mercy and salvation.

The Almighty has done great things for me,
    and holy is his Name.
He has mercy on those who fear him
    in every generation.

℟. **My soul rejoices in my God.**

He has filled the hungry with good things,
    and the rich he has sent away empty.
He has come to the help of his servant Israel
    for he has remembered his promise of mercy.

℟. **My soul rejoices in my God.**

| Lect. No. 8 | **SECOND READING: 1 Thessalonians 5:16-24** |

This part of Saint Paul's First Letter to the Thessalonians is called the paranesis. It is a section of last-minute instructions found at the end of most of Paul's Letters.

Two of the themes found all throughout this letter are joy and prayer. Joy is the sense of peace that we find when we do God's will, and prayer is a means of discerning God's will.

We should not quench the Spirit, but we must test everything. We must be open to God's speaking in our hearts, but we also need to recognize that we do not have a monopoly on the truth. We must also listen to the Spirit speaking through the hierarchy.

A reading from the first Letter of Saint Paul to the Thessalonians

Brothers and sisters:
Rejoice always. Pray without ceasing.
In all circumstances give thanks,
    for this is the will of God for you in Christ Jesus.
Do not quench the Spirit.
Do not despise prophetic utterances.
Test everything; retain what is good.
Refrain from every kind of evil.

May the God of peace make you perfectly holy
    and may you entirely, spirit, soul, and body,
      be preserved blameless for the coming of our
        Lord Jesus Christ.
The one who calls you is faithful,
    and he will also accomplish it.

The word of the Lord.

Lect.
No. 8

ALLELUIA: Isaiah 61:1 (cited in Luke 4:18)

The Alleluia Verse repeats the verse concerning the Spirit of the Lord being upon the Messiah, which we saw in the First Reading and which Jesus applies to himself in the Gospel of Luke.

℞. **Alleluia, alleluia.**

The Spirit of the Lord is upon me,
because he has anointed me
to bring glad tidings to the poor.

℞. **Alleluia, alleluia.**

Lect.
No. 8

GOSPEL: John 1:6-8, 19-28

In the Synoptic Gospels, John the Baptist calls people to conversion in order to prepare them for the coming of the Messiah by proclaiming a time of repentance.

In the Gospel of John, the Baptist's role is somewhat different. In the first verses of this reading, we hear that he gave testimony (witness) to the fact that Jesus is the Messiah and that he (John the Baptist) is not.

In the days of Jesus, there were people (called Mandaeans) who claimed that John the Baptist was the Messiah—and some continue to make this claim today. By having John the Baptist himself deny this, the evangelist is stating that everything John said and did pointed toward Jesus as the true Messiah.

John considered his role as one of preparing the way of the Lord, making straight the path through a conversion of hearts to justice and righteousness.

A reading from the holy Gospel according to John

A man named John was sent from God.
  He came for testimony, to testify to the light,
so that all might believe through him.
He was not the light,
  but came to testify to the light.

And this is the testimony of John.
When the Jews from Jerusalem sent priests and
      Levites to him
  to ask him, "Who are you?"
  he admitted and did not deny it,
  but admitted, "I am not the Christ."
So they asked him,
  "What are you then? Are you Elijah?"
And he said, "I am not."
"Are you the Prophet?"
He answered, "No."
So they said to him,
  "Who are you, so we can give an answer to those
      who sent us?
What do you have to say for yourself?"
He said:
  "I am *the voice of one crying out in the desert,*
  'make straight the way of the Lord,'
  as Isaiah the prophet said."

John the Baptist cannot untie Jesus' sandal both because he cannot touch the least significant of Jesus' garments and because the act of untying sandals is part of the Levirite marriage ceremony. In this ceremony, the next of kin would marry a widow who had not had a son. In this Gospel, Israel is the widow (for she had married God in the Old Covenant) and Jesus is the bridegroom who will marry her (the New Covenant). John the Baptist cannot untie the sandal because he is not the bridegroom (the Messiah)—Jesus is.

Some Pharisees were also sent.
They asked him,
    "Why then do you baptize
    if you are not the Christ or Elijah or the Prophet?"
John answered them,
    "I baptize with water;
    but there is one among you whom you do not recognize,
    the one who is coming after me,
    whose sandal strap I am not worthy to untie."
This happened in Bethany across the Jordan,
    where John was baptizing.

The Gospel of the Lord.

PASTORAL REFLECTIONS

The Third Sunday of Advent is traditionally called Gaudete *Sunday. (The word* Gaudete *means "rejoice.") It is a time to rejoice because our Advent journey has almost come to an end. It is also, however, a time to rejoice because we have been able to simplify our lives and draw our hearts closer to God's ways throughout Advent. This brings us true joy.*

Our society sometimes presents the message that the more we accumulate, the happier we will be. This is especially true in the shopping season before Christmas when we are told that love is measured by how much we spend on one another. True joy comes from the peace that we find when we become simple and childlike. Our turning away from sin and bad habits helps us to reach that state.

December 24, 2017

FOURTH SUNDAY OF ADVENT

Lect. No. 11

FIRST READING:

2 Samuel 7:1-5, 8b-12, 14a, 16

The Old Testament contains a series of covenants. There is one made with Noah, one with Abraham, one with Moses, and one with Joshua. Today we hear about the covenant made with David.

David approached Nathan (who was court prophet, a type of counselor) to speak about building a temple for the LORD. When David conquered Jerusalem, he brought the Ark of the Covenant into that city, but he had not yet built a temple for it. Now that David had been incredibly successful in his conquests and had established an empire that extended from river to river (the Nile to the Euphrates), he was ready to honor the LORD by building him a temple.

We hear that the LORD refused David's idea. There are two reasons given in Scripture for this refusal. In the Book of Chronicles it says that David could not build the temple because he had shed too much blood. In this reading the reason is much more the arrogance of David. It is almost as if he thinks that he is doing God a big favor.

The LORD's response reestablishes the correct order.

A reading from the second Book of Samuel

When King David was settled in his palace,
and the LORD had given him rest from his enemies on every side,
he said to Nathan the prophet,
"Here I am living in a house of cedar,
while the ark of God dwells in a tent!"
Nathan answered the king,
"Go, do whatever you have in mind,
for the LORD is with you."
But that night the LORD spoke to Nathan and said:
"Go, tell my servant David, 'Thus says the LORD:
Should you build me a house to dwell in?

"'It was I who took you from the pasture
and from the care of the flock
to be commander of my people Israel.
I have been with you wherever you went,
and I have destroyed all your enemies before you.
And I will make you famous like the great ones of
the earth.
I will fix a place for my people Israel;
I will plant them so that they may dwell in their
place
without further disturbance.
Neither shall the wicked continue to afflict them as
they did of old,
since the time I first appointed judges over my
people Israel.
I will give you rest from all your enemies.
The LORD also reveals to you
that he will establish a house for you.

He tells David that he will be the one to create a house for David (a dynasty). If David and his sons are faithful to the ways of the LORD, they will reign in Israel forever.

God will be close and loving to David and his descendants, as a father loves a son. This promise is only fully realized in the birth of Jesus, the son of David.

And when your time comes and you rest with your ancestors,
    I will raise up your heir after you, sprung from your loins,
    and I will make his kingdom firm.
I will be a father to him,
    and he shall be a son to me.
Your house and your kingdom shall endure forever before me;
    your throne shall stand firm forever.' "

The word of the Lord.

Lect. No. 11

RESPONSORIAL PSALM: Ps 89:2-3, 4-5, 27, 29 (℟.: 2a)

The Responsorial Psalm celebrates the fidelity of the LORD. God made a covenant with David, and he will fulfill his promises both to David and to Israel. The psalmist uses words like faithfulness and kindness to describe the LORD.

Furthermore, God will be a father, rock, and savior to them. *Father* is a title that speaks of the LORD's tender concern and care for Israel. The term *rock* speaks of God's fidelity, for God always remains faithful to his promises. He and we will never be shaken. Finally, God is our *savior,* for he will rescue us from all of our enemies.

The only appropriate response to all of this is to proclaim the goodness of the LORD. The psalmist promises to sing forever and to praise God for all that he has done.

℟. **For ever I will sing the goodness of the Lord.**

The promises of the LORD I will sing forever;
    through all generations my mouth shall proclaim your faithfulness.
For you have said, "My kindness is established forever";
    in heaven you have confirmed your faithfulness.

℟. **For ever I will sing the goodness of the Lord.**

"I have made a covenant with my chosen one,
    I have sworn to David my servant:
forever will I confirm your posterity
    and establish your throne for all generations."

℟. **For ever I will sing the goodness of the Lord.**

"He shall say of me, 'You are my father,
    my God, the Rock, my savior.'
Forever I will maintain my kindness toward him,
    and my covenant with him stands firm."

℟. **For ever I will sing the goodness of the Lord.**

Lect. No. 11

SECOND READING: Romans 16:25-27

This reading is actually a prayer or doxology (hymn of praise). These hymns are found at the end of most of Saint Paul's letters.

Like the First Reading and the psalm, this reading celebrates the goodness of the Lord who is faithful to all of his promises. God revealed his promises long ago through the law and the prophets, and now he has fulfilled them through the birth of Jesus in our midst.

This miracle of grace was proclaimed not only to the people of Israel but also to all of the nations on the earth.

A reading from the Letter of Saint Paul
to the Romans

Brothers and sisters:
To him who can strengthen you,
  according to my gospel and the proclamation of
    Jesus Christ,
  according to the revelation of the mystery kept
    secret for long ages
  but now manifested through the prophetic writ-
    ings and,
  according to the command of the eternal God,
  made known to all nations to bring about the obe-
    dience of faith,
  to the only wise God, through Jesus Christ
be glory forever and ever. Amen.

The word of the Lord.

Lect. No. 11

ALLELUIA: Luke 1:38

The Alleluia Verse introduces us to the words of Mary that we will hear in the Gospel today, the words by which Mary placed herself at the service of the Lord.

℟. **Alleluia, alleluia.**
Behold, I am the handmaid of the Lord.
May it be done to me according to your word.

℟. **Alleluia, alleluia.**

Lect. No. 11

GOSPEL: Luke 1:26-38

The Gospel is the account of the Annunciation through which Jesus became incarnate in our world. Saint Luke presents an account that is a parallel to the story of the annunciation of the birth of John the Baptist—but while the annunciation of John was great, that of Jesus far surpasses it.

A reading from the holy Gospel according to Luke

The angel Gabriel was sent from God
  to a town of Galilee called Nazareth,
to a virgin betrothed to a man named Joseph,
of the house of David,
  and the virgin's name was Mary.

The angel Gabriel appears to Mary. (We are not told the exact circumstances but given only a quick account of the dialogue.) He greets her, calling her one who is full of grace. The particular form in which this phrase is written makes it obvious that Mary was already filled with grace even before the angel greeted her.

Gabriel asks Mary to be the mother of the Son of God. Because Mary was immaculate from the moment of her conception, she is able to respond to God's invitation with great generosity.

She does not seek her own advancement, but rather places herself at the disposition of God, saying that she is God's handmaid. She answers God's call even though she does not yet fully understand what it all means.

The child is to be called Jesus, a name that means "Yahweh saves." He will be the fulfillment of Nathan's promise to David, for he will be a king with an eternal reign.

All of this happens, even though Mary is a virgin. This is impossible according to worldly logic, but nothing is impossible for God. God, who gave Elizabeth a child even though she was advanced in years, could certainly give a child to Mary.

And coming to her, he said,
"Hail, full of grace! The Lord is with you."
But she was greatly troubled at what was said
and pondered what sort of greeting this might be.
Then the angel said to her,
"Do not be afraid, Mary,
for you have found favor with God.

"Behold, you will conceive in your womb and bear a son,
and you shall name him Jesus.
He will be great and will be called Son of the Most High,
and the Lord God will give him the throne of David his father,
and he will rule over the house of Jacob forever,
and of his kingdom there will be no end."
But Mary said to the angel,
"How can this be,
since I have no relations with a man?"
And the angel said to her in reply,
"The Holy Spirit will come upon you,
and the power of the Most High will overshadow you.
Therefore the child to be born
will be called holy, the Son of God.
And behold, Elizabeth, your relative,
has also conceived a son in her old age,
and this is the sixth month for her who was called barren;
for nothing will be impossible for God."
Mary said, "Behold, I am the handmaid of the Lord.
May it be done to me according to your word."
Then the angel departed from her.

The Gospel of the Lord.

December 24, 2017

THE NATIVITY OF THE LORD [CHRISTMAS]

AT THE VIGIL MASS

Lect. No. 13

FIRST READING: Isaiah 62:1-5

This prophecy speaks of the restoration of the people of Israel. They had suffered terribly during the years of exile and during the difficult years when they first came back from exile. They wondered whether God had forgotten them or possibly was still angry at them.

This reading makes it clear that this is not God's attitude. Using matrimonial symbolism, the prophet speaks of the remarkable restoration that would take place.

The LORD would espouse his people. They would be given a new name that expresses the delight of the LORD. This reading is filled with a sense of joy and new possibilities. The promise that it expresses was fulfilled when God established a new covenant with his chosen people.

The hymn is written with parallelism, saying the same thing a second time with slightly different words.

A reading from the Book of the Prophet Isaiah

For Zion's sake I will not be silent,
for Jerusalem's sake I will not be quiet,
until her vindication shines forth like the dawn
and her victory like a burning torch.

Nations shall behold your vindication,
and all the kings your glory;
you shall be called by a new name
pronounced by the mouth of the LORD.
You shall be a glorious crown in the hand of the LORD,
a royal diadem held by your God.
No more shall people call you "Forsaken,"
or your land "Desolate,"
but you shall be called "My Delight,"
and your land "Espoused."
For the LORD delights in you
and makes your land his spouse.
As a young man marries a virgin,
your Builder shall marry you;
and as a bridegroom rejoices in his bride
so shall your God rejoice in you.

The word of the Lord.

Lect. No. 13

RESPONSORIAL PSALM: Ps 89:4-5, 16-17, 27, 29 (℟.: 2a)

The psalm celebrates the covenant that God has made with his people as well as with King David. God will always remain faithful to his covenant. Even if we sin, God will not abandon his promises. We never have to worry about God hiding his face or forgetting us, for we will walk in the light of his countenance.

The only possible response to this remarkable generosity is great joy. We are filled with awe at the goodness of God.

We are also filled with confidence, for we know that God will always defend us against our enemies. Thus, we can call God, "my father, my God, the Rock, my savior."

℟. **For ever I will sing the goodness of the Lord.**

I have made a covenant with my chosen one,
 I have sworn to David my servant:
forever will I confirm your posterity
 and establish your throne for all generations.

℟. **For ever I will sing the goodness of the Lord.**

Blessed the people who know the joyful shout;
 in the light of your countenance, O LORD, they walk.
At your name they rejoice all the day,
 and through your justice they are exalted.

℟. **For ever I will sing the goodness of the Lord.**

He shall say of me, "You are my father,
 my God, the Rock, my savior."
Forever I will maintain my kindness toward him,
 and my covenant with him stands firm.

℟. **For ever I will sing the goodness of the Lord.**

Lect. No. 13

SECOND READING: Acts 13:16-17, 22-25

This speech presents a form of the early "kerygma," the things that Saint Paul would preach when he first entered a new city.

This kerygma is very Jewish in tone for Paul is speaking in a synagogue. He wants to present the message in such a way that they could understand who Jesus was and what he meant for them.

Notice that two kings are mentioned in the course of the speech: Saul and David. This is actually a subtle threat to the community.

A reading from the Acts of the Apostles

When Paul reached Antioch in Pisidia and entered the synagogue,
 he stood up, motioned with his hand, and said,
 "Fellow Israelites and you others who are God-fearing, listen.
The God of this people Israel chose our ancestors
 and exalted the people during their sojourn in the land of Egypt.
With uplifted arm he led them out of it.
Then he removed Saul and raised up David as king;
 of him he testified,
 'I have found David, son of Jesse, a man after my own heart;
 he will carry out my every wish.'

Saul had been chosen by the Lord to be king, but he displeased the Lord and was rejected. God then chose David to be the new king of Israel.

Paul was warning the community that the same could happen to them. They, too, considered themselves to be the chosen, but if they did not accept his message, they, too, could be rejected. Their only recourse was to accept Jesus as their Messiah and be baptized.

From this man's descendants God, according to his promise,
   has brought to Israel a savior, Jesus.
John heralded his coming by proclaiming a baptism of repentance
   to all the people of Israel;
   and as John was completing his course, he would say,
'What do you suppose that I am? I am not he.
Behold, one is coming after me;
   I am not worthy to unfasten the sandals of his feet.'"

The word of the Lord.

Lect. No. 13

The birth of the child Jesus in Bethlehem destroys the power of wickedness upon the earth. He is love incarnate, and nothing that is opposed to that love can defeat him.

ALLELUIA

℟. **Alleluia, alleluia.**

Tomorrow the wickedness of the earth will be destroyed:
the Savior of the world will reign over us.

℟. **Alleluia, alleluia.**

Lect. No. 13

GOSPEL: A Longer Form: Matthew 1:1-25

Matthew presents an extensive genealogy to demonstrate that Jesus is a true son of David, son of Abraham. This will show that Jesus is the fulfillment of all God's promises to his people.

Abraham was the founder of the Jewish people. By tracing Jesus' genealogy back to Abraham, Matthew is showing that Jesus is the Messiah whom Yahweh had sent to his chosen people.

A reading from the holy Gospel according to Matthew

The book of the genealogy of Jesus Christ,
   the son of David, the son of Abraham.

Abraham became the father of Isaac,
   Isaac the father of Jacob,
   Jacob the father of Judah and his brothers.
Judah became the father of Perez and Zerah,
   whose mother was Tamar.
Perez became the father of Hezron,
   Hezron the father of Ram,
   Ram the father of Amminadab.
Amminadab became the father of Nahshon,

David was the great king of Israel and model of what the Messiah should be. Jesus was a true son of David, and he would inherit his eternal throne.

The list of Jesus' ancestors is a bit unhistorical. Matthew tries to make three sets of fourteen names each. The middle set of names skips a few generations in order to make the list add up to fourteen names.

The number fourteen is important for that is the symbolic number for the name David. By producing three lists of fourteen, Matthew is saying that Jesus is three times more important than David. Hebrew had no superlative degree, so saying a word three times in a row was their way of expressing that idea (e.g., holy, holy, holy means the holiest). Jesus was three times "David," and he was therefore the "Davidest."

There are a number of women mentioned in the list. This is unusual. Normally genealogies only had the names of men. Furthermore, the women mentioned had unusual pasts. One was an adulteress, one a foreigner, one committed incest, and one was a prostitute. Matthew was trying to say that God had worked in most unusual ways throughout history. He had chosen most unexpected people to be instruments of his will. This was also true of the fifth woman on his list, a poor virgin named Mary.

After the genealogy, we hear about the birth of Jesus.

Nahshon the father of Salmon,
Salmon the father of Boaz,
whose mother was Rahab.
Boaz became the father of Obed,
whose mother was Ruth.
Obed became the father of Jesse,
Jesse the father of David the king.

David became the father of Solomon,
whose mother had been the wife of Uriah.
Solomon became the father of Rehoboam,
Rehoboam the father of Abijah,
Abijah the father of Asaph.
Asaph became the father of Jehoshaphat,
Jehoshaphat the father of Joram,
Joram the father of Uzziah.
Uzziah became the father of Jotham,
Jotham the father of Ahaz,
Ahaz the father of Hezekiah.
Hezekiah became the father of Manasseh,
Manasseh the father of Amos,
Amos the father of Josiah.
Josiah became the father of Jechoniah and his brothers
at the time of the Babylonian exile.

After the Babylonian exile,
Jechoniah became the father of Shealtiel,
Shealtiel the father of Zerubbabel,
Zerubbabel the father of Abiud.
Abiud became the father of Eliakim,
Eliakim the father of Azor,
Azor the father of Zadok.
Zadok became the father of Achim,
Achim the father of Eliud,
Eliud the father of Eleazar.
Eleazar became the father of Matthan,
Matthan the father of Jacob,
Jacob the father of Joseph, the husband of Mary.
Of her was born Jesus who is called the Christ.

Mary and Joseph were betrothed. This means that they were engaged but not yet living together.

We hear that the child was conceived through the action of the Holy Spirit.

The phrase about Joseph being a righteous man is not clear. A truly righteous man (in the Jewish definition) would have had Mary killed. Matthew might have meant to say that although he was righteous, he decided to divorce her. Whatever Matthew might have meant, he probably wants to show Joseph as a truly righteous man (one who exhibits the traits of New Testament righteousness = compassion).

Joseph is warned in a dream to accept Mary and her child. Joseph is named after Joseph the Patriarch, the dreamer, of the Old Testament, so like him he received his revelations through dreams.

Matthew also shows how Jesus fulfills all of the predictions about the Messiah contained in the law and the prophets. Jesus is Emmanuel, a name that means "God is with us."

The passage ends with us hearing that Joseph had no relations with his wife before the child was born. This does not mean that they had relations after, only that there could be absolutely no doubt that the child was the Son of God. Catholic tradition holds that Mary remained a virgin throughout her life.

Thus the total number of generations
　　from Abraham to David
　　is fourteen generations;
　　from David to the Babylonian exile,
　　fourteen generations;
　　from the Babylonian exile to the Christ,
　　fourteen generations.

Now this is how the birth of Jesus Christ came about.
When his mother Mary was betrothed to Joseph,
　　but before they lived together,
　　she was found with child through the Holy Spirit.
Joseph her husband, since he was a righteous man,
　　yet unwilling to expose her to shame,
　　decided to divorce her quietly.
Such was his intention when, behold,
　　the angel of the Lord appeared to him in a dream
　　　　and said,
　　"Joseph, son of David,
　　do not be afraid to take Mary your wife into your
　　　　home.
For it is through the Holy Spirit
　　that this child has been conceived in her.
She will bear a son and you are to name him Jesus,
　　because he will save his people from their sins."
All this took place to fulfill
　　what the Lord had said through the prophet:
　　　　Behold, the virgin shall conceive and bear a son,
　　　　　　and they shall name him Emmanuel,
　　which means "God is with us."
When Joseph awoke,
　　he did as the angel of the Lord had commanded him
　　and took his wife into his home.
He had no relations with her until she bore a son,
　　and he named him Jesus.

The Gospel of the Lord.

| Lect.
No. 13 | **GOSPEL:** **B** Shorter Form: Matthew 1:18-25 |

We hear that the child was conceived through the action of the Holy Spirit.

The phrase about Joseph being a righteous man is not clear. A truly righteous man (in the Jewish definition) would have had Mary killed. Matthew might have meant to say that although he was righteous, he decided to divorce her. Whatever Matthew might have meant, he probably wants to show Joseph as a truly righteous man (one who exhibits the traits of New Testament righteousness = compassion).

Joseph is warned in a dream to accept Mary and her child. Joseph is named after Joseph the Patriarch, the dreamer, of the Old Testament, so like him he received his revelations through dreams.

Matthew also shows how Jesus fulfills all of the predictions about the Messiah contained in the law and the prophets. Jesus is Emmanuel, a name that means "God is with us."

The passage ends with us hearing that Joseph had no relations with his wife before the child was born. This does not mean that they had relations after, only that there could be absolutely no doubt that the child was the Son of God. Catholic tradition holds that Mary remained a virgin throughout her life.

A reading from the holy Gospel according to Matthew

This is how the birth of Jesus Christ came about.
    When his mother Mary was betrothed to Joseph,
    but before they lived together,
    she was found with child through the Holy Spirit.
Joseph her husband, since he was a righteous man,
    yet unwilling to expose her to shame,
    decided to divorce her quietly.
Such was his intention when, behold,
    the angel of the Lord appeared to him in a dream
        and said,
    "Joseph, son of David,
    do not be afraid to take Mary your wife into your
        home.
For it is through the Holy Spirit
    that this child has been conceived in her.
She will bear a son and you are to name him Jesus,
    because he will save his people from their sins."
All this took place to fulfill
    what the Lord had said through the prophet:
        Behold, the virgin shall conceive and bear a son,
            and they shall name him Emmanuel,
    which means "God is with us."
When Joseph awoke,
    he did as the angel of the Lord had commanded
        him
    and took his wife into his home.
He had no relations with her until she bore a son,
    and he named him Jesus.

The Gospel of the Lord.

December 25, 2017

THE NATIVITY OF THE LORD [CHRISTMAS]

AT THE MASS DURING THE NIGHT

Lect. No. 14

FIRST READING: Isaiah 9:1-6

This passage is taken from a series of prophecies about the Messiah. Isaiah had long hoped that the kings of Israel would reform and prove to be faithful to their anointing. They all disappointed him, however, and Isaiah realized that things would change only if God sent a chosen one. This would have to be more than a messiah—it would have to be the Messiah.

This Messiah would change the world. The Israelites who were enslaved and burdened would be liberated. They had lived in gloom, but they would see a great light. They had been filled with sadness and confusion, but now they would be filled with joy.

The Messiah would have a series of symbolic names that would describe him. This was typical of ancient kings who would receive a series of symbolic names when they were enthroned.

He would be called Wonder-Counselor, God-Hero, Father-Forever, and Prince of Peace. He would inherit David's throne and reign forever. His reign would be marked by justice and peace.

A reading from the Book of the Prophet Isaiah

The people who walked in darkness
    have seen a great light;
upon those who dwelt in the land of gloom
    a light has shone.
You have brought them abundant joy
    and great rejoicing,
as they rejoice before you as at the harvest,
    as people make merry when dividing spoils.
For the yoke that burdened them,
    the pole on their shoulder,
and the rod of their taskmaster
    you have smashed, as on the day of Midian.
For every boot that tramped in battle,
    every cloak rolled in blood,
    will be burned as fuel for flames.
For a child is born to us, a son is given us;
    upon his shoulder dominion rests.
They name him Wonder–Counselor, God–Hero,
    Father–Forever, Prince of Peace.
His dominion is vast
    and forever peaceful,
from David's throne, and over his kingdom,
    which he confirms and sustains
by judgment and justice,
    both now and forever.
The zeal of the LORD of hosts will do this!

The word of the Lord.

Lect. No. 14 — RESPONSORIAL PSALM: Ps 96:1-2, 2-3, 11-12, 13 (℟.: Luke 2:11)

This hymn of praise invites us to sing a new song. There are two words for new in ancient languages. One word means that which is not old; the other means that which is radically new.

We are celebrating something radically new, an intervention of God in our history that makes all previous interventions seem insignificant. God becomes incarnate and thus fills this created world with his majesty.

The only possible response to this wondrous situation is to be filled with awe and to praise God. We even invite creation to praise God. Saint Paul tells us how creation was imprisoned in futility by our sin. Jesus now liberates it by becoming a creature. He restores creation to what God meant it to be when it was first created. Thus, the world and everyone who is in it should raise their voices to praise the Lord.

℟. **Today is born our Savior, Christ the Lord.**

Sing to the LORD a new song;
  sing to the LORD, all you lands.
Sing to the LORD; bless his name.

℟. **Today is born our Savior, Christ the Lord.**

Announce his salvation, day after day.
  Tell his glory among the nations;
  among all peoples, his wondrous deeds.

℟. **Today is born our Savior, Christ the Lord.**

Let the heavens be glad and the earth rejoice;
  let the sea and what fills it resound;
  let the plains be joyful and all that is in them!
Then shall all the trees of the forest exult.

℟. **Today is born our Savior, Christ the Lord.**

They shall exult before the LORD, for he comes;
  for he comes to rule the earth.
He shall rule the world with justice
  and the peoples with his constancy.

℟. **Today is born our Savior, Christ the Lord.**

Lect. No. 14 — SECOND READING: Titus 2:11-14

The Second Reading reminds us that the birth of Jesus is not just a time to rejoice, it is also a time to call us to account.

Jesus is born into our world in order to sanctify us and call us to live a righteous life. Therefore, we must reject those things that separate us from God's love.

A reading from the Letter of Saint Paul to Titus

Beloved:
  The grace of God has appeared, saving all
  and training us to reject godless ways and worldly
    desires
  and to live temperately, justly, and devoutly in this
    age,
  as we await the blessed hope,

We also recall in this reading that while we celebrate the first coming of Jesus into the world, we also are preparing for his return in glory at the end of time. This, too, is a joyous expectation, for we do not fear the return of the Lord. Our prayer is *Maranatha,* "Come, Lord Jesus."

Lect.
No. 14

The Alleluia Verse repeats the words of the angels to the shepherds, that Jesus is our savior and he is born for us all. This is a message of great joy, for it meant that we no longer have to live futile and meaningless lives.

Lect.
No. 14

Luke includes many of his major themes in this account of the birth of Jesus.

He starts his account by placing the birth in the context of world history by reciting the names of kings and governors. By mentioning that the great Caesar Augustus called a worldwide census, Luke is reminding us that the child being born in a small village in the corner of the Roman empire would transform the entire world. We see this implicit prophecy fulfilled at the end of the Acts of the Apostles when Saint Paul proclaims the gospel in Rome, the political center of the world.

the appearance of the glory of our great God
and savior Jesus Christ,
who gave himself for us to deliver us from all lawlessness
and to cleanse for himself a people as his own,
eager to do what is good.

The word of the Lord.

ALLELUIA: Luke 2:10-11

℟. **Alleluia, alleluia.**

I proclaim to you good news of great joy:
today a Savior is born for us,
Christ the Lord.

℟. **Alleluia, alleluia.**

GOSPEL: Luke 2:1-14

A reading from the holy Gospel according to Luke

In those days a decree went out from Caesar Augustus
that the whole world should be enrolled.
This was the first enrollment,
when Quirinius was governor of Syria.
So all went to be enrolled, each to his own town.
And Joseph too went up from Galilee from the town of Nazareth
to Judea, to the city of David that is called Bethlehem,
because he was of the house and family of David,
to be enrolled with Mary, his betrothed, who was with child.
While they were there,
the time came for her to have her child,
and she gave birth to her firstborn son.

Certain of the details in this account are exactly the same as in Matthew's version of the story. Those common details have a high level of credibility. In both accounts, the mother is Mary, a virgin betrothed to a man named Joseph. The child's name is Jesus, a name revealed by God. The child was conceived through the power of the Holy Spirit. Jesus was born in Bethlehem and grew up in Nazareth. When one considers how many of the central details are in agreement, it is astounding. Some of the secondary details, e.g., whether shepherds or Magi visited the baby, etc. are secondary.

The story emphasizes the poverty of the Holy Family. The child is born in a cave and laid in a manger for there was no room in the inn.

The first people in Luke to visit baby Jesus were the shepherds. At the time of Jesus, shepherds were considered to be untrustworthy and their work made them ceremonially unclean. They were social outcasts. The message Luke is presenting is that God sent the message of salvation first to those who most needed it.

She wrapped him in swaddling clothes and laid him
    in a manger,
because there was no room for them in the inn.

Now there were shepherds in that region living in
    the fields
and keeping the night watch over their flock.
The angel of the Lord appeared to them
    and the glory of the Lord shone around them,
    and they were struck with great fear.
The angel said to them,
    "Do not be afraid;
    for behold, I proclaim to you good news of great
        joy
    that will be for all the people.
For today in the city of David
    a savior has been born for you who is Christ and
        Lord.
And this will be a sign for you:
    you will find an infant wrapped in swaddling
        clothes
    and lying in a manger."
And suddenly there was a multitude of the heavenly
    host with the angel,
    praising God and saying:
        "Glory to God in the highest
            and on earth peace to those on whom his
                favor rests."

The Gospel of the Lord.

PASTORAL REFLECTIONS

Even as God invited the poor and the broken (e.g., the shepherds) to the first Christmas, we should also invite that type of person into our own Christmas celebrations (e.g., difficult relatives, estranged friends, etc.).

December 25, 2017
THE NATIVITY OF THE LORD
[CHRISTMAS]
AT THE MASS AT DAWN

Lect. No. 15

FIRST READING: Isaiah 62:11-12

The First Reading this morning celebrates the promise of salvation given to the people of Israel. It is a proclamation that should reach to the ends of the earth. Everyone had seen Israel when she was punished, and now they must witness her restoration.

Israel will be a holy people. The word "holy" means that they are set apart for a sacred purpose, to proclaim the goodness of the LORD. They are also redeemed, bought back from slavery.

A reading from the Book of the Prophet Isaiah

See, the LORD proclaims
to the ends of the earth:
say to daughter Zion,
    your savior comes!
Here is his reward with him,
    his recompense before him.
They shall be called the holy people,
    the redeemed of the LORD,
and you shall be called "Frequented,"
    a city that is not forsaken.

The word of the Lord.

Lect. No. 15

RESPONSORIAL PSALM: Ps 97:1, 6, 11-12

Psalm 97 is an exuberant song of joy for the salvation that the LORD is accomplishing upon the earth.

When the psalmist speaks of the heavens and the earth rejoicing, he is using a typical Hebrew symbolism. By citing the two extremes, he means that everything in between is also engaged in this act of praise.

We are filled with joy, for once we were in the darkness and now we have seen the light; once we were imprisoned in sin, and now we are free.

℟. **A light will shine on us this day: the Lord is born for us.**

The LORD is king; let the earth rejoice;
    let the many isles be glad.
The heavens proclaim his justice,
    and all peoples see his glory.

℟. **A light will shine on us this day: the Lord is born for us.**

Light dawns for the just;
    and gladness, for the upright of heart.
Be glad in the LORD, you just,
    and give thanks to his holy name.

℟. **A light will shine on us this day: the Lord is born for us.**

Lect.
No. 15

SECOND READING: Titus 3:4-7

This morning we celebrate new birth, that of the babe of Bethlehem and also our own re-birth through the Sacrament of Baptism. Both of these births are signs of mercy. We have not earned God's love; it is a gracious gift.

Justified by God's grace, we hear that we have become heirs in hope of eternal life. This means that God has established a relationship of peace with us through the death and resurrection of his Son Jesus. Now we live in hope, for if God would allow his Son to die for us, certainly he will call us into his glory.

A reading from the Letter of Saint Paul to Titus

Beloved:
When the kindness and generous love
   of God our savior appeared,
not because of any righteous deeds we had done
   but because of his mercy,
he saved us through the bath of rebirth
   and renewal by the Holy Spirit,
whom he richly poured out on us
   through Jesus Christ our savior,
so that we might be justified by his grace
   and become heirs in hope of eternal life.

The word of the Lord.

Lect.
No. 15

ALLELUIA: Luke 2:14

We join the angels as they sing to proclaim the glory of God in order to celebrate the birth of God's Son in Bethlehem. He is the one who truly brings peace to the world.

℟. **Alleluia, alleluia.**

Glory to God in the highest,
and on earth peace to those
on whom his favor rests.

℟. **Alleluia, alleluia.**

PASTORAL REFLECTIONS

The Second Reading speaks of being reborn in the Sacrament of Baptism. What exactly does that mean and what consequences does this rebirth produce?

Lect.
No. 15

GOSPEL: Luke 2:15-20

This is the account of the shepherds who visited the baby and his parents. Everything in the account is filled with wonder and joy.

The last thing that the Holy Family would have expected is for shepherds to arrive in order to pay homage. Shepherds in the days of Jesus were feared and avoided. They were regarded as untrustworthy and their work made them ceremonially unclean. They were social outcasts. Yet, they pay homage to the newborn king of the Jews and give praise and glory to God for his wondrous deeds.

Mary ponders these things in her heart. In Biblical symbolism, the heart is the organ of thinking, not feeling. (One feels with one's guts or stomach.) Thus, Mary is wondering about the meaning of the things that were happening.

A reading from the holy Gospel according to Luke

When the angels went away from them to heaven,
    the shepherds said to one another,
    "Let us go, then, to Bethlehem
    to see this thing that has taken place,
    which the Lord has made known to us."
So they went in haste and found Mary and Joseph,
    and the infant lying in the manger.
When they saw this,
    they made known the message
    that had been told them about this child.
All who heard it were amazed
    by what had been told them by the shepherds.
And Mary kept all these things,
    reflecting on them in her heart.
Then the shepherds returned,
    glorifying and praising God
    for all they had heard and seen,
    just as it had been told to them.

The Gospel of the Lord.

PASTORAL REFLECTIONS

We sometimes overidealize what our Christmas celebrations should be. We want to create the perfect Christmas for ourselves and our family. Yet, no Christmas can ever match our unrealistic expectations. Even the first Christmas had disappointments and frustrations. The Holy Family found refuge in a cave (cold, smelly, probably filled with fleas and lice). Then, the first to arrive were the shepherds, the very last people that the Holy Family would have wanted to see. Yet, it was a holy Christmas. Maybe if we lower our expectations a bit, we will enjoy the holiday better.

December 25, 2017
THE NATIVITY OF THE LORD [CHRISTMAS]
AT THE MASS DURING THE DAY

Lect. No. 16

FIRST READING: Isaiah 52:7-10

In this First Reading we hear of how the LORD comforts his people. This is, in fact, the major theme of this section of the Book of the Prophet Isaiah. It begins, "Comfort, be comforted my people" (Isaiah 40:1).

We also hear that it is the LORD himself who will comfort his people. Throughout these chapters the LORD insists that he himself will intervene. We hear phrases like "I will rescue," "I will redeem," "I will create," etc. This is fulfilled in the birth of the babe of Bethlehem, for the child is God among us.

The prophet struggles to find words appropriate to this announcement, for it is glad tidings, an announcement of peace, and of good news.

A reading from the Book of the Prophet Isaiah

How beautiful upon the mountains
    are the feet of him who brings glad tidings,
announcing peace, bearing good news,
    announcing salvation, and saying to Zion,
    "Your God is King!"

Hark! Your sentinels raise a cry,
    together they shout for joy,
for they see directly, before their eyes,
    the LORD restoring Zion.
Break out together in song,
    O ruins of Jerusalem!
For the LORD comforts his people,
    he redeems Jerusalem.
The LORD has bared his holy arm
    in the sight of all the nations;
all the ends of the earth will behold
    the salvation of our God.

The word of the Lord.

Lect. No. 16

RESPONSORIAL PSALM: Ps 98:1, 2-3, 3-4, 5-6 (℟.: 3c)

This entire psalm is a hymn of praise for the wondrous deeds that God has done for his chosen people.

Normally when the people of Israel praised God for acts of

℟. **All the ends of the earth have seen the saving power of God.**

Sing to the LORD a new song,
    for he has done wondrous deeds;
his right hand has won victory for him,
    his holy arm.

salvation, it was a remembrance of the Exodus experience.

This psalm, however, seems to have been written later, and probably refers to the salvation that the Lord worked through the second exodus, the return of the Israelites from Babylon.

Yet, there is also a third application, that of the birth of Jesus, whose very name means "Yahweh saves."

The psalmist praises the Lord by singing a new song. There are two forms of the word new in Biblical languages. One word simply means that it is not old. The other word means that it is radically new.

The salvation of the Lord would be for all the nations of the earth. It was no longer restricted to one people or one time.

The psalmist calls upon the community to use every musical instrument to praise the Lord.

℞. **All the ends of the earth have seen the saving power of God.**

The LORD has made his salvation known:
   in the sight of the nations he has revealed his justice.
He has remembered his kindness and his faithfulness
   toward the house of Israel.

℞. **All the ends of the earth have seen the saving power of God.**

All the ends of the earth have seen
   the salvation by our God.
Sing joyfully to the LORD, all you lands;
   break into song; sing praise.

℞. **All the ends of the earth have seen the saving power of God.**

Sing praise to the LORD with the harp,
   with the harp and melodious song.
With trumpets and the sound of the horn
   sing joyfully before the King, the LORD.

℞. **All the ends of the earth have seen the saving power of God.**

Lect. No. 16

SECOND READING: Hebrews 1:1-6

The author of the Letter to the Hebrews combines Jewish learning and Greek philosophy to proclaim Jesus as our High Priest.

He speaks of how God revealed his word through the prophets of old. This was a wonderful gift, but the prophets could never fully communicate God's

A reading from the beginning of the
Letter to the Hebrews

Brothers and sisters:
In times past, God spoke in partial and various ways
   to our ancestors through the prophets;
in these last days, he has spoken to us through the
   Son,

word in human words. Human words always fall short. That is why there had to be many prophets, because none was ever fully successful in revealing God's word to his people.

This is why God chose to send his own Son. Jesus, the only-begotten Son of God, is the Word of God, the perfect expression of who God is and what he asks of us. It is only through him that we can truly know God.

The last part of this reading tries to show how Jesus is superior to the angels. In Greek philosophy, totally spiritual beings were superior to material beings. Jesus took on our flesh, so some wondered if angels were superior to him. Our author argues that Jesus is the Son of God and above every angel.

whom he made heir of all things
and through whom he created the universe,
> who is the refulgence of his glory, the very imprint of his being,
> and who sustains all things by his mighty word.
> When he had accomplished purification from sins,
> he took his seat at the right hand of the Majesty on high,
> as far superior to the angels
> as the name he has inherited is more excellent than theirs.

For to which of the angels did God ever say:
> *You are my son; this day I have begotten you?*
Or again:
> *I will be a father to him, and he shall be a son to me?*
And again, when he leads the firstborn into the world, he says:
> *Let all the angels of God worship him.*

The word of the Lord.

Lect. No. 16

As the Lord Jesus comes to proclaim his Gospel to us, we rise to greet him and adore him as the light of the world. He lights a path for us through the darkness of our world.

ALLELUIA

℟. **Alleluia, alleluia.**

A holy day has dawned upon us.
Come, you nations, and adore the Lord.
For today a great light has come upon the earth.

℟. **Alleluia, alleluia.**

GOSPEL: A Longer Form: John 1:1-18

The Prologue of the Gospel of John presents Jesus as the Word of God. The author of this hymn is presenting Jesus as wisdom incarnate. This was a way of saying that even before Jesus was born in the flesh in Bethlehem, he already existed. Our author is saying that although the Old Testament authors did not know it, they were actually writing about Jesus whenever they wrote about Wisdom.

John the Baptist was a witness to the fact that Jesus is the Son of God. Unlike the other Gospels where John the Baptist is constantly calling people to conversion, in the Gospel of John he continuously gives witness to the identity of Jesus. John proclaims that Jesus is the Messiah and that he, himself, is not.

When this hymn speaks about the Word being in the world and the world not knowing it, it is not speaking about the rejection of Jesus. It is speaking about Israel's rejection of all of the prophets whom Yahweh sent to call her to conversion.

In verse 14 we begin to speak about Jesus incarnate. We hear that the Word became flesh. This means that God did not consider our material world to be evil, but rather decided to join us and thus bless and consecrate this created world.

A reading from the holy Gospel according to John

In the beginning was the Word,
  and the Word was with God,
  and the Word was God.
He was in the beginning with God.
All things came to be through him,
  and without him nothing came to be.
What came to be through him was life,
  and this life was the light of the human race;
the light shines in the darkness,
  and the darkness has not overcome it.
A man named John was sent from God.
He came for testimony, to testify to the light,
  so that all might believe through him.
He was not the light,
  but came to testify to the light.
The true light, which enlightens everyone, was coming into the world.
  He was in the world,
    and the world came to be through him,
    but the world did not know him.
  He came to what was his own,
    but his own people did not accept him.

But to those who did accept him
  he gave power to become children of God,
  to those who believe in his name,
  who were born not by natural generation
  nor by human choice nor by a man's decision
  but of God.
    And the Word became flesh
      and made his dwelling among us,
      and we saw his glory,

Jesus is full of grace and truth. These two words are actually Old Testament ideas: that God loves us with a covenant love and God is always faithful. Jesus is God's love and faithfulness incarnate.

Jesus is the only Son of God. In the Old Testament, "the son of God" was often used as a synonym for "hero," but to be the only Son of God is to be the eternally begotten Son of God.

Finally, we hear that Jesus reveals who God is. As the wisdom of God, Jesus can fill us with knowledge of God. We cannot hope to understand who God is except through Jesus.

the glory as of the Father's only Son,
  full of grace and truth.
John testified to him and cried out, saying,
  "This was he of whom I said,
  'The one who is coming after me ranks ahead of me
  because he existed before me.'"
From his fullness we have all received,
  grace in place of grace,
  because while the law was given through Moses,
  grace and truth came through Jesus Christ.
No one has ever seen God.
The only Son, God, who is at the Father's side,
  has revealed him.

The Gospel of the Lord.

| Lect. No. 16 |

GOSPEL: B Shorter Form: John 1:1-5, 9-14

The Prologue of the Gospel of John presents Jesus as the Word of God. The author of this hymn is presenting Jesus as wisdom incarnate. This was a way of saying that even before Jesus was born in the flesh in Bethlehem, he already existed. Our author is saying that although the Old Testament authors did not know it, they were actually writing about Jesus whenever they wrote about Wisdom.

When this hymn speaks about the Word being in the world and the world not knowing it, it is not speaking about the rejection of Jesus. It is speaking about Israel's rejection of all of the prophets whom Yahweh sent to call her to conversion.

A reading from the holy Gospel according to John

In the beginning was the Word,
  and the Word was with God,
  and the Word was God.
He was in the beginning with God.
All things came to be through him,
  and without him nothing came to be.
What came to be through him was life,
  and this life was the light of the human race;
the light shines in the darkness,
  and the darkness has not overcome it.
The true light, which enlightens everyone, was coming into the world.
He was in the world,
  and the world came to be through him,
  but the world did not know him.

In verse 14 we begin to speak about Jesus incarnate. We hear that the Word became flesh. This means that God did not consider our material world to be evil, but rather decided to join us and thus bless and consecrate this created world.

Jesus is full of grace and truth. These two words are actually Old Testament ideas: that God loves us with a covenant love and God is always faithful. Jesus is God's love and faithfulness incarnate.

Jesus is the only Son of God. In the Old Testament, "the son of God" was often used as a synonym for "hero," but to be the only Son of God is to be the eternally begotten Son of God.

He came to what was his own,
    but his own people did not accept him.

But to those who did accept him
    he gave power to become children of God,
    to those who believe in his name,
    who were born not by natural generation
    nor by human choice nor by a man's decision
    but of God.
        And the Word became flesh
            and made his dwelling among us,
            and we saw his glory,
            the glory as of the Father's only Son,
            full of grace and truth.

The Gospel of the Lord.

PASTORAL REFLECTIONS

There are different ways to speak about the Christmas story. Even the Gospels present Magi in one account (Matthew) and shepherds in another (Luke). Then in John, we have a philosophical presentation that speaks about the eternal Word of God that becomes human.

We retell the Christmas story in the way that we celebrate this day and season and in the way that we carry forth God's love throughout the year. Christ and his message are reborn in our hearts and we make him present to the world again in our lives and our love.

December 31, 2017

THE HOLY FAMILY OF JESUS, MARY, AND JOSEPH

The A, B, C readings given on pp. 54-57 may be used in place of these B readings.

Lect. No. 17

FIRST READING: Genesis 15:1-6; 21:1-3

The First Reading is one of the accounts of the covenant that God made with Abraham. A covenant is a formal promise or treaty made between nations, a king and his servants, or two equals. In this case, covenant describes a commitment on the part of God to be Abrabam's God and protector.

At the beginning of the account, we hear that Abraham's original name was Abram. His name was changed as a result of his encounter with God. (This is reported in chapter 17 of Genesis.) Likewise, Sarah's name was also changed from its original form: Sarai.

God had called Abraham from his homeland to the land of Canaan, which God promised that Abraham would inherit. He had also promised Abraham that he would have a numerous descendance. Yet, until this point, Abraham did not have any children. Abraham began to wonder whether God would fulfill his promises.

God renews his promise to Abraham in these verses. The latter part of the reading, which is found in chapter 21, tells of the fulfillment of God's promise with the birth of Isaac.

A reading from the Book of Genesis

The word of the LORD came to Abram in a vision, saying:
"Fear not, Abram!
I am your shield;
I will make your reward very great."
But Abram said,
"O Lord GOD, what good will your gifts be,
if I keep on being childless
and have as my heir the steward of my house, Eliezer?"
Abram continued,
"See, you have given me no offspring,
and so one of my servants will be my heir."
Then the word of the LORD came to him:
"No, that one shall not be your heir;
your own issue shall be your heir."
The Lord took Abram outside and said,
"Look up at the sky and count the stars, if you can.
Just so," he added, "shall your descendants be."
Abram put his faith in the LORD,
who credited it to him as an act of righteousness.

The LORD took note of Sarah as he had said he would;
he did for her as he had promised.
Sarah became pregnant and bore Abraham a son in his old age,
at the set time that God had stated.
Abraham gave the name Isaac to this son of his whom Sarah bore him.

The word of the Lord.

RESPONSORIAL PSALM: Ps 105:1-2, 3-4, 6-7, 8-9 (℟.: 7a, 8a)

Lect. No. 17

The people of Israel encountered God through his intervention in their history. Psalm 105 celebrates this fact, emphasizing how God first called Abraham and made a covenant with him, and then how God fulfilled that covenant by rescuing his people from slavery in Egypt through the exodus.

We use the first part of that psalm today, for it ties in well with the First and Second Readings, which speak of God's fulfillment of his promise in the days of Abraham, but also with the Gospel, which speaks of the greater fulfillment of that promise through the birth of Jesus (for the covenant with Abraham was binding for one thousand generations).

Even the nations, which means the pagans, should be filled with wonder at the fact that God is so good and powerful. He is the God of all the earth, and not only of the nation of Israel. This means that Jesus is the source of salvation for all the peoples upon the earth.

℟. **The Lord remembers his covenant for ever.**

Give thanks to the LORD, invoke his name;
 make known among the nations his deeds.
Sing to him, sing his praise,
 proclaim all his wondrous deeds.

℟. **The Lord remembers his covenant for ever.**

Glory in his holy name;
 rejoice, O hearts that seek the LORD!
Look to the LORD in his strength;
 constantly seek his face.

℟. **The Lord remembers his covenant for ever.**

You descendants of Abraham, his servants,
 sons of Jacob, his chosen ones!
He, the LORD, is our God;
 throughout the earth his judgments prevail.

℟. **The Lord remembers his covenant for ever.**

He remembers forever his covenant
 which he made binding for a thousand generations
which he entered into with Abraham
 and by his oath to Isaac.

℟. **The Lord remembers his covenant for ever.**

SECOND READING: Hebrews 11:8, 11-12, 17-19

Lect. No. 17

Today's Second Reading is taken from the Letter to the Hebrews. It speaks of the faith of the great heroes of Israel's history. In this case, we hear of the faith of Abraham. God called him to leave his homeland and travel to the land of Israel.

A reading from the Letter to the Hebrews

Brothers and sisters:
 By faith Abraham obeyed when he was called to go out to a place
that he was to receive as an inheritance;

God also promised Abraham and Sarah as many descendants as the sand on the shore of the sea and the stars in the sky. Yet Abraham had to trust that God would fulfill his promise, especially when he and Sarah grew old. Although they could hardly believe it (for they even met the news with laughter), Sarah became pregnant and gave birth to a son whom they named Isaac.

God tested Abraham further. He asked him to sacrifice his only son Isaac (for God had already ordered him to send Ishmael, the son of Hagar, into the desert). Although Abraham could not understand why God would endanger the fulfillment of his covenant, he obeyed and thus showed his faith in the LORD.

By faith he received power to generate,
    even though he was past the normal age
    —and Sarah herself was sterile—
    for he thought that the one who had made the
        promise was trustworthy.
So it was that there came forth from one man,
    himself as good as dead,
    descendants as numerous as the stars in the sky
    and as countless as the sands on the seashore.

By faith Abraham, when put to the test, offered up
        Isaac,
    and he who had received the promises was ready
        to offer his only son,
    of whom it was said,
    "Through Isaac descendants shall bear your
        name."
He reasoned that God was able to raise even from
        the dead,
    and he received Isaac back as a symbol.

The word of the Lord.

Lect.
No. 17

The Alleluia Verse quotes the first couple of verses of the Letter to the Hebrews. While God revealed many words to Israel throughout history, he revealed the one Word of God in the birth of his only Son.

ALLELUIA: Hebrews 1:1-2

℟. **Alleluia, alleluia.**

In the past God spoke to our ancestors through the
        prophets;
in these last days, he has spoken to us through the
        Son.

℟. **Alleluia, alleluia.**

Lect.
No. 17

This account of the purification in the temple shows that although Luke respected Jewish tradition, he himself was not a

GOSPEL: A Longer Form: Luke 2:22-40

A reading from the holy Gospel according to Luke

When the days were completed for their purification according to the law of Moses,
    they took him up to Jerusalem

Jew. He occasionally misquotes Jewish ideas.

He speaks of "their" purification, implying Mary and the baby Jesus. Mary was going to the temple for her purification, but the rite that was being performed for Jesus was different. It was a rite of redemption.

Ever since the firstborn of the Israelites were saved from death during the exodus from Egypt, God somehow had a right over the firstborn. They were ritually bought back from the Lord through the sacrifice of turtledoves or pigeons.

The Holy Family meets Simeon, a righteous and devout man who awaited the birth of the Savior of Israel. This is a constant theme in Luke's Gospel, that there were many righteous people in Israel who followed Jesus. The difference between following Jesus or not was not based upon race, but upon the purity of one's heart.

Simeon's hymn is probably a hymn that the evangelist borrowed from early Christian liturgies. It might have served as a hymn to be sung at funerals. (Listen to the words contained in it.)

This technique of using outside material that is then attributed to characters inside the story is typical of ancient authors. The theory was that the ideas contained in the hymn well describe what Simeon's attitude would have been at this moment.

to present him to the Lord,
just as it is written in the law of the Lord,
Every male that opens the womb shall be consecrated to the Lord,
and to offer the sacrifice of
a pair of turtledoves or two young pigeons,
in accordance with the dictate in the law of the Lord.

Now there was a man in Jerusalem whose name was Simeon.
This man was righteous and devout,
awaiting the consolation of Israel,
and the Holy Spirit was upon him.
It had been revealed to him by the Holy Spirit
that he should not see death
before he had seen the Christ of the Lord.
He came in the Spirit into the temple;
and when the parents brought in the child Jesus
to perform the custom of the law in regard to him,
he took him into his arms and blessed God, saying:
"Now, Master, you may let your servant go
in peace, according to your word,
for my eyes have seen your salvation,
which you prepared in sight of all the peoples,
a light for revelation to the Gentiles,
and glory for your people Israel."
The child's father and mother were amazed at what was said about him;
and Simeon blessed them and said to Mary his mother,
"Behold, this child is destined
for the fall and rise of many in Israel,
and to be a sign that will be contradicted
—and you yourself a sword will pierce—
so that the thoughts of many hearts may be revealed."
There was also a prophetess, Anna,
the daughter of Phanuel, of the tribe of Asher.

Simeon speaks of a sword that will pierce Mary's heart. This is often understood as being the sword of sorrow, but in the Bible the heart is where one thinks and not where one feels. The sword is the Word of God. Simeon is saying that the birth of Jesus will force Mary to discern who her Son is.

While Mary knew that her Son was Messiah, it was quite another thing to believe that her Son was God. This was all but impossible to believe.

Yet the fact that Luke pictures Mary as being present at the descent of the Holy Spirit means that Luke holds that she did believe what seemed to be impossible—that Jesus was truly the Son of God.

She was advanced in years,
    having lived seven years with her husband after her marriage,
    and then as a widow until she was eighty–four.
She never left the temple,
    but worshiped night and day with fasting and prayer.
And coming forward at that very time,
    she gave thanks to God and spoke about the child
    to all who were awaiting the redemption of Jerusalem.

When they had fulfilled all the prescriptions
    of the law of the Lord,
    they returned to Galilee,
    to their own town of Nazareth.
The child grew and became strong, filled with wisdom;
    and the favor of God was upon him.

The word of the Lord.

Lect. No. 17

GOSPEL: B Shorter Form: Luke 2:22, 39-40

The shorter form of this Gospel speaks of the Holy Family fulfilling all of the prescriptions of the Jewish law. Saint Luke believes that God has a plan for all people, and that it is only when we follow that plan that we can hope to find peace and joy.

The Holy Family is a model of obedience to the will of God.

The child is seen as living in the favor of the Lord. Today we would call this grace. The child is anointed to be the Savior of Israel.

A reading from the holy Gospel according to Luke

When the days were completed for their purification according to the law of Moses,
    they took him up to Jerusalem
    to present him to the Lord.

When they had fulfilled all the prescriptions
    of the law of the Lord,
    they returned to Galilee,
    to their own town of Nazareth.
The child grew and became strong, filled with wisdom;
    and the favor of God was upon him.

The Gospel of the Lord.

The following A, B, C readings may be used in place of the previous readings.

Lect. No. 17

FIRST READING: Sirach 3:2-6, 12-14

The Book of Sirach was written late in the Old Testament period when Jewish society was strongly influenced by Greek culture.

A Greek ideal was to live an ordered life that would give public witness to the values that were the core of one's beliefs.

The author of Sirach combined this ideal with the traditional respect for parents and the family. Together they produce this beautiful appeal for a family life in which one's parents are treated with great respect.

Although this portrait is idealized, it also shows signs of realism. It acknowledges that the situation might arise in which one's parents are no longer mentally alert. Nevertheless, care for parents is a sacred responsibility.

A reading from the Book of Sirach

God sets a father in honor over his children;
a mother's authority he confirms over her sons.
Whoever honors his father atones for sins,
and preserves himself from them.
When he prays, he is heard;
he stores up riches who reveres his mother.
Whoever honors his father is gladdened by children,
and, when he prays, is heard.
Whoever reveres his father will live a long life;
he who obeys his father brings comfort to his mother.

My son, take care of your father when he is old;
grieve him not as long as he lives.
Even if his mind fail, be considerate of him;
revile him not all the days of his life;
kindness to a father will not be forgotten,
firmly planted against the debt of your sins
—a house raised in justice to you.

The word of the Lord.

Lect. No. 17

RESPONSORIAL PSALM: Ps 128:1-2, 3, 4-5 (℟.: cf. 1)

Like the First Reading, Psalm 128 is taken from the Wisdom tradition of Old Testament literature. Wisdom literature answered the question, "How can we live a good and virtuous life?"

This psalm responds that one must fear the LORD. This expression is often misunderstood. People sometimes think

℟. **Blessed are those who fear the Lord and walk in his ways.**

Blessed is everyone who fears the LORD,
who walks in his ways!
For you shall eat the fruit of your handiwork;
blessed shall you be, and favored.

℟. **Blessed are those who fear the Lord and walk in his ways.**

that we must be afraid that God might judge us as worthy of punishment.

Fear of the LORD is really a profound sense of reverence and awe when one considers the greatness of God. We are creatures, while God is the creator of all. We cannot even begin to understand the wonder of God's majesty.

If we have this attitude toward God, our everyday lives will reflect it and we will observe his law. Then our families will be blessed, for our lifestyles will be respectful and gracious. We will not be selfish and egocentric.

Your wife shall be like a fruitful vine
　　in the recesses of your home;
your children like olive plants
　　around your table.

℟. **Blessed are those who fear the Lord and walk in his ways.**

Behold, thus is the man blessed
　　who fears the LORD.
The LORD bless you from Zion:
　　may you see the prosperity of Jerusalem
　　all the days of your life.

℟. **Blessed are those who fear the Lord and walk in his ways.**

| Lect. No. 17 | **SECOND READING:** **A** Longer Form: Colossians 3:12-21 |

The first part of this reading exhorts the community to a life of virtue. Early Christians felt that it was essential for them to live at peace with one another so that pagans could see how virtuous their calling was and might be led to conversion. This is why they were to live in compassion, kindness, humility, gentleness, and patience, etc. Christ was to guide their hearts.

This ideal is just as important today. One often hears of people who go to Mass but do not live their faith on an everyday basis, especially in the way they treat their own family.

We cannot hope to live our Christian calling if we are not filled with a sense of gratitude. It is the virtue that reminds us how much we depend upon the Lord. This reading encourages

A reading from the Letter of Saint Paul to the Colossians

Brothers and sisters:
　Put on, as God's chosen ones, holy and beloved,
　heartfelt compassion, kindness, humility, gentleness, and patience,
　bearing with one another and forgiving one another,
　if one has a grievance against another;
　as the Lord has forgiven you, so must you also do.
And over all these put on love,
　that is, the bond of perfection.
And let the peace of Christ control your hearts,
　the peace into which you were also called in one body.
And be thankful.
Let the word of Christ dwell in you richly,
　as in all wisdom you teach and admonish one another,

expressions of gratitude toward the Lord for all that we have received.

The latter part of the reading exhorts family members to live the relationships that the community felt were established by God.

Notice, though, rather than emphasizing the control of one member over another, the letter stresses the mutual responsibilities of one family member toward the others.

singing psalms, hymns, and spiritual songs
　with gratitude in your hearts to God.
And whatever you do, in word or in deed,
　do everything in the name of the Lord Jesus,
　giving thanks to God the Father through him.

Wives, be subordinate to your husbands,
　as is proper in the Lord.
Husbands, love your wives,
　and avoid any bitterness toward them.
Children, obey your parents in everything,
　for this is pleasing to the Lord.
Fathers, do not provoke your children,
　so they may not become discouraged.

The word of the Lord.

Lect. No. 17

SECOND READING: B Shorter Form: Colossians 3:12-17

The first part of this reading exhorts the community to a life of virtue. Early Christians felt that it was essential for them to live at peace with one another so that pagans could see how virtuous their calling was and might be led to conversion. This is why they were to live in compassion, kindness, humility, gentleness, and patience, etc. Christ would lead them to virtue and peace.

This ideal is just as important today. One often hears of people who go to Mass but do not live their faith on an everyday basis, especially in the way they treat their own family.

We cannot hope to live our Christian calling if we are not filled with a sense of gratitude. It is the virtue that reminds us how much we depend upon

A reading from the Letter of Saint Paul
to the Colossians

Brothers and sisters:
　Put on, as God's chosen ones, holy and beloved,
heartfelt compassion, kindness, humility, gentleness, and patience,
　bearing with one another and forgiving one another,
　if one has a grievance against another;
　as the Lord has forgiven you, so must you also do.
And over all these put on love,
　that is, the bond of perfection.
And let the peace of Christ control your hearts,
　the peace into which you were also called in one body.
And be thankful.
Let the word of Christ dwell in you richly,
　as in all wisdom you teach and admonish one another,

the Lord. This reading encourages expressions of gratitude toward the Lord for everything we have, for everything that we have comes from the Lord.

singing psalms, hymns, and spiritual songs
    with gratitude in your hearts to God.
And whatever you do, in word or in deed,
    do everything in the name of the Lord Jesus,
    giving thanks to God the Father through him.

The word of the Lord.

Lect. No. 17

The only way that our families can be peace-filled is by making Christ the center of our lives.

ALLELUIA: Colossians 3:15a, 16a

℟. **Alleluia, alleluia.**

Let the peace of Christ control your hearts;
let the word of Christ dwell in you richly.

℟. **Alleluia, alleluia.**

Lect. No. 17

See p. 51.

GOSPEL: A Longer Form: Luke 2:22-40

PASTORAL REFLECTIONS

There are really no perfect families upon the earth. They only seem that way at times because we don't know what is going on inside of their homes. Even the Holy Family had its difficulties, e.g., homeless, in exile, etc. Yet, they responded to those difficulties in a way that made these things into occasions of grace. We have the same challenge today with our own family problems.

January 1, 2018

THE OCTAVE DAY OF THE NATIVITY OF THE LORD [CHRISTMAS]

SOLEMNITY OF MARY, THE HOLY MOTHER OF GOD

Lect. No. 18

FIRST READING: Numbers 6:22-27

The First Reading for this feast records the blessing that the LORD gave to Moses to invoke over the people of Israel.

It is the presence of God in our lives that is the true definition of blessing. Our lives, in fact, only have meaning inasmuch as we make God the center.

This blessing is also called the blessing of Saint Francis for he recommended this greeting to his followers.

A reading from the Book of Numbers

The LORD said to Moses:
"Speak to Aaron and his sons and tell them:
This is how you shall bless the Israelites.
Say to them:
The LORD bless you and keep you!
The LORD let his face shine upon you, and be gracious to you!
The LORD look upon you kindly and give you peace!
So shall they invoke my name upon the Israelites,
and I will bless them."

The word of the Lord.

Lect. No. 18

RESPONSORIAL PSALM: Ps 67:2-3, 5, 6, 8 (℟.: 2a)

The psalm continues the theme that the only true blessing is that which is found in the presence of the LORD. God is the source of mercy. God is the source of our salvation.

We should remember that there are two meanings for the word salvation.

Saint Paul always speaks about salvation as what will

℟. **May God bless us in his mercy.**

May God have pity on us and bless us;
    may he let his face shine upon us.
So may your way be known upon earth;
    among all nations, your salvation.

℟. **May God bless us in his mercy.**

May the nations be glad and exult
    because you rule the peoples in equity;
    the nations on the earth you guide.

℟. **May God bless us in his mercy.**

happen to us when God welcomes us into heaven.

Saint Luke speaks about salvation as something that is already happening to us now. The minute we make Jesus a part of our lives, we already are experiencing the joys of heaven.

May the peoples praise you, O God;
  may all the peoples praise you!
May God bless us,
  and may all the ends of the earth fear him!

℟. **May God bless us in his mercy.**

Lect. No. 18

SECOND READING: Galatians 4:4-7

There are two words for time in Greek. One word simply means the passing of one minute to the next. The other, that which Saint Paul uses here, signifies time that is sacred time.

This is the first reference in Scripture to the birth of Jesus (written over a decade before the first Gospel).

God sends the Holy Spirit into our hearts so that we can know how much God loves us. This means that when we ask ourselves what we would most like to hear from God, the answer is not so much ours as that of the Spirit speaking in our hearts.

A reading from the Letter of Saint Paul
to the Galatians

Brothers and sisters:
  When the fullness of time had come, God sent his Son,
  born of a woman, born under the law,
  to ransom those under the law,
  so that we might receive adoption as sons.
As proof that you are sons,
  God sent the Spirit of his Son into our hearts,
  crying out, "Abba, Father!"
So you are no longer a slave but a son,
  and if a son then also an heir, through God.

The word of the Lord.

Lect. No. 18

ALLELUIA: Hebrews 1:1-2

The Alleluia Verse quotes the first couple of verses of the Letter to the Hebrews. While God revealed many words to Israel throughout history, he revealed the one Word of God in the birth of his only Son.

℟. **Alleluia, alleluia.**

In the past God spoke to our ancestors through the prophets;
in these last days, he has spoken to us through the Son.

℟. **Alleluia, alleluia.**

Lect.
No. 18

GOSPEL: Luke 2:16-21

This passage from the Gospel of Luke recounts some of the wondrous events that accompanied the birth of Jesus. Note especially that Mary pondered all of these things in her heart. In Biblical symbolism, the heart is where one thinks. Thus, Mary is pictured as wondering what the meaning of all these things could be.

It is also important to remember that shepherds were not considered to be reputable people. They were social outcasts, thieves, and worse. The message of salvation was given first of all to those who most needed it.

Mary and Joseph, being good Jews, fulfill all of the prescriptions of the law by circumcising Jesus eight days after he was born and giving him the name that had been revealed to them by the archangel Gabriel.

A reading from the holy Gospel according to Luke

The shepherds went in haste to Bethlehem and
found Mary and Joseph,
and the infant lying in the manger.
When they saw this,
they made known the message
that had been told them about this child.
All who heard it were amazed
by what had been told them by the shepherds.
And Mary kept all these things,
reflecting on them in her heart.
Then the shepherds returned,
glorifying and praising God
for all they had heard and seen,
just as it had been told to them.

When eight days were completed for his circumcision,
he was named Jesus, the name given him by the angel
before he was conceived in the womb.

The Gospel of the Lord.

PASTORAL REFLECTIONS

In 431 A.D., bishops from all over the world met in Ephesus (Turkey) and declared Mary to be the Mother of God. (The term they used was Theotokos.*) This declaration actually had more to do with Jesus than Mary. By it, the Council Fathers were declaring that the Word of God did not pretend to unite with human flesh. Jesus truly had two natures (human and divine) united in one person. This feast of the Blessed Virgin reminds us that our devotion to Mary should always be Christ-centered, for she always points to her Son and says, "Follow him!"*

THE EPIPHANY OF THE LORD

Lect. No. 20

FIRST READING: Isaiah 60:1-6

This part of the Book of the Prophet Isaiah was written shortly after the Jews returned from exile in Babylon (c. 539 B.C.).

In the previous part of this book, we had heard of how Yahweh would restore the fortune of his beloved people. Thus, when the Persian emperor Cyrus allowed the Jewish people to return to their homeland, they were exultant. Yet, when they arrived home, all they found was devastation.

In this part of Isaiah, we hear that God would still fulfill the promises found in Second Isaiah (chs. 40—55).

The glory of God would be upon Israel to such an extent that even the Gentile peoples would come in pilgrimage to Jerusalem to pay homage to the LORD. No longer would the pagans carry the Israelites off into exile. Now the pagans would bring their riches and submit themselves to the God of Israel. This promise would be fulfilled with the arrival of the Magi.

A reading from the Book of the Prophet Isaiah

Rise up in splendor, Jerusalem! Your light has come,
the glory of the Lord shines upon you.
See, darkness covers the earth,
and thick clouds cover the peoples;
but upon you the LORD shines,
and over you appears his glory.
Nations shall walk by your light,
and kings by your shining radiance.
Raise your eyes and look about;
they all gather and come to you:
your sons come from afar,
and your daughters in the arms of their nurses.

Then you shall be radiant at what you see,
your heart shall throb and overflow,
for the riches of the sea shall be emptied out before you,
the wealth of nations shall be brought to you.
Caravans of camels shall fill you,
dromedaries from Midian and Ephah;
all from Sheba shall come
bearing gold and frankincense,
and proclaiming the praises of the LORD.

The word of the Lord.

RESPONSORIAL PSALM: Ps 72:1-2, 7-8, 10-11, 12-13 (℟.: cf. 11)

Lect. No. 20

Psalm 72 gives a description of the perfect king of Israel. He would be someone who was filled with wisdom like Solomon, as well as being a great warrior who could enlarge the boundaries of Israel from sea to sea, one of David's accomplishments. He would also guarantee justice in the land, especially to the poor.

As with the First Reading, we hear that even Gentile kings would recognize the splendor of that king's reign and come to pay him homage.

None of the kings of Israel would fulfill all of these expectations. Every time that the prophets spoke of a king whom they hoped would finally do the will of the LORD, they ended up being disillusioned. Thus, they began to speak about an anointed one in the future who would be unlike all of the other kings of Israel.

The arrival of the Magi to pay homage to baby Jesus, the Messiah of the LORD who would inaugurate the reign of God, was the fulfillment of this prophecy.

℟. **Lord, every nation on earth will adore you.**

O God, with your judgment endow the king,
　　and with your justice, the king's son;
he shall govern your people with justice
　　and your afflicted ones with judgment.

℟. **Lord, every nation on earth will adore you.**

Justice shall flower in his days,
　　and profound peace, till the moon be no more.
May he rule from sea to sea,
　　and from the River to the ends of the earth.

℟. **Lord, every nation on earth will adore you.**

The kings of Tarshish and the Isles shall offer gifts;
　　the kings of Arabia and Seba shall bring tribute.
All kings shall pay him homage,
　　all nations shall serve him.

℟. **Lord, every nation on earth will adore you.**

For he shall rescue the poor when he cries out,
　　and the afflicted when he has no one to help him.
He shall have pity for the lowly and the poor;
　　the lives of the poor he shall save.

℟. **Lord, every nation on earth will adore you.**

SECOND READING: Ephesians 3:2-3a, 5-6

Lect. No. 20

In the Old Covenant, only the Jewish people received the promise. They were the chosen people and heirs of the promises that God had made to the patriarchs and the prophets of Israel.

A reading from the Letter of Saint Paul
to the Ephesians

Brothers and sisters:
You have heard of the stewardship of God's grace
that was given to me for your benefit,

In the New Covenant all peoples will participate in the grace of the Lord. There will be no distinction between Jew and Greek, slave or free, male or female. They all are chosen by the Lord. All will participate in the promise of the Gospel. They all are part of the body of Christ, which is the Church. This is the mystery of salvation: the bounty of God's love for all people.

Lect. No. 20

The Magi saw a star rising in the sky and risked all to pay homage to the newborn king of the Jews. As we proclaim this Alleluia Verse, we promise to follow wherever God leads us.

Lect. No. 20

The feast of the Epiphany celebrates the arrival of the Magi to pay homage to baby Jesus. Epiphany means "manifestation," for we are commemorating the day when the glory of God's Messiah was made manifest to the pagans (in the person of the Magi).

Magi were astrologers. They were not kings (although that title is often used for them) nor does it say that there were three. (That is the number of gifts.) The account speaks of them coming from the east (possibly Persia or Babylon).

namely, that the mystery was made known to me
  by revelation.
It was not made known to people in other generations
  as it has now been revealed
  to his holy apostles and prophets by the Spirit:
  that the Gentiles are coheirs, members of the
    same body,
  and copartners in the promise in Christ Jesus
    through the gospel.

The word of the Lord.

ALLELUIA: Matthew 2:2

℟. **Alleluia, alleluia.**

We saw his star at its rising
and have come to do him homage.

℟. **Alleluia, alleluia.**

GOSPEL: Matthew 2:1-12

A reading from the holy Gospel according
  to Matthew

When Jesus was born in Bethlehem of Judea,
  in the days of King Herod,
  behold, magi from the east arrived in Jerusalem,
    saying,
  "Where is the newborn king of the Jews?
We saw his star at its rising
  and have come to do him homage."
When King Herod heard this,
  he was greatly troubled,
  and all Jerusalem with him.
Assembling all the chief priests and the scribes of
    the people,

It is possible that the star that they saw was the elision of the three planets, Mars, Jupiter, and Saturn, which occurred around 7 B.C. The technical name for this type of elision is syzygy.

The Magi would naturally have gone to Jerusalem to inquire about the birth of a Jewish king. Herod intends to use them to murder what he considers to be a rival to his throne. From many sources we know that Herod was a murderous paranoid when it came to his throne. He murdered a wife, three sons, and a brother-in-law, who was the high priest.

Jewish scholars use a passage taken from Micah to determine that the Messiah was to be born in Bethlehem. This is typical of Matthew who always shows how Jesus fulfills the law and the prophets.

The Magi bring gold, frankincense, and myrrh. They would have brought these products because they were easy to carry and valuable. Later authors found symbolic meaning in these gifts. They spoke of gold as a gift one would give a king, frankincense as an incense one would burn to honor a god, and myrrh as an ointment used in burials, foretelling how Jesus would save us.

he inquired of them where the Christ was to be born.

They said to him, "In Bethlehem of Judea,
  for thus it has been written through the prophet:
    And you, Bethlehem, land of Judah,
      are by no means least among the rulers of Judah;
    since from you shall come a ruler,
      who is to shepherd my people Israel."

Then Herod called the magi secretly
  and ascertained from them the time of the star's appearance.

He sent them to Bethlehem and said,
  "Go and search diligently for the child.

When you have found him, bring me word,
  that I too may go and do him homage."

After their audience with the king they set out.

And behold, the star that they had seen at its rising
  preceded them,
  until it came and stopped over the place where the child was.

They were overjoyed at seeing the star,
  and on entering the house
  they saw the child with Mary his mother.

They prostrated themselves and did him homage.

Then they opened their treasures
  and offered him gifts of gold, frankincense, and myrrh.

And having been warned in a dream not to return to Herod,
  they departed for their country by another way.

The Gospel of the Lord.

PASTORAL REFLECTIONS

This feast, with its stars and the arrival of the Magi, reminds us that God has a plan that is worked out in time (whether Biblical time or the time of our own lives).

January 14, 2018

SECOND SUNDAY IN ORDINARY TIME

Lect. No. 65 **FIRST READING: 1 Samuel 3:3b-10, 19**

With this Sunday we begin the readings of Ordinary Time. The normal pattern for readings throughout this season is to take a reading from the main Gospel of the year (this year Mark). We then have a First Reading that relates to the theme of that Gospel passage. The Second Reading, on the other hand, is a passage taken from one of the New Testament Epistles (and is not related to the theme found in the other two readings).

This week, by exception, the Gospel is taken from John and speaks of the call of the first disciples. The theme developed in it and in the First Reading is God's call and our response.

The First Reading speaks of the call of Samuel, the last of the judges of Israel. A judge was a leader who also served as prophet and priest.

Samuel had been conceived through a miraculous intervention of the LORD and he was dedicated by Hannah, his mother, to the service of God while he was still a baby. He responded to God's call in the middle of the night, and God thus gave his every word authority and power.

A reading from the first Book of Samuel

Samuel was sleeping in the temple of the LORD where the ark of God was.

The LORD called to Samuel, who answered, "Here I am."

Samuel ran to Eli and said, "Here I am. You called me."

"I did not call you," Eli said. "Go back to sleep."

So he went back to sleep.

Again the LORD called Samuel, who rose and went to Eli.

"Here I am," he said. "You called me."

But Eli answered, "I did not call you, my son. Go back to sleep."

At that time Samuel was not familiar with the LORD,
because the LORD had not revealed anything to him as yet.

The LORD called Samuel again, for the third time.

Getting up and going to Eli, he said, "Here I am. You called me."

Then Eli understood that the LORD was calling the youth.

So he said to Samuel, "Go to sleep, and if you are called, reply,
Speak, LORD, for your servant is listening."

When Samuel went to sleep in his place,
the LORD came and revealed his presence,
calling out as before, "Samuel, Samuel!"

Samuel answered, "Speak, for your servant is listening."

Samuel grew up, and the LORD was with him,
not permitting any word of his to be without effect.

The word of the Lord.

RESPONSORIAL PSALM: Ps 40:2, 4, 7-8, 8-9, 10 (℟.: 8a and 9a)

Lect. No. 65

The theme of today's Mass is the call of God and our response. Thus, Psalm 40 speaks of what God really asks of us.

God does not want us to perform sacrifices of holocausts or sin-offerings. Those are external actions that do not always reflect what is going on in our hearts. God wants us to follow him with our whole heart and will.

Thus, we will announce God's justice to everyone whom we meet. This psalm certainly calls us to live our Christian calling with courage and to give public witness to what we believe (both in word and in action).

This is the only thing that will bring us true joy. Hiding who we are or giving our Christian calling a half-hearted response will bring us only emptiness and frustration.

℟. **Here am I, Lord; I come to do your will.**

I have waited, waited for the LORD,
    and he stooped toward me and heard my cry.
And he put a new song into my mouth,
    a hymn to our God.

℟. **Here am I, Lord; I come to do your will.**

Sacrifice or offering you wished not,
    but ears open to obedience you gave me.
Holocausts or sin–offerings you sought not;
    then said I, "Behold I come."

℟. **Here am I, Lord; I come to do your will.**

"In the written scroll it is prescribed for me,
to do your will, O my God, is my delight,
    and your law is within my heart!"

℟. **Here am I, Lord; I come to do your will.**

I announced your justice in the vast assembly;
    I did not restrain my lips, as you, O LORD, know.

℟. **Here am I, Lord; I come to do your will.**

SECOND READING: 1 Corinthians 6:13c-15a, 17-20

Lect. No. 65

The Second Readings for today and the next three weeks are taken from the First Letter to the Corinthians.

This letter was written to a community that was mostly Gentile. Pagans were famous for their sexual immorality, so Saint Paul must remind his readers that their bodies are to be used with modesty.

God created our bodies as good, but sin has caused us to

A reading from the first Letter of Saint Paul to the Corinthians

Brothers and sisters:
The body is not for immorality, but for the Lord, and the Lord is for the body;
God raised the Lord and will also raise us by his power.

Do you not know that your bodies are members of Christ?
But whoever is joined to the Lord becomes one Spirit with him.

use them for evil purposes (e.g., using ourselves and others as objects instead of treating them with respect).

Jesus died on the cross to give us a new chance. He asks us to use our bodies in a way that proclaims God's goodness. We are temples of the Holy Spirit, and we should not allow ourselves or others to be degraded or manipulated.

Avoid immorality.
Every other sin a person commits is outside the body,
  but the immoral person sins against his own body.
Do you not know that your body
  is a temple of the Holy Spirit within you,
  whom you have from God, and that you are not
    your own?
For you have been purchased at a price.
Therefore glorify God in your body.

The word of the Lord.

Lect. No. 65

Jesus is the only truth in our lives that does not fail us. He is the source of grace, which is such profound life in God that even death cannot defeat it.

ALLELUIA: John 1:41, 17b

℟. **Alleluia, alleluia.**

We have found the Messiah:
Jesus Christ, who brings us truth and grace.

℟. **Alleluia, alleluia.**

Lect. No. 65

John the Baptist proclaims Jesus to be the Lamb of God. In Aramaic, the language that John spoke, this phrase is a wordplay. It could mean the Lamb of God as we see (referring to Jesus' death, which freed us from our sins) or it could mean the Servant of God (again, referring to Jesus' death, which expiated our sins).

Two of John's disciples follow Jesus to see who he is. One is Andrew, the brother of Peter. The other disciple remains unnamed. Many believe that this is the beloved disciple.

It is Andrew who calls Peter to meet and follow Jesus. He

GOSPEL: John 1:35-42

A reading from the holy Gospel according to John

John was standing with two of his disciples,
  and as he watched Jesus walk by, he said,
  "Behold, the Lamb of God."
The two disciples heard what he said and followed
    Jesus.
Jesus turned and saw them following him and said
    to them,
  "What are you looking for?"
They said to him, "Rabbi"—which translated means
    Teacher—,
  "where are you staying?"
He said to them, "Come, and you will see."
So they went and saw where Jesus was staying,
  and they stayed with him that day.

tells Peter that Jesus is the Messiah. Notice that this text translates "the Messiah" into Greek ("the Christ"). The reason for this is that most of the readers of the Gospel of John probably spoke Greek as their mother tongue.

Peter receives a new name, "Cephas" in Aramaic (which is translated as "Peter" in Greek). This name means rock. In Matthew this is explained as Peter being the solid foundation of the Church.

It was about four in the afternoon.
Andrew, the brother of Simon Peter,
    was one of the two who heard John and followed Jesus.
He first found his own brother Simon and told him,
    "We have found the Messiah"—which is translated Christ—.
Then he brought him to Jesus.
Jesus looked at him and said,
    "You are Simon the son of John;
    you will be called Cephas"—which is translated Peter.

The Gospel of the Lord.

PASTORAL REFLECTIONS

We all have received a vocation, a call from God. At its most basic level, we all have received a call to salvation. Several times in the New Testament we hear that our names have been written in the Book of Life before the foundation of the world.

We also have received a more specific call on how we are to live out this more general call. Some of us are called to be married, others single. This is not a question of personal preference—it is a response to God's call.

Finally, our work is also part of our response to our vocation. We are not simply earning a living; we also are responding to God's call in whatever work we do. If we keep this fact in mind, then we can see how whatever work we might do, even forms of work that seem to be quite humble, can be for us an expression of our dedication to the spreading of the Kingdom of God.

In today's Gospel we hear Jesus proclaim that the Kingdom of God is at hand and he calls us to conversion.

This is, more or less, the theme of the First Reading as well. Jonah goes to Nineveh, a pagan city, and he preaches that God is ready to punish the city for all of its sins.

The people respond to this announcement with a call to repentance. The king decrees a fast for everyone in the city. He reasons that God might relent and forgive them their sins (which is exactly what happens).

Today, as at every Mass, we are called to examine our lives and turn from our sinful paths so that we might respond to God's call.

Lect. No. 68

FIRST READING: Jonah 3:1-5, 10

A reading from the Book of the Prophet Jonah

The word of the LORD came to Jonah, saying:
"Set out for the great city of Nineveh,
and announce to it the message that I will tell you."
So Jonah made ready and went to Nineveh,
according to the LORD's bidding.
Now Nineveh was an enormously large city;
it took three days to go through it.
Jonah began his journey through the city,
and had gone but a single day's walk announcing,
"Forty days more and Nineveh shall be destroyed,"
when the people of Nineveh believed God;
they proclaimed a fast
and all of them, great and small, put on sackcloth.

When God saw by their actions how they turned
from their evil way,
he repented of the evil that he had threatened to
do to them;
he did not carry it out.

The word of the Lord.

Lect. No. 68

RESPONSORIAL PSALM: Ps 25:4-5, 6-7, 8-9 (℞.: 4a)

In the Responsorial Psalm we beg the LORD to reveal his paths to us. We cannot hope to live in God's ways with a purely human effort. Sooner or later we will lose our way and turn toward sin and selfishness, but if God instructs us in his ways, then we can hope to do what is pleasing in his sight.

This truly shows us that God is loving and compassionate. We experience God's compassion not only in the fact that he forgives us our sins, but also in the fact that he teaches us how to avoid sin. God does not leave us to fend for ourselves. Rather, God treats us like a loving parent treats a child, for he guides and instructs us in his ways. He teaches us how to be good and upright and humble.

℞. **Teach me your ways, O Lord.**

Your ways, O LORD, make known to me;
   teach me your paths,
guide me in your truth and teach me,
   for you are God my savior.

℞. **Teach me your ways, O Lord.**

Remember that your compassion, O LORD,
   and your love are from of old.
In your kindness remember me,
   because of your goodness, O LORD.

℞. **Teach me your ways, O Lord.**

Good and upright is the LORD;
   thus he shows sinners the way.
He guides the humble to justice
   and teaches the humble his way.

℞. **Teach me your ways, O Lord.**

PASTORAL REFLECTIONS

The Lord instructs us in many different ways. We can study the moral teachings of our Church. We can read Scripture and discern what it calls us to do. We can simply look at life around us and evaluate whether we and others are living in a dignified and grace-filled way.

| Lect.
| No. 68 |

SECOND READING: 1 Corinthians 7:29-31

Christians in the early days of the Church believed that the end of the world was at hand. Thus, Saint Paul instructed this community to live as if our worldly concerns were no longer important.

We do not know when the world will end, but we can still maintain a proper perspective on our problems if we view them in light of eternity (if we do not allow ourselves to get caught up in our everyday concerns).

A reading from the first Letter of Saint Paul to the Corinthians

I tell you, brothers and sisters, the time is running out.
  From now on, let those having wives act as not having them,
  those weeping as not weeping,
  those rejoicing as not rejoicing,
  those buying as not owning,
  those using the world as not using it fully.
For the world in its present form is passing away.

The word of the Lord.

| Lect.
| No. 68 |

ALLELUIA: Mark 1:15

The Kingdom (or reign) of God dawns when we make the law of love the guide of our lives and our hearts. This is what true repentance means; this is what the Gospel teaches us to do.

℟. **Alleluia, alleluia.**

The kingdom of God is at hand.
Repent and believe in the Gospel.

℟. **Alleluia, alleluia.**

PASTORAL REFLECTIONS

When we suffer from a serious illness or have a bad accident, we often gain perspective on how precarious life can be. One moment we are here, and the next we might be gone. This helps us discern what is really important and what is secondary. St. Paul asks the community in Corinth to have this type of perspective every day of their lives so that they live each moment to the fullest.

| Lect. |
| No. 68 |

GOSPEL: Mark 1:14-20

This Gospel passage recounts the call of the first apostles: Peter and Andrew, James and John. Both pairs of brothers were fishermen, and Jesus called them from their activities to become proclaimers of the Word of God.

The time of fulfillment and the Kingdom of God are that time when God's law would be observed in righteousness. All people would turn their hearts back to the ways of the Lord. Jesus both proclaimed the dawning of that era and was the personification of the Kingdom of God. This is the good news (Gospel) that Jesus proclaims.

These first apostles left all that they had and they followed Jesus wherever he went. This is our call as well. We do not necessarily have to leave our homes and families, but we do have to live our Christian calling in such a way that everything else (work, possessions, status, etc.) is secondary.

A reading from the holy Gospel according to Mark

After John had been arrested,
Jesus came to Galilee proclaiming the gospel of God:
"This is the time of fulfillment.
The kingdom of God is at hand.
Repent, and believe in the gospel."

As he passed by the Sea of Galilee,
he saw Simon and his brother Andrew casting their nets into the sea;
they were fishermen.
Jesus said to them,
"Come after me, and I will make you fishers of men."
Then they abandoned their nets and followed him.
He walked along a little farther
and saw James, the son of Zebedee, and his brother John.
They too were in a boat mending their nets.
Then he called them.
So they left their father Zebedee in the boat
along with the hired men and followed him.

The Gospel of the Lord.

PASTORAL REFLECTIONS

Conversion always involves saying "yes" to God's call and "no" to those things that would hinder us from answering that call. Even things that are good can get in the way if they become too important in our lives (e.g., relationships, food, etc.).

January 28, 2018

FOURTH SUNDAY IN ORDINARY TIME

Lect. No. 71 **FIRST READING: Deuteronomy 18:15-20**

The First Reading comes from the Book of Deuteronomy. The word "deuteronomy" means the "second law," for it was a collection of laws found in the temple during the religious reform of King Josiah (c. 621 B.C.). It is not clear when it was produced, but it seems to have been written hundreds of years after many of the laws that had been given on Mount Sinai.

Moses is promising a continuity of the prophetic tradition in Israel. God would not leave his chosen people without the guidance that they needed to walk in the ways of the LORD.

Typical of many of the passages of the Old Testament, this prediction came to be understood in a different way as time went on. It was seen more and more as a prediction of a Messiah.

This is one of the reasons why we see Moses in the Transfiguration, to show that Jesus was truly the fulfillment of the promise that Moses had made.

A reading from the Book of Deuteronomy

Moses spoke to all the people, saying:
"A prophet like me will the LORD, your God, raise up for you
from among your own kin;
to him you shall listen.
This is exactly what you requested of the LORD, your God, at Horeb
on the day of the assembly, when you said,
'Let us not again hear the voice of the LORD, our God,
nor see this great fire any more, lest we die.'
And the LORD said to me, 'This was well said.
I will raise up for them a prophet like you from among their kin,
and will put my words into his mouth;
he shall tell them all that I command him.
Whoever will not listen to my words which he speaks in my name,
I myself will make him answer for it.
But if a prophet presumes to speak in my name
an oracle that I have not commanded him to speak,
or speaks in the name of other gods, he shall die.'"

The word of the Lord.

PASTORAL REFLECTIONS

A prophet is not so much someone who foretells the future as much as someone who sees and speaks from God's viewpoint.

Lect. No. 71

RESPONSORIAL PSALM: Ps 95:1-2, 6-7, 7-9 (R̷.: 8)

The first part of this Responsorial Psalm celebrates God as our king and our shepherd. We acclaim his power and mercy with great majesty. He is filled with power and authority (something that, in the Gospel, we will see Jesus also has).

The proper response to this glory is to fall on our knees and worship. It is important to recognize how great God is and how insignificant we are. This is not an act of self-humiliation; it is an acknowledgment of the awesome nature of God. The LORD is not only a companion and friend, he is also the creator of all that exists and the holy one who is beyond our understanding.

The second part of the psalm is a call to obedience and conversion. If God is really our king and shepherd, then we should live obedient and righteous lives.

R̷. **If today you hear his voice, harden not your hearts.**

Come, let us sing joyfully to the LORD;
   let us acclaim the rock of our salvation.
Let us come into his presence with thanksgiving;
   let us joyfully sing psalms to him.

R̷. **If today you hear his voice, harden not your hearts.**

Come, let us bow down in worship;
   let us kneel before the LORD who made us.
For he is our God,
   and we are the people he shepherds, the flock he guides.

R̷. **If today you hear his voice, harden not your hearts.**

Oh, that today you would hear his voice:
   "Harden not your hearts as at Meribah,
   as in the day of Massah in the desert,
where your fathers tempted me;
   they tested me though they had seen my works."

R̷. **If today you hear his voice, harden not your hearts.**

Lect. No. 71

SECOND READING: 1 Corinthians 7:32-35

In the Second Reading Saint Paul recommends that it is better for people to remain single rather than get married so that they can dedicate themselves to the service of the Lord. This is based partly on Paul's view that the end of the world was at hand and that everyone should

A reading from the first Letter of Saint Paul to the Corinthians

Brothers and sisters:
   I should like you to be free of anxieties.
An unmarried man is anxious about the things of the Lord,
   how he may please the Lord.

prepare for it. Therefore, everyone in the community should be preaching and trying to draw others to the faith while there was time.

This theology implies that if someone is serving one's own family, then that person is not serving the Lord. The Second Vatican Council proposed another theology in which virginity and the married state were both seen as valued lifestyles, and God called each of us to one or the other. Service of family is not anxious, wasted effort; it is loving service.

But a married man is anxious about the things of the world,
    how he may please his wife, and he is divided.
An unmarried woman or a virgin is anxious about
    the things of the Lord,
    so that she may be holy in both body and spirit.
A married woman, on the other hand,
    is anxious about the things of the world,
    how she may please her husband.
I am telling you this for your own benefit,
    not to impose a restraint upon you,
    but for the sake of propriety
    and adherence to the Lord without distraction.

The word of the Lord.

Lect. No. 71

Christ is the light of the world, and it is he who will guide us through the darkness. His light is so powerful that it has even conquered the darkness of death, for when we die we will be invited into Christ's kingdom of light.

ALLELUIA: Matthew 4:16

℟. **Alleluia, alleluia.**

The people who sit in darkness have seen a great
    light;
on those dwelling in a land overshadowed by death,
light has arisen.

℟. **Alleluia, alleluia.**

Lect. No. 71

Today's Gospel comes from the account of Jesus' first day in Capernaum. Scholars believe that Saint Mark received this information from Saint Peter himself, for the latter was an eyewitness to these events.

Although this account is short, we hear more than once that Jesus speaks with authority. We also see an example of

GOSPEL: Mark 1:21-28

A reading from the holy Gospel according to Mark

Then they came to Capernaum,
    and on the sabbath Jesus entered the synagogue
    and taught.
The people were astonished at his teaching,
    for he taught them as one having authority and
    not as the scribes.
In their synagogue was a man with an unclean
    spirit;

his exercise of authority when he causes an unclean spirit to come out of a man who is possessed.

The unclean spirit, being a spiritual creature, knows the truth about Jesus. It is not confused by appearances, for it recognizes that Jesus is the Holy One of God.

The people are filled with awe. This is a common reaction to seeing something so wondrous that one cannot understand it. They do not yet know who Jesus is, but they already know that something very holy is happening in their midst.

he cried out, "What have you to do with us, Jesus of Nazareth?

Have you come to destroy us?

I know who you are—the Holy One of God!"

Jesus rebuked him and said,

"Quiet! Come out of him!"

The unclean spirit convulsed him and with a loud cry came out of him.

All were amazed and asked one another,

"What is this?

A new teaching with authority.

He commands even the unclean spirits and they obey him."

His fame spread everywhere throughout the whole region of Galilee.

The Gospel of the Lord.

PASTORAL REFLECTIONS

How do we know if what we have decided is truly coming from God (for being a prophet means to see things from God's perspective)?

We have to pray, fast, ask advice, etc. We must also discern our motivations. We often feel we are doing something from totally pure motivations, but there are frequently hidden levels of motivation (at times even hidden from ourselves). We must be brutally honest with ourselves as to why we want something. We must admit that a part of our motivation is almost always selfish. When we recognize these less than noble motives, we can purify them and unite our intentions more closely to those of God.

FIFTH SUNDAY IN ORDINARY TIME

Lect.
No. 74

There is an interesting contrast between the message of the First Reading and that of the Gospel today. This reading from the Book of Job emphasizes the futility and frustration of human life. It is short; it passes as quickly as a spool that flies from one end to another of a weaver's shuttle. Likewise, it is filled with woe (e.g., months of misery and troubled nights). Remember, these are Job's reflections after he has lost everything that he had and was scraping sores off his body while sitting on a dunghill.

The Gospel presents the response to this reading: Jesus. When he comes into our lives, we find healing.

FIRST READING: Job 7:1-4, 6-7

A reading from the Book of Job

Job spoke, saying:
Is not man's life on earth a drudgery?
 Are not his days those of hirelings?
He is a slave who longs for the shade,
 a hireling who waits for his wages.
So I have been assigned months of misery,
 and troubled nights have been allotted to me.
If in bed I say, "When shall I arise?"
 then the night drags on;
 I am filled with restlessness until the dawn.
My days are swifter than a weaver's shuttle;
 they come to an end without hope.
Remember that my life is like the wind;
 I shall not see happiness again.

The word of the Lord.

PASTORAL REFLECTIONS

We do not fully understand why there is suffering. We only know that we are called to trust in God's love even in the midst of our suffering.

This is not easy, for when we are suffering we often feel abandoned and helpless. Yet, Jesus joined us in our suffering (the cross) so that we will never be alone again.

It also can help to join our suffering to that of others. We can say, "Lord, if my suffering can in any way lighten N's burden, then let me carry the cross with N."

Lect. No. 74

RESPONSORIAL PSALM: Ps 147:1-2, 3-4, 5-6 (℟.: cf. 3a)

This psalm calls upon us to praise the LORD and speaks of how good God is. It is a recognition that no matter how good we try to be, we will always fail if we rely upon our own strength.

God, on the other hand, is omnipotent and omniscient. Everything that exists depends upon him. We see this in the fact that he can call each star by its name. Stars exist at the very extreme of our human consciousness, and yet God can name them. The act of naming is one of dominion (which is why it was forbidden to say the name Yahweh out loud, for it would imply that one had power over God). God also knows all things. There is no limit to his wisdom.

Yet God reaches down and sustains the lowly and humble. He gathers those who are dispersed and rebuilds Jerusalem. He heals the brokenhearted. Even though God is great, he will never forget the weak and the powerless.

Finally, the psalm closes, as most wisdom psalms do, with the declaration that the wicked will be punished for their arrogance.

℟. **Praise the Lord, who heals the brokenhearted.**

or:

℟. **Alleluia.**

Praise the LORD, for he is good;
    sing praise to our God, for he is gracious;
    it is fitting to praise him.
The LORD rebuilds Jerusalem;
    the dispersed of Israel he gathers.

℟. **Praise the Lord, who heals the brokenhearted.**

or:

℟. **Alleluia.**

He heals the brokenhearted
    and binds up their wounds.
He tells the number of the stars;
    he calls each by name.

℟. **Praise the Lord, who heals the brokenhearted.**

or:

℟. **Alleluia.**

Great is our Lord and mighty in power;
    to his wisdom there is no limit.
The LORD sustains the lowly;
    the wicked he casts to the ground.

℟. **Praise the Lord, who heals the brokenhearted.**

or:

℟. **Alleluia.**

Lect. No. 74

SECOND READING: 1 Corinthians 9:16-19, 22-23

This reading is from the First Letter to the Corinthians. Saint Paul was writing to some who insisted upon their rights and were only concerned with what they could get out of life.

Paul responds by speaking of the greatest reward he received in his ministry. It was to share the message of God free of charge. The reward for doing good deeds is the possibility of doing good deeds. God has given us the opportunity to share our talents and love with others. Our greatest self-fulfillment lies in giving ourselves to others, for that is when we are most like God.

Paul also speaks of how he tried to act in a way that would not prove a hindrance to the acceptance of the Gospel message. It is not that he was willing to flip-flop; rather, he realized that the Gospel can only be accepted if it is presented in an acceptable manner.

A reading from the first Letter of Saint Paul to the Corinthians

Brothers and sisters:
If I preach the gospel, this is no reason for me to boast,
  for an obligation has been imposed on me,
  and woe to me if I do not preach it!
If I do so willingly, I have a recompense,
  but if unwillingly, then I have been entrusted with a stewardship.
What then is my recompense?
That, when I preach,
  I offer the gospel free of charge
  so as not to make full use of my right in the gospel.

Although I am free in regard to all,
  I have made myself a slave to all
  so as to win over as many as possible.
To the weak I became weak, to win over the weak.
I have become all things to all, to save at least some.
All this I do for the sake of the gospel,
  so that I too may have a share in it.

The word of the Lord.

Lect. No. 74

ALLELUIA: Matthew 8:17

The Alleluia Verse gives us an indication of the central theme of the Gospel today: Jesus is the healer of our soul and our body.

℟. Alleluia, alleluia.

Christ took away our infirmities
and bore our diseases.

℟. Alleluia, alleluia.

Lect. No. 74

Our Gospel is a continuation of the account of Jesus' first day in Capernaum. As we saw last week, this material was probably given to Saint Mark by Saint Peter, who was an eyewitness to these events.

We hear about the healing of Peter's mother-in-law. What is very interesting about this particular account is that she is one of the few people who receives a miracle in this Gospel and responds in an appropriate manner. Instead of drawing attention to herself, she responds to Jesus' gracious action by service.

When Jesus healed many in the village, he refused to allow the demons to speak because they knew him. They would have proclaimed that Jesus was the Messiah, and Jesus knew that the crowd would have misunderstood his role.

He did not intend to be seen as a political leader or a miracle worker. He was there to heal hearts and to call people to conversion. He was not the Messiah whom they wanted, but rather he was the Messiah whom they needed.

This is why, after he had prayed in a deserted spot for a while, he goes to the other villages in the area to proclaim the Word of God.

GOSPEL: Mark 1:29-39

A reading from the holy Gospel according to Mark

On leaving the synagogue
Jesus entered the house of Simon and Andrew
with James and John.
Simon's mother–in–law lay sick with a fever.
They immediately told him about her.
He approached, grasped her hand, and helped her up.
Then the fever left her and she waited on them.

When it was evening, after sunset,
they brought to him all who were ill or possessed by demons.
The whole town was gathered at the door.
He cured many who were sick with various diseases,
and he drove out many demons,
not permitting them to speak because they knew him.

Rising very early before dawn, he left
and went off to a deserted place, where he prayed.
Simon and those who were with him pursued him
and on finding him said, "Everyone is looking for you."
He told them, "Let us go on to the nearby villages
that I may preach there also.
For this purpose have I come."
So he went into their synagogues,
preaching and driving out demons throughout the whole of Galilee.

The Gospel of the Lord.

February 11, 2018

SIXTH SUNDAY IN ORDINARY TIME

The Gospel today will speak about a healing of someone who had leprosy. It refers to the law of Moses concerning what to do when someone in the community had this disease. The First Reading today gives us an account of that law.

Leprosy was especially feared in the ancient world. It was so dreaded that anyone who had any sort of skin disease (even severe acne or eczema) was considered to be leprous.

All who had any sort of skin disease were severely segregated. They lost any right to participate in normal society. This was true at a civil and religious level (for priests were involved in the official declaration of uncleanness and that someone had been healed).

Lect. No. 77 **FIRST READING: Leviticus 13:1-2, 44-46**

A reading from the Book of Leviticus

The LORD said to Moses and Aaron,
"If someone has on his skin a scab or pustule or blotch
which appears to be the sore of leprosy,
he shall be brought to Aaron, the priest,
or to one of the priests among his descendants.
If the man is leprous and unclean,
the priest shall declare him unclean
by reason of the sore on his head.

"The one who bears the sore of leprosy
shall keep his garments rent and his head bare,
and shall muffle his beard;
he shall cry out, 'Unclean, unclean!'
As long as the sore is on him he shall declare himself unclean,
since he is in fact unclean.
He shall dwell apart, making his abode outside the camp."

The word of the Lord.

Lect. No. 77 **RESPONSORIAL PSALM: Ps 32:1-2, 5, 11 (℟.: 7)**

The Responsorial Psalm speaks of the healing that God will grant us. The Gospel describes that healing in terms of being healed from physical diseases. This psalm speaks of the more important healing that only God can give, a healing of our hearts.

℟. **I turn to you, Lord, in time of trouble, and you fill me with the joy of salvation.**

Blessed is he whose fault is taken away,
whose sin is covered.
Blessed the man to whom the LORD imputes not guilt,
in whose spirit there is no guile.

God offers us healing, but we can only be healed if we ask for it. We have to admit our sinfulness and seek pardon.

Sin is doing things that deny the love we should have for ourselves and others. When we sin, we are telling ourselves and others that we are trash, and that we might as well act like trash.

God does not treat us this way. God treats us with more respect than we think we deserve. God loves us even when we do not know enough to love ourselves.

℟. **I turn to you, Lord, in time of trouble, and you fill me with the joy of salvation.**

Then I acknowledged my sin to you,
    my guilt I covered not.
I said, "I confess my faults to the LORD,"
    and you took away the guilt of my sin.

℟. **I turn to you, Lord, in time of trouble, and you fill me with the joy of salvation.**

Be glad in the LORD and rejoice, you just;
    exult, all you upright of heart.

℟. **I turn to you, Lord, in time of trouble, and you fill me with the joy of salvation.**

Lect. No. 77

SECOND READING: 1 Corinthians 10:31—11:1

The Second Reading speaks of the attitude that we must adopt in our service of God and each other. Everything must be done in a way that will bring others to God. We cannot think only of ourselves and what we want. We must ultimately be imitators of Christ.

Saint Paul also tells the community that they should imitate him. This is not pride or arrogance, but rather is simple honesty; for, as Paul says elsewhere, he had already chosen to live only in and for the Lord.

A reading from the first Letter of Saint Paul to the Corinthians

Brothers and sisters,
    Whether you eat or drink, or whatever you do,
    do everything for the glory of God.
Avoid giving offense, whether to the Jews or Greeks
        or the church of God,
    just as I try to please everyone in every way,
    not seeking my own benefit but that of the many,
    that they may be saved.
Be imitators of me, as I am of Christ.

The word of the Lord.

Lect. No. 77

The Alleluia Verse presents Jesus as a great prophet. This does not mean that he is not the Son of God, but rather that he is the one who most clearly communicates the word of God to us.

ALLELUIA: Luke 7:16

℟. **Alleluia, alleluia.**

A great prophet has arisen in our midst,
God has visited his people.

℟. **Alleluia, alleluia.**

Lect.
No. 77

The Gospel today is the account of a miracle. Most miracle stories have four elements: a description of the situation, an appeal for help, an intervention on the part of Jesus, and a reaction of the people who witnessed that miracle.

Jesus healed this man because he was moved with pity. In this Gospel and others Jesus often heals because of compassion.

Jesus heals the man and orders him not to tell anyone except for the priests who could certify his healing (and thus allow him to reenter society from which he had been excluded because of his disease).

Jesus' command not to say anything about what had happened to him is typical of the Gospel of Mark wherein Jesus does not want to become famous as a miracle worker, for his mission is much more profound than that. In spite of this command, Jesus' fame spread throughout the land.

GOSPEL: Mark 1:40-45

A reading from the holy Gospel according
to Mark

A leper came to Jesus and kneeling down begged
him and said,
"If you wish, you can make me clean."
Moved with pity, he stretched out his hand,
touched him, and said to him,
"I do will it. Be made clean."
The leprosy left him immediately, and he was made
clean.
Then, warning him sternly, he dismissed him at
once.

He said to him, "See that you tell no one anything,
but go, show yourself to the priest
and offer for your cleansing what Moses prescribed;
that will be proof for them."

The man went away and began to publicize the
whole matter.
He spread the report abroad
so that it was impossible for Jesus to enter a town
openly.
He remained outside in deserted places,
and people kept coming to him from everywhere.

The Gospel of the Lord.

PASTORAL REFLECTIONS

Many forms of illness make people feel isolated (e.g., cancer, AIDS, etc.). It is a true work of mercy to reach out to those who feel isolated and let them know that they are accepted and loved.

February 14, 2018
ASH WEDNESDAY*

These readings are found in the Lectionary, Vol. II, no. 219.

Lect.
Vol. II
No. 219

FIRST READING: Joel 2:12-18

Lent is a time to examine our lives carefully and to root out those things that keep us from loving God and each other.

In the First Reading, Joel speaks of how God is ready to forgive us. We, however, must decide to seek that pardon. If we are not willing to admit that we are sinners and broken, then God cannot heal us.

It is not that God does not want to heal us, only that we cannot receive his healing until we open our hearts to it.

It is never too late to turn back to God. Consider the story of the owner of the vineyard who rewarded everyone who worked for him, even those who worked for only a very short while.

At the same time, however, we should not presume upon God's mercy. We must use this blessed season to change our ways.

The reading speaks of weeping and mourning as signs of our willingness to turn away from sin and to return to God. Our sign today is ashes, which are an external sign of our own willingness to change both our hearts and our actions.

A reading from the Book of the Prophet Joel

Even now, says the LORD,
   return to me with your whole heart,
     with fasting, and weeping, and mourning;
Rend your hearts, not your garments,
     and return to the LORD, your God.
For gracious and merciful is he,
     slow to anger, rich in kindness,
     and relenting in punishment.
Perhaps he will again relent
     and leave behind him a blessing,
Offerings and libations
     for the LORD, your God.

Blow the trumpet in Zion!
     proclaim a fast,
     call an assembly;
Gather the people,
     notify the congregation;
Assemble the elders,
     gather the children
     and the infants at the breast;
Let the bridegroom quit his room
     and the bride her chamber.
Between the porch and the altar
     let the priests, the ministers of the LORD, weep,
And say, "Spare, O LORD, your people,
     and make not your heritage a reproach,
     with the nations ruling over them!
Why should they say among the peoples,
     'Where is their God?'"

When we do this, we can truly accept the love and mercy that God offers us in this holy season.

Then the LORD was stirred to concern for his land
and took pity on his people.

The word of the Lord.

Lect. Vol. II No. 219

RESPONSORIAL PSALM: Ps 51:3-4, 5-6ab, 12-13, 14 and 17 (℟.: see 3a)

Psalm 51 is a beautiful penitential psalm. It is dedicated to the memory of that moment when the Prophet Nathan confronted King David concerning his act of adultery with Bathsheba and his murder of Uriah the Hittite.

The psalm recognizes many of the facets of turning away from sin and back to God. It speaks of how we can only be cleansed through the intervention of God.

We recognize the fact that we are sinners and worthy of condemnation. Yet, we beseech God for healing.

If God recreates us with his Spirit, we will be alive in God again. Our sin has made us like creatures that have lost their life, but now God has breathed his Spirit back into us. We will be filled with the joy of God, for he is the source of our salvation.

℟. **Be merciful, O Lord, for we have sinned.**

Have mercy on me, O God, in your goodness;
    in the greatness of your compassion wipe out my
        offense.
Thoroughly wash me from my guilt
    and of my sin cleanse me.

℟. **Be merciful, O Lord, for we have sinned.**

For I acknowledge my offense,
    and my sin is before me always:
"Against you only have I sinned,
    and done what is evil in your sight."

℟. **Be merciful, O Lord, for we have sinned.**

A clean heart create for me, O God,
    and a steadfast spirit renew within me.
Cast me not out from your presence,
    and your Holy Spirit take not from me.

℟. **Be merciful, O Lord, for we have sinned.**

Give me back the joy of your salvation,
    and a willing spirit sustain in me.
O Lord, open my lips,
    and my mouth shall proclaim your praise.

℟. **Be merciful, O Lord, for we have sinned.**

PASTORAL REFLECTIONS

Psalm 51 was probably not written by King David. It was dedicated to his memory.

Lect.
Vol. II
No. 219

SECOND READING: 2 Corinthians 5:20—6:2

Saint Paul speaks of being an ambassador for the message of salvation. His entire life's work was to proclaim the salvation that God offers us through the death and resurrection of Jesus.

Now is the time to accept that salvation into our lives. The beginning of Lent is a blessed time for us to turn from our mistaken ways and to find the path of truth.

This is all that God wants of us. That is why God created us: to be saved. We see this in the fact that Jesus took our human condition upon himself, even suffering and dying, although he had done nothing wrong. He became sin (adopted our sinful flesh) to set us free from our sin.

A reading from the second Letter of Saint Paul to the Corinthians

Brothers and sisters:
We are ambassadors for Christ,
   as if God were appealing through us.
We implore you on behalf of Christ,
   be reconciled to God.
For our sake he made him to be sin who did not know sin,
   so that we might become the righteousness of God in him.

Working together, then,
   we appeal to you not to receive the grace of God in vain.
For he says:

In an acceptable time I heard you,
   and on the day of salvation I helped you.

Behold, now is a very acceptable time;
   behold, now is the day of salvation.

The word of the Lord.

Lect.
Vol. II
No. 219

VERSE BEFORE THE GOSPEL: See Psalm 95:8

Now is the time to turn from our sin and to embrace God with all our hearts. Today is the day of our salvation.

If today you hear his voice,
harden not your hearts.

**Lect.
Vol. II
No. 219**

GOSPEL: Matthew 6:1-6,16-18

When the temple in Jerusalem was destroyed in 70 A.D., the Jewish people lost the place where they could expiate their sins. Previously, they had performed sacrifices that won them forgiveness for their sins.

Sin had brought death into their lives. The blood of their sacrifices gave them life again (for blood was a sign of life).

The people asked the rabbis what they could do to obtain forgiveness for their sins now that there was nowhere that they could offer sacrifices.

The rabbis answered that there were three things that brought forgiveness of sins: almsgiving, fasting, and praying.

These are the exact things that our reading asks us to do. Saint Matthew's message is that the rabbis were right, but they were wrong in the way that they did these things. They often did them to look good before others.

That is not the reason why we should do these things. We should do them out of a profound willingness to change our lives. They should be reflections of a change of heart. Without that, these actions are nothing more than superficial deeds that do us no good.

Therefore, today we dedicate ourselves to acts of penance.

A reading from the holy Gospel according to Matthew

Jesus said to his disciples:
"Take care not to perform righteous deeds
in order that people may see them;
otherwise, you will have no recompense from
your heavenly Father.
When you give alms,
do not blow a trumpet before you,
as the hypocrites do in the synagogues and in the
streets
to win the praise of others.
Amen, I say to you,
they have received their reward.
But when you give alms,
do not let your left hand know what your right is
doing,
so that your almsgiving may be secret.
And your Father who sees in secret will repay you.

"When you pray,
do not be like the hypocrites,
who love to stand and pray in the synagogues and
on street corners
so that others may see them.
Amen, I say to you,
they have received their reward.
But when you pray, go to your inner room,
close the door, and pray to your Father in secret.
And your Father who sees in secret will repay you.

"When you fast,
do not look gloomy like the hypocrites.
They neglect their appearance,
so that they may appear to others to be fasting.
Amen, I say to you, they have received their reward.

These actions are signs of our willingness to make this Lent meaningful. We commit ourselves to prayer, to acts of charity, and to acts of mortification.

These things do not have to be spectacular. (In fact, it is always prudent to plan things that are reasonable lest we overcommit ourselves and lose heart after a few days.) However, they must be honest signs of willingness to live for and in God our Father.

But when you fast,
  anoint your head and wash your face,
  so that you may not appear to be fasting,
  except to your Father who is hidden.
And your Father who sees what is hidden will repay
  you."

The Gospel of the Lord.

PASTORAL REFLECTIONS

There are several reasons why we fast. One of them is that we often abuse food. We eat too much, too little, or the wrong thing. Fasting helps us to break away from our obsession to food and it gives us perspective.

Fasting also teaches us discipline for it teaches us how to be able to say "no" to certain things so that we might say "yes" to God.

Fasting reminds us, too, who is really important in our lives. The hunger pains remind us of our commitment to God, and they also remind us of the poor (who are God's children) who are hungry each day.

In addition, fasting heals some of the wounds that we have brought into our lives through sin. Every time that we sin, we weaken ourselves and make it easier for us to sin in the future. By making the loving choice to fast, we are strengthening our choice to love.

When one fasts with the proper disposition, it leads to a tremendous sense of lightness and joy, for it is an action of love.

February 18, 2018

FIRST SUNDAY OF LENT

Lect. No. 23

FIRST READING: Genesis 9:8-15

Today's First Reading is taken from the end of the story of Noah and the flood. God had punished humanity for their sinfulness by sending a flood that destroyed everything that lived (with the exception of Noah and his family and the animals he saved on the ark).

After the flood had receded, Noah and his family opened the ark and stepped onto dry land. The first thing that they did was to offer a sacrifice of thanksgiving to the LORD. This greatly pleased God.

God, on his part, made a covenant with Noah and with all creatures that he would never destroy the world again with a flood.

He did not make this pact with them because they were so good, for in a passage that immediately precedes this reading, God admits that human hearts are corrupt from their birth. Rather, he made this promise as an act of mercy.

Finally, God gave the rainbow as a reminder to all who would see it of this covenant that he would uphold forever.

A reading from the Book of Genesis

God said to Noah and to his sons with him:
"See, I am now establishing my covenant with you
and your descendants after you
and with every living creature that was with you:
all the birds, and the various tame and wild animals
that were with you and came out of the ark.
I will establish my covenant with you,
that never again shall all bodily creatures be destroyed
by the waters of a flood;
there shall not be another flood to devastate the earth."
God added:
"This is the sign that I am giving for all ages to come,
of the covenant between me and you
and every living creature with you:
I set my bow in the clouds to serve as a sign
of the covenant between me and the earth.
When I bring clouds over the earth,
and the bow appears in the clouds,
I will recall the covenant I have made
between me and you and all living beings,
so that the waters shall never again become a flood
to destroy all mortal beings."

The word of the Lord.

Lect. No. 23

RESPONSORIAL PSALM: Ps 25:4-5, 6-7, 8-9 (℟.: cf. 10)

God is forever faithful to his covenant, but we are not always as consistent.

All too often we fall into sins that betray the love God has shown us. No matter how we try to be faithful, we do not seem to have the strength to be good.

This is why we reach out to God. We depend upon God to show us the right path, and then to give us the courage to do what is right.

God promises to instruct and guide us. This is the greatest sign of his mercy, that he will not abandon us to futile and frustrating attempts to do what is right.

This psalm reminds us that our Lenten conversion is not simply an act of will on our part, but rather a surrender to the guidance of God, for we cannot hope to change our ways by ourselves.

℟. **Your ways, O Lord, are love and truth to those who keep your covenant.**

Your ways, O LORD, make known to me;
   teach me your paths.
Guide me in your truth and teach me,
   for you are God my savior.

℟. **Your ways, O Lord, are love and truth to those who keep your covenant.**

Remember that your compassion, O LORD,
   and your love are from of old.
In your kindness remember me,
   because of your goodness, O LORD.

℟. **Your ways, O Lord, are love and truth to those who keep your covenant.**

Good and upright is the LORD,
   thus he shows sinners the way.
He guides the humble to justice,
   and he teaches the humble his way.

℟. **Your ways, O Lord, are love and truth to those who keep your covenant.**

Lect. No. 23

SECOND READING: 1 Peter 3:18-22

This reading from the First Letter of Peter is rather complicated. The entire Letter has a baptismal theme, which is also found here.

Baptism is seen as a washing to remove the contagion of sin (and not the cleansing from physical dirtiness). The ark that saved Noah from the flood is a type of prefiguring of the Sacrament of Baptism (for in Baptism

A reading from the first Letter of Saint Peter

Beloved:
Christ suffered for sins once,
   the righteous for the sake of the unrighteous,
   that he might lead you to God.
Put to death in the flesh,
   he was brought to life in the Spirit.
In it he also went to preach to the spirits in prison,
   who had once been disobedient
   while God patiently waited in the days of Noah

we are saved from the flood of sin and lies that surrounds us).

The verse that speaks about Jesus preaching to those who were in prison seems to be a reference to the belief that, after Jesus died on the cross, he descended down into the underworld (sometimes called hell or hades or Sheol).

He did this in order to proclaim his message of salvation to those who had died before he was born.

during the building of the ark,
  in which a few persons, eight in all,
  were saved through water.
This prefigured baptism, which saves you now.
It is not a removal of dirt from the body
  but an appeal to God for a clear conscience,
  through the resurrection of Jesus Christ,
  who has gone into heaven
  and is at the right hand of God,
  with angels, authorities, and powers subject to
    him.

The word of the Lord.

Lect. No. 23

VERSE BEFORE THE GOSPEL: Matthew 4:4b

In this time of fasting, we are reminded that we need to nourish not only our bodies but also our souls.

One does not live on bread alone,
  but on every word that comes forth from the
    mouth of God.

Lect. No. 23

GOSPEL: Mark 1:12-15

The account of the temptation in the desert in the Gospel of Mark is the simplest of the three Synoptic versions. There is no mention of the three separate temptations as there is in Luke and Matthew. All we are told is that Jesus was tempted for forty days.

The kingdom of God (or more accurately, the reign of God) will be manifested when people turn their hearts to the Lord. This is why we repent during Lent: to allow God (and not other things) to be at the center of our lives.

A reading from the holy Gospel according
  to Mark

The Spirit drove Jesus out into the desert,
  and he remained in the desert for forty days,
    tempted by Satan.
He was among wild beasts,
  and the angels ministered to him.

After John had been arrested,
  Jesus came to Galilee proclaiming the gospel of
    God:
"This is the time of fulfillment.
The kingdom of God is at hand.
Repent, and believe in the gospel."

The Gospel of the Lord.

February 25, 2018
SECOND SUNDAY OF LENT

FIRST READING:

Genesis 22:1-2, 9a, 10-13, 15-18

Both the First Reading and the Gospel today present events that take place on the tops of mountains, but the two stories are significantly different.

The first story involves Abraham and Isaac. God calls Abraham and tests his faith by asking him to sacrifice his only son.

Isaac is Abraham's only son because God had already told Abraham to listen to the complaints of Sarah and send his other son, Ishmael, the son of Hagar the slave, into the desert.

This is not only the story of a test that involves the life of an only child, which would already be an incredible thing to ask of Abraham. It is also the question of putting God's word to the test.

God had promised Abraham the land in which he was dwelling (of which he possessed nothing) and a large descendance (and he had only one son). Was God going to fulfill his promises?

Abraham places all of his trust in the LORD and he does exactly as he was ordered.

God responds to this act of faith with great beneficence. He protects the child Isaac, and

A reading from the Book of Genesis

God put Abraham to the test.
He called to him, "Abraham!"
"Here I am!" he replied.
Then God said:
   "Take your son Isaac, your only one, whom you
      love,
   and go to the land of Moriah.
There you shall offer him up as a holocaust
   on a height that I will point out to you."

When they came to the place of which God had told
      him,
   Abraham built an altar there and arranged the
      wood on it.
Then he reached out and took the knife to slaughter
   his son.
But the LORD's messenger called to him from heaven,
   "Abraham, Abraham!"
"Here I am!" he answered.
"Do not lay your hand on the boy," said the messenger.
"Do not do the least thing to him.
I know now how devoted you are to God,
   since you did not withhold from me your own
      beloved son."
As Abraham looked about,
   he spied a ram caught by its horns in the thicket.
So he went and took the ram
   and offered it up as a holocaust in place of his son.

Again the LORD's messenger called to Abraham from
      heaven and said:
   "I swear by myself, declares the LORD,

then he renews his promise to Abraham.

We might ask why God would put Abraham to the test if God already knows everything that is going to happen.

The response is that Abraham did not know everything. He learned how much he could trust and love God through this test (as we often learn through our own times of trial).

that because you acted as you did
in not withholding from me your beloved son,
I will bless you abundantly
and make your descendants as countless
as the stars of the sky and the sands of the
    seashore;
your descendants shall take possession
of the gates of their enemies,
and in your descendants all the nations of the earth
    shall find blessing—
all this because you obeyed my command."
The word of the Lord.

Lect. No. 26

RESPONSORIAL PSALM: Ps 116: 10, 15, 16-17, 18-19 (℟.: 9)

Today's Responsorial Psalm is actually a series of verses taken out of Psalm 116. The entire psalm is a thanksgiving psalm to celebrate a deliverance through the intervention of the LORD.

The verses that have been chosen for today speak of the Psalmist's trust in God. Although the Psalmist was greatly afflicted, he was delivered from his adversity. It never quite says what the problem was, which leaves this psalm more open-ended for both the Psalmist and ourselves.

The only possible way that he can respond to this goodness is to sing a hymn of thanksgiving.

He will dedicate himself to the service of God. He will give witness to all who will listen that it is God who saved him.

℟. **I will walk before the Lord, in the land of the living.**

I believed, even when I said,
    "I am greatly afflicted."
Precious in the eyes of the LORD
    is the death of his faithful ones.

℟. **I will walk before the Lord, in the land of the living.**

O LORD, I am your servant;
    I am your servant, the son of your handmaid;
    you have loosed my bonds.
To you will I offer sacrifice of thanksgiving,
    and I will call upon the name of the LORD.

℟. **I will walk before the Lord, in the land of the living.**

My vows to the LORD I will pay
    in the presence of all his people,
in the courts of the house of the LORD,
    in your midst, O Jerusalem.

℟. **I will walk before the Lord, in the land of the living.**

Lect. No. 26

SECOND READING: Romans 8:31b-34

In the earlier chapters of the Letter to the Romans, Saint Paul had spoken of the fact that we deserved to be condemned for our sins, but God chose to shower his mercy upon us. He loved us so much that it was his will that Jesus die for us.

If this is true, then how can we fear anyone or anything?

God is on our side; he has already proven that abundantly. What other power exists that could destroy the peace and love we have found in the Lord?

A reading from the Letter of Saint Paul to the Romans

Brothers and sisters:
If God is for us, who can be against us?
He who did not spare his own Son
    but handed him over for us all,
    how will he not also give us everything else along
      with him?
Who will bring a charge against God's chosen ones?
    It is God who acquits us. Who will condemn?
Christ Jesus it is who died—or, rather, was raised—
    who also is at the right hand of God,
    who indeed intercedes for us.

The word of the Lord.

Lect. No. 26

VERSE BEFORE THE GOSPEL: cf. Matthew 17:5

This verse introduces the words that we will hear God the Father proclaim in the Gospel.

From the shining cloud the Father's voice is heard:
This is my beloved Son, listen to him.

Lect. No. 26

GOSPEL: Mark 9:2-10

The Gospel is the account of the Transfiguration. Jesus took Peter, James, and John up the mountain with him.

Whenever something important happens in the Gospel, it usually involves these three. Upon the mountain Jesus is transfigured and appears in glorious raiment.

Moses and Elijah appear, for Jesus is both the fulfillment of the Law (represented by Moses who received the Law on Mount

A reading from the holy Gospel according to Mark

Jesus took Peter, James, and John
    and led them up a high mountain apart by themselves.
And he was transfigured before them,
    and his clothes became dazzling white,
    such as no fuller on earth could bleach them.
Then Elijah appeared to them along with Moses,
    and they were conversing with Jesus.
Then Peter said to Jesus in reply,
    "Rabbi, it is good that we are here!

Jewish people rest from sunset on Friday until sunset the next evening. Christians observe this weekly rest on Sunday to pay respect to the day of Jesus' resurrection.

The other seven commandments concern our obligations toward our brothers and sisters. It must be remembered that these commandments give the absolute minimum in terms of how we should treat others.

Even if one were to keep all of these commandments, it does not mean that one is necessarily a good Christian (especially if one does not also act in charity toward others).

This is why the Beatitudes, a type of Christian commandments, ask for more than the minimum; they invite one to generosity.

No work may be done then either by you, or your
    son or daughter,
    or your male or female slave, or your beast,
    or by the alien who lives with you.
In six days the Lord made the heavens and the
    earth,
    the sea and all that is in them;
    but on the seventh day he rested.
That is why the Lord has blessed the sabbath day
    and made it holy.

"Honor your father and your mother,
    that you may have a long life in the land
    which the Lord, your God, is giving you.
You shall not kill.
You shall not commit adultery.
You shall not steal.
You shall not bear false witness against your neighbor.
You shall not covet your neighbor's house.
You shall not covet your neighbor's wife,
    nor his male or female slave, nor his ox or ass,
    nor anything else that belongs to him."

The word of the Lord.

Lect. No. 29 **FIRST READING: B Shorter Form: Exodus 20:1-3, 7-8, 12-17**

The First Reading gives an account of the reception of the Ten Commandments. The first three commandments concern our obligation to God. We are told that we are not to create idols or worship strange gods (e.g., the gods of work, prestige, etc., or even practices such as horoscopes and psychics).

We should treat God's name and the Sabbath, the day of rest, with sacred respect. We are told that the Sabbath obli-

A reading from the Book of Exodus

In those days, God delivered all these commandments:
    "I, the Lord, am your God,
    who brought you out of the land of Egypt, that
    place of slavery.
You shall not have other gods besides me.

"You shall not take the name of the Lord, your God,
    in vain.
For the Lord will not leave unpunished
    the one who takes his name in vain.

gation dates back to the first days of creation when God worked for six days and then rested on the seventh.

Jewish people rest from sunset on Friday until sunset the next evening. Christians observe this weekly rest on Sunday to pay respect to the day of Jesus' resurrection.

The other seven commandments concern our obligations toward our brothers and sisters. These commandments give the absolute minimum in terms of how we should treat others.

"Remember to keep holy the sabbath day.
Honor your father and your mother,
    that you may have a long life in the land
    which the LORD, your God, is giving you.
You shall not kill.
You shall not commit adultery.
You shall not steal.
You shall not bear false witness against your neighbor.
You shall not covet your neighbor's house.
You shall not covet your neighbor's wife,
    nor his male or female slave, nor his ox or ass,
    nor anything else that belongs to him."

The word of the Lord.

| Lect. No. 29 |

RESPONSORIAL PSALM: Ps 19:8, 9, 10, 11 (℟.: Jn 6:68c)

The second half of Psalm 19 is a hymn that celebrates the Law. Six different synonyms are used for the Law, all of which speak of the goodness of the Law.

It is unusual that the author used six synonyms. Seven is the perfect number in the Bible, and one would have expected to find this many attributes of the Law.

The seventh reference is actually found at the end of the psalm (which is not included in the Responsorial Psalm today).

The author prays that the words of his mouth and the meditation of his heart be pleasing in the sight of the LORD. The meaning of this is that the Law does not really become perfect until it is interiorized in one's heart and professed by one's life.

℟. **Lord, you have the words of everlasting life.**

The law of the LORD is perfect,
    refreshing the soul;
the decree of the LORD is trustworthy,
    giving wisdom to the simple.

℟. **Lord, you have the words of everlasting life.**

The precepts of the LORD are right,
    rejoicing the heart;
the command of the LORD is clear,
    enlightening the eye.

℟. **Lord, you have the words of everlasting life.**

The fear of the LORD is pure,
    enduring forever;
the ordinances of the LORD are true,
    all of them just.

℟. **Lord, you have the words of everlasting life.**

They are more precious than gold,
    than a heap of purest gold;
sweeter also than syrup
    or honey from the comb.

℟. **Lord, you have the words of everlasting life.**

Lect. No. 29

SECOND READING: 1 Corinthians 1:22-25

The ways of the world are not necessarily like the ways of the Lord. The world expected God to send a Messiah who was powerful (which is what Jews considered to be wisdom) and God to remain totally spiritual and removed from this material world (which is what the Greeks considered to be wisdom).

Instead of this, Jesus was born in the flesh as a baby in Bethlehem and died for us on the cross (which is the wisdom of God). The love of God, expressed in this most incarnate manner, puts to shame the concepts of wisdom professed by the world.

A reading from the first Letter of Saint Paul to the Corinthians

Brothers and sisters:
Jews demand signs and Greeks look for wisdom,
but we proclaim Christ crucified,
a stumbling block to Jews and foolishness to Gentiles,
but to those who are called, Jews and Greeks alike,
Christ the power of God and the wisdom of God.
For the foolishness of God is wiser than human wisdom,
and the weakness of God is stronger than human strength.

The word of the Lord.

Lect. No. 29

VERSE BEFORE THE GOSPEL: John 3:16

This text contains a truth that should be of great comfort to us, that God's attitude toward the world is one of profound love.

God so loved the world that he gave his only Son,
so that everyone who believes in him might have eternal life.

Lect. No. 29

GOSPEL: John 2:13-25

In the Synoptic Gospels (Matthew, Mark, and Luke), Jesus cleanses the temple at the end of his ministry. In those Gospels, it is the proximate reason why the leaders of the Jews decide to put Jesus to death.

In the Gospel of John that we hear today, the cleansing of the temple occurs at the beginning

A reading from the holy Gospel according to John

Since the Passover of the Jews was near,
Jesus went up to Jerusalem.
He found in the temple area those who sold oxen, sheep, and doves,
as well as the money changers seated there.
He made a whip out of cords
and drove them all out of the temple area, with the sheep and oxen,

of his ministry (for the entire ministry of Jesus is a revelation of the Father's love for us that can only end upon the cross).

Animals were needed for the daily sacrifices performed in the temple, and coins had to be changed (for one could only donate Jewish coins in the temple since most pagan coins had images of pagan gods on them).

Yet those who were performing this necessary function had begun to abuse their role and act in a way that was at least undignified, and more probably scandalous.

Jesus spoke of the destruction of the temple of his body, but those listening to him misunderstood what he was saying and thought he was referring to the temple. This might explain why they later accused him of trying to destroy the temple.

Many who followed Jesus did so to see him perform miracles (called "signs" in this Gospel).

Their faith was superficial, for they only wanted to see a miracle worker. They were only concerned with what they could get out of this relationship. They did not want to commit their lives and their love to Jesus.

and spilled the coins of the money changers
and overturned their tables,
and to those who sold doves he said,
"Take these out of here,
and stop making my Father's house a marketplace."
His disciples recalled the words of Scripture,
Zeal for your house will consume me.
At this the Jews answered and said to him,
"What sign can you show us for doing this?"
Jesus answered and said to them,
"Destroy this temple and in three days I will raise it up."
The Jews said,
"This temple has been under construction for forty-six years,
and you will raise it up in three days?"
But he was speaking about the temple of his body.
Therefore, when he was raised from the dead,
his disciples remembered that he had said this,
and they came to believe the Scripture
and the word Jesus had spoken.

While he was in Jerusalem for the feast of Passover,
many began to believe in his name
when they saw the signs he was doing.
But Jesus would not trust himself to them because he knew them all,
and did not need anyone to testify about human nature.
He himself understood it well.

The Gospel of the Lord.

PASTORAL REFLECTIONS

The wisdom of the cross which is spoken of in the Second Reading is the measure by which we Christians measure true success.

The following readings given for Year A, no. 28, may be used in place of the previous readings.

Lect. No. 28

FIRST READING: Exodus 17:3-7

The Lord had just freed the Israelites from slavery in Egypt, intervening with powerful miracles to convince the Egyptians to let his people go, but they still grumbled against Moses and the Lord. They refused to believe that the Lord would continue to protect them and provide for their needs.

This lack of gratitude is astounding, and yet the Lord responds with another act of generosity. He provides them with water from the rock.

This was a pattern that occurred over and over again throughout the Exodus experience. This is why the Israelites had to remain in the desert for forty years, to learn how to trust in the Lord.

Before we condemn the Israelites, though, it is good to admit that, in spite of all the ways we have seen God's goodness in our lives, we still doubt his presence all too often. We often hedge our bets by relying on God but also upon our own resources.

A reading from the Book of Exodus

In those days, in their thirst for water,
the people grumbled against Moses,
saying, "Why did you ever make us leave Egypt?
Was it just to have us die here of thirst
with our children and our livestock?"
So Moses cried out to the Lord,
"What shall I do with this people?
A little more and they will stone me!"
The Lord answered Moses,
"Go over there in front of the people,
along with some of the elders of Israel,
holding in your hand, as you go,
the staff with which you struck the river.
I will be standing there in front of you on the rock in
Horeb.
Strike the rock, and the water will flow from it
for the people to drink."
This Moses did, in the presence of the elders of
Israel.
The place was called Massah and Meribah,
because the Israelites quarreled there
and tested the Lord, saying,
"Is the Lord in our midst or not?"

The word of the Lord.

Lect. No. 28

RESPONSORIAL PSALM: Ps 95:1-2, 6-7, 8-9 (℟.: 8)

This is above all a hymn of praise to the Lord who is our strength and salvation. We must recognize how much we need God to be a part of our lives.

When we acknowledge how important God is for us, then we

℟. **If today you hear his voice, harden not your hearts.**

Come, let us sing joyfully to the Lord;
let us acclaim the Rock of our salvation.
Let us come into his presence with thanksgiving;
let us joyfully sing psalms to him.

must fall down on our knees to worship him.

One of the goals of Lent is to do exactly that. We must discover those things that we have set at the center of our lives in the place of God and root them out. We must return God to his proper place in our lives. We must fall down on our knees in gratitude and awe.

This is why the last part of our Responsorial Psalm is a warning against arrogance and pride. We are always being tempted to self-sufficiency and the illusion that we can solve all of our own problems if we just try hard enough. Only in God can we find a response to our need; only in our heavenly Father can we find peace.

R̷. **If today you hear his voice, harden not your hearts.**

Come, let us bow down in worship;
   let us kneel before the LORD who made us.
For he is our God,
   and we are the people he shepherds, the flock he guides.

R̷. **If today you hear his voice, harden not your hearts.**

Oh, that today you would hear his voice:
   "Harden not your hearts as at Meribah,
   as in the day of Massah in the desert,
where your fathers tempted me;
   they tested me though they had seen my works."

R̷. **If today you hear his voice, harden not your hearts.**

Lect. No. 28

SECOND READING: Romans 5:1-2, 5-8

Saint Paul outlines his theology of salvation in this letter to the Christian community in Rome.

According to Paul, Christ paid the price for our redemption on the cross. When we accept the free gift of his love through our response of faith, we are justified. Justification means that we are living at peace with our God.

This gift is incredible. It was given to us not because of something that we have done, but quite the opposite. We have sinned and rejected God's love, and God responded to that offense with a greater outpouring of love.

A reading from the Letter of Saint Paul
to the Romans

Brothers and sisters:
   Since we have been justified by faith,
we have peace with God through our Lord Jesus Christ,
through whom we have gained access by faith
to this grace in which we stand,
and we boast in hope of the glory of God.

And hope does not disappoint,
   because the love of God has been poured out into our hearts
   through the Holy Spirit who has been given to us.
For Christ, while we were still helpless,
   died at the appointed time for the ungodly.

If God did this for us while we were still sinners, then what is in store for us now that we are living at peace with him (justified)! Paul marvels at the greatness of God's love for us and the glory into which we have been called to live for all eternity.

Indeed, only with difficulty does one die for a just person,
    though perhaps for a good person one might even find courage to die.
But God proves his love for us
    in that while we were still sinners Christ died for us.

The word of the Lord.

Lect. No. 28

VERSE BEFORE THE GOSPEL: cf. John 4:42, 15

Jesus is both the savior of the world and our own individual savior. We thirst for his love and grace, and he responds to our need with great generosity.

Lord, you are truly the Savior of the world;
give me living water, that I may never thirst again.

Lect. No. 28

GOSPEL: **A** Longer Form: John 4:5-42

Throughout the Old Testament there are several "well" stories. In each of them, a person meets his or her spouse (e.g., Isaac, Jacob, Moses, and Ruth). The technical term for this type of pattern is "leitmotif." The differences in each of the stories give us insights into the characters involved in these encounters.

The evangelist used the well story pattern in this account to speak of God's relationship to the Samaritans and pagans. They had not been part of the original covenant, which was a type of marriage between God and the people of Israel. God was now going to invite them into the new covenant.

The Samaritan woman in this story represents the Samaritans and pagans. This is typical

A reading from the holy Gospel according to John

Jesus came to a town of Samaria called Sychar,
    near the plot of land that Jacob had given to his son Joseph.
Jacob's well was there.
Jesus, tired from his journey, sat down there at the well.
It was about noon.

A woman of Samaria came to draw water.
Jesus said to her,
    "Give me a drink."
His disciples had gone into the town to buy food.
The Samaritan woman said to him,
    "How can you, a Jew, ask me, a Samaritan woman, for a drink?"
—For Jews use nothing in common with Samaritans.—
Jesus answered and said to her,
    "If you knew the gift of God
    and who is saying to you, 'Give me a drink,'

of John's Gospel, for every time that a character is referred to by a title and not a name (e.g., man born blind, Samaritan woman), that character plays a symbolic role.

The woman goes to the well at the the sixth hour, which is noon. That is unusual, for it was too hot at that hour to go to the well for water. This woman was afraid to meet others because of her reputation, and so she avoided them by going to the well when they were not there.

Even when Jesus begins to speak to her, she is hesitant. Jesus continues to treat her with great dignity and respect— one could say with more respect than that with which she treated herself.

Jesus offers her "living water." This phrase is ambiguous for it could mean flowing water or water that gives life. She only understands flowing water.

Jesus promises that this water will become a font overflowing within her. This means that she will be filled to overflowing with God's grace and life.

The woman does not understand anything that Jesus is saying, so he instructs her to call her husband. She has had five and is now living with another man, which makes six. These husbands represent all of the gods that her people have served.

The perfect number in the Bible is seven. Jesus, by offering her water, is becoming her

you would have asked him
　and he would have given you living water."
The woman said to him,
　"Sir, you do not even have a bucket and the cistern is deep;
　where then can you get this living water?
Are you greater than our father Jacob,
　who gave us this cistern and drank from it himself
　with his children and his flocks?"
Jesus answered and said to her,
　"Everyone who drinks this water will be thirsty again;
　but whoever drinks the water I shall give will never thirst;
　the water I shall give will become in him
　a spring of water welling up to eternal life."
The woman said to him,
　"Sir, give me this water, so that I may not be thirsty
　or have to keep coming here to draw water."

Jesus said to her,
　"Go call your husband and come back."
The woman answered and said to him,
　"I do not have a husband."
Jesus answered her,
　"You are right in saying, 'I do not have a husband.'
For you have had five husbands,
　and the one you have now is not your husband.
What you have said is true."
The woman said to him,
　"Sir, I can see that you are a prophet.
Our ancestors worshiped on this mountain;
　but you people say that the place to worship is in Jerusalem."
Jesus said to her,
　"Believe me, woman, the hour is coming
　when you will worship the Father
　neither on this mountain nor in Jerusalem.

seventh. He is inviting the Samaritan people and the pagans into a marriage (covenant) with God. (Always remember that this is a symbolic marriage.)

The Samaritan woman asks whether Jesus might be the Messiah. The Samaritan concept of the Messiah was very different from the Jewish concept. The Jewish people expected a conquering hero, but the Samaritans expected one who would reveal the secrets of God to them. This was exactly what Jesus was doing, for he was able to reveal all of the woman's secrets.

We hear that we are to worship the Father in Spirit and in Truth. The Spirit is the Holy Spirit, and the Truth is Jesus. We worship the Father in and through Jesus and the Holy Spirit.

The woman leaves her water jar, for, as Jesus promised, his grace has become a font of living water inside of her. She proclaims her message to the people from her village. Before she avoided them (going to the well at noon to avoid speaking to them); now she shares her discovery with them and she helps to bring them to salvation.

Jesus does not need the nourishment that the disciples can offer for he is totally sustained by the Father.

Jesus tells his disciples that the grain is already white for the harvest ("ripe" is a bit of a mistranslation). He is not pointing

You people worship what you do not understand;
   we worship what we understand,
   because salvation is from the Jews.
But the hour is coming, and is now here,
   when true worshipers will worship the Father in
      Spirit and truth;
   and indeed the Father seeks such people to wor-
      ship him.
God is Spirit, and those who worship him
   must worship in Spirit and truth."
The woman said to him,
   "I know that the Messiah is coming, the one called
      the Christ;
   when he comes, he will tell us everything."
Jesus said to her,
   "I am he, the one speaking with you."

At that moment his disciples returned,
   and were amazed that he was talking with a
      woman,
   but still no one said, "What are you looking for?"
   or "Why are you talking with her?"
The woman left her water jar
   and went into the town and said to the people,
   "Come see a man who told me everything I have
      done.
Could he possibly be the Christ?"
They went out of the town and came to him.
Meanwhile, the disciples urged him, "Rabbi, eat."
But he said to them,
   "I have food to eat of which you do not know."
So the disciples said to one another,
   "Could someone have brought him something to
      eat?"
Jesus said to them,
   "My food is to do the will of the one who sent me
   and to finish his work.
Do you not say, 'In four months the harvest will be
      here'?

to the grain fields; he is pointing at the Samaritans who were coming out of the village. Samaritans wore white robes, and they were the harvest of which Jesus was speaking. The one who sowed that harvest was the Samaritan woman; now the disciples were being called to harvest what she had planted.

The Samaritans then encounter Jesus and come to a more profound faith. They no longer believe in him because of what the woman said, but because they had experienced him themselves.

This is a powerful story of conversion. A woman who previously had been filled with fear was now filled to overflowing with love.

This is also the story of a people who had searched for love in the many gods whom they worshiped, but had not found true love or peace.

Finally, this is a reminder to us. We often have our own set of gods whom we worship: work, possessions, power, etc.

I tell you, look up and see the fields ripe for the harvest.
The reaper is already receiving payment
    and gathering crops for eternal life,
    so that the sower and reaper can rejoice together.
For here the saying is verified that 'One sows and
    another reaps.'
I sent you to reap what you have not worked for;
    others have done the work,
    and you are sharing the fruits of their work."

Many of the Samaritans of that town began to believe in him
    because of the word of the woman who testified,
    "He told me everything I have done."
When the Samaritans came to him,
    they invited him to stay with them;
    and he stayed there two days.
Many more began to believe in him because of his word,
    and they said to the woman,
    "We no longer believe because of your word;
    for we have heard for ourselves,
    and we know that this is truly the savior of the world."

The Gospel of the Lord.

Lect. No. 28

GOSPEL: **B** Shorter Form: John 4:5-15, 19b-26, 39a, 40-42

Throughout the Old Testament there are several "well" stories. In each of them, a person meets his or her spouse (e.g., Isaac, Jacob, Moses, and Ruth). The technical term for this type of pattern is "leitmotif." The differences in each of the stories give us insights into the characters involved in these encounters.

A reading from the holy Gospel according to John

Jesus came to a town of Samaria called Sychar,
    near the plot of land that Jacob had given to his
    son Joseph.
Jacob's well was there.
Jesus, tired from his journey, sat down there at the
    well.
It was about noon.

The Samaritan woman in this story represents the Samaritans and the pagans. When Jesus begins to speak to the Samaritan woman at the well, she is hesitant. Jesus treats her with great dignity and respect—one could say with more respect than that with which she treated herself.

Jesus offers her "living water." This phrase is ambiguous for it could mean flowing water or water that gives life. She only understands flowing water.

Jesus promises that this water will become a font overflowing within her. This means that she will be filled to overflowing with God's grace and life.

The woman does not understand anything that Jesus is saying, so he instructs her to call her husband.

She has had five and is now living with another man, which makes six.

These husbands represent all of the gods that her people have served.

The perfect number in the Bible is seven. Jesus, by offering her water, is becoming her seventh.

He is inviting the Samaritan people and the pagans into a marriage (covenant) with God. (Always remember that this is a symbolic marriage.)

The Samaritan woman asks whether Jesus might be the Messiah. The Samaritan concept of Messiah was very differ-

A woman of Samaria came to draw water.
Jesus said to her,
   "Give me a drink."
His disciples had gone into the town to buy food.
The Samaritan woman said to him,
   "How can you, a Jew, ask me, a Samaritan woman, for a drink?"
—For Jews use nothing in common with Samaritans.—
Jesus answered and said to her,
   "If you knew the gift of God
   and who is saying to you, 'Give me a drink,'
   you would have asked him
   and he would have given you living water."
The woman said to him,
   "Sir, you do not even have a bucket and the cistern is deep;
   where then can you get this living water?
Are you greater than our father Jacob,
   who gave us this cistern and drank from it himself
   with his children and his flocks?"
Jesus answered and said to her,
   "Everyone who drinks this water will be thirsty again;
   but whoever drinks the water I shall give will never thirst;
   the water I shall give will become in him
   a spring of water welling up to eternal life."
The woman said to him,
   "Sir, give me this water, so that I may not be thirsty
   or have to keep coming here to draw water.

"I can see that you are a prophet.
Our ancestors worshiped on this mountain;
   but you people say that the place to worship is in Jerusalem."
Jesus said to her,
   "Believe me, woman, the hour is coming

ent from the Jewish concept. The Jewish people expected a conquering hero, but the Samaritans expected one who would reveal the secrets of God to them. This was exactly what Jesus was doing, for he was able to reveal all of the woman's secrets.

We hear that we are to worship the Father in Spirit and in Truth. The Spirit is the Holy Spirit, and the Truth is Jesus. We worship the Father in and through Jesus and the Holy Spirit.

The woman leaves her water jar, for, as Jesus promised, his grace has become a font of living water inside of her. She proclaims her message to the people from her village. Before she avoided them (going to the well at noon to avoid speaking to them); now she shares her discovery with them and she helps to bring them to salvation.

The Samaritans then encounter Jesus and come to a more profound faith. They no longer believe in him because of what the woman said, but because they had experienced him themselves.

This is a reminder to us. We often have our own set of gods whom we worship: work, possessions, power, etc.

when you will worship the Father
  neither on this mountain nor in Jerusalem.
You people worship what you do not understand;
  we worship what we understand,
  because salvation is from the Jews.
But the hour is coming, and is now here,
  when true worshipers will worship the Father in
    Spirit and truth;
  and indeed the Father seeks such people to wor-
    ship him.
God is Spirit, and those who worship him
  must worship in Spirit and truth."
The woman said to him,
  "I know that the Messiah is coming, the one called
    the Christ;
  when he comes, he will tell us everything."
Jesus said to her,
  "I am he, the one who is speaking with you."

Many of the Samaritans of that town began to be-
    lieve in him.
When the Samaritans came to him,
  they invited him to stay with them;
  and he stayed there two days.
Many more began to believe in him because of his
    word,
  and they said to the woman,
  "We no longer believe because of your word;
  for we have heard for ourselves,
  and we know that this is truly the savior of the
    world."

The Gospel of the Lord.

PASTORAL REFLECTIONS

It is easy to point to the many mistakes others have made (e.g., this Samaritan woman), not realizing that we are in the same condition as they are. (Possibly our faults are more subtle or hidden—e.g., judgmentalism.)

FOURTH SUNDAY OF LENT

The readings given for Year A, no. 31, pp. 113-120, may be used in place of these B readings.

| Lect. No. 32 |

FIRST READING:

2 Chronicles 36:14-16, 19-23

The First Reading comes from the Second Book of Chronicles. The two Books of Chronicles are a rewriting of the historical books of the Bible. The author highly edited those historic books to remove some of the more scandalous passages, e.g., King David's sins.

This particular reading gives an overview of the history of Judah from just before the exile until the Israelites returned from Babylon.

The reason for the exile is made abundantly clear: because the people and their leaders (princes and priests) refused to live in the ways of the LORD. God had sent them prophets to call them back to righteousness, but they stubbornly refused to change their ways.

Therefore, the LORD gave them up into the hands of their enemies. Notice how the author makes it absolutely clear that the defeat of Judah and the exile was not God's fault; it was entirely the people's fault.

Neither was the exile an accident of history. God had foretold

A reading from the second Book of Chronicles

In those days, all the princes of Judah, the priests, and the people
added infidelity to infidelity,
practicing all the abominations of the nations
and polluting the LORD's temple
which he had consecrated in Jerusalem.

Early and often did the LORD, the God of their fathers,
send his messengers to them,
for he had compassion on his people and his dwelling place.
But they mocked the messengers of God,
despised his warnings, and scoffed at his prophets,
until the anger of the LORD against his people was so inflamed
that there was no remedy.
Their enemies burnt the house of God,
tore down the walls of Jerusalem,
set all its palaces afire,
and destroyed all its precious objects.
Those who escaped the sword were carried captive to Babylon,
where they became servants of the king of the Chaldeans and his sons
until the kingdom of the Persians came to power.

what was going to happen through the mouth of his prophet Jeremiah.

God, however, would not abandon his people forever. He sent Cyrus, the emperor of the Persians and the conqueror of Babylon, to liberate his people from exile. It was Cyrus' policy to send captive peoples back to their original homeland.

Notice, though, how the author makes it clear that it is the LORD himself and not Cyrus who is the instigator of this liberation. Cyrus was only an instrument in the hands of the LORD.

In Isaiah, in fact, Cyrus is called an anointed one of the LORD (a messiah), for Cyrus served the LORD even though he did not even know the LORD by name.

All this was to fulfill the word of the LORD spoken
    by Jeremiah:
    "Until the land has retrieved its lost sabbaths,
    during all the time it lies waste it shall have rest
    while seventy years are fulfilled."

In the first year of Cyrus, king of Persia,
    in order to fulfill the word of the LORD spoken by
        Jeremiah,
    the LORD inspired King Cyrus of Persia
    to issue this proclamation throughout his kingdom,
    both by word of mouth and in writing:
    "Thus says Cyrus, king of Persia:
    All the kingdoms of the earth
    the LORD, the God of heaven, has given to me,
    and he has also charged me to build him a house
    in Jerusalem, which is in Judah.
Whoever, therefore, among you belongs to any part
    of his people,
    let him go up, and may his God be with him!"

The word of the Lord.

Lect. No. 32

RESPONSORIAL PSALM: Ps 137:1-2, 3, 4-5, 6 (℟.: 6ab)

The Responsorial Psalm quotes a type of lamentation and curse song that was written during the exile of the Jewish people in Babylon.

The Babylonians wanted the captives to go on living as if nothing had happened. They even wanted them to sing their songs to them. The Jews steadfastly refused for they did not want to pretend that everything was fine. It was important for them to remember that this was not their home, and they had to hope for a deliverance.

℟. **Let my tongue be silenced, if I ever forget you!**

By the streams of Babylon
    we sat and wept when we remembered Zion.
On the aspens of that land
    we hung up our harps.

℟. **Let my tongue be silenced, if I ever forget you!**

For there our captors asked of us
    the lyrics of our songs,
and our despoilers urged us to be joyous:
    "Sing for us the songs of Zion!"

℟. **Let my tongue be silenced, if I ever forget you!**

What could this psalm written during the exile teach us during this Lenten season? Like the people of Judah, we have forced ourselves into exile through our sinful choices. We have created a distance between ourselves and God. This is not what God wants, so we have to make a choice to return to his love and mercy. We have to remember that this is not our true home—the arms of the LORD are where we truly belong.

How could we sing a song of the LORD
   in a foreign land?
If I forget you, Jerusalem,
   may my right hand be forgotten!

℟. **Let my tongue be silenced, if I ever forget you!**

May my tongue cleave to my palate
   if I remember you not,
if I place not Jerusalem
   ahead of my joy.

℟. **Let my tongue be silenced, if I ever forget you!**

Lect.
No. 32

SECOND READING: Ephesians 2:4-10

Like the First Reading, this passage from the Letter to the Ephesians speaks of how we created a horrible situation for ourselves through our sinfulness. (In the First Reading it was exile; here it is a state of death caused by our transgressions.) Yet, in both of these readings, the emphasis is not so much on our sin and guilt as on the mercy of God that has liberated us from this horrific state.

God is so generous that, even though we do not in any way deserve it, he has saved us and called us into his glory. It was not our good works or pious practices that bought us this freedom; it was God's gracious generosity and loving care.

Now that God has done this for us, we must respond with gratitude by doing good works and practicing generosity with those around us.

A reading from the Letter of Saint Paul
to the Ephesians

Brothers and sisters:
  God, who is rich in mercy,
   because of the great love he had for us,
   even when we were dead in our transgressions,
   brought us to life with Christ—by grace you have
     been saved—,
   raised us up with him,
   and seated us with him in the heavens in Christ
     Jesus,
   that in the ages to come
   he might show the immeasurable riches of his
     grace
   in his kindness to us in Christ Jesus.
For by grace you have been saved through faith,
   and this is not from you; it is the gift of God;
   it is not from works, so no one may boast.
For we are his handiwork, created in Christ Jesus
     for the good works
   that God has prepared in advance,
   that we should live in them.

The word of the Lord.

Lect. No. 32

God sent his Son into the world to reveal how much he truly loves us. If we live in that love, then we are already experiencing the joys of heaven.

Lect. No. 32

This passage comes from the second half of Jesus' discourse with Nicodemus.

Jesus speaks of the Son of Man being lifted up. This phrase is ambiguous in Greek and can refer either to his being lifted up on the cross or to his being lifted up in the Ascension into heaven.

The message being presented is that we have all but killed ourselves through our sin, and now the only way we can be saved is by looking up at Jesus who died for us and having faith in him (believing in his love).

This love is not something new. God never wanted to condemn us. That is the point of Jesus coming into the world: to reveal to us how much God truly loves us. Still, we have to choose to accept and live in that love.

Those who do not accept that love have already condemned themselves (because now they will have to live outside of God's love). Those who accept that love have already received their reward (the possibility of living in that love).

VERSE BEFORE THE GOSPEL: John 3:16

God so loved the world that he gave his only Son,
so everyone who believes in him might have eternal life.

GOSPEL: John 3:14-21

A reading from the holy Gospel according to John

Jesus said to Nicodemus:
"Just as Moses lifted up the serpent in the desert,
so must the Son of Man be lifted up,
so that everyone who believes in him may have eternal life."

For God so loved the world that he gave his only Son,
so that everyone who believes in him might not perish
but might have eternal life.
For God did not send his Son into the world to condemn the world,
but that the world might be saved through him.
Whoever believes in him will not be condemned,
but whoever does not believe has already been condemned,
because he has not believed in the name of the only Son of God.
And this is the verdict,
that the light came into the world,
but people preferred darkness to light,
because their works were evil.
For everyone who does wicked things hates the light
and does not come toward the light,
so that his works might not be exposed.
But whoever lives the truth comes to the light,
so that his works may be clearly seen as done in God.
The Gospel of the Lord.

The following readings given for Year A, no. 31, may be used in place of the previous readings.

Lect.
No. 31

FIRST READING: 1 Samuel 16:1b, 6-7, 10-13a

The Israelites had asked the LORD for a king to rule over them. The LORD indicated to Samuel, the last of the judges, that Saul was to be that king. (Judges were charismatically chosen leaders who acted as king, prophet, priest, and judge.) For a while, all went well and Saul led Israel against their enemies. However, Saul did what was evil in the sight of the LORD, so the LORD rejected Saul and sent Samuel to anoint another king of Israel in his place.

The LORD sent Samuel to Bethlehem, a small city in the area settled by the tribe of Judah. There Samuel spoke to Jesse and asked to see his sons. He saw one after another of the sons, and all of them seemed to be handsome and courageous. If Samuel had made the choice on appearances, he could have chosen any one of them.

However, the LORD chooses according to what is in a person's heart. David was to be the new king of Israel, for he was a man according to the LORD's own heart.

Samuel anointed David, making him an anointed of the LORD. Remember that the word "anointed" in Hebrew is messiah, but while David was a messiah, only Jesus would be the Messiah. Nevertheless, David would be regarded as the model of what the future Messiah should

A reading from the first Book of Samuel

The LORD said to Samuel:
    "Fill your horn with oil, and be on your way.
I am sending you to Jesse of Bethlehem,
    for I have chosen my king from among his sons."

As Jesse and his sons came to the sacrifice,
    Samuel looked at Eliab and thought,
    "Surely the LORD's anointed is here before him."
But the LORD said to Samuel:
    "Do not judge from his appearance or from his
        lofty stature,
    because I have rejected him.
Not as man sees does God see,
    because man sees the appearance
    but the LORD looks into the heart."
In the same way Jesse presented seven sons before
        Samuel,
    but Samuel said to Jesse,
    "The LORD has not chosen any one of these."
Then Samuel asked Jesse,
    "Are these all the sons you have?"
Jesse replied,
    "There is still the youngest, who is tending the
        sheep."
Samuel said to Jesse,
    "Send for him;
    we will not begin the sacrificial banquet until he
        arrives here."
Jesse sent and had the young man brought to them.
He was ruddy, a youth handsome to behold
    and making a splendid appearance.
The LORD said,
    "There—anoint him, for this is the one!"

be. This is why the Gospel of Matthew mentions that Jesus is a son of David in its genealogy.

The Spirit of the LORD rushed upon David, even as the Spirit of the LORD would anoint Jesus to proclaim a year of favor.

Then Samuel, with the horn of oil in hand,
　　anointed David in the presence of his brothers;
　　and from that day on, the spirit of the LORD
　　rushed upon David.

The word of the Lord.

Lect. No. 31

RESPONSORIAL PSALM: Ps 23:1-3a, 3b-4, 5, 6 (℟.: 1)

This psalm is a beautiful hymn of trust in the goodness of the LORD. It was probably written during the exile in Babylon when the people of Israel desperately needed the consolation of knowing that the LORD was leading them and had not forgotten or abandoned them because of their sinfulness.

Before the exile, the prophets had often complained that the kings of Israel were evil shepherds who did not guide their flocks in the ways of the LORD. Now God himself would guide them.

There are several images presented in the first part of the psalm to show how God is a good shepherd. He brings the flock to verdant pastures and leads them to restful waters. (Remember the importance of that in an arid climate.) He also leads them through dangerous places. The valley through which we are led is called the "dark valley" (more popularly known as the "valley of death"). The Hebrew meaning is a valley that is as dark as death.

His rod and staff give us comfort for while we are wandering in the dark, we can nevertheless feel his presence as he gently touches us with them.

℟. **The Lord is my shepherd; there is nothing I shall want.**

The LORD is my shepherd; I shall not want.
　　In verdant pastures he gives me repose;
beside restful waters he leads me;
　　he refreshes my soul.

℟. **The Lord is my shepherd; there is nothing I shall want.**

He guides me in right paths
　　for his name's sake.
Even though I walk in the dark valley
　　I fear no evil; for you are at my side
with your rod and your staff
　　that give me courage.

℟. **The Lord is my shepherd; there is nothing I shall want.**

You spread the table before me
　　in the sight of my foes;
you anoint my head with oil;
　　my cup overflows.

℟. **The Lord is my shepherd; there is nothing I shall want.**

Only goodness and kindness follow me
　　all the days of my life;
and I shall dwell in the house of the LORD
　　for years to come.

℟. **The Lord is my shepherd; there is nothing I shall want.**

Lect. No. 31

SECOND READING: Ephesians 5:8-14

The Second Reading develops the theme of light and darkness. These two opposites were often used as a synonym for good and evil. We must choose the good and reject evil. Otherwise, we will be children of the dark, children of the evil one.

We see this same theme developed in other places in Scripture. Jesus, for example, calls himself the light of the world. He gives light to the man born blind. On the other hand, we hear that after Judas departed from the Last Supper it was dark.

One of the goals of our Lenten conversion is transparency. We should do everything in such a way that we will never be embarrassed if others see what we have done. We have to allow the light of Christ to shine through us.

A reading from the Letter of Saint Paul
to the Ephesians

Brothers and sisters:
    You were once darkness,
  but now you are light in the Lord.
Live as children of light,
    for light produces every kind of goodness
    and righteousness and truth.
Try to learn what is pleasing to the Lord.
Take no part in the fruitless works of darkness;
    rather expose them, for it is shameful even to mention
    the things done by them in secret;
    but everything exposed by the light becomes visible,
    for everything that becomes visible is light.
Therefore, it says:
    "Awake, O sleeper,
    and arise from the dead,
    and Christ will give you light."

The word of the Lord.

Lect. No. 31

VERSE BEFORE THE GOSPEL: John 8:12

Jesus is the light of the world. He is the source of guidance for our journey and the light toward which we travel.

I am the light of the world, says the Lord;
whoever follows me will have the light of life.

Lect.
No. 31 **GOSPEL:** **A** **Longer Form: John 9:1-41**

This story is presented at two levels of meaning. The first (superficial) level is the story of a miracle that Jesus performed during his public ministry. The second (deeper symbolic level) is a story of a community that came to faith in Jesus Christ as the light of the world.

The disciples ask whether the man born blind is a sinner or whether his parents are sinners to explain why he should have been born blind. They are using a theology in which individual maladies are the result of particular sins.

Jesus rejects their question (which was rude considering that the blind man could hear what they were saying). He speaks of God manifesting his power through him. Jesus treats the man with great respect, beginning the healing of his spirit even before he heals him physically.

Jesus uses saliva to heal the man, something that many miracle workers in his day would have done. (The Pharisees would later object for the very act of making mud was considered to be work, an act forbidden on the Sabbath.) He then sends the man to wash at the pool of Siloam.

The man was immediately healed. The people who were his neighbors never really knew

A reading from the holy Gospel according to John

As Jesus passed by he saw a man blind from birth.
  His disciples asked him,
"Rabbi, who sinned, this man or his parents,
that he was born blind?"
Jesus answered,
  "Neither he nor his parents sinned;
  it is so that the works of God might be made visible through him.
We have to do the works of the one who sent me
    while it is day.
Night is coming when no one can work.
While I am in the world, I am the light of the world."
When he had said this, he spat on the ground
    and made clay with the saliva,
    and smeared the clay on his eyes, and said to him,
    "Go wash in the Pool of Siloam"—which means
      Sent—.
So he went and washed, and came back able to see.

His neighbors and those who had seen him earlier
    as a beggar said,
"Isn't this the one who used to sit and beg?"
Some said, "It is,"
    but others said, "No, he just looks like him."
He said, "I am."
So they said to him, "How were your eyes opened?"
He replied,
    "The man called Jesus made clay and anointed my eyes
    and told me, 'Go to Siloam and wash.'
So I went there and washed and was able to see."
And they said to him, "Where is he?"
He said, "I don't know."

him as a person, they only knew him as a disability. (Notice that they do not use his name.) That is why they cannot identify him when he is healed.

The man is brought before the Pharisees. It is only then that we hear that Jesus healed the man on the Sabbath. This is intentional, for while it was not important to Jesus that it was the Sabbath, it was important to the Pharisees. They could not understand why Jesus would not wait until the next day to heal him, for it was against the law to heal him if he were not in danger of death. Jesus, on the other hand, would not make him wait even one more minute.

The fact that the man is interrogated only before the Pharisees and not as one would expect, before the full Sanhedrin, which was composed of both the Pharisees and the Sadducees is a sign that this story has a second level, one that occurred toward the end of the century when the Sadducees had ceased to exist.

The man born blind is not given a name because he also plays a symbolic role in this Gospel. He represents the members of the community of the Beloved Disciple that had come to believe in Jesus.

Before they converted they had been blind, for they had not known the light of the world. Jesus came into their lives, and he healed them. He brought them to faith, and they were able to see the truth; like the man born blind, they suffered for their beliefs, for they were expelled from the synagogue.

They brought the one who was once blind to the Pharisees.
Now Jesus had made clay and opened his eyes on a sabbath.
So then the Pharisees also asked him how he was able to see.
He said to them,
  "He put clay on my eyes, and I washed, and now I can see."
So some of the Pharisees said,
  "This man is not from God,
  because he does not keep the sabbath."
But others said,
  "How can a sinful man do such signs?"
And there was a division among them.
So they said to the blind man again,
  "What do you have to say about him,
  since he opened your eyes?"
He said, "He is a prophet."

Now the Jews did not believe
  that he had been blind and gained his sight
  until they summoned the parents of the one who
    had gained his sight.
They asked them,
  "Is this your son, who you say was born blind?
How does he now see?"
His parents answered and said,
  "We know that this is our son and that he was
    born blind.
We do not know how he sees now,
  nor do we know who opened his eyes.
Ask him, he is of age;
  he can speak for himself."
His parents said this because they were afraid
  of the Jews, for the Jews had already agreed
  that if anyone acknowledged him as the Christ,
  he would be expelled from the synagogue.

The parents of the man born blind seem to represent that part of the Christian community that denied their faith in order to remain within the synagogue. They are often called crypto-Christians, i.e., hidden Christians. They let fear guide their lives and denied the one they knew to be the Messiah. They are a warning to us when we subtly deny our faith by failing to give witness to who or what we are.

The man born blind humiliates the great doctors of the law with his simplicity and truth. He has no formal learning, but his wisdom is much more profound than theirs. It is the wisdom of the cross being more powerful than the wisdom of the world.

Throughout the account the man born blind has used various titles for Jesus such as "the man called Jesus," "a prophet," "a man . . . from God," etc. After he is expelled from the presence of the Pharisees (which represents the synagogue), he comes to recognize who Jesus is. He calls him his "Lord" and he worships him. "Lord" is a title used for Yahweh in the Old Testament. The name Yahweh was so holy that whenever one found it in Scripture, one would pronounce its substitute word, *Adonai,* which means "LORD." By saying that Jesus is "LORD," the author is saying that Jesus is the same thing that Yahweh is: God. Also, one only worships God; therefore, when the man worships Jesus, he is proclaiming him to be God.

It was when the man suffered and was expelled from the synagogue that he came to recognize who Jesus was for him.

For this reason his parents said,
   "He is of age; question him."
So a second time they called the man who had been blind
   and said to him, "Give God the praise!
We know that this man is a sinner."
He replied,
   "If he is a sinner, I do not know.
One thing I do know is that I was blind and now I see."
So they said to him,
   "What did he do to you?
   How did he open your eyes?"
He answered them,
   "I told you already and you did not listen.
Why do you want to hear it again?
Do you want to become his disciples, too?"
They ridiculed him and said,
   "You are that man's disciple;
   we are disciples of Moses!
We know that God spoke to Moses,
   but we do not know where this one is from."
The man answered and said to them,
   "This is what is so amazing,
   that you do not know where he is from, yet he opened my eyes.
We know that God does not listen to sinners,
   but if one is devout and does his will, he listens to him.
It is unheard of that anyone ever opened the eyes of a person born blind.
If this man were not from God,
   he would not be able to do anything."
They answered and said to him,
   "You were born totally in sin,
   and are you trying to teach us?"
Then they threw him out.

The same is often true for us, that it is in times of suffering that we finally recognize who God really is for us.

Throughout this story there has been a recurring theme of sin. The disciples thought that the man was blind as a punishment for sin. The Pharisees accused both Jesus and the man born blind of being sinners.

It is the Pharisees who are the true sinners for they had the ability to recognize who Jesus was, and they refused to see. They chose to remain in their blindness, so they were condemned to remain in the hell they had made for themselves.

Throughout this Gospel we hear that Jesus has come for judgment. He does not want to condemn us. We condemn ourselves if we choose against the Lord and against the truth. Likewise, by choosing Jesus to be the center of our lives, we have already received our reward, for Jesus will be a part of our lives.

When Jesus heard that they had thrown him out,
he found him and said, "Do you believe in the Son of Man?"
He answered and said,
"Who is he, sir, that I may believe in him?"
Jesus said to him,
"You have seen him,
and the one speaking with you is he."
He said,
"I do believe, Lord," and he worshiped him.
Then Jesus said,
"I came into this world for judgment,
so that those who do not see might see,
and those who do see might become blind."

Some of the Pharisees who were with him heard this
and said to him, "Surely we are not also blind, are we?"
Jesus said to them,
"If you were blind, you would have no sin;
but now you are saying, 'We see,' so your sin remains."

The Gospel of the Lord.

| Lect. No. 31 | **GOSPEL: B Shorter Form: John 9:1, 6-9, 13-17, 34-38** |

This story is presented at two levels of meaning. The first (superficial) level is the story of a miracle that Jesus performed during his public ministry. The second (deeper symbolic level) is a story of a community that came to faith in Jesus Christ as the light of the world.

Jesus uses saliva to heal the man born blind and sends him to wash at the pool of Siloam.

A reading from the holy Gospel according to John

As Jesus passed by he saw a man blind from birth. He spat on the ground and made clay with the saliva,
and smeared the clay on his eyes, and said to him,
"Go wash in the Pool of Siloam"—which means Sent—.
So he went and washed, and came back able to see.

His neighbors and those who had seen him earlier as a beggar said,

The man born blind is not given a name because he also plays a symbolic role in this Gospel. He represents the members of the community of the Beloved Disciple who had come to believe in Jesus.

Before they converted they had been blind, for they had not known the light of the world. Jesus came into their lives, and he healed them. He brought them to faith, and they were able to see the truth; like the man born blind, they suffered for their beliefs, for they were expelled from the synagogue. The man born blind humiliates the great doctors of the law with his simplicity and truth. He has no formal learning, but his wisdom is much more profound than theirs. It is the wisdom of the cross—more powerful than the wisdom of the world.

Throughout the account the man born blind has used various titles for Jesus such as "the man called Jesus," "a prophet," "a man . . . from God," etc. After he is expelled from the presence of the Pharisees (which represents the synagogue), he comes to recognize who Jesus is. He calls him his "Lord" and he worships him. "Lord" is a title used for Yahweh in the Old Testament. The name Yahweh was so holy that whenever one found it in Scripture, one would pronounce its substitute word, *Adonai,* which means "Lord." By saying that Jesus is "Lord," the author is saying that Jesus is the same thing that Yahweh is: God. Furthermore, one only worships God; so when the man worships Jesus, he is proclaiming him to be God.

"Isn't this the one who used to sit and beg?"
Some said, "It is,"
    but others said, "No, he just looks like him."
He said, "I am."

They brought the one who was once blind to the
        Pharisees.
Now Jesus had made clay and opened his eyes on a
        sabbath.
So then the Pharisees also asked him how he was
        able to see.
He said to them,
    "He put clay on my eyes, and I washed, and now I
        can see."
So some of the Pharisees said,
    "This man is not from God,
    because he does not keep the sabbath."
But others said,
    "How can a sinful man do such signs?"
And there was a division among them.
So they said to the blind man again,
    "What do you have to say about him,
    since he opened your eyes?"
He said, "He is a prophet."

They answered and said to him,
    "You were born totally in sin,
    and are you trying to teach us?"
Then they threw him out.

When Jesus heard that they had thrown him out,
    he found him and said, "Do you believe in the Son
        of Man?"
He answered and said,
    "Who is he, sir, that I may believe in him?"
Jesus said to him,
    "You have seen him,
    and the one speaking with you is he."
He said,
    "I do believe, Lord," and he worshiped him.

The Gospel of the Lord.

FIFTH SUNDAY OF LENT

The readings given for Year A, no. 34, pp. 124-131, may be used in place of these B readings.

The readings given for Year A, no. 34, pp. 124-131, may be used in place of these B readings.

| Lect. No. 35 | **FIRST READING: Jeremiah 31:31-34** |

A reading from the Book of the Prophet Jeremiah

The days are coming, says the LORD,
　when I will make a new covenant with the house of Israel
and the house of Judah.
It will not be like the covenant I made with their fathers
　the day I took them by the hand
　to lead them forth from the land of Egypt;
　for they broke my covenant,
　and I had to show myself their master, says the LORD.
But this is the covenant that I will make
　with the house of Israel after those days, says the LORD.
I will place my law within them and write it upon their hearts;
　I will be their God, and they shall be my people.
No longer will they have need to teach their friends and relatives
　how to know the LORD.
All, from least to greatest, shall know me, says the LORD,
　for I will forgive their evildoing and remember their sin no more.

The word of the Lord.

The earlier chapters of the Book of the Prophet Jeremiah are an almost continuous condemnation of Israel for its infidelity. We are told how severe God's punishment would be upon his faithless people.

Yet, even if the people of Israel were faithless, God would not abandon them.

In today's First Reading we hear how the LORD would create a new covenant with them that would be much more profound and internalized than the old covenant, which had been written upon tablets of stone.

This covenant would be placed upon their very hearts. Remember, the heart in the Bible does not symbolize the center of one's affections but rather the source of one's intellect (so the covenant written on their hearts means that they would be filled with knowledge of the ways of the LORD).

They would not need anyone to teach them about these things for God's ways would be as natural to them as breathing.

| Lect. |
| No. 35 |

RESPONSORIAL PSALM: Ps 51:3-4, 12-13, 14-15 (℟.: 12a)

The Responsorial Psalm contains verses taken from Psalm 51, the great penitential psalm.

The author of this psalm asks for forgiveness for his sins, and also that the LORD would renew him (create a new heart within him). By sinning, he had chosen death (for sin was considered to be a type of spiritual death). The only way that he could live again was if the LORD would restore his Holy Spirit (the breath of God) to him.

The author promises that if he were to experience the joy of salvation once again, he would surely share knowledge of the ways of the LORD with others. This would lead not only to his deliverance, but also the conversion of many who had turned away from the paths of the LORD.

℟. **Create a clean heart in me, O God.**

Have mercy on me, O God, in your goodness;
  in the greatness of your compassion wipe out my
    offense.
Thoroughly wash me from my guilt
  and of my sin cleanse me.

℟. **Create a clean heart in me, O God.**

A clean heart create for me, O God,
  and a steadfast spirit renew within me.
Cast me not out from your presence,
  and your Holy Spirit take not from me.

℟. **Create a clean heart in me, O God.**

Give me back the joy of your salvation,
  and a willing spirit sustain in me.
I will teach transgressors your ways,
  and sinners shall return to you.

℟. **Create a clean heart in me, O God.**

| Lect. |
| No. 35 |

SECOND READING: Hebrews 5:7-9

Jesus implored the Father for his assistance, and the Father raised him from the dead. The trust and obedience that Jesus displayed made him perfect. The word "perfect" is really a play on words, for this was the word used for the act by which a man in Old Testament times became a priest. Thus, Jesus became our high priest and advocate before the Father. He is both the priest who offers the victim and the victim being offered through which we obtain forgiveness of our sins.

A reading from the Letter to the Hebrews

In the days when Christ Jesus was in the flesh,
  he offered prayers and supplications with loud
    cries and tears
  to the one who was able to save him from death,
  and he was heard because of his reverence.
Son though he was, he learned obedience from what
    he suffered;
  and when he was made perfect,
  he became the source of eternal salvation for all
    who obey him.

The word of the Lord.

Lect.
No. 35

VERSE BEFORE THE GOSPEL: John 12:26

The call to discipleship leads inevitably to the cross, but Jesus will also always be there for us.

Whoever serves me must follow me, says the Lord; and where I am, there also will my servant be.

Lect.
No. 35

GOSPEL: John 12:20-33

This discourse comes at the end of the first part of the Gospel of John, not too much before the account of the Last Supper. There is a sense of the story drawing to a conclusion, something that is appropriate on the Sunday before Palm Sunday.

One of the words that is repeated in this passage is "glory." Normally this word is understood as being a synonym for power or magnificence.

If that were how the word was being used in this Gospel, then one would expect the hour of Jesus' glory to be the Transfiguration or the Resurrection. Instead, the hour of glory is the cross, for the word has been redefined in this Gospel.

Here it means an outpouring of love. Jesus most manifests the love of God for us when he is dying on the cross, for the cross is the Sacrament (visible sign of the invisible reality) of God's love for us.

The voice that comes from heaven is said to sound like thunder. This is a bit of a word-play, for the Hebrew word for thunder is "qol," which could be

A reading from the holy Gospel according to John

Some Greeks who had come to worship at the Passover Feast
came to Philip, who was from Bethsaida in Galilee,
and asked him, "Sir, we would like to see Jesus."
Philip went and told Andrew;
then Andrew and Philip went and told Jesus.
Jesus answered them,
"The hour has come for the Son of Man to be glorified.
Amen, amen, I say to you,
unless a grain of wheat falls to the ground and dies,
it remains just a grain of wheat;
but if it dies, it produces much fruit.
Whoever loves his life loses it,
and whoever hates his life in this world
will preserve it for eternal life.
Whoever serves me must follow me,
and where I am, there also will my servant be.
The Father will honor whoever serves me.

"I am troubled now. Yet what should I say?
'Father, save me from this hour'?
But it was for this purpose that I came to this hour.
Father, glorify your name."
Then a voice came from heaven,
"I have glorified it and will glorify it again."
The crowd there heard it and said it was thunder;
but others said, "An angel has spoken to him."
Jesus answered and said,

translated as "thunder" or "the voice of God."

Jesus is about to be lifted up (on the cross). This was the moment of judgment, for one had to choose between life (which is found in Jesus) and death (the realm of Satan, ruler of this world).

"This voice did not come for my sake but for yours.
Now is the time of judgment on this world;
    now the ruler of this world will be driven out.
And when I am lifted up from the earth,
    I will draw everyone to myself."
He said this indicating the kind of death he would die.

The Gospel of the Lord.

The following readings given for Year A, no. 34, may be used in place of the previous readings.

Lect. No. 34

FIRST READING: Ezekiel 37:12-14

This prophecy is taken from a passage that speaks about the resurrection of the dead. Ezekiel describes a plain filled with the dry bones of those who had died. He preaches to the bones and they are filled with God's breath and Spirit and brought back to life.

It appears as if Ezekiel was originally speaking about the resurrection of the nation, but his words could also be applied to the resurrection of the individual. It is the Spirit of the LORD who gives us true life, life that will never end.

A reading from the Book of the Prophet Ezekiel

Thus says the Lord GOD:
    O my people, I will open your graves
    and have you rise from them,
    and bring you back to the land of Israel.
Then you shall know that I am the LORD,
    when I open your graves and have you rise from them,
    O my people!
I will put my spirit in you that you may live,
    and I will settle you upon your land;
    thus you shall know that I am the LORD.
I have promised, and I will do it, says the LORD.

The word of the Lord.

Lect. No. 34

RESPONSORIAL PSALM: Ps 130:1-2, 3-4, 5-6, 7-8 (℞.: 7)

Psalm 130 is an individual lament. It begins with an almost desperate appeal to the LORD for an intervention. Then there is a series of verses which speak of the things tormenting the psalmist. Finally, there is a todah. This is a thanksgiving for

℞. **With the Lord there is mercy and fullness of redemption.**

Out of the depths I cry to you, O LORD;
    LORD, hear my voice!
Let your ears be attentive
    to my voice in supplication.

the deliverance that the psalmist is sure Yahweh will deliver.

There is a sense of urgency in this psalm, as if things had gone so far that there were only moments of life left. The image of the sentinel waiting for the dawn is especially appropriate. The dark is filled with danger and confusion, but with the dawn comes a restoration of hope. Throughout the Old Testament, the dawn was considered to be the hour of the day when God would intervene to save us from our enemies.

The psalmist readily admits that the disasters that had befallen him were probably due to his own sins. He even states that if the LORD were to mark his iniquities, he would have no chance of standing. He and Israel deserve everything that they were getting. Nevertheless, he is filled with hope that the LORD will deliver them from their dangers, for the LORD is truly merciful and gracious.

℞. **With the Lord there is mercy and fullness of redemption.**

If you, O LORD, mark iniquities,
    Lord, who can stand?
But with you is forgiveness,
    that you may be revered.

℞. **With the Lord there is mercy and fullness of redemption.**

I trust in the LORD;
    my soul trusts in his word.
More than sentinels wait for the dawn,
    let Israel wait for the LORD.

℞. **With the Lord there is mercy and fullness of redemption.**

For with the LORD is kindness
    and with him is plenteous redemption;
and he will redeem Israel
    from all their iniquities.

℞. **With the Lord there is mercy and fullness of redemption.**

Lect.
No. 34

SECOND READING: Romans 8:8-11

In this passage from Saint Paul's Letter to the Romans we hear of the contrast between living according to the flesh and living according to the Spirit. By using the word flesh, Paul is not speaking about our bodies or the created world. He is speaking about that part of us which drags us down, which will lead us to sin. Saint Augustine calls this concupiscence.

The Spirit, on the other hand, is the gift of the Holy Spirit that we have received in our Bap-

A reading from the Letter of Saint Paul
to the Romans

Brothers and sisters:
    Those who are in the flesh cannot please God.
But you are not in the flesh;
    on the contrary, you are in the spirit,
    if only the Spirit of God dwells in you.
Whoever does not have the Spirit of Christ does not
    belong to him.
But if Christ is in you,
    although the body is dead because of sin,
    the spirit is alive because of righteousness.

tism. We can live in the Spirit by choosing to live in God's love.

The life that we receive from the Spirit is so profound that even our mortal bodies will be filled with eternal life in the resurrection from the dead.

If the Spirit of the One who raised Jesus from the
 dead dwells in you,
the One who raised Christ from the dead
will give life to your mortal bodies also,
through his Spirit dwelling in you.

The word of the Lord.

| Lect. No. 34 |

VERSE BEFORE THE GOSPEL: John 11:25a, 26

Jesus is the source and the goal of our lives. Life has no meaning if it is not lived in him and for him.

I am the resurrection and the life, says the Lord;
whoever believes in me, even if he dies, will never
 die.

| Lect. No. 34 |

GOSPEL: A Longer Form: John 11:1-45

Lazarus was a common name at the time of Jesus (a form of the name Eliezer, which means that "God aids") and this Lazarus should not be confused with the poor Lazarus of the parable in Luke's Gospel.

Jesus stayed at the house of Lazarus and his sisters Martha and Mary during the Jewish feast days. There were so many pilgrims in Jerusalem at those times that pilgrims often stayed in the suburbs of Jerusalem. Bethany, the town where Lazarus and Mary his sister lived, was only a short distance outside of Jerusalem.

Although Mary does not anoint the feet of Jesus until chapter 12, the action is placed in the past tense. In this Gospel the readers and the author already know all of the events recorded in this Gospel.

It is odd that Jesus remained where he was after he had heard

A reading from the holy Gospel according to John

Now a man was ill, Lazarus from Bethany,
 the village of Mary and her sister Martha.
Mary was the one who had anointed the Lord with
 perfumed oil
and dried his feet with her hair;
it was her brother Lazarus who was ill.
So the sisters sent word to Jesus, saying,
 "Master, the one you love is ill."
When Jesus heard this he said,
 "This illness is not to end in death,
 but is for the glory of God,
 that the Son of God may be glorified through it."
Now Jesus loved Martha and her sister and
 Lazarus.
So when he heard that he was ill,
 he remained for two days in the place where he
 was.
Then after this he said to his disciples,
 "Let us go back to Judea."
The disciples said to him,
 "Rabbi, the Jews were just trying to stone you,
 and you want to go back there?"

of the illness of his friend. It is almost as if he wanted him to die. This is only explainable if one remembers that this will be a powerful sign of God's love. In fact, it will be a sign of God's glory.

Jesus' hour of glory in this Gospel is the cross and not the resurrection as one might expect. In the greatest irony of the Gospel, Jesus is put to death by the Jewish leaders specifically because he brought Lazarus back to life. The Jewish leaders wanted people to be under their control; they did not want them to be free or truly alive.

We hear that Lazarus was dead for four days already. The Jewish people believed that the soul remained in the body for the first three days after the person died. To say that someone was dead for four days was to say that they were irretrievably dead.

Martha and Mary both respond to Jesus' arrival with statements that show a mix of annoyance at the fact that he had taken so long to get there and an expression of hope that he would still do something to help them.

Jesus responds that he is "the resurrection and the life." What is interesting about this phrase is that he is not saying that he will grant the resurrection; he is saying that he is the resurrection.

When one comes to know Jesus, one is already in some way risen. One's life is so full and profound that even if one

Jesus answered,
　　"Are there not twelve hours in a day?
If one walks during the day, he does not stumble,
　　because he sees the light of this world.
But if one walks at night, he stumbles,
　　because the light is not in him."
He said this, and then told them,
　　"Our friend Lazarus is asleep,
　　but I am going to awaken him."
So the disciples said to him,
　　"Master, if he is asleep, he will be saved."
But Jesus was talking about his death,
　　while they thought that he meant ordinary sleep.
So then Jesus said to them clearly,
　　"Lazarus has died.
And I am glad for you that I was not there,
　　that you may believe.
Let us go to him."
So Thomas, called Didymus, said to his fellow disciples,
　　"Let us also go to die with him."

When Jesus arrived, he found that Lazarus
　　had already been in the tomb for four days.
Now Bethany was near Jerusalem, only about two
　　miles away.
And many of the Jews had come to Martha and Mary
　　to comfort them about their brother.
When Martha heard that Jesus was coming,
　　she went to meet him;
　　but Mary sat at home.
Martha said to Jesus,
　　"Lord, if you had been here,
　　my brother would not have died.
But even now I know that whatever you ask of God,
　　God will give you."

were to die, one would continue to live in him. Eschatology speaks about the things that will occur at the end of time. This Gospel has a "realized eschatology," for we do not have to wait until the end of time to receive our eternal reward. We have already begun to experience it when we came to know Jesus (although we will experience it even more fully after we die).

Jesus is described as being perturbed and deeply troubled. At first we might think that he is disturbed because the Jewish people and Mary are crying (which he might have interpreted as a sign of their lack of faith in him), but he himself cries within a few minutes. It is more probable that he is angry at death itself, which has robbed him of his beloved friend. He also cries to express his grief at the death of Lazarus.

Christian hope at the death of a beloved does not mean that we have to deny our emotions. It means that we express them, but also try to maintain hope.

There are several expressions of irony throughout the story. Thomas says that the disciples should follow Jesus to die with him (while they do the exact opposite). The people watching Jesus ask whether he could not have saved Lazarus from death (which he, of course, could have). This is typical of the Gospel of John where we, the readers, often know more than the characters involved in the story.

Jesus said to her,
"Your brother will rise."
Martha said to him,
"I know he will rise,
in the resurrection on the last day."
Jesus told her,
"I am the resurrection and the life;
whoever believes in me, even if he dies, will live,
and everyone who lives and believes in me will never die.
Do you believe this?"
She said to him, "Yes, Lord.
I have come to believe that you are the Christ, the Son of God,
the one who is coming into the world."

When she had said this,
she went and called her sister Mary secretly, saying,
"The teacher is here and is asking for you."
As soon as she heard this,
she rose quickly and went to him.
For Jesus had not yet come into the village,
but was still where Martha had met him.
So when the Jews who were with her in the house comforting her
saw Mary get up quickly and go out,
they followed her,
presuming that she was going to the tomb to weep there.
When Mary came to where Jesus was and saw him,
she fell at his feet and said to him,
"Lord, if you had been here,
my brother would not have died."
When Jesus saw her weeping and the Jews who had come with her weeping,
he became perturbed and deeply troubled, and said,

Jesus proclaims a rather unusual prayer. It is almost as if it is being said for the sake of the audience so that they will know that Jesus is doing this deed of power through the intervention of the Father. Jesus does absolutely nothing in this Gospel on his own. Everything he does is in obedience to the will of the Father.

Lazarus is not actually resurrected, he is reanimated. The difference is that Lazarus is brought back to life, but he would still have to die again someday.

Jesus, on the other hand, when he is resurrected, will never die again. He has a glorified body that is not subject to the limitations of our mortal bodies. Such is not the case with Lazarus who someday would die again.

Jesus instructs those with him to untie Lazarus. This has often been used as an image of how Jesus unbinds us from everything that imprisons us, whether it be sin or fear or the habits that leave us lonely and confused. We cannot do this by ourselves; we must seek the assistance of Jesus to set us free.

The end of the account speaks of those who had come to see Mary and Martha. The purpose is to show that this was a very public miracle and it explains why this particular miracle would be brought to the attention of the leaders of the Jews in the next verses of this story.

"Where have you laid him?"

They said to him, "Sir, come and see."

And Jesus wept.

So the Jews said, "See how he loved him."

But some of them said,

"Could not the one who opened the eyes of the blind man
have done something so that this man would not have died?"

So Jesus, perturbed again, came to the tomb.

It was a cave, and a stone lay across it.

Jesus said, "Take away the stone."

Martha, the dead man's sister, said to him,

"Lord, by now there will be a stench;
he has been dead for four days."

Jesus said to her,

"Did I not tell you that if you believe
you will see the glory of God?"

So they took away the stone.

And Jesus raised his eyes and said,

"Father, I thank you for hearing me.

I know that you always hear me;
but because of the crowd here I have said this,
that they may believe that you sent me."

And when he had said this,

he cried out in a loud voice,
"Lazarus, come out!"

The dead man came out,

tied hand and foot with burial bands,
and his face was wrapped in a cloth.

So Jesus said to them,

"Untie him and let him go."

Now many of the Jews who had come to Mary
and seen what he had done began to believe in him.

The Gospel of the Lord.

Lect.
No. 34 **GOSPEL:** **B** **Shorter Form: John 11:3-7, 17, 20-27, 33b-45**

It is odd that Jesus remained where he was after he had heard of the illness of his friend Lazarus. It is almost as if he wanted him to die. This is only explainable if one remembers that this will be a powerful sign of God's love. In fact, it will be a sign of God's glory.

We hear that Lazarus was dead for four days already. The Jewish people believed that the soul remained in the body for the first three days after the person died. To say that someone was dead for four days was to say that that person was irretrievably dead.

Martha and Mary both respond to Jesus' arrival with statements that show a mix of annoyance at the fact that he had taken so long to get there and an expression of hope that he would still do something to help them.

Jesus responds that he is "the resurrection and the life." What is interesting about this phrase is that he is not saying that he will grant the resurrection; he is saying that he is the resurrection.

When one comes to know Jesus, one is already in some way risen. One's life is so full and profound that even if one were to die, one would continue to live in him. Eschatology speaks about the things that will occur at the end of time. This Gospel has a "realized eschatology," for we do not have to wait until the end of time to re-

A reading from the holy Gospel according to John

The sisters of Lazarus sent word to Jesus, saying, "Master, the one you love is ill."
When Jesus heard this he said,
    "This illness is not to end in death,
    but is for the glory of God,
    that the Son of God may be glorified through it."
Now Jesus loved Martha and her sister and Lazarus.
So when he heard that he was ill,
    he remained for two days in the place where he
        was.
Then after this he said to his disciples,
    "Let us go back to Judea."

When Jesus arrived, he found that Lazarus
    had already been in the tomb for four days.
When Martha heard that Jesus was coming,
    she went to meet him;
    but Mary sat at home.
Martha said to Jesus,
    "Lord, if you had been here,
    my brother would not have died.
But even now I know that whatever you ask of God,
    God will give you."
Jesus said to her,
    "Your brother will rise."
Martha said,
    "I know he will rise,
    in the resurrection on the last day."
Jesus told her,
    "I am the resurrection and the life;
    whoever believes in me, even if he dies, will live,
    and everyone who lives and believes in me will
        never die.
Do you believe this?"
She said to him, "Yes, Lord.

ceive our eternal reward. We have already begun to experience it when we came to know Jesus (although we will experience it even more fully after we die).

Jesus is described as being perturbed and deeply troubled. At first we might think that he is disturbed because the Jewish people and Mary are crying (which he might have interpreted as a sign of their lack of faith in him), but he himself cries within a few minutes. It is more probable that he is angry at death itself, which has robbed him of his beloved friend. He also cries to express his grief at the death of Lazarus.

Christian hope at the death of a beloved does not mean that we have to deny our emotions. It means that we express them, but also try to maintain hope.

Lazarus is not actually resurrected, he is reanimated. The difference is that Lazarus is brought back to life, but he would still have to die again someday.

Jesus, on the other hand, when he is resurrected, will never die again. He has a glorified body that is not subject to the limitations of our mortal bodies. Such is not the case with Lazarus who someday would die again.

The end of the account speaks of those who had come to see Mary and Martha. The purpose is to show that this was a very public miracle and it explains why this particular miracle would be brought to the attention of the leaders of the Jews in the next verses of this story.

I have come to believe that you are the Christ, the Son of God,

the one who is coming into the world."

He became perturbed and deeply troubled, and said, "Where have you laid him?"

They said to him, "Sir, come and see."

And Jesus wept.

So the Jews said, "See how he loved him."

But some of them said,

"Could not the one who opened the eyes of the blind man

have done something so that this man would not have died?"

So Jesus, perturbed again, came to the tomb.

It was a cave, and a stone lay across it.

Jesus said, "Take away the stone."

Martha, the dead man's sister, said to him,

"Lord, by now there will be a stench;

he has been dead for four days."

Jesus said to her,

"Did I not tell you that if you believe

you will see the glory of God?"

So they took away the stone.

And Jesus raised his eyes and said,

"Father, I thank you for hearing me.

I know that you always hear me;

but because of the crowd here I have said this,

that they may believe that you sent me."

And when he had said this,

he cried out in a loud voice,

"Lazarus, come out!"

The dead man came out,

tied hand and foot with burial bands,

and his face was wrapped in a cloth.

So Jesus said to them,

"Untie him and let him go."

Now many of the Jews who had come to Mary

and seen what he had done began to believe in him.

The Gospel of the Lord.

March 25, 2018

PALM SUNDAY OF THE PASSION OF THE LORD

At the Procession with Palms

Lect. No. 37 **GOSPEL:** **A** **Mark 11:1-10**

It appears that when Jesus entered Jerusalem on Palm Sunday, he chose to perform certain symbolic actions so that the crowd would understand what was occurring.

He approached Jerusalem by way of the Mount of Olives. In the Old Testament, the Mount of Olives was associated with the dawning of the Day of the Lord, that day when God would reign with power upon the earth.

We also see Jesus riding a donkey. In Zechariah we hear how the Messiah would enter the holy city riding on a donkey. Zechariah was contrasting how the pagan conquerors had entered Jerusalem and how the Jewish Messiah would enter it.

The pagan kings had entered with a haughty display of their power; the Jewish Messiah was going to enter it with meekness and humility.

Jesus knew both of these prophecies and decided to enter Jerusalem in this manner to give the implicit message that he was the fulfillment of what had been prophesied.

A reading from the holy Gospel according to Mark

When Jesus and his disciples drew near to Jerusalem,
to Bethphage and Bethany at the Mount of Olives,
he sent two of his disciples and said to them,
"Go into the village opposite you,
and immediately on entering it,
you will find a colt tethered on which no one has
ever sat.
Untie it and bring it here.
If anyone should say to you,
'Why are you doing this?' reply,
'The Master has need of it
and will send it back here at once.'"
So they went off
and found a colt tethered at a gate outside on the
street,
and they untied it.
Some of the bystanders said to them,
"What are you doing, untying the colt?"
They answered them just as Jesus had told them to,
and they permitted them to do it.
So they brought the colt to Jesus
and put their cloaks over it.
And he sat on it.
Many people spread their cloaks on the road,
and others spread leafy branches
that they had cut from the fields.

The crowd cries out "Hosanna." This phrase means, "Lord, save us."

They also speak of David. This was bound to cause difficulties, for Jerusalem was so crowded in those days that the Romans were frightened that a rebellion would break out. Proclaiming Jesus as a Jewish king would have been interpreted as the battle cry of that outbreak.

Lect.
No. 37

In John's version of Palm Sunday, we hear many of the same phrases found in the Synoptic Gospels. The crowd cries out "Hosanna" (a phrase meaning "Lord, save us") and they proclaim Jesus as the Jewish king, something that would have provoked a reaction from the leaders of the Jews and the Romans.

Jesus rides into Jerusalem on a donkey. This fulfills Zechariah's prophecy that the Jewish Messiah would enter the holy city in a meek and gentle manner, riding on a donkey and not on a great battle steed like the pagan conquerors.

The disciples did not understand this until Jesus was glorified. (His hour of glory is on the cross when he is the king of love.)

Those preceding him as well as those following kept crying out:

"Hosanna!
Blessed is he who comes in the name of the Lord!
Blessed is the kingdom of our father David that is to come!
Hosanna in the highest!"

The Gospel of the Lord.

OR:

GOSPEL: B John 12:12-16

A reading from the holy Gospel according to John

When the great crowd that had come to the feast heard
that Jesus was coming to Jerusalem,
they took palm branches and went out to meet him, and cried out:
"Hosanna!
"Blessed is he who comes in the name of the Lord,
the king of Israel."
Jesus found an ass and sat upon it, as is written:
Fear no more, O daughter Zion;
see, your king comes, seated upon an ass's colt.
His disciples did not understand this at first,
but when Jesus had been glorified
they remembered that these things were written about him
and that they had done this for him.

The Gospel of the Lord.

At the Mass

FIRST READING: Isaiah 50:4-7

This reading is taken from the third song of the Suffering Servant. It speaks of the Servant as one who brings consolation to the weary, even while he suffers terribly. We will hear in the fourth song that he suffers to bring us forgiveness of our sins.

It was never exactly clear who this figure was supposed to be during Old Testament times. Jesus, through many of the things he said, showed that he considered himself to be the fulfillment of this prophecy.

In spite of the agony of the Servant, he remained obedient to the will of God. He professed his faith in the LORD for he knew that God would deliver him from all of his distress. This deliverance was fulfilled when the Father raised Jesus from the dead on Easter Sunday.

A reading from the Book of the Prophet Isaiah

The Lord GOD has given me
a well-trained tongue,
that I might know how to speak to the weary
a word that will rouse them.
Morning after morning
he opens my ear that I may hear;
and I have not rebelled,
have not turned back.
I gave my back to those who beat me,
my cheeks to those who plucked my beard;
my face I did not shield
from buffets and spitting.

The Lord GOD is my help,
therefore I am not disgraced;
I have set my face like flint,
knowing that I shall not be put to shame.

The word of the Lord.

RESPONSORIAL PSALM: Ps 22:8-9, 17-18, 19-20, 23-24 (℟.: 2a)

This is the psalm that Jesus quoted while he was hanging on the cross. It is a lamentation, and typical of all lamentations, it begins with an appeal, continues with a list of the sufferings that the psalmist is undergoing, and closes with a short hymn of praise in which the psalmist declares his faith in his eventual deliverance.

When Jesus quoted the first verse of this psalm, he was

℟. **My God, my God, why have you abandoned me?**

All who see me scoff at me;
they mock me with parted lips, they wag their heads:
"He relied on the LORD; let him deliver him,
let him rescue him, if he loves him."

℟. **My God, my God, why have you abandoned me?**

identifying with the psalmist's feeling of abandonment, but he was at the same time professing his faith in the fact that God would deliver him. He agreed with the sentiments found in the psalm, "I will proclaim your name to my brethren; in the midst of the assembly I will praise you."

The similarities between this psalm and what actually occurred to Jesus on the cross are astounding. It speaks of hands and feet being pierced, garments being divided, lots being cast, etc.

We can easily forget that Psalm 22 was written several hundreds of years before the time of Jesus. It fills us with a sense of awe, for here we see the Holy Spirit inspiring the psalmist in a powerful way.

Indeed, many dogs surround me,
    a pack of evildoers closes in upon me;
they have pierced my hands and my feet;
    I can count all my bones.

℟. **My God, my God, why have you abandoned me?**

They divide my garments among them,
    and for my vesture they cast lots.
But you, O LORD, be not far from me;
    O my help, hasten to aid me.

℟. **My God, my God, why have you abandoned me?**

I will proclaim your name to my brethren;
    in the midst of the assembly I will praise you:
"You who fear the LORD, praise him;
    all you descendants of Jacob, give glory to him;
    revere him, all you descendants of Israel!"

℟. **My God, my God, why have you abandoned me?**

Lect. No. 38

SECOND READING: Philippians 2:6-11

Saint Paul presents this hymn as an example of the profound humility of Jesus. It is also a teaching about Jesus who surrendered his prerogatives as God to serve us as a human.

The phrase, "form of God," means that Jesus is God, even as God the Father is God. Yet Jesus emptied himself of his godliness. The word "empty," *kenosis* in Greek, signifies a spirituality of surrender and humility. It does not mean that he stopped being God.

A reading from the Letter of Saint Paul to the Philippians

Christ Jesus, though he was in the form of God,
    did not regard equality with God
    something to be grasped.
Rather, he emptied himself,
    taking the form of a slave,
    coming in human likeness;
    and found human in appearance,
    he humbled himself,
    becoming obedient to the point of death,
    even death on a cross.
Because of this, God greatly exalted him

The ultimate degree of humility was to be obedient to the Father, even to the point of dying on the cross. We might think that this expression of humility was humiliating for Jesus, but he did not see it that way. He saw it as the fullest expression of his love and trust in the Father. God the Father responded to this trust by proclaiming Jesus as Lord, a title which affirms his divinity.

and bestowed on him the name
which is above every name,
that at the name of Jesus
every knee should bend,
of those in heaven and on earth and under the
    earth,
and every tongue confess that
Jesus Christ is Lord,
to the glory of God the Father.

The word of the Lord.

Lect. No. 38

VERSE BEFORE THE GOSPEL: Philippians 2:8-9

The Verse Before the Gospel repeats the heart of the Philippians' hymn. It celebrates the obedience of Jesus upon the cross and his exaltation in his resurrection.

Christ became obedient to the point of death,
even death on a cross.
Because of this, God greatly exalted him
and bestowed on him the name which is above
    every name.

Lect. No. 38

GOSPEL: 🅐 Longer Form: Mark 14:1—15:47

There was always a tremendous influx of pilgrims during the Feast of Passover. This is why the chief priests were hesitant to arrest Jesus at that time, for whenever great crowds of people gather together, one cannot really control how they might react.

In Mark's Gospel, Jesus is anointed by a woman at Simon the Leper's house. In John's Gospel it is by Mary, the sister of Martha and Lazarus. In both cases, the ointment used is a form of nard, an incredibly expensive perfume made from a plant that only grows in the

The Passion of our Lord Jesus Christ
according to Mark

The Passover and the Feast of Unleavened Bread
were to take place in two days' time.
So the chief priests and the scribes were seeking a
    way
    to arrest him by treachery and put him to death.
They said, "Not during the festival,
    for fear that there may be a riot among the people."

When he was in Bethany reclining at table
    in the house of Simon the leper,
    a woman came with an alabaster jar of perfumed
        oil,
    costly genuine spikenard.

Himalaya Mountains. It is said to have been worth more than three hundred days' salary (or almost a year's income).

Jesus' remark on serving the poor should not be interpreted as being callous. He is simply pointing out that she is performing a loving act of service to him, and that she should not be hindered. Often, when we serve the poor, we do acts of charity that can be manipulative, using others as recipients of our acts of kindness, which make us feel good about ourselves. Saint Vincent de Paul said we only hope that the poor will forgive us our charity. The alternative is to serve the person in front of us as an act of love, exactly what this woman was doing.

The account of the plot to betray Jesus is very short, simply stating that those who made it waited for their opportunity.

The meal that Jesus eats with his apostles is the Passover meal. (In the Gospel of John, Jesus anticipates the feast by one day.)

Jesus gives instructions to his disciples concerning the preparations that they were to make for the room where they would eat the Passover meal. The fact that a man would be carrying a water jar indicates that Jesus ate the Last Supper in the Essene section of the city. Normally women carried water home, but the Essenes were concerned with ritual impurity so men among them carried water jars.

She broke the alabaster jar and poured it on his head.
There were some who were indignant.
"Why has there been this waste of perfumed oil?
It could have been sold for more than three hundred
    days' wages
  and the money given to the poor."
They were infuriated with her.
Jesus said, "Let her alone.
Why do you make trouble for her?
She has done a good thing for me.
The poor you will always have with you,
  and whenever you wish you can do good to them,
  but you will not always have me.
She has done what she could.
She has anticipated anointing my body for burial.
Amen, I say to you,
  wherever the gospel is proclaimed to the whole
    world,
  what she has done will be told in memory of her."

Then Judas Iscariot, one of the Twelve,
  went off to the chief priests to hand him over to
    them.
When they heard him they were pleased and promised to pay him money.
Then he looked for an opportunity to hand him over.

On the first day of the Feast of Unleavened Bread,
  when they sacrificed the Passover lamb,
  his disciples said to him,
  "Where do you want us to go
  and prepare for you to eat the Passover?"
He sent two of his disciples and said to them,
  "Go into the city and a man will meet you,
  carrying a jar of water.
Follow him.
Wherever he enters, say to the master of the house,
  'The Teacher says, "Where is my guest room
  where I may eat the Passover with my disciples?"'

The tenor of the words concerning who would betray him makes it appear that Jesus knew this at a very profound level of his person.

Jesus and the twelve reclined at table, for the table was only about 18 inches high.

During the meal, people would dip herbs into a haroset sauce. It is not clear whether Jesus intended one particular action, or simply the fact that he was sharing table fellowship with him.

Although the death of Jesus had been predicted and this was all in obedience to the will of God, it does not mean that the person who would betray Jesus was without guilt. Here Jesus speaks of how it would have been better if the betrayer had never been born.

In the course of the meal we hear the words of consecration over the bread and the wine that become the body and blood of Jesus. This version of the words is very close to that found in the Gospel of Matthew, and probably represents a more primitive tradition than the words found in Luke and First Corinthians.

The blood of the covenant (a phrase implying the initiation of a new covenant) is shed for the many. This is an Aramaic way of saying "for everyone."

The Passover meal traditionally ended with the singing of the Hallel hymns praising the

Then he will show you a large upper room furnished and ready.
Make the preparations for us there."
The disciples then went off, entered the city,
and found it just as he had told them;
and they prepared the Passover.

When it was evening, he came with the Twelve.
And as they reclined at table and were eating, Jesus said,
"Amen, I say to you, one of you will betray me,
one who is eating with me."
They began to be distressed and to say to him, one by one,
"Surely it is not I?"
He said to them,
"One of the Twelve, the one who dips with me into the dish.
For the Son of Man indeed goes, as it is written of him,
but woe to that man by whom the Son of Man is betrayed.
It would be better for that man if he had never been born."

While they were eating,
he took bread, said the blessing,
broke it, and gave it to them, and said,
"Take it; this is my body."
Then he took a cup, gave thanks, and gave it to them,
and they all drank from it.
He said to them,
"This is my blood of the covenant,
which will be shed for many.
Amen, I say to you,
I shall not drink again the fruit of the vine
until the day when I drink it new in the kingdom of God."

Lord. Jesus and the disciples walked to the Mount of Olives (a hill on the east side of Jerusalem) where he prayed in the Garden of Gethsemane.

This mountain was always associated with the dawning of the end times in Old Testament prophecies.

On the way, he predicted his passion (which he had already done a number of times throughout the Gospel). Peter reacts with a response of bravura that Jesus cuts short when he predicts Peter's denial.

Jesus enters the garden and proceeds with Peter, James, and John (the three disciples who always accompany Jesus in some of the most important events of his ministry). He asks them to keep vigil and goes a little farther on to pray.

They fail miserably because all three times that Jesus returns to check on them, the three have fallen asleep. We are certainly able to see the irony here, for Peter professed that he would die for Jesus. He cannot even stay awake for a short time.

The depth of emotion that Jesus is feeling is obvious from the description in these verses. He says, "My soul is sorrowful even to death."

Jesus prays to the Father that the cup be taken away from him, but he also professes himself ready to do what the Father wanted.

Then, after singing a hymn,
> they went out to the Mount of Olives.

Then Jesus said to them,
> "All of you will have your faith shaken, for it is written:
>> *I will strike the shepherd,*
>>> *and the sheep will be dispersed.*
> But after I have been raised up,
>> I shall go before you to Galilee."
Peter said to him,
> "Even though all should have their faith shaken,
> mine will not be."
Then Jesus said to him,
> "Amen, I say to you,
> this very night before the cock crows twice
> you will deny me three times."
But he vehemently replied,
> "Even though I should have to die with you,
> I will not deny you."
And they all spoke similarly.

Then they came to a place named Gethsemane,
> and he said to his disciples,
> "Sit here while I pray."
He took with him Peter, James, and John,
> and began to be troubled and distressed.
Then he said to them, "My soul is sorrowful even to
> death.
Remain here and keep watch."
He advanced a little and fell to the ground and
> prayed
> that if it were possible the hour might pass by
> him;
> he said, "Abba, Father, all things are possible to
> you.
Take this cup away from me,
> but not what I will but what you will."
When he returned he found them asleep.

In this Gospel, there is no angel to console Jesus. Rather, there is absolute silence.

Jesus must proceed with total faith, even though he has not received any concrete signs of the concern of the Father.

Mark intends this to be a lesson for all of us. Often, we are asked to do God's will and to trust in God's love, even when we cannot understand why nor have received any sign from God that he is near to console us.

The Jewish elders came with Judas to arrest Jesus in the garden. They had agreed upon a sign, that Judas would kiss him. Remember, Jesus was from Galilee, and not all of the Jewish officials knew him by sight.

Furthermore, it was dark in the garden, so they might have needed a very clear sign to point out who Jesus was in the midst of the crowd of disciples.

Jesus asks why the Jewish leaders came to arrest him so heavily armed. He implies that they were performing an act of cowardice, for they could have easily taken him while he was in the temple during the day but had not.

This accusation is actually true, as we saw earlier, for they were afraid of the mob of pilgrims who might have hindered Jesus' arrest if it had been attempted during the day.

He said to Peter, "Simon, are you asleep?
Could you not keep watch for one hour?
Watch and pray that you may not undergo the test.
The spirit is willing but the flesh is weak."
Withdrawing again, he prayed, saying the same
    thing.
Then he returned once more and found them asleep,
    for they could not keep their eyes open
    and did not know what to answer him.
He returned a third time and said to them,
    "Are you still sleeping and taking your rest?
It is enough. The hour has come.
Behold, the Son of Man is to be handed over to sin-
    ners.
Get up, let us go.
See, my betrayer is at hand."

Then, while he was still speaking,
    Judas, one of the Twelve, arrived,
    accompanied by a crowd with swords and clubs
    who had come from the chief priests,
    the scribes, and the elders.
His betrayer had arranged a signal with them, say-
    ing,
    "The man I shall kiss is the one;
    arrest him and lead him away securely."
He came and immediately went over to him and
    said,
    "Rabbi." And he kissed him.
At this they laid hands on him and arrested him.
One of the bystanders drew his sword,
    struck the high priest's servant, and cut off his
    ear.
Jesus said to them in reply,
    "Have you come out as against a robber,
    with swords and clubs, to seize me?
Day after day I was with you teaching in the temple
    area,

We are not sure who the young man is who loses his clothes. It is possible that this is a remembrance of Mark himself (one of the few moments when he might have followed Jesus during his public ministry).

It is also possible that this figure is symbolically tied to the man dressed in white in the tomb. It could be a baptismal symbol. (We lose our clothes when we die with Christ in Baptism, and then we are vested in white when we rise with him.)

We are told that the entire Sanhedrin met to try Jesus. Many scholars doubt this, for it was the middle of the night, and as far as we know, night meetings of the Sanhedrin were not permitted. They suggest that this was more of a plot among some of the leaders of the Jews.

In spite of the fact that they had produced false witnesses, the leaders of the Jews could not make any of the charges stick (for they were trying to condemn the source of truth himself).

The high priest then asks Jesus whether he is the Christ (the Messiah), the Son of the Blessed One. Jesus responds that he is with the phrase, "I am." He speaks of himself as being the fulfillment of the prophecy in Daniel 7, where the Son of Man would receive power and dominion and authority.

yet you did not arrest me;
but that the Scriptures may be fulfilled."
And they all left him and fled.
Now a young man followed him
wearing nothing but a linen cloth about his body.
They seized him,
but he left the cloth behind and ran off naked.

They led Jesus away to the high priest,
and all the chief priests and the elders and the
scribes came together.
Peter followed him at a distance into the high
priest's courtyard
and was seated with the guards, warming himself
at the fire.
The chief priests and the entire Sanhedrin
kept trying to obtain testimony against Jesus
in order to put him to death, but they found none.
Many gave false witness against him,
but their testimony did not agree.
Some took the stand and testified falsely against
him,
alleging, "We heard him say,
'I will destroy this temple made with hands
and within three days I will build another
not made with hands.'"
Even so their testimony did not agree.
The high priest rose before the assembly and questioned Jesus,
saying, "Have you no answer?
What are these men testifying against you?"
But he was silent and answered nothing.
Again the high priest asked him and said to him,
"Are you the Christ, the son of the Blessed One?"
Then Jesus answered, "I am;
and 'you will see the Son of Man
seated at the right hand of the Power
and coming with the clouds of heaven.'"

The high priest finds this phrase blasphemous. Yet, technically, it is not blasphemy, for Jesus is not exactly saying he is God, only that he is the chosen and anointed one.

But, he had certainly proclaimed that he had a special relationship with the Father and had applied certain prerogatives to himself that belong to God (such as the forgiveness of sins), so one might make an argument that a Jewish leader would consider what he said to be blasphemy.

The guards then beat and tried to humiliate Jesus, something that was always done to condemned prisoners at that time.

In the meantime, Peter is being asked by bystanders to give witness to his discipleship, and he fails. Before the cock crowed twice that evening, he had denied Jesus three times.

Before his third denial, the bystanders mentioned that he was a Galilean. People who came from Galilee had a noticeable accent when they spoke Aramaic, so those listening were able to pick him out.

The description of Peter's reaction after the third denial is powerful. It implies someone who is distraught with grief. One pious legend even speaks of the lines that were carved into Peter's face from the tears that he shed that night.

At that the high priest tore his garments and said,
  "What further need have we of witnesses?
You have heard the blasphemy.
What do you think?"
They all condemned him as deserving to die.
Some began to spit on him.
They blindfolded him and struck him and said to
    him, "Prophesy!"
And the guards greeted him with blows.

While Peter was below in the courtyard,
  one of the high priest's maids came along.
Seeing Peter warming himself,
  she looked intently at him and said,
  "You too were with the Nazarene, Jesus."
But he denied it saying,
  "I neither know nor understand what you are
    talking about."
So he went out into the outer court.
Then the cock crowed.
The maid saw him and began again to say to the by-
    standers,
  "This man is one of them."
Once again he denied it.
A little later the bystanders said to Peter once more,
  "Surely you are one of them; for you too are a
    Galilean."
He began to curse and to swear,
  "I do not know this man about whom you are
    talking."
And immediately a cock crowed a second time.
Then Peter remembered the word that Jesus had
    said to him,
  "Before the cock crows twice you will deny me
    three times."
He broke down and wept.

As soon as morning came,
  the chief priests with the elders and the scribes,
  that is, the whole Sanhedrin, held a council.

Jesus is then sent to Pilate, for the Jewish leaders did not have authority to put anyone to death. They wanted Pilate to do it for them.

They had probably told Pilate that Jesus was planning a rebellion, for the governor asks Jesus whether he is the king of the Jews.

Jesus' odd silence in response to Pilate's questions almost gives the interrogation a tone of Jesus being in charge and Pilate being the subordinate.

The account speaks of a custom of releasing a prisoner during Passover time. We have no outside evidence of this custom from other sources, but all four Gospels agree that this is what happened, so there is no reason to doubt the account.

The crowd does not want Jesus to be freed, but rather cries out for the release of Barabbas. The various Gospel accounts speak of Barabbas in different ways. Here he is called a rebel who had committed murder during a rebellion.

The sense of the account is that Pilate did not really want to kill Jesus, but the crowd forced his hands.

Finally, he ordered Barabbas released and had Jesus scourged, a preliminary to carrying out the sentence of having him crucified.

They bound Jesus, led him away, and handed him
over to Pilate.
Pilate questioned him,
"Are you the king of the Jews?"
He said to him in reply, "You say so."
The chief priests accused him of many things.
Again Pilate questioned him,
"Have you no answer?
See how many things they accuse you of."
Jesus gave him no further answer, so that Pilate was
amazed.

Now on the occasion of the feast he used to release
to them
one prisoner whom they requested.
A man called Barabbas was then in prison
along with the rebels who had committed murder
in a rebellion.
The crowd came forward and began to ask him
to do for them as he was accustomed.
Pilate answered,
"Do you want me to release to you the king of the
Jews?"
For he knew that it was out of envy
that the chief priests had handed him over.
But the chief priests stirred up the crowd
to have him release Barabbas for them instead.
Pilate again said to them in reply,
"Then what do you want me to do
with the man you call the king of the Jews?"
They shouted again, "Crucify him."
Pilate said to them, "Why? What evil has he done?"
They only shouted the louder, "Crucify him."
So Pilate, wishing to satisfy the crowd,
released Barabbas to them and, after he had Jesus
scourged,
handed him over to be crucified.

The guards further torture and humiliate Jesus by crowning him with thorns and putting a purple cloak around him. They hail him as the king of the Jews. We know from historic records that the praetorian guard often played these games with prisoners whom they were about to put to death. We are not sure about the purple robe, however, for purple was a royal color and was rare. Matthew speaks of a scarlet robe, which might be the more accurate description.

The soldiers force a passerby to assist. His name is Simon, and he is described as the father of Alexander and Rufus (possibly two early Christians).

They take Jesus to the Place of the Skull, Golgotha (probably so named because it was an outcrop of rock that resembled the shape of a skull). This was found in a used-out quarry, and the stone into which the cross was placed had been left because it contained a flaw. Thus, the stone rejected by the builders had become the cornerstone.

They offer Jesus wine mixed with myrrh (possibly a narcotic to dull the pain), but he refuses it. At the Last Supper he said that he would not drink wine again until he came into the kingdom of God.

This account speaks of him being crucified around nine, while the other Gospels speak of noon. This was before accurate ways to measure time, so it might have been mid- to late morning.

The soldiers led him away inside the palace,
>   that is, the praetorium, and assembled the whole cohort.
They clothed him in purple and,
>   weaving a crown of thorns, placed it on him.
They began to salute him with, "Hail, King of the Jews!"
>   and kept striking his head with a reed and spitting upon him.
They knelt before him in homage.
And when they had mocked him,
>   they stripped him of the purple cloak,
>   dressed him in his own clothes,
>   and led him out to crucify him.

They pressed into service a passer-by, Simon,
>   a Cyrenian, who was coming in from the country,
>   the father of Alexander and Rufus,
>   to carry his cross.

They brought him to the place of Golgotha
>   —which is translated Place of the Skull—.
They gave him wine drugged with myrrh,
>   but he did not take it.
Then they crucified him and divided his garments
>   by casting lots for them to see what each should take.
It was nine o'clock in the morning when they crucified him.
The inscription of the charge against him read,
>   "The King of the Jews."
With him they crucified two revolutionaries,
>   one on his right and one on his left.
Those passing by reviled him,
>   shaking their heads and saying,
>   "Aha! You who would destroy the temple
>   and rebuild it in three days,
>   save yourself by coming down from the cross."
Likewise the chief priests, with the scribes,

Jesus is mocked by the passersby and by the two thieves crucified with him. There is no good thief in this account—that story is found only in the Gospel of Luke.

We hear of a darkness that covered the whole land (which could mean the area around Jerusalem or the whole earth) from noon until three.

Jesus is heard to cry out, *"Eloi, Eloi, lema sabachthani?"* This is the first verse of Psalm 22 in Aramaic, the language that Jesus spoke.

Psalm 22 is a lamentation that speaks about how the psalmist feels abandoned by the LORD. It describes the suffering of the psalmist in terms that are hauntingly similar to the sufferings that Jesus actually underwent.

The last verse of this lamentation is a profession of trust in the LORD for what the psalmist was sure would be a deliverance from danger.

The description of Jesus' death is simple: he cries out and breathes his last. This is typical of the simplicity of Mark's Gospel accounts.

The Roman centurion, a pagan, proclaims Jesus as the Son of God. By having a pagan make this proclamation, Mark is showing that Jesus is not simply a hero (the Old Testament meaning of the term), but truly the only-begotten Son of God.

mocked him among themselves and said,
"He saved others; he cannot save himself.
Let the Christ, the King of Israel,
come down now from the cross
that we may see and believe."
Those who were crucified with him also kept abusing him.

At noon darkness came over the whole land
until three in the afternoon.
And at three o'clock Jesus cried out in a loud voice,
"Eloi, Eloi, lema sabachthani?"
which is translated,
"My God, my God, why have you forsaken me?"
Some of the bystanders who heard it said,
"Look, he is calling Elijah."
One of them ran, soaked a sponge with wine, put it on a reed
and gave it to him to drink saying,
"Wait, let us see if Elijah comes to take him down."
Jesus gave a loud cry and breathed his last.

Here all kneel and pause for a short time.

The veil of the sanctuary was torn in two from top to bottom.
When the centurion who stood facing him
saw how he breathed his last he said,
"Truly this man was the Son of God!"
There were also women looking on from a distance.
Among them were Mary Magdalene,
Mary the mother of the younger James and of Joses, and Salome.
These women had followed him when he was in Galilee
and ministered to him.
There were also many other women
who had come up with him to Jerusalem.

When it was already evening,
since it was the day of preparation,

The women who ministered to Jesus are present at the crucifixion (although notice that Mary, his mother, is not present in this account).

Joseph of Arimathea, a member of the council, had the courage to ask for the body of Jesus and to bury it. There is no mention of anointing the body in preparation for burial.

This is why the women would return there on Easter Sunday morning, to anoint the body for there had not been time to do this on Friday.

They laid Jesus in a tomb hewn out of the rock (a tomb of a relatively prosperous person, probably belonging to Joseph himself).

the day before the sabbath, Joseph of Arimathea,
   a distinguished member of the council,
   who was himself awaiting the kingdom of God,
   came and courageously went to Pilate
   and asked for the body of Jesus.
Pilate was amazed that he was already dead.
He summoned the centurion
   and asked him if Jesus had already died.
And when he learned of it from the centurion,
   he gave the body to Joseph.
Having bought a linen cloth, he took him down,
   wrapped him in the linen cloth,
   and laid him in a tomb that had been hewn out of
      the rock.
Then he rolled a stone against the entrance to the
      tomb.
Mary Magdalene and Mary the mother of Joses
   watched where he was laid.

The Gospel of the Lord.

Lect.
No. 38

GOSPEL: 🅑 Shorter Form: Mark 15:1-39

Jesus was sent to Pilate by the Jewish leaders because they did not have the authority to put anyone to death. They wanted Pilate to do their dirty work.

They had probably told Pilate that Jesus was planning a rebellion, for the governor asks Jesus whether he is the king of the Jews. This was an especially dangerous accusation to make against someone during Passover time when tensions ran high.

The Passion of our Lord Jesus Christ
according to Mark

As soon as morning came,
   the chief priests with the elders and the scribes,
   that is, the whole Sanhedrin, held a council.
They bound Jesus, led him away, and handed him
      over to Pilate.
Pilate questioned him,
   "Are you the king of the Jews?"
He said to him in reply, "You say so."
The chief priests accused him of many things.
Again Pilate questioned him,
   "Have you no answer?
See how many things they accuse you of."

Jesus' odd silence in response to Pilate's questions almost gives the interrogation a tone of Jesus being in charge and Pilate being the subordinate.

The account speaks of a custom of releasing a prisoner during Passover time. We have no outside evidence of this custom from other sources, but all four Gospels agree that this is what happened, so there is no reason to doubt the account.

The crowd does not want Jesus to be freed, but rather cries out for the release of Barabbas. The various Gospel accounts speak of Barabbas in different ways. Here he is called a rebel who had committed murder during a rebellion.

The sense of the account is that Pilate did not really want to kill Jesus, but the crowd forced his hands. Finally, he ordered Barabbas released and had Jesus scourged, a preliminary to carrying out the sentence of having him crucified.

The guards further torture and humiliate Jesus by crowning him with thorns and putting a purple cloak around him. They hail him as the king of the Jews.

We know from historic records that the praetorian guard often played these games with prisoners whom they were about to put to death.

We are not sure about the purple robe, however, for purple was a royal color and was rare.

Jesus gave him no further answer, so that Pilate was
    amazed.

Now on the occasion of the feast he used to release
    to them
    one prisoner whom they requested.
A man called Barabbas was then in prison
    along with the rebels who had committed murder
    in a rebellion.
The crowd came forward and began to ask him
    to do for them as he was accustomed.
Pilate answered,
    "Do you want me to release to you the king of the
    Jews?"
For he knew that it was out of envy
    that the chief priests had handed him over.
But the chief priests stirred up the crowd
    to have him release Barabbas for them instead.
Pilate again said to them in reply,
    "Then what do you want me to do
    with the man you call the king of the Jews?"
They shouted again, "Crucify him."
Pilate said to them, "Why? What evil has he done?"
They only shouted the louder, "Crucify him."
So Pilate, wishing to satisfy the crowd,
    released Barabbas to them and, after he had Jesus
    scourged,
    handed him over to be crucified.

The soldiers led him away inside the palace,
    that is, the praetorium, and assembled the whole
    cohort.
They clothed him in purple and,
    weaving a crown of thorns, placed it on him.
They began to salute him with, "Hail, King of the
    Jews!"
    and kept striking his head with a reed and spitting upon him.
They knelt before him in homage.

Matthew speaks of a scarlet robe.

The soldiers force a passerby to assist. His name is Simon, the father of Alexander and Rufus (possibly two early Christians).

They take Jesus to the Place of the Skull, Golgotha (probably so named because it was an outcrop of rock that resembled the shape of a skull). This was found in a used-out quarry, and the stone into which the cross was placed had been left because it contained a flaw. Thus, the stone rejected by the builders had become the cornerstone.

They offer Jesus wine mixed with myrrh (possibly a narcotic to dull the pain), but he refuses it. At the Last Supper he said that he would not drink wine again until he came into the kingdom of God.

This account speaks of him being crucified around nine, while the other Gospels speak of noon. This was before accurate ways to measure time, so it might have been mid- to late morning.

Jesus is mocked by the passersby and by the two thieves crucified with him. There is no good thief in this account—that story is found only in the Gospel of Luke.

We hear of a darkness that covered the whole land (meaning either the area around Jerusalem or the whole earth) from noon until three.

Jesus is heard to cry out, "*Eloi, Eloi, lema sabachthani?*" the first verse of Psalm 22 in

And when they had mocked him,
    they stripped him of the purple cloak,
    dressed him in his own clothes,
    and led him out to crucify him.

They pressed into service a passer–by, Simon,
    a Cyrenian, who was coming in from the country,
    the father of Alexander and Rufus,
    to carry his cross.

They brought him to the place of Golgotha
    —which is translated Place of the Skull—.
They gave him wine drugged with myrrh,
    but he did not take it.
Then they crucified him and divided his garments
    by casting lots for them to see what each should take.
It was nine o'clock in the morning when they crucified him.
The inscription of the charge against him read,
    "The King of the Jews."
With him they crucified two revolutionaries,
    one on his right and one on his left.
Those passing by reviled him,
    shaking their heads and saying,
    "Aha! You who would destroy the temple
    and rebuild it in three days,
    save yourself by coming down from the cross."
Likewise the chief priests, with the scribes,
    mocked him among themselves and said,
    "He saved others; he cannot save himself.
Let the Christ, the King of Israel,
    come down now from the cross
    that we may see and believe."
Those who were crucified with him also kept abusing him.

At noon darkness came over the whole land
    until three in the afternoon.
And at three o'clock Jesus cried out in a loud voice,

Aramaic. Psalm 22 is a lamentation that describes sufferings that are hauntingly similar to those which Jesus endured. The last verse of this lamentation has a profession of trust in the LORD for what the psalmist was sure would be a deliverance.

The description of Jesus' death is simple: he cries out and breathes his last. This is typical of the simplicity of Mark's Gospel accounts.

The Roman centurion, a pagan, proclaims Jesus as the Son of God. Mark is showing that Jesus is not simply a hero (the Old Testament meaning of the term), but truly the only-begotten Son of God.

"Eloi, Eloi, lema sabachthani?"
which is translated,
"My God, my God, why have you forsaken me?"
Some of the bystanders who heard it said,
"Look, he is calling Elijah."
One of them ran, soaked a sponge with wine, put it on a reed
and gave it to him to drink saying,
"Wait, let us see if Elijah comes to take him down."
Jesus gave a loud cry and breathed his last.

Here all kneel and pause for a short time.

The veil of the sanctuary was torn in two from top to bottom.
When the centurion who stood facing him
saw how he breathed his last he said,
"Truly this man was the Son of God!"

The Gospel of the Lord.

PASTORAL REFLECTIONS

The proclamation of the Passion of Jesus today gives us an opportunity to reflect upon the meaning of remembrance.

The Jewish concept of remembrance was much more powerful than simply calling something to mind. By remembering, one somehow made that thing present. Thus, when Jewish people read the account of the Passover, they believed that they were somehow participating in those events.

Likewise, as we enter into the commemoration of Holy Week, we are passing outside of our everyday life and entering into the mystery of Jesus' death and resurrection.

March 29, 2018

THURSDAY OF HOLY WEEK
[HOLY THURSDAY]

THE CHRISM MASS

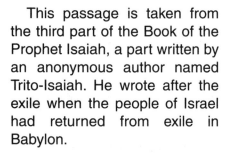

Lect. No. 260

FIRST READING:

Isaiah 61:1-3ab, 6a, 8b-9

This passage is taken from the third part of the Book of the Prophet Isaiah, a part written by an anonymous author named Trito-Isaiah. He wrote after the exile when the people of Israel had returned from exile in Babylon.

The author speaks of an anointed one who would bring a year of favor to his people. This was to be the fulfillment of the Jubilee Year.

Every seven years the people did not plant crops because they wanted to show their faith in the providence of the LORD. Every seventh seven, there was a Jubilee Year. Debts were forgiven, slaves were freed, properties were returned to their original owners, etc. It was to be a year of profound dedication to justice. The people were to share the providence they had received from the LORD.

The Messiah spoken of in this passage was to establish that year of favor. He was to bring consolation to a people burdened by their difficulties. He would be able to do this because he was filled with the anointing of the Spirit of the LORD.

A reading from the Book of the Prophet Isaiah

The Spirit of the Lord GOD is upon me,
because the LORD has anointed me;
He has sent me to bring glad tidings to the poor,
to heal the brokenhearted,
To proclaim liberty to the captives
and release to the prisoners,
To announce a year of favor from the LORD
and a day of vindication by our God,
to comfort all who mourn;
To place on those who mourn in Zion
a diadem instead of ashes,
To give them oil of gladness in place of mourning,
a glorious mantle instead of a listless spirit.

You yourselves shall be named priests of the LORD,
ministers of our God you shall be called.

I will give them their recompense faithfully,
a lasting covenant I will make with them.
Their descendants shall be renowned among the nations,
and their offspring among the peoples;
All who see them shall acknowledge them
as a race the LORD has blessed.

The word of the Lord.

150

Lect. No. 260

RESPONSORIAL PSALM: Ps 89:21-22, 25 and 27 (℟.: 2a)

At the Chrism Mass we bless the sacred oils that will be used throughout the year. This oil will be used for consecrating, anointing for healing, and setting apart for God.

These verses speak of the effects of an anointing. David, the anointed of the LORD, was filled with the strength, faithfulness, and kindness of the LORD.

Anointing establishes a special relationship between us and God, who is our father, our rock, and our savior.

℟. **For ever I will sing the goodness of the Lord.**

"I have found David, my servant;
    with my holy oil I have anointed him.
That my hand may be always with him;
    and that my arm may make him strong."

℟. **For ever I will sing the goodness of the Lord.**

"My faithfulness and my mercy shall be with him;
    and through my name shall his horn be exalted.
He shall say of me, 'You are my father,
    my God, the Rock, my savior!'"

℟. **For ever I will sing the goodness of the Lord.**

Lect. No. 260

SECOND READING: Revelation 1:5-8

The Book of Revelation is filled with liturgical hymns. This one lauds Jesus who is the faithful witness. The word for witness in Greek is "martureo," the source of the English word "martyr."

Jesus has made us coheirs with him in the glory of God, for he has adopted us as his brothers and sisters.

We have also become priests through our baptismal anointing. We share in the priesthood of Jesus, and like him, we are both the priest offering up the sacrifice and the sacrifice itself. We lift up an offering of our life and love, our successes and failures, our hopes and even our fears.

God is our Alpha and Omega for he is the source of everything we have and are, and also the goal toward which we journey.

A reading from the Book of Revelation

[Grace to you and peace] from Jesus Christ,
    who is the faithful witness,
    the firstborn of the dead and ruler of the kings of
        the earth.
To him who loves us and has freed us from our sins by
        his Blood,
    who has made us into a Kingdom, priests for his
        God and Father,
    to him be glory and power forever and ever. Amen.

    Behold, he is coming amid the clouds,
        and every eye will see him,
        even those who pierced him.
    All the peoples of the earth will lament him.
        Yes. Amen.

"I am the Alpha and the Omega," says the Lord God,
    "the one who is and who was
        and who is to come, the Almighty."

The word of the Lord.

**Lect.
No. 260**

VERSE BEFORE THE GOSPEL: Isaiah 61:1 (cited in Luke 4:18)

This Verse speaks of the sacred anointing through which the Holy Spirit calls us to serve the poorest of the poor.

The Spirit of the LORD is upon me
for he sent me to bring glad tidings to the poor.

**Lect.
No. 260**

GOSPEL: Luke 4:16-21

Early in his public ministry, Jesus goes into the synagogue in his hometown and identifies himself as the anointed one of God.

This anointing proclaims Jesus as the fulfillment of the Jubilee Year of the Lord. We would not have to wait fifty years in order to experience God's justice. When we encounter Jesus and the love he offers, we are changed.

We cannot treat ourselves and others with the lack of respect that we sometimes showed them. We must love them with the same love with which Jesus loved us. This is especially true of those who most need our care and love, those who are broken and hurting.

As we receive the anointing of the Spirit of the Lord (using the oils blessed at this Mass), we share in Jesus' ministry to proclaim that year of favor to the world.

A reading from the holy Gospel according to Luke

Jesus came to Nazareth, where he had grown up,
and went according to his custom
into the synagogue on the sabbath day.
He stood up to read and was handed a scroll of the
    prophet Isaiah.
He unrolled the scroll and found the passage
    where it was written:
    The Spirit of the Lord is upon me,
    because he has anointed me
        to bring glad tidings to the poor.
    He has sent me to proclaim liberty to captives
        and recovery of sight to the blind,
        to let the oppressed go free,
    and to proclaim a year acceptable to the Lord.
Rolling up the scroll, he handed it back to the attendant and sat down,
    and the eyes of all in the synagogue looked intently at him.
He said to them,
    "Today this Scripture passage is fulfilled in your
        hearing."

The Gospel of the Lord.

March 29, 2018
THURSDAY OF THE LORD'S SUPPER [HOLY THURSDAY]
AT THE EVENING MASS

Lect. No. 39

FIRST READING: Exodus 12:1-8, 11-14

The First Reading for Holy Thursday is a recounting of the events of the first Passover of the Exodus. Scholars now believe that the Jewish people celebrated Passover before the Exodus as an agricultural feast (possibly associated with the birth of the Spring lambs). The Hebrew word for Passover, "Pesach," means leaping, probably referring to the leaping of the newborn lambs.

After the Exodus, it was linked with the events that occurred in Egypt. The passing over was now understood as both the angel of death passing over Egypt and the Israelites passing over the Red Sea.

The month of the Passover was to be considered the first month of the year. This changed when the Israelites were in exile in Babylon. During the exile they adopted the Babylonian calendar, which marked the fall as the beginning of the year. Jewish people celebrate Rosh Hashana (New Year's Day) in September.

The meal was to be eaten as if they were preparing for a journey (with loins girt and sandals on their feet). They were, in fact, to relive the events every time they commemorated them.

A reading from the Book of Exodus

The LORD said to Moses and Aaron in the land of Egypt,
"This month shall stand at the head of your calendar;
you shall reckon it the first month of the year.
Tell the whole community of Israel:
On the tenth of this month every one of your families
must procure for itself a lamb, one apiece for each household.
If a family is too small for a whole lamb,
it shall join the nearest household in procuring one
and shall share in the lamb
in proportion to the number of persons who partake of it.
The lamb must be a year-old male and without blemish.
You may take it from either the sheep or the goats.
You shall keep it until the fourteenth day of this month,
and then, with the whole assembly of Israel present,
it shall be slaughtered during the evening twilight.
They shall take some of its blood
and apply it to the two doorposts and the lintel
of every house in which they partake of the lamb.
That same night they shall eat its roasted flesh
with unleavened bread and bitter herbs.

The Israelites ate a lamb and used the blood of the lamb to mark their doorposts and lintel. This mark protected them from the depredations of the angel of death who destroyed the first-born of all of the Egyptians.

It is appropriate that the doorposts should be marked with blood. In Old Testament symbolism blood signified life. The blood saved the lives of the Israelites.

The closing verses of this reading remind the Israelites that this was to be a celebration among the Jews forever, and also that it was intended to be a pilgrimage festival. During the days of Jesus, it was believed that as many as a quarter of a million pilgrims arrived in Jerusalem to celebrate the feast.

"This is how you are to eat it:
  with your loins girt, sandals on your feet and your staff in hand,
  you shall eat like those who are in flight.
It is the Passover of the LORD.
For on this same night I will go through Egypt,
  striking down every firstborn of the land, both man and beast,
  and executing judgment on all the gods of Egypt—I, the LORD!
But the blood will mark the houses where you are.
Seeing the blood, I will pass over you;
  thus, when I strike the land of Egypt,
  no destructive blow will come upon you.

"This day shall be a memorial feast for you,
  which all your generations shall celebrate
  with pilgrimage to the LORD, as a perpetual institution."
The word of the Lord.

Lect. No. 39

RESPONSORIAL PSALM: Ps 116:12-13, 15-16bc, 17-18

(℟.: cf. 1 Corinthians 10:16)

Psalm 116 is a thanksgiving psalm prayed in gratitude to the LORD for a deliverance. The psalmist had been at the point of death, but the LORD then loosed his bonds (the bonds of death).

The LORD had granted him the cup of salvation (allowed him to taste the effects of the LORD's salvation). Now, he would offer him a sacrifice of thanksgiving.

Both of these sacrificial images are appropriate for our celebration this evening. The Eucharist is both a powerful gift of salvation (celebrating the salvation offered upon the cross)

℟. **Our blessing-cup is a communion with the Blood of Christ.**

How shall I make a return to the LORD
  for all the good he has done for me?
The cup of salvation I will take up,
  and I will call upon the name of the LORD.

℟. **Our blessing-cup is a communion with the Blood of Christ.**

Precious in the eyes of the LORD
  is the death of his faithful ones.
I am your servant, the son of your handmaid;
  you have loosed my bonds.

℟. **Our blessing-cup is a communion with the Blood of Christ.**

and an act of thanksgiving. The word "Eucharist" in Greek actually means "to give thanks." Our only possible response to the incredible generosity and benevolence of God is to live our commitments to him with integrity.

To you will I offer sacrifice of thanksgiving,
and I will call upon the name of the LORD.
My vows to the LORD I will pay
in the presence of all his people.

℟. **Our blessing-cup is a communion with the Blood of Christ.**

Lect. No. 39

SECOND READING: 1 Corinthians 11:23-26

Paul wrote this account of the institution of the Eucharist to the Corinthian community because they seem to have forgotten the significance of this event. They were celebrating the Lord's Supper but not living in communion with their sisters and brothers. Some in the community had more than enough to eat when they gathered together, while others were all but starving.

Paul accused them of sinning against the communion they were celebrating when they participated in the Eucharist. He told them to examine their consciences before they received the Eucharist. In other words, they were to make absolutely sure they understood the significance of what they were doing.

A reading from the first Letter of Saint Paul to the Corinthians

Brothers and sisters:
I received from the Lord what I also handed on to you,
that the Lord Jesus, on the night he was handed over,
took bread, and, after he had given thanks,
broke it and said, "This is my body that is for you.
Do this in remembrance of me."
In the same way also the cup, after supper, saying,
"This cup is the new covenant in my blood.
Do this, as often as you drink it, in remembrance of me."
For as often as you eat this bread and drink the cup,
you proclaim the death of the Lord until he comes.

The word of the Lord.

Lect. No. 39

VERSE BEFORE THE GOSPEL: John 13:34

We hear a passage from the Gospel of John about loving one another. This command is the core of the Sacrament we are celebrating.

I give you a new commandment, says the Lord:
love one another as I have loved you.

Lect.
No. 39

The account of the Last Supper found in the Gospel of John does not include an account of the institution of the Eucharist. Rather, it speaks of how Jesus washed the feet of his disciples and invited them to do the same to each other. It is not that this Gospel ignores the Eucharist (quite the opposite, for it speaks of the Eucharist here, in chapter 6, and also in chapter 21).

Rather, John presents this scene to teach us the spiritual significance of the Sacrament of the Eucharist. It is the Sacrament through which Jesus serves us in a most profound manner, and in which he invites us to be of service to each other. This is what his ministry in this Gospel is all about. Jesus came into this world to save us.

This is why the beginning of the account mentions certain things. First of all, we hear that the feast of the Passover was near. (In John the Last Supper is an anticipation of the Passover meal, for in this Gospel Passover does not begin until Good Friday night.)

We also hear that Jesus is acting in the love of the Father. Thus, his action of humility is not one performed because he did not know he was God, but rather the opposite. As we hear in the First Letter of John, God is love. Therefore, we hear of the great love he had for his disciples, a love shown in humble service.

GOSPEL: John 13:1-15

A reading from the holy Gospel according to John

Before the feast of Passover, Jesus knew that his hour had come
    to pass from this world to the Father.
He loved his own in the world and he loved them to the end.
The devil had already induced Judas, son of Simon the Iscariot, to hand him over.
So, during supper,
    fully aware that the Father had put everything into his power
    and that he had come from God and was returning to God,
    he rose from supper and took off his outer garments.
He took a towel and tied it around his waist.
Then he poured water into a basin
    and began to wash the disciples' feet
    and dry them with the towel around his waist.
He came to Simon Peter, who said to him,
    "Master, are you going to wash my feet?"
Jesus answered and said to him,
    "What I am doing, you do not understand now,
    but you will understand later."
Peter said to him, "You will never wash my feet."
Jesus answered him,
    "Unless I wash you, you will have no inheritance with me."
Simon Peter said to him,
    "Master, then not only my feet, but my hands and head as well."
Jesus said to him,
    "Whoever has bathed has no need except to have his feet washed,

Peter does not want his feet to be washed, possibly because he fears vulnerability (being served). Yet, both service and vulnerability are necessary dimensions of the love of Christ. We must both serve and allow ourselves to be served.

This chapter presents the Sacrament of the Eucharist as a verb, an act of service, and an invitation to serve others. This portrayal is balanced by chapter 6, where the Eucharist is presented as a noun (the real presence of Jesus) and chapter 21, where the meal on the shore after the miraculous catch of fish has Eucharistic overtones and presents the Eucharist as a call to mission.

for he is clean all over;
so you are clean, but not all."
For he knew who would betray him;
for this reason, he said, "Not all of you are clean."

So when he had washed their feet
and put his garments back on and reclined at table again,
he said to them, "Do you realize what I have done for you?
You call me 'teacher' and 'master,' and rightly so, for indeed I am.
If I, therefore, the master and teacher, have washed your feet,
you ought to wash one another's feet.
I have given you a model to follow,
so that as I have done for you, you should also do."

The Gospel of the Lord.

PASTORAL REFLECTIONS

The theology of the Sacrament of the Eucharist is much too rich to be expressed with one set of images. The Gospel of John was written at the end of the 1st century A.D., and already it contains three depictions of the Eucharist (ch. 6, 13, and 21).

In chapter 6 we see the vertical dimension of the Eucharist. Jesus, as the Good Shepherd, multiplies the loaves and fish, and he then proclaims the bread of life to be his body and the drink of life to be his blood. The Eucharist is thus seen to be Jesus truly present in this sacrament.

Chapter 13 presents the horizontal dimension of the Eucharist. The Eucharist is Jesus serving us (in this meal and also on the cross). He also asks us to serve each other.

Finally, in chapter 21 when the multiplication of the fish is emphasized because Jesus is calling the disciples to be fishers of men, we see the mission dimension of the Eucharist. After we have received this great love from Jesus, we must share it with others.

March 30, 2018

FRIDAY OF THE PASSION OF THE LORD [GOOD FRIDAY]

Lect. No. 40 **FIRST READING: Isaiah 52:13—53:12**

This is the fourth of the songs of the Suffering Servant of Yahweh. These songs were incorporated into the second part of the Book of the Prophet Isaiah. They are attributed to an anonymous author called Second Isaiah. (He prophesied during the Babylonian exile.)

These songs speak about a mysterious figure who would suffer to fulfill the mission of the LORD. This mission was to bring about an era of justice and peace. This wondrous future would be given not only to the people of the nation of Israel, but also to all the nations (the Hebrew phrase for the Gentiles).

The Servant would not bring about this new dispensation through violence. He would be meek and gentle and would not crush a bruised reed.

The author of the song speaks of the awe that this figure evokes (both at his willingness to suffer and at the extent of that suffering).

It was not known in ancient times who this Servant was. Some said that it was the personification of the nation of Israel, others that it was one of the prophets (possibly Jeremiah). It was Jesus who first applied these prophecies to himself.

A reading from the Book of the Prophet Isaiah

See, my servant shall prosper,
    he shall be raised high and greatly exalted.
Even as many were amazed at him—
    so marred was his look beyond human semblance
    and his appearance beyond that of the sons of man—
so shall he startle many nations,
    because of him kings shall stand speechless;
for those who have not been told shall see,
    those who have not heard shall ponder it.

Who would believe what we have heard?
    To whom has the arm of the LORD been revealed?
He grew up like a sapling before him,
    like a shoot from the parched earth;
there was in him no stately bearing to make us look at him,
    nor appearance that would attract us to him.
He was spurned and avoided by people,
    a man of suffering, accustomed to infirmity,
one of those from whom people hide their faces,
    spurned, and we held him in no esteem.

Yet it was our infirmities that he bore,
    our sufferings that he endured,
while we thought of him as stricken,
    as one smitten by God and afflicted.
But he was pierced for our offenses,
    crushed for our sins;

The fourth song is the most poignant in its description. It contains two elements that were not part of the theology of the era in which it was written.

First of all, it speaks about the ultimate exaltation of the Servant after he had been killed in the service of the LORD. This means his resurrection from the dead, an idea that had not yet become fully developed in theology of Israel.

Even stranger for this era was the idea that this Servant would bear the sins of the people upon himself: expiation. The Jewish people did not believe that the suffering and death of any person could bring about good. Their Messiah was to conquer, not to be killed.

What is being described is what Saint Paul speaks of as being the wisdom of God or the wisdom of the cross. In that wisdom, one must die in order to live forever.

The description of the sufferings of this Servant are similar to those of Psalm 22 and are uncannily similar to what actually happened to Jesus. He was like a sheep led to the slaughter, cut off from the land of the living, buried among wrongdoers, crushed.

Yet, because he was obedient to the will of the Father, he won pardon for our offenses and would be exalted in glory and proclaimed as Lord of everything that exists in heaven, on the earth, and under the earth.

upon him was the chastisement that makes us whole,
　　by his stripes we were healed.
We had all gone astray like sheep,
　　each following his own way;
but the LORD laid upon him
　　the guilt of us all.

Though he was harshly treated, he submitted
　　and opened not his mouth;
like a lamb led to the slaughter
　　or a sheep before the shearers,
　　he was silent and opened not his mouth.
Oppressed and condemned, he was taken away,
　　and who would have thought any more of his destiny?
When he was cut off from the land of the living,
　　and smitten for the sin of his people,
a grave was assigned him among the wicked
　　and a burial place with evildoers,
though he had done no wrong
　　nor spoken any falsehood.
But the LORD was pleased
　　to crush him in infirmity.

If he gives his life as an offering for sin,
　　he shall see his descendants in a long life,
　　and the will of the LORD shall be accomplished
　　　through him.

Because of his affliction
　　he shall see the light in fullness of days;
through his suffering, my servant shall justify many,
　　and their guilt he shall bear.
Therefore I will give him his portion among the great,
　　and he shall divide the spoils with the mighty,
because he surrendered himself to death
　　and was counted among the wicked;
and he shall take away the sins of many,
　　and win pardon for their offenses.

The word of the Lord.

Lect. No. 40

RESPONSORIAL PSALM: Ps 31:2, 6, 12-13, 15-16, 17, 25
(℟.: Luke 23:46)

Psalm 31 is a psalm of thanksgiving written by one who had been delivered from horrible life-threatening dangers. It expresses faith in the fact that God would surely deliver that person, for the LORD is truly a refuge.

It might seem odd to be reciting this psalm today, since it almost seems too positive in tone. Yet, there is a strong sense of hope in our commemoration for we are certain that the defeat on the cross will be followed by the triumph of the resurrection. This also reminds us that not all of our deliverances will be in this life. We must live in hope of a future fulfillment of God's promises in our resurrection from the dead.

Even on Good Friday Jesus expressed this same hope. He was citing Psalm 22 when he prayed, "My God, my God, why have you forsaken me?" These are the first words of this psalm of lamentation. All lamentations end with a profession of faith in God's ultimate deliverance. While Jesus was speaking of his feelings of abandonment, he was also professing his faith that the LORD, his Father, would deliver him.

℟. **Father, into your hands I commend my spirit.**

In you, O LORD, I take refuge;
　let me never be put to shame.
In your justice rescue me.
Into your hands I commend my spirit;
　you will redeem me, O LORD, O faithful God.

℟. **Father, into your hands I commend my spirit.**

For all my foes I am an object of reproach,
　a laughingstock to my neighbors, and a dread to
　　my friends;
they who see me abroad flee from me.
I am forgotten like the unremembered dead;
　I am like a dish that is broken.

℟. **Father, into your hands I commend my spirit.**

But my trust is in you, O LORD;
　I say, "You are my God.
In your hands is my destiny; rescue me
　from the clutches of my enemies and my persecu-
　　tors."

℟. **Father, into your hands I commend my spirit.**

Let your face shine upon your servant;
　save me in your kindness.
Take courage and be stouthearted,
　all you who hope in the LORD.

℟. **Father, into your hands I commend my spirit.**

Lect. No. 40

SECOND READING: Hebrews 4:14-16; 5:7-9

One of the major themes developed in the Letter to the Hebrews is that Jesus is our High Priest. Unlike the high priests of the Old Testament, Jesus was not a sinner. Being totally sinless, he therefore did not have to perform sacrifices for his own sins. His sacrifice was performed totally for our benefit.

Yet, in spite of the fact that Jesus was perfect and without sin, he nevertheless was able to empathize with us (because he shared our human condition). He was like us in all things but sin.

The second part of the reading speaks of Jesus' obedience to the will of the Father. This should not be understood as a blind obedience that denigrated Jesus. Rather, by being obedient, he was most fully who he really is. He was perfect in his response to God's will. Likewise, when we sin, we are rejecting who God made us to be, while when we live in obedience to God's will, we are actually most fully ourselves.

A reading from the Letter to the Hebrews

Brothers and sisters:
Since we have a great high priest who has
    passed through the heavens,
Jesus, the Son of God,
let us hold fast to our confession.
For we do not have a high priest
    who is unable to sympathize with our weaknesses,
    but one who has similarly been tested in every
        way,
    yet without sin.
So let us confidently approach the throne of grace
    to receive mercy and to find grace for timely help.

In the days when Christ was in the flesh,
    he offered prayers and supplications with loud
        cries and tears
    to the one who was able to save him from death,
    and he was heard because of his reverence.
Son though he was, he learned obedience from what
    he suffered;
    and when he was made perfect,
    he became the source of eternal salvation for all
        who obey him.

The word of the Lord.

Lect. No. 40

VERSE BEFORE THE GOSPEL: Philippians 2:8-9

This verse, taken from the Philippians' hymn, speaks of Jesus' profound obedience to the will of the Father and his exaltation as LORD.

Christ became obedient to the point of death,
    even death on a cross.
Because of this, God greatly exalted him
    and bestowed on him the name which is above
        every other name.

Lect.
No. 40

GOSPEL: John 18:1—19:42

The passion narrative in the Gospel of John agrees with the other Gospels in most details except those that are specifically Johannine. One example of this is that wherever possible the divinity of Jesus is emphasized. Jesus knows all things and controls all things from the beginning to the end of the account.

Although the place where Jesus led the disciples is not mentioned by name, it is obviously the garden of Gethsemane. We can see the violent intent of the soldiers of the high priests by the weapons they are carrying. This contrasts with the way that Jesus meets the troops, totally without arms. He is able to defeat them simply with the truth.

Jesus asks them whom they seek. They respond, "Jesus the Nazorean," and he tells them, "I AM." This phrase is the same as the meaning of the name of God in the Old Testament: Yahweh. Thus, Jesus is identifying himself as God. Those who had come to arrest Jesus fall down in fear and awe, for they are in the presence of the living God.

Peter tries to defend Jesus with a sword, cutting off Malchus' ear. Only in this Gospel is the violent disciple identified as Peter. It is compatible with his personality, which is a bit impetuous throughout this Gospel. Jesus tells him to put away his sword because he is

The Passion of our Lord Jesus Christ according to John

Jesus went out with his disciples across the Kidron valley
  to where there was a garden,
  into which he and his disciples entered.
Judas his betrayer also knew the place,
  because Jesus had often met there with his disciples.
So Judas got a band of soldiers and guards
  from the chief priests and the Pharisees
  and went there with lanterns, torches, and weapons.
Jesus, knowing everything that was going to happen to him,
  went out and said to them, "Whom are you looking for?"
They answered him, "Jesus the Nazorean."
He said to them, "I AM."
Judas his betrayer was also with them.
When he said to them, "I AM,"
  they turned away and fell to the ground.
So he again asked them,
  "Whom are you looking for?"
They said, "Jesus the Nazorean."
Jesus answered,
  "I told you that I AM.
So if you are looking for me, let these men go."
This was to fulfill what he had said,
  "I have not lost any of those you gave me."
Then Simon Peter, who had a sword, drew it,
  struck the high priest's slave, and cut off his right ear.
The slave's name was Malchus.

not going to confront violence with violence. Jesus wants to show that only love conquers.

Jesus is brought to the high priest's house. We hear how Caiaphas had predicted that it was better for one person to die for the sake of the people. Caiaphas had meant that it was better to kill him before a rebellion began, but the Holy Spirit had given him a revelation that he did not even understand. Jesus was going to die for the people, for the forgiveness of our sins.

The leaders of the Jews were offended by the fact that Jesus claimed divine prerogatives for himself. He was also considered to be a political danger, for the Jewish leaders feared he might start a rebellion in which they would lose their privileges.

The other disciple, who is probably the beloved disciple, is able to enter the high priest's house. He also arranges to bring Peter into the courtyard.

Jesus answers the questions of the high priest with diffidence. He is the very presence of God, and it is absurd that they should be questioning him. Furthermore, he is truth itself, and had spoken in the light. They were the ones who were working in the dark to hide their evil deeds.

The temple guards are enraged that Jesus would respond to the high priest in this manner and one strikes Jesus. He is trying to protect the dignity of the high priest, but there is an

Jesus said to Peter,
  "Put your sword into its scabbard.
Shall I not drink the cup that the Father gave me?"

So the band of soldiers, the tribune, and the Jewish
    guards seized Jesus,
  bound him, and brought him to Annas first.
He was the father-in-law of Caiaphas,
  who was high priest that year.
It was Caiaphas who had counseled the Jews
  that it was better that one man should die rather
    than the people.

Simon Peter and another disciple followed Jesus.
Now the other disciple was known to the high
    priest,
  and he entered the courtyard of the high priest
    with Jesus.
But Peter stood at the gate outside.
So the other disciple, the acquaintance of the high
    priest,
  went out and spoke to the gatekeeper and brought
    Peter in.
Then the maid who was the gatekeeper said to
    Peter,
  "You are not one of this man's disciples, are you?"
He said, "I am not."
Now the slaves and the guards were standing
    around a charcoal fire
  that they had made, because it was cold,
  and were warming themselves.
Peter was also standing there keeping warm.

The high priest questioned Jesus
  about his disciples and about his doctrine.
Jesus answered him,
  "I have spoken publicly to the world.
I have always taught in a synagogue
  or in the temple area where all the Jews gather,
  and in secret I have said nothing. Why ask me?

irony here. How much more important is Jesus, and yet the guard fails to recognize the honor he should be paying him.

We hear of Peter's denial of Jesus (an abbreviated version as compared to that in the Synoptics). Typical of this Gospel is the subtle comparison between Peter who denies Jesus and the beloved disciple who is courageous enough to accompany Jesus to the cross.

Jesus is brought to the palace of Pilate. The leaders of the Jews do not want to enter the palace because that would make them ritually impure and they would not be able to celebrate the Passover meal that night. John's Gospel presents the Last Supper as an anticipated Passover meal. In the Gospel of John, Jesus dies on Good Friday, but Passover begins on Friday night and not on Thursday night as in the Synoptic Gospels. The best studies on this topic have suggested that John was probably right.

The interrogation of Jesus before Pilate is a brilliant scene. There are seven sections to the drama (divided by leaving or entering the palace). The first and last, second and second last, third and third last sections are related. The central section is the passage where Jesus is hailed as the King of the Jews. This is the core message of this extended section. Jesus, despite appearances, is the true King of the Jews. Yet, he is a King who rules from the cross, and his crown is not one of gold but one made of thorns.

Ask those who heard me what I said to them.
They know what I said."
When he had said this,
    one of the temple guards standing there struck
        Jesus and said,
    "Is this the way you answer the high priest?"
Jesus answered him,
    "If I have spoken wrongly, testify to the wrong;
    but if I have spoken rightly, why do you strike
        me?"
Then Annas sent him bound to Caiaphas the high
        priest.

Now Simon Peter was standing there keeping
        warm.
And they said to him,
    "You are not one of his disciples, are you?"
He denied it and said,
    "I am not."
One of the slaves of the high priest,
    a relative of the one whose ear Peter had cut off,
        said,
    "Didn't I see you in the garden with him?"
Again Peter denied it.
And immediately the cock crowed.

Then they brought Jesus from Caiaphas to the prae-
        torium.
It was morning.
And they themselves did not enter the praetorium,
    in order not to be defiled so that they could eat
        the Passover.
So Pilate came out to them and said,
    "What charge do you bring against this man?"
They answered and said to him,
    "If he were not a criminal,
    we would not have handed him over to you."
At this, Pilate said to them,

In the first and last sections, Pilate uses Jesus as a pawn to get back at the Jews (whom he hated). He tells the Jews to judge him according to their own law. They respond that they cannot put him to death (which is quoting Roman law and not Jewish law). They have thus implicitly denied their own law.

Likewise, in the last section Pilate asks whether he should put their King to death. They respond that they have no king but Caesar. By saying that, they are denying their King (both Jesus and Yahweh).

In the second and second last portions we see Pilate questioning Jesus. In the second there are questions concerning Jesus' kingdom and truth, and in the second last section there are questions concerning Pilate's authority. Both of them examine who has the real authority, Pilate or Jesus.

The way that Jesus responds to Pilate throughout this section shows that Jesus possesses the true authority while that of Pilate is illusory. All authority comes from God (even that exercised by earthly rulers).

Furthermore, when Pilate asks the question, "What is truth?" he is not asking a philosophical question. He is stating a political opinion, "What does truth matter when he could gain political advantage." He knew that Jesus was innocent, but yet he would let Jesus die in order to get back at the Jews.

"Take him yourselves, and judge him according to
    your law."
The Jews answered him,
    "We do not have the right to execute anyone,"
    in order that the word of Jesus might be fulfilled
    that he said indicating the kind of death he would
        die.
So Pilate went back into the praetorium
    and summoned Jesus and said to him,
    "Are you the King of the Jews?"
Jesus answered,
    "Do you say this on your own
    or have others told you about me?"
Pilate answered,
    "I am not a Jew, am I?
Your own nation and the chief priests handed you
        over to me.
What have you done?"
Jesus answered,
    "My kingdom does not belong to this world.
If my kingdom did belong to this world,
    my attendants would be fighting
    to keep me from being handed over to the Jews.
But as it is, my kingdom is not here."
So Pilate said to him,
    "Then you are a king?"
Jesus answered,
    "You say I am a king.
For this I was born and for this I came into the
        world,
    to testify to the truth.
Everyone who belongs to the truth listens to my
        voice."
Pilate said to him, "What is truth?"

When he had said this,
    he again went out to the Jews and said to them,
    "I find no guilt in him.

In the third and third last sections we see Pilate speaking with the Jewish leaders. He gives them a choice between Jesus and Barabbas in the third, and presents the beaten and humiliated Jesus in the third last. Neither of these presentations quiets their bloodlust. They still seek to crucify him.

As mentioned above, the core to understanding all that is going on in this trial is found in the central section where the soldiers treat Jesus as a king. They intend to humiliate him, but in great irony they are actually proclaiming the hidden truth about Jesus.

All of the characters involved (Pilate, the leaders of the Jews, the soldiers) thought that they were controlling what was going on. Jesus is the true King, and he was in control in spite of what they thought.

The purple cloak they use is a bit problematic. Purple was very rare and it was not clear how they would have obtained it. The Gospel of Matthew speaks of a scarlet robe.

Pilate asks Jesus where he is from. This is a common theme throughout the Gospel. People often wonder where Jesus comes from, for they do not recognize that he comes from the Father. He comes from above, and he leads us back there.

After this drama is played out, it is time for all to be completed. Jesus is led out to the place of judgment.

But you have a custom that I release one prisoner to
you at Passover.
Do you want me to release to you the King of the
Jews?"
They cried out again,
"Not this one but Barabbas!"
Now Barabbas was a revolutionary.

Then Pilate took Jesus and had him scourged.
And the soldiers wove a crown out of thorns and
placed it on his head,
and clothed him in a purple cloak,
and they came to him and said,
"Hail, King of the Jews!"
And they struck him repeatedly.
Once more Pilate went out and said to them,
"Look, I am bringing him out to you,
so that you may know that I find no guilt in him."
So Jesus came out,
wearing the crown of thorns and the purple cloak.
And he said to them, "Behold, the man!"
When the chief priests and the guards saw him they
cried out,
"Crucify him, crucify him!"
Pilate said to them,
"Take him yourselves and crucify him.
I find no guilt in him."
The Jews answered,
"We have a law, and according to that law he
ought to die,
because he made himself the Son of God."
Now when Pilate heard this statement,
he became even more afraid,
and went back into the praetorium and said to
Jesus,
"Where are you from?"
Jesus did not answer him.
So Pilate said to him,

It is important to remember that all of this is occurring on the preparation day for the Passover celebration. Jesus was being led out to his crucifixion at the very moment that the Passover lambs were being taken to the temple to be killed for the Passover meal. In this we see how Jesus is the new Passover Lamb. This symbolism is continued later in the account where we hear about the fact that none of his bones was broken. This was one of the requirements for the Passover lamb, and it was true of Jesus as well.

The leaders of the Jews are strongly blamed for the death of Jesus in this Gospel. This Gospel and Matthew have often been used as proof texts for anti-Semitism. That is not a correct reading of these texts. It was not "the Jews" who had Jesus put to death. It was their leaders with the collaboration of the Roman authorities. We should remember, however, that we are ultimately responsible for the death of Jesus. He died because of our sins.

Pilate proclaims Jesus as King of the Jews in the inscription that he ordered to be hung over the head of Jesus. The leaders of the Jews objected to the phrase "King of the Jews," but Pilate insisted that it remain.

Jesus is crucified on Golgotha, a small outcropping of rock in a used-out quarry. His cross was anchored in a rock that had a natural flaw and was therefore rejected by the builders (hence, the fulfillment of the verse that speaks of the stone rejected by the builders becoming the cornerstone).

"Do you not speak to me?
Do you not know that I have power to release you
    and I have power to crucify you?"
Jesus answered him,
    "You would have no power over me
    if it had not been given to you from above.
For this reason the one who handed me over to you
    has the greater sin."
Consequently, Pilate tried to release him; but the
        Jews cried out,
    "If you release him, you are not a Friend of Cae-
        sar.
Everyone who makes himself a king opposes Cae-
        sar."

When Pilate heard these words he brought Jesus out
    and seated him on the judge's bench
    in the place called Stone Pavement, in Hebrew,
        Gabbatha.
It was preparation day for Passover, and it was
        about noon.
And he said to the Jews,
    "Behold, your king!"
They cried out,
    "Take him away, take him away! Crucify him!"
Pilate said to them,
    "Shall I crucify your king?"
The chief priests answered,
    "We have no king but Caesar."
Then he handed him over to them to be crucified.

So they took Jesus, and, carrying the cross himself,
    he went out to what is called the Place of the
        Skull,
    in Hebrew, Golgotha.
There they crucified him, and with him two others,
    one on either side, with Jesus in the middle.
Pilate also had an inscription written and put on the
        cross.

The leaders of the Jews object to the inscription placed over the head of Jesus stating that he was the King of the Jews. Ironically, it was a pagan who insisted upon sustaining the truth while Jesus' own people were rejecting their own King.

The soldiers divide Jesus' garments, but they do not cut his cloak, which was a seamless garment.

The mother of Jesus is standing below the cross along with Mary, the wife of Clopas, Mary of Magdala, and the beloved disciple.

Jesus hands his mother over into the care of the beloved disciple. Tradition holds that he cared for her for the rest of her life.

This passage also has a symbolic meaning. Jesus married the Church on the cross (in fulfillment of the matrimonial symbolism found throughout the Gospel). According to Jewish tradition, if a man died without having children, his next of kin was to marry the widow to have a child who would bear the deceased man's name.

Jesus had no children from his marriage to the Church, so he adopted the beloved disciple as his brother so that the brother would produce children who would bear his name (Christians).

Jesus is in control until the very minute of his death. He fulfills all that was prophesied

It read,
"Jesus the Nazorean, the King of the Jews."
Now many of the Jews read this inscription,
because the place where Jesus was crucified was near the city;
and it was written in Hebrew, Latin, and Greek.
So the chief priests of the Jews said to Pilate,
"Do not write 'The King of the Jews,'
but that he said, 'I am the King of the Jews.'"
Pilate answered,
"What I have written, I have written."

When the soldiers had crucified Jesus,
they took his clothes and divided them into four shares,
a share for each soldier.
They also took his tunic, but the tunic was seamless,
woven in one piece from the top down.
So they said to one another,
"Let's not tear it, but cast lots for it to see whose it will be,"
in order that the passage of Scripture might be fulfilled that says:
They divided my garments among them,
and for my vesture they cast lots.
This is what the soldiers did.
Standing by the cross of Jesus were his mother
and his mother's sister, Mary the wife of Clopas,
and Mary of Magdala.
When Jesus saw his mother and the disciple there whom he loved
he said to his mother, "Woman, behold, your son."
Then he said to the disciple,
"Behold, your mother."
And from that hour the disciple took her into his home.

After this, aware that everything was now finished,
in order that the Scripture might be fulfilled,

about his death, and he then hands over his spirit. It was he who decided when it was time to die.

The soldiers were sent to break the legs of those who had been crucified. A person died on the cross due to suffocation when he no longer had the strength to push his body up to catch his breath. By breaking the legs of those who had been crucified, the soldiers hastened their death for they could not push up to breathe.

When they came to Jesus, he was already dead. Therefore, they did not break his legs.

This fulfilled the Paschal Lamb symbolism that none of the lamb's bones were to be broken.

It also fulfilled matrimonial symbolism. God created Adam's wife Eve by placing Adam in a deep sleep and taking a rib from his side. God created the second Adam's (Jesus') wife, the Church, by allowing Jesus to descend into a deep sleep (death) and opening his side (the pierced side), which gave forth blood and water (the symbols for the Eucharist and Baptism).

The burial is problematic. The Synoptics speak of the women going to the tomb on Easter morning to anoint the body because there had been no time to do so on Friday. The myrrh and aloes, therefore, might be a symbolic allusion to Psalm 45 in which the groom's robes are fragrant with myrrh and aloes.

Jesus said, "I thirst."
There was a vessel filled with common wine.
So they put a sponge soaked in wine on a sprig of hyssop
and put it up to his mouth.
When Jesus had taken the wine, he said,
"It is finished."
And bowing his head, he handed over the spirit.

Here all kneel and pause for a short time.

Now since it was preparation day,
in order that the bodies might not remain on the cross on the sabbath,
for the sabbath day of that week was a solemn one,
the Jews asked Pilate that their legs be broken
and that they be taken down.
So the soldiers came and broke the legs of the first
and then of the other one who was crucified with Jesus.
But when they came to Jesus and saw that he was already dead,
they did not break his legs,
but one soldier thrust his lance into his side,
and immediately blood and water flowed out.
An eyewitness has testified, and his testimony is true;
he knows that he is speaking the truth,
so that you also may come to believe.
For this happened so that the Scripture passage might be fulfilled:
Not a bone of it will be broken.
And again another passage says:
They will look upon him whom they have pierced.

After this, Joseph of Arimathea,
secretly a disciple of Jesus for fear of the Jews,
asked Pilate if he could remove the body of Jesus.
And Pilate permitted it.

This is the only Gospel where we see Nicodemus assisting Joseph of Arimathea. Nicodemus appears three times in this Gospel. The first time is when he comes to Jesus by night (for he was afraid). The second time is when it is suggested in the Sanhedrin that Jesus be put to death. Nicodemus objects that this is not the proper legal procedure. Notice that he is not defending Jesus as much as citing the law.

This is the third time we see Nicodemus. Here he courageously assists in the burial of Jesus, a convicted criminal according to Roman law. He risks his life to render this sign of respect toward Jesus. These three appearances show a growth in his faith from fear to lukewarm commitment to the point where he is willing to die for Jesus.

So he came and took his body.

Nicodemus, the one who had first come to him at night,

    also came bringing a mixture of myrrh and aloes weighing about one hundred pounds.

They took the body of Jesus

    and bound it with burial cloths along with the spices,

according to the Jewish burial custom.

Now in the place where he had been crucified there was a garden,

    and in the garden a new tomb, in which no one had yet been buried.

So they laid Jesus there because of the Jewish preparation day;

    for the tomb was close by.

The Gospel of the Lord.

PASTORAL REFLECTIONS

The liturgy of Good Friday is one of the starkest liturgies throughout the year. There is much less music, fewer decorations, and the liturgy begins and ends in silence with the altar stripped and the tabernacle empty.

It is appropriate that the liturgy signals that something unusual is happening. Good Friday, the day when we commemorate the death of Jesus, is not like any other day. It is the day when the person who loved us most died a violent death for our sake.

We should foster this spirit of differentness throughout the day. The Church calls us to fast. We could turn off our TVs and radios (at least from 12:00 to 3:00 P.M.). If we can, we could leave work early and attend the commemoration of the Lord's Passion in our parish church (usually held at 3:00 P.M.).

THE EASTER VIGIL IN THE HOLY NIGHT

Lect. No. 41

FIRST READING:

A Longer Form: Genesis 1:1—2:2

A reading from the Book of Genesis

In the beginning, when God created the heavens and the earth,
the earth was a formless wasteland, and darkness covered the abyss,
while a mighty wind swept over the waters.

Then God said,
"Let there be light," and there was light.
God saw how good the light was.
God then separated the light from the darkness.
God called the light "day," and the darkness he called "night."
Thus evening came, and morning followed—the first day.

Then God said,
"Let there be a dome in the middle of the waters,
to separate one body of water from the other."
And so it happened:
God made the dome,
and it separated the water above the dome from the water below it.
God called the dome "the sky."
Evening came, and morning followed—the second day.

Then God said,
"Let the water under the sky be gathered into a single basin,
so that the dry land may appear."

We begin our Easter Vigil readings with the Priestly account of creation. This account was written during the Babylonian exile, and shows signs of either agreeing with or rejecting the theology that the Jewish people encountered there.

By using the phrases, "In the beginning" and "create," the author is speaking about creation *ex nihilo*, the fact that God created everything that exists from nothing.

The first thing that God creates is light. Ancient people believed that light was the most ethereal of all the things that existed, so it was the first thing created. One should not ask where the light came from. (The sun and moon and stars are not created until the fourth day.) God is the ultimate source of light.

God creates through the word. He speaks and all is made. This creation story, in fact, has God speaking ten times. The law of God was very important to the authors who wrote this account, and so God is seen as creating with the ten words. (The word "decalogue" means both ten words and ten commandments.) God also names all the things that he creates, showing that he has dominion over them.

God not only creates, he also separates. He separates the light from darkness, water from dry land, etc. God establishes order in our universe and gives it certain laws that it must obey. This is the source for the idea of the "laws of nature" (and also "the natural law").

The ancients pictured the sky as a type of bowl that protected the world from the flood of waters over it. Thus, when the great flood occurs in the day of Noah, God opens the floodgates in the heavens. This reminds us of the fragility of creation. If God withholds his care for but a moment, it would cease to exist.

On the third day God commands the earth to bring forth vegetation. This phrasing retains a bit of the idea of Mother Nature, for God uses the earth as his intermediary. Plants were not considered to be living creatures by the Jews. Things had to have breath and blood in order to be considered living creatures.

When God creates the lights in the heavens, he names neither the sun nor the moon. The reason for this is that the names for moon and sun in Hebrew were also names of pagan gods. In order to keep all traces of pagan beliefs out of this account, the author does not even mention the names of these heavenly bodies (lest a reader believe that Yahweh had created the moon and the sun as minor deities). They are clearly creatures created by and subject to the LORD alone.

And so it happened:
   the water under the sky was gathered into its basin,
   and the dry land appeared.
God called the dry land "the earth,"
   and the basin of the water he called "the sea."
God saw how good it was.
Then God said,
   "Let the earth bring forth vegetation:
   every kind of plant that bears seed
   and every kind of fruit tree on earth
   that bears fruit with its seed in it."
And so it happened:
   the earth brought forth every kind of plant that bears seed
   and every kind of fruit tree on earth
   that bears fruit with its seed in it.
God saw how good it was.
Evening came, and morning followed—the third day.

Then God said:
   "Let there be lights in the dome of the sky,
   to separate day from night.
Let them mark the fixed times, the days and the years,
   and serve as luminaries in the dome of the sky,
   to shed light upon the earth."
And so it happened:
   God made the two great lights,
   the greater one to govern the day,
   and the lesser one to govern the night;
   and he made the stars.
God set them in the dome of the sky,
   to shed light upon the earth,
   to govern the day and the night,
   and to separate the light from the darkness.
God saw how good it was.

Note that evening precedes the morning throughout the account. Jewish people believe that the day begins with sunset (specifically, when one can look into the sky and see three stars at the same glance).

On the fifth day God creates fish, sea creatures, and birds. These creatures are at the edge of the world in which we exist. Those creatures closer to us are created the sixth day. Note that the author uses the word "create" on the fifth day. This is the second use of this phrase, for on the first day God created things that were not living, and he was now creating living creatures.

God even created the sea creatures. This is a reference to Leviathan and Rahab, the primordial sea creatures. Pagans believed them to be gods. This author states clearly that they were created by the Lord God. One of the psalms even speaks of how God created them so that he could play with them, as if they were a child's playthings.

The rabbis speculated on when God created the angels. They had two possible answers. Some said that God created the angels on the second day for that is when he created the heavens. Others said that he created the angels on the fifth day, for that is when he created winged creatures.

Throughout the account we continue to hear how good creation is. God created this world to be good. Evil entered through sin, not because the world had been created that way.

Evening came, and morning followed—the fourth day.

Then God said,
"Let the water teem with an abundance of living creatures,
and on the earth let birds fly beneath the dome of the sky."
And so it happened:
God created the great sea monsters
and all kinds of swimming creatures with which the water teems,
and all kinds of winged birds.
God saw how good it was, and God blessed them, saying,
"Be fertile, multiply, and fill the water of the seas;
and let the birds multiply on the earth."
Evening came, and morning followed—the fifth day.

Then God said,
"Let the earth bring forth all kinds of living creatures:
cattle, creeping things, and wild animals of all kinds."
And so it happened:
God made all kinds of wild animals, all kinds of cattle,
and all kinds of creeping things of the earth.
God saw how good it was.

Then God said:
"Let us make man in our image, after our likeness.
Let them have dominion over the fish of the sea,
the birds of the air, and the cattle,
and over all the wild animals
and all the creatures that crawl on the ground."
God created man in his image;
in the image of God he created him;
male and female he created them.

The creation of the human race involves a special intervention on God's part. (Notice the three uses of the word "create.") Humanity is created as both male and female, implying that we are not complete without each other.

We are created in God's likeness and image. This means that we have been given dominion over all that was created. We have been made God's viceroys and representatives upon the earth. This does not mean that we should be arrogant and misuse creation.

Psalm 8 explains that dominion is treating the world as a small child might who sings the glory of God's creation. Dominion means to celebrate creation, not abuse it.

All that was created is placed at our disposition. This is how greatly God esteems us.

On the seventh day God rests and consecrates the Sabbath. The weekly day of rest is not another commandment that we must obey, but rather a time when we can imitate God himself. As Jesus said, the Sabbath was created for us, for it gives us a chance to rest, meditate on life and praise God for all his goodness.

God blessed them, saying:
   "Be fertile and multiply;
   fill the earth and subdue it.
Have dominion over the fish of the sea, the birds of
      the air,
   and all the living things that move on the earth."
God also said:
   "See, I give you every seed-bearing plant all over
      the earth
   and every tree that has seed-bearing fruit on it to
      be your food;
   and to all the animals of the land, all the birds of
      the air,
   and all the living creatures that crawl on the
      ground,
   I give all the green plants for food."
And so it happened.
God looked at everything he had made, and he
      found it very good.
Evening came, and morning followed—the sixth
      day.

Thus the heavens and the earth and all their array
      were completed.
Since on the seventh day God was finished
   with the work he had been doing,
   he rested on the seventh day from all the work he
      had undertaken.

The word of the Lord.

Lect. No. 41

FIRST READING: B Shorter Form: Genesis 1:1, 26-31a

We begin our Easter Vigil readings with the Priestly account of creation. By using the phrases, "In the beginning" and "create," the author is speaking about creation *ex nihilo*, the fact that God created everything that exists from nothing.

God creates through the word. He speaks and everything is made, and all that God makes is good.

The creation of the human race involves a special intervention on God's part. (Notice the three uses of the word "create.") Humanity is created as both male and female, implying that we are not complete without each other.

We are created in God's likeness and image. This means that we have been given dominion over all that was created.

We have been made God's viceroys and representatives upon the earth. This does not mean that we should be arrogant and misuse creation.

Psalm 8 explains that dominion is treating the world as a small child might who sings the glory of God's creation. Dominion means to celebrate creation, not abuse it.

All that was created is placed at our disposition. This is how greatly God esteems us.

A reading from the Book of Genesis

In the beginning, when God created the heavens and the earth,

God said: "Let us make man in our image, after our likeness.

Let them have dominion over the fish of the sea,
    the birds of the air, and the cattle,
    and over all the wild animals
    and all the creatures that crawl on the ground."

God created man in his image;
        in the image of God he created him;
        male and female he created them.

God blessed them, saying:
    "Be fertile and multiply;
    fill the earth and subdue it.

Have dominion over the fish of the sea, the birds of the air,
    and all the living things that move on the earth."

God also said:
    "See, I give you every seed-bearing plant all over the earth
    and every tree that has seed-bearing fruit on it to be your food;
    and to all the animals of the land, all the birds of the air,
    and all the living creatures that crawl on the ground,
    I give all the green plants for food."

And so it happened.

God looked at everything he had made, and he found it very good.

The word of the Lord.

Lect. No. 41 RESPONSORIAL PSALM: ◼A Ps 104:1-2, 5-6, 10, 12, 13-14, 24, 35 (℟.: 30)

Psalm 104 is a hymn of thanksgiving to praise the LORD as the God of creation.

The response requests that God send forth his Spirit and renew the face of the earth. This is a recognition that God created everything that exists through his Spirit.

The word for Spirit in Hebrew is the same word as breath and wind. God spoke, sent forth the breath of his mouth, and all was created.

On Easter, we celebrate the first creation and also the new creation which occurred in the death and resurrection of Jesus and the descent of the Holy Spirit upon the earth.

In this hymn we see both the power of the LORD (for he can command the earth and waters to occupy a place from which they will not move) and also God's loving concern (for he waters the earth, gives vegetation for the needs of its animals, etc.).

Just by looking at the world and all that it contains, the psalmist is led to glorify the God of creation. One cannot look at a bird or flower and not realize that it was created by a loving God. One cannot look into a microscope or a telescope and not realize that God is great and generous and good. It fills us with a sense of awe and gratitude.

℟. **Lord, send out your Spirit, and renew the face of the earth.**

Bless the LORD, O my soul!
　O LORD, my God, you are great indeed!
You are clothed with majesty and glory,
　robed in light as with a cloak.

℟. **Lord, send out your Spirit, and renew the face of the earth.**

You fixed the earth upon its foundation,
　not to be moved forever;
with the ocean, as with a garment, you covered it;
　above the mountains the waters stood.

℟. **Lord, send out your Spirit, and renew the face of the earth.**

You send forth springs into the watercourses
　that wind among the mountains.
Beside them the birds of heaven dwell;
　from among the branches they send forth their song.

℟. **Lord, send out your Spirit, and renew the face of the earth.**

You water the mountains from your palace;
　the earth is replete with the fruit of your works.
You raise grass for the cattle,
　and vegetation for man's use,
producing bread from the earth.

℟. **Lord, send out your Spirit, and renew the face of the earth.**

How manifold are your works, O LORD!
　In wisdom you have wrought them all—
the earth is full of your creatures.
　Bless the LORD, O my soul!

℟. **Lord, send out your Spirit, and renew the face of the earth.**

RESPONSORIAL PSALM: **B** Ps 33:4-5, 6-7, 12-13, 20 and 22 (℟.: 5b)

Lect. No. 41

Psalm 33 is both a hymn to praise the God of creation and a hymn of trust in the goodness of the LORD.

God's word created the world in goodness. He continuously proclaimed all that he created to be good. His word is trustworthy. His law manifests his justice and righteousness, for the law is an expression of his divine will.

Blessed, indeed, is the nation that has such a just and merciful God. This is a God who not only created all things, but also continues to care for them with gentle compassion.

We might sometimes wonder if God could really be concerned with us. We wonder if God knows what is happening to us or cares. This psalm celebrates the fact that God, who created all things, will still respond to our every need. We truly can place our hope in him. He is our shield and refuge, our help and our hope.

℟. **The earth is full of the goodness of the Lord.**

Upright is the word of the LORD,
   and all his works are trustworthy.
He loves justice and right;
   of the kindness of the LORD the earth is full.

℟. **The earth is full of the goodness of the Lord.**

By the word of the LORD the heavens were made;
   by the breath of his mouth all their host.
He gathers the waters of the sea as in a flask;
   in cellars he confines the deep.

℟. **The earth is full of the goodness of the Lord.**

Blessed the nation whose God is the LORD,
   the people he has chosen for his own inheritance.
From heaven the LORD looks down;
   he sees all mankind.

℟. **The earth is full of the goodness of the Lord.**

Our soul waits for the LORD,
   who is our help and our shield.
May your kindness, O LORD, be upon us
   who have put our hope in you.

℟. **The earth is full of the goodness of the Lord.**

SECOND READING: **A** Longer Form: Genesis 22:1-18

Lect. No. 41

The Second Reading this evening is the story of the sacrifice of Isaac. (This is also called the binding of Isaac in Jewish literature.) It is an esteemed story in both the Jewish and the Christian traditions.

A reading from the Book of Genesis

God put Abraham to the test.
   He called to him, "Abraham!"
"Here I am," he replied.
Then God said:

God calls Abraham and asks him to sacrifice his only son to the LORD. There is tremendous irony in this command, for Abraham had had another son, Ishmael. Ishmael tried to harm Isaac, and Ishmael was sent away into the desert. Furthermore, God asks for the son "whom you love." God knew exactly how great this sacrifice would be for Abraham.

He is also asking for a tremendous act of trust, for the boy Isaac was the only visible sign of God's fulfillment of his promise. Even though God had promised a great land and a descendance as numerous as the sand on the shore of the sea and the stars in the sky, Abraham nevertheless did not yet have any land and only one son (for as far as Abraham knew, his other son Ishmael was dead or at least as good as dead to Abraham).

However, Abraham proves his obedience to the will of the LORD by taking his son to Mount Moriah where he fully intends to sacrifice him. The journey is made pathetic by the fact that Abraham carries the knife and fire on the journey up the mountainwhile his son carries the wood. Abraham is carrying those objects that might harm the boy.

Then it is even worse when the son asks where the sacrifice is, and Abraham responds that the LORD will provide. Abraham is saying this thinking of the son that the LORD had already provided, but the LORD would give these words new meaning.

"Take your son Isaac, your only one, whom you love,

and go to the land of Moriah.

There you shall offer him up as a holocaust

on a height that I will point out to you."

Early the next morning Abraham saddled his donkey,

took with him his son Isaac and two of his servants as well,

and with the wood that he had cut for the holocaust,

set out for the place of which God had told him.

On the third day Abraham got sight of the place from afar.

Then he said to his servants:

"Both of you stay here with the donkey,

while the boy and I go on over yonder.

We will worship and then come back to you."

Thereupon Abraham took the wood for the holocaust

and laid it on his son Isaac's shoulders,

while he himself carried the fire and the knife.

As the two walked on together, Isaac spoke to his father Abraham:

"Father!" Isaac said.

"Yes, son," he replied.

Isaac continued, "Here are the fire and the wood,

but where is the sheep for the holocaust?"

"Son," Abraham answered,

"God himself will provide the sheep for the holocaust."

Then the two continued going forward.

When they came to the place of which God had told him,

Abraham built an altar there and arranged the wood on it.

Next he tied up his son Isaac,

and put him on top of the wood on the altar.

When the LORD saw that Abraham was totally obedient, he halted the sacrifice. What Abraham had said about the LORD providing was fulfilled when Abraham saw a ram caught in the thicket and sacrificed that animal in place of his son.

Some scholars say that this was originally a story of how the Israelite people rejected human sacrifices. That might even be true, but the form of the story contained in Genesis is clearly a story about the demands of faith. One must be willing to die to oneself and sacrifice everything in order to follow God's will.

This event is a prefiguring of what happened to Jesus on the cross. We had sinned and deserved to be punished. We were to be the holocaust, but God sent a substitute in our place: Jesus, his only beloved Son. Thus, he saved his beloved children through the death of his only Son.

Why did God test Abraham in this manner? Certainly he knew Abraham's faith. Is it possible that this test was for Abraham's benefit, so that he could learn the depths of his trust? This is true in our own faith lives, for we often learn what trust means in times of crisis and suffering.

The account closes with a reaffirmation of God's covenantial promises to Abraham. Until the day he died Abraham would have to continue to trust, for his immediate descendance was not very numerous nor did he possess much land (for he only owned his burial cave).

Then he reached out and took the knife to slaughter
    his son.
But the LORD'S messenger called to him from
    heaven,
    "Abraham, Abraham!"
"Here I am," he answered.
"Do not lay your hand on the boy," said the messen-
    ger.
"Do not do the least thing to him.
I know now how devoted you are to God,
    since you did not withhold from me your own
      beloved son."
As Abraham looked about,
    he spied a ram caught by its horns in the thicket.
So he went and took the ram
    and offered it up as a holocaust in place of his
      son.
Abraham named the site Yahweh-yireh;
    hence people now say, "On the mountain the LORD
      will see."

Again the LORD'S messenger called to Abraham
    from heaven and said:
    "I swear by myself, declares the LORD,
    that because you acted as you did
    in not withholding from me your beloved son,
    I will bless you abundantly
    and make your descendants as countless
    as the stars of the sky and the sands of the
      seashore;
    your descendants shall take possession
    of the gates of their enemies,
    and in your descendants all the nations of the
      earth shall find blessing—
    all this because you obeyed my command."

The word of the Lord.

Lect. No. 41 **SECOND READING:** **B** **Shorter Form: Genesis 22:1-2, 9a, 10-13, 15-18**

God calls Abraham and asks him to sacrifice his only son to the LORD. He is asking for the son "whom you love." God knew exactly how great this sacrifice would be for Abraham.

He is also asking for a tremendous act of trust, for the boy Isaac was the only visible sign of God's fulfillment of his promise. Even though God had promised a great land and a descendance as numerous as the sand on the shore of the sea and the stars in the sky, Abraham nevertheless did not yet have any land and only one son (for as far as Abraham knew, his other son Ishmael was dead or at least as good as dead to Abraham).

However, Abraham proves his obedience to the will of the LORD by taking his son to Mount Moriah where he fully intends to sacrifice him.

When the LORD saw that Abraham was totally obedient, he halted the sacrifice. What Abraham had said about the LORD providing was fulfilled when Abraham saw a ram caught in the thicket and sacrificed that animal in place of his son.

This story is clearly about the demands of faith. One must be willing to die to self and sacrifice everything in order to follow God's will.

A reading from the Book of Genesis

God put Abraham to the test.
He called to him, "Abraham!"
"Here I am," he replied.
Then God said:
  "Take your son Isaac, your only one, whom you love,
  and go to the land of Moriah.
There you shall offer him up as a holocaust
  on a height that I will point out to you."

When they came to the place of which God had told him,
  Abraham built an altar there and arranged the wood on it.
Then he reached out and took the knife to slaughter his son.
But the LORD's messenger called to him from heaven,
  "Abraham, Abraham!"
"Here I am," he answered.
"Do not lay your hand on the boy," said the messenger.
"Do not do the least thing to him.
I know now how devoted you are to God,
  since you did not withhold from me your own beloved son."
As Abraham looked about,
  he spied a ram caught by its horns in the thicket.
So he went and took the ram
  and offered it up as a holocaust in place of his son.

Again the LORD's messenger called to Abraham from heaven and said:

This event is a prefiguring of what happened to Jesus on the cross. We had sinned and deserved to be punished. We were to be the holocaust, but God sent a substitute in our place: Jesus, his only beloved Son. Thus, he saved his beloved children through the death of his only Son.

Why did God test Abraham in this manner? Certainly he knew Abraham's faith. Is it possible that this test was for Abraham's benefit, so that he could learn the depths of his trust? This is true in our own lives, for we often learn what trust means in times of crisis and suffering.

"I swear by myself, declares the LORD,

that because you acted as you did

in not withholding from me your beloved son,

I will bless you abundantly

and make your descendants as countless

as the stars of the sky and the sands of the
    seashore;

your descendants shall take possession

of the gates of their enemies,

and in your descendants all the nations of the
    earth shall find blessing—

all this because you obeyed my command."

The word of the Lord.

Lect. No. 41

RESPONSORIAL PSALM: Ps 16:5, 8, 9-10, 11 (℟.: 1)

Psalm 16 is a powerful expression of trust in the LORD. Not only will God deliver us; God is our entire inheritance. He is our allotted portion and our cup.

This is an appropriate response to the story that we have just read. Abraham risked everything on the LORD. He believed in the LORD's promise even when there was no sign that the LORD was going to be faithful.

God was just as faithful to his own Son when he died on the cross. He did not allow his Son to undergo corruption or to be abandoned to the netherworld. This is also true of us, for we have become adopted children of the LORD. We are heirs to his promise and coheirs with Jesus.

℟. **You are my inheritance, O Lord.**

O LORD, my allotted portion and my cup,
    you it is who hold fast my lot.
I set the LORD ever before me;
    with him at my right hand I shall not be disturbed.

℟. **You are my inheritance, O Lord.**

Therefore my heart is glad and my soul rejoices,
    my body, too, abides in confidence;
because you will not abandon my soul to the netherworld,
    nor will you suffer your faithful one to undergo
    corruption.

℟. **You are my inheritance, O Lord.**

You will show me the path to life,
    fullness of joys in your presence,
    the delights at your right hand forever.

℟. **You are my inheritance, O Lord.**

Lect.
No. 41

THIRD READING: Exodus 14:15—15:1

Our Third Reading tells us of the Exodus of the Israelites from slavery in Egypt to freedom in the promised land.

Although the Pharaoh had promised to let the Israelites go free, he repented his decision and followed them with all of his troops. He intended to cut them off and kill them.

The LORD ordered Moses to hold his staff over the waters of the Red Sea. The waters split, and the Israelites were able to pass through the sea without harm.

Various explanations have been given in recent years to interpret what happened. Some have spoken of earthquakes, volcanic explosions, El Niño, etc. God often works through natural means to further his plan. Whatever, the Israelites and we have one explanation for what happened: God delivered his chosen people from certain destruction at the hands of Pharaoh and his soldiers.

We could also speak about the soldiers. God did not want the Israelites to travel to the promised land by the sea route lest they become afraid and return to Egypt. He knew that his people were not courageous. Maybe they even needed the soldiers at their backs to force them across the sea lest they turn back out of fear. This has

A reading from the Book of Exodus

The LORD said to Moses, "Why are you crying out to me?

Tell the Israelites to go forward.

And you, lift up your staff and, with hand outstretched over the sea,

split the sea in two,

that the Israelites may pass through it on dry land.

But I will make the Egyptians so obstinate

that they will go in after them.

Then I will receive glory through Pharaoh and all his army,

his chariots and charioteers.

The Egyptians shall know that I am the LORD,

when I receive glory through Pharaoh

and his chariots and charioteers."

The angel of God, who had been leading Israel's camp,

now moved and went around behind them.

The column of cloud also, leaving the front,

took up its place behind them,

so that it came between the camp of the Egyptians

and that of Israel.

But the cloud now became dark, and thus the night passed

without the rival camps coming any closer together all night long.

Then Moses stretched out his hand over the sea,

and the LORD swept the sea

with a strong east wind throughout the night

and so turned it into dry land.

often been used as a symbol of the fact that God sometimes allows us to feel the consequences of our sins in order to push us across the sea from slavery to sin into the freedom of God's children.

We become bogged down in our sinful habits, and it often looks more comfortable to stay in our sins than to convert from them. The sins have become familiar (even if they are a form of slavery), while conversion is the unknown (like marching off into the desert).

God brings us to the point where staying in our sins grows so uncomfortable that we finally have the courage to leave them and wander into the unknown. We have to recognize for ourselves how much our sins are hurting us before we can reject them and choose the freedom of the children of God.

The Egyptians followed the Israelites, but their heavy chariots became clogged down in the mud of the recently dried sea bottom. Thus, when Moses stretched his hands out over the sea again and the waters flowed back, they could not extricate themselves and they drowned. The defeat was total, for one cannot fight against the LORD.

The Israelites, who had by now reached dry land, were filled with a sense of awe and wonder. They realized that they owed their entire victory to the LORD. The only thing they could do was to thank and praise the LORD.

When the water was thus divided,
    the Israelites marched into the midst of the sea on
        dry land,
    with the water like a wall to their right and to
        their left.

The Egyptians followed in pursuit;
    all Pharaoh's horses and chariots and charioteers
        went after them
    right into the midst of the sea.
In the night watch just before dawn
    the LORD cast through the column of the fiery cloud
    upon the Egyptian force a glance that threw it
        into a panic;
    and he so clogged their chariot wheels
    that they could hardly drive.
With that the Egyptians sounded the retreat before
        Israel,
    because the LORD was fighting for them against
        the Egyptians.

Then the LORD told Moses, "Stretch out your hand
        over the sea,
    that the water may flow back upon the Egyptians,
    upon their chariots and their charioteers."
So Moses stretched out his hand over the sea,
    and at dawn the sea flowed back to its normal
        depth.
The Egyptians were fleeing head on toward the sea,
    when the LORD hurled them into its midst.
As the water flowed back,
    it covered the chariots and the charioteers of
        Pharaoh's whole army
    which had followed the Israelites into the sea.
Not a single one of them escaped.
But the Israelites had marched on dry land
    through the midst of the sea,
    with the water like a wall to their right and to
        their left.

The Israelites sang a great victory song to celebrate their wondrous deliverance. Their song, which is called the Song of Miriam, is one of the oldest parts of the Old Testament to have been written. It represents a very ancient tradition.

By studying the language of the hymn, scholars have determined that it dates back to at least the 11th century B.C. In other words, the hymn that is now found in the Book of Exodus might be the actual hymn that the Israelites sang on that glorious day when the LORD led them through the sea on dry land.

Thus the LORD saved Israel on that day
　from the power of the Egyptians.
When Israel saw the Egyptians lying dead on the
　　seashore
　and beheld the great power that the LORD
　had shown against the Egyptians,
　they feared the LORD and believed in him and in
　　his servant Moses.

Then Moses and the Israelites sang this song to the
　　LORD:
I will sing to the LORD, for he is gloriously tri-
　　umphant;
　horse and chariot he has cast into the sea.

The word of the Lord.

Lect. No. 41 **RESPONSORIAL PSALM: Exodus 15:1-2, 3-4, 5-6, 17-18 (℞.: 1b)**

As we have just seen, this might be one of the oldest hymns of the Bible. It was sung in celebration of the victory that God had given to the Israelite people at the Reed Sea.

One of the important aspects of the hymn is the pattern of parallelism that occurs throughout it. The author repeats the same idea over and over again, using slightly different words each time.

In this hymn the LORD is lauded as being a great warrior. He defeated both the forces of Pharaoh and also those of the sea.

In the Old Testament, the sea was often thought of as being opposed to the will of God. It was where the great sea monster Leviathan lived. If God can

℞. **Let us sing to the Lord; he has covered himself in glory.**

I will sing to the LORD, for he is gloriously tri-
　　umphant;
　horse and chariot he has cast into the sea.
My strength and my courage is the LORD,
　and he has been my savior.
He is my God, I praise him;
　the God of my father, I extol him.

℞. **Let us sing to the Lord; he has covered himself in glory.**

The LORD is a warrior,
　LORD is his name!
Pharaoh's chariots and army he hurled into the sea;
　the elite of his officers were submerged in the Red
　　Sea.

℞. **Let us sing to the Lord; he has covered himself in glory.**

use it to further his plans, then he is truly LORD of earth and sea.

God not only redeemed the Israelites, he also brought them and planted them on the mountain of his inheritance.

Some scholars believe that this part of the hymn was written at a later date, for it speaks of Mount Zion (the mountain upon which Solomon built the temple in Jerusalem a few hundred years after the Exodus). Still, others argue that it actually represents the same ancient tradition in which God is pictured as living on a great mountain (like Mount Sinai).

The flood waters covered them,
　　they sank into the depths like a stone.
Your right hand, O LORD, magnificent in power,
　　your right hand, O LORD, has shattered the enemy.

℟. **Let us sing to the Lord; he has covered himself in glory.**

You brought in the people you redeemed
　　and planted them on the mountain of your inheritance—
the place where you made your seat, O LORD,
　　the sanctuary, LORD, which your hands established.
The LORD shall reign forever and ever.

℟. **Let us sing to the Lord; he has covered himself in glory.**

Lect.
No. 41

FOURTH READING: Isaiah 54:5-14

This reading comes from the Book of the Prophet Isaiah, from the section of the book written by Second Isaiah. It was composed during the exile in Babylon, and it is a promise of consolation for a people who had been sorely tried by their suffering.

When the Israelites were defeated by the Babylonians, they wondered why the LORD had allowed them to lose to their enemies. They wondered whether Yahweh might be less powerful than Marduk, the national god of the Babylonians. Might Yahweh be angry with them and have rejected them? Was he still angry at them? Would he ever forgive them?

A reading from the Book of the Prophet Isaiah

The One who has become your husband is your Maker;
　　his name is the LORD of hosts;
your redeemer is the Holy One of Israel,
　　called God of all the earth.
The LORD calls you back,
　　like a wife forsaken and grieved in spirit,
　　a wife married in youth and then cast off,
　　says your God.
For a brief moment I abandoned you,
　　but with great tenderness I will take you back.
In an outburst of wrath, for a moment
　　I hid my face from you;
but with enduring love I take pity on you,
　　says the LORD, your redeemer.

This reading speaks of the commitment that God had made toward them. He was their maker, their spouse. He might have been angry at them for a while, but they were now forgiven. The LORD speaks of his anger as being something that was momentary, forever to be forgotten.

Even though nature itself would be shaken, even though mountains and hills were brought low, God's love for Israel would never be in question. God would rebuild their cities with great splendor. He himself would redeem them and deliver them from the hands of their enemies.

The LORD would also instruct his people so that they would know his will and never again fall from his favor. They would live in justice and peace forever.

This is for me like the days of Noah,
when I swore that the waters of Noah
should never again deluge the earth;
so I have sworn not to be angry with you,
or to rebuke you.
Though the mountains leave their place
and the hills be shaken,
my love shall never leave you
nor my covenant of peace be shaken,
says the LORD, who has mercy on you.
O afflicted one, storm-battered and unconsoled,
I lay your pavements in carnelians,
and your foundations in sapphires;
I will make your battlements of rubies,
your gates of carbuncles,
and all your walls of precious stones.
All your children shall be taught by the LORD,
and great shall be the peace of your children.
In justice shall you be established,
far from the fear of oppression,
where destruction cannot come near you.

The word of the Lord.

Lect. No. 41 **RESPONSORIAL PSALM: Ps 30:2, 4, 5-6, 11-12, 13 (℟.: 2a)**

Psalm 30 is a thanksgiving for a deliverance. The psalmist was at the point of death and was sure that he had fallen into the hands of his enemies.

The LORD intervened in a miraculous manner and saved him from all of his enemies' plots. The LORD is truly merciful and generous. Even when he becomes angry at his people for their sins, his anger lasts but a moment.

℟. **I will praise you, Lord, for you have rescued me.**

I will extol you, O LORD, for you drew me clear
and did not let my enemies rejoice over me.
O LORD, you brought me up from the netherworld;
you preserved me from among those going down
into the pit.

℟. **I will praise you, Lord, for you have rescued me.**

Sing praise to the LORD, you his faithful ones,
and give thanks to his holy name.

We can ask how to apply this psalm to our Christian lives. It is obvious that we are reading this psalm at the Easter Vigil because we are celebrating Jesus' defeat over our worst enemies: sin, alienation, death, etc.

Our other enemies, people who hurt us, are no longer to be hated because we are a Gospel people. We do not want to hurt or destroy them; we want to love them into healing (just as the LORD has done to us).

For his anger lasts but a moment;
　　a lifetime, his good will.
At nightfall, weeping enters in,
　　but with the dawn, rejoicing.

　　℟. **I will praise you, Lord, for you have rescued me.**

Hear, O LORD, and have pity on me;
　　O LORD, be my helper.
You changed my mourning into dancing;
　　O LORD, my God, forever will I give you thanks.

　　℟. **I will praise you, Lord, for you have rescued me.**

Lect.
No. 41

FIFTH READING: Isaiah 55:1-11

The Fifth Reading is another passage from the Book of the Prophet Isaiah, from the writings of Second Isaiah.

The central theme of this prophet is consolation. The first words of his prophecy are, in fact, "be consoled" (Is 40:1).

This consolation is not something to be earned. God has already paid the price. We should not seek after other sources of comfort for the pain in our hearts. God alone can provide that love and that healing which will bring us true peace.

This healing is so powerful that nations will seek it from afar. If we give witness to the peace we have found in God, people will seek to find the same peace in their own lives. Even if we never mention the name of the LORD, they will

A reading from the Book of the Prophet Isaiah

Thus says the LORD:
　　All you who are thirsty,
　　come to the water!
You who have no money,
　　come, receive grain and eat;
come, without paying and without cost,
　　drink wine and milk!
Why spend your money for what is not bread,
　　your wages for what fails to satisfy?
Heed me, and you shall eat well,
　　you shall delight in rich fare.
Come to me heedfully,
　　listen, that you may have life.
I will renew with you the everlasting covenant,
　　the benefits assured to David.
As I made him a witness to the peoples,
　　a leader and commander of nations,
so shall you summon a nation you knew not,
　　and nations that knew you not shall run to you,

sense that there is something different about us and they will ask to share in the gift that we have received.

Now is the time to seek God. It is time to abandon all foolishness and sinfulness. We must admit our fundamental need for the mercy of God and seek him with all our strength. This is not a time for compromise or hesitation. We must make a leap of faith and place our trust in God.

This leap of faith means adopting a different way of viewing reality, for we must look at things through the eyes of God. This means learning the wisdom of God and living by its precepts.

The word of God has been showered down upon the earth and into our hearts. We must allow it to take root and become fertile. God's word is effective. (Remember how the world was created through God's word.) However, God also gives us freedom. God will not force himself upon us: we must choose to make our hearts a home for his word.

because of the LORD, your God,
  the Holy One of Israel, who has glorified you.

Seek the LORD while he may be found,
  call him while he is near.
Let the scoundrel forsake his way,
  and the wicked man his thoughts;
let him turn to the LORD for mercy;
  to our God, who is generous in forgiving.
For my thoughts are not your thoughts,
  nor are your ways my ways, says the LORD.
As high as the heavens are above the earth,
  so high are my ways above your ways
  and my thoughts above your thoughts.

For just as from the heavens
  the rain and snow come down
and do not return there
  till they have watered the earth,
  making it fertile and fruitful,
giving seed to the one who sows
  and bread to the one who eats,
so shall my word be
  that goes forth from my mouth;
my word shall not return to me void,
  but shall do my will,
  achieving the end for which I sent it.

The word of the Lord.

Lect.
No. 41

RESPONSORIAL PSALM: Isaiah 12:2-3, 4, 5-6 (℟.: 3)

This Responsorial Psalm is not even a psalm; it is a hymn found in the first part of the Book of the Prophet Isaiah.

It celebrates the actions of the LORD who is Israel's savior. When this hymn was written, it especially meant that God would save Israel from their earthly enemies. However, as we have seen in

℟. **You will draw water joyfully from the springs of salvation.**

God indeed is my savior;
  I am confident and unafraid.
My strength and my courage is the LORD,
  and he has been my savior.
With joy you will draw water
  at the fountain of salvation.

the previous readings, we must spiritualize this hymn and speak of how God saves us from the worst of our enemies: sin, fear, alienation, death, etc.

We proclaim God as our deliverer. We must praise God with great gratitude. We must recognize how God has showered his blessing upon us and we give thanks.

This is already an action that produces a powerful witness to our faith, for when we speak about how God has blessed us, people will begin to see God working in their own lives.

℟. **You will draw water joyfully from the springs of salvation.**

Give thanks to the Lord, acclaim his name;
   among the nations make known his deeds,
   proclaim how exalted is his name.

℟. **You will draw water joyfully from the springs of salvation.**

Sing praise to the Lord for his glorious achievement;
   let this be known throughout all the earth.
Shout with exultation, O city of Zion,
   for great in your midst
   is the Holy One of Israel!

℟. **You will draw water joyfully from the springs of salvation.**

Lect. No. 41

SIXTH READING: Baruch 3:9-15, 32—4:4

This Sixth Reading has been attributed to Baruch, the secretary of Jeremiah the Prophet. The book is actually a collection of various fragments that have been assembled together. It is not clear if it was actually written by Baruch.

This particular section speaks about wisdom and the law. Wisdom was considered to be the revelation of the will of God. We could not possibly know what God wanted if he had not revealed it to us.

The fullest expression of this revelation, according to this reading, is the law. God has not left us in the darkness like

A reading from the Book of the Prophet Baruch

Hear, O Israel, the commandments of life:
   listen, and know prudence!
How is it, Israel,
   that you are in the land of your foes,
   grown old in a foreign land,
defiled with the dead,
   accounted with those destined for the netherworld?
You have forsaken the fountain of wisdom!
   Had you walked in the way of God,
   you would have dwelt in enduring peace.
Learn where prudence is,
   where strength, where understanding;
that you may know also
   where are length of days, and life,
   where light of the eyes, and peace.

other peoples. They did not know how to please their gods. Our God has revealed exactly what is pleasing in his sight through the law.

That is why we should reexamine our ways and observe the law with all our heart. If we live the law, then we will find true joy. Our lives will be filled with meaning. If we do not follow it, then we will find that we have abandoned the will of God and we will not find peace.

This wisdom, the law of the LORD, is already ingrained in creation. We saw this in the First Reading that we heard this evening, when we saw how God created with ten words (the decalogue).

These ten words, the ten commandments, are the foundation and blueprint of creation. If we observe nature, we should be able to see the order that exists in it and be able to learn what God wants from us.

As Christians, our law is the law of love seen in the Gospels. We do not observe precepts for the sake of consistency, but rather as a response to God's revelation of love for us. Only by living God's law can our hearts be receptive to the love of God.

Who has found the place of wisdom,
  who has entered into her treasuries?

The One who knows all things knows her;
  he has probed her by his knowledge—
the One who established the earth for all time,
  and filled it with four-footed beasts;
he who dismisses the light, and it departs,
  calls it, and it obeys him trembling;
before whom the stars at their posts
  shine and rejoice;
when he calls them, they answer, "Here we are!"
  shining with joy for their Maker.
Such is our God;
  no other is to be compared to him:
he has traced out the whole way of understanding,
  and has given her to Jacob, his servant,
  to Israel, his beloved son.

Since then she has appeared on earth,
  and moved among people.
She is the book of the precepts of God,
  the law that endures forever;
all who cling to her will live,
  but those will die who forsake her.
Turn, O Jacob, and receive her:
  walk by her light toward splendor.
Give not your glory to another,
  your privileges to an alien race.
Blessed are we, O Israel;
  for what pleases God is known to us!

The word of the Lord.

We celebrate the new covenant that Jesus inaugurated with his passion, death, and resurrection.

You shall live in the land I gave your fathers;
  you shall be my people, and I will be your God.

The word of the Lord.

**Lect.
No. 41**

RESPONSORIAL PSALM:

When baptism is celebrated, responsorial psalm A is used; when baptism is not celebrated, responsorial psalm B or C is used.

A

Ps 42:3, 5; 43:3, 4 (℟.: 42:2)

Psalms 42 and 43 were probably originally written as one lamentation psalm. Here we use selected verses from the two psalms to add to the spirit of joy and desire for the things of the LORD.

This psalm was probably written by a priest or levite. It speaks of the incredible joy that he felt when he celebrated the liturgy of the LORD. This was, for him, the greatest reward for all that he did. Its memory was all that gave him hope in times of suffering.

He even speaks of his desire for the LORD as being a thirsting, like the deer that longs for running water. We have to remember that this was written in a highly arid climate, and water was the difference between life and death.

This evening we could say that our relationship with God is the difference for us between life that is meaningful and an existence that has no ultimate meaning.

Thus, as we either make or renew our baptismal promises, we vow ourselves to life in God.

When baptism is celebrated

℟. **Like a deer that longs for running streams, my soul longs for you, my God.**

Athirst is my soul for God, the living God.
  When shall I go and behold the face of God?

℟. **Like a deer that longs for running streams, my soul longs for you, my God.**

I went with the throng
  and led them in procession to the house of God,
amid loud cries of joy and thanksgiving,
  with the multitude keeping festival.

℟. **Like a deer that longs for running streams, my soul longs for you, my God.**

Send forth your light and your fidelity;
  they shall lead me on
and bring me to your holy mountain,
  to your dwelling-place.

℟. **Like a deer that longs for running streams, my soul longs for you, my God.**

Then will I go in to the altar of God,
  the God of my gladness and joy;
then will I give you thanks upon the harp,
  O God, my God!

℟. **Like a deer that longs for running streams, my soul longs for you, my God.**

B

Isaiah 12:2-3, 4bcd, 5-6 (℟.: 3)

When baptism is not celebrated

In our readings this evening we have celebrated our creation, our call, and our rebirth in the new covenant written upon our hearts and our spirits.

These are all ways that God has shown himself to be our savior, and God continues to be our savior for he continues to protect us from our enemies.

Therefore, we proclaim his name and glory before all the nations. This is especially important considering what we have just read: that our conduct often gives scandal and betrays our commitment to the covenant.

People know that we call ourselves Christian, but all too often we fail to live as such. We have to make our words and actions powerful witnesses to God's love and mercy. We have to become more of what we say we are: people whose every word and deed show us to be followers of Christ.

℟. **You will draw water joyfully from the springs of salvation.**

God indeed is my savior;
     I am confident and unafraid.
My strength and my courage is the LORD,
     and he has been my savior.
With joy you will draw water
     at the fountain of salvation.

℟. **You will draw water joyfully from the springs of salvation.**

Give thanks to the LORD, acclaim his name;
     among the nations make known his deeds,
     proclaim how exalted is his name.

℟. **You will draw water joyfully from the springs of salvation.**

Sing praise to the LORD for his glorious achievement;
     let this be known throughout all the earth.
Shout with exultation, O city of Zion,
     for great in your midst
     is the Holy One of Israel!

℟. **You will draw water joyfully from the springs of salvation.**

C

Ps 51:12-13, 14-15, 18-19 (℟.: 12a)

When baptism is not celebrated

Our last reading spoke about the rebirth that God offers us, for he places a new heart and a new spirit within us.

This psalm is a penitential psalm that speaks of the need for this rebirth. We cannot hope to turn from sin if we do

℟. **Create a clean heart in me, O God.**

A clean heart create for me, O God,
     and a steadfast spirit renew within me.
Cast me not out from your presence,
     and your Holy Spirit take not from me.

℟. **Create a clean heart in me, O God.**

not receive the grace to do so from God.

We, for our part, must admit our brokenness and need. We cannot be arrogant, pretending that we can do it all by ourselves. We have to have humble and contrite hearts.

In this psalm we also promise to be instruments of God's mercy, for we will share our insights into his mercy with those who do not yet know how much he loves them.

Give me back the joy of your salvation,
　and a willing spirit sustain in me.
I will teach transgressors your ways,
　and sinners shall return to you.

℟. **Create a clean heart in me, O God.**

For you are not pleased with sacrifices;
　should I offer a holocaust, you would not accept it.
My sacrifice, O God, is a contrite spirit;
　a heart contrite and humbled, O God, you will not
　spurn.

℟. **Create a clean heart in me, O God.**

| Lect. |
| No. 41 |

When Jesus rose from the dead, he was not reanimated like Lazarus and the widow of Naim's son. They were brought back to life, but one day they would die again. They were still subject to all of the limitations of this mortal existence.

That was not the case with Jesus. When he rose from the dead, he received a glorified body that no longer suffers from the limitations of this world. He will no longer die. He is so filled with the life of God that death no longer has any power over him.

When we were baptized, we died to this world in order to live with Christ. Saint Paul speaks of being crucified to this world. We have rejected our previous lifestyle in which we were slaves to sin. We have chosen to live Christ's life and love, but now we have to live in a manner that is consistent with this choice.

EPISTLE: Romans 6:3-11

A reading from the Letter of Saint Paul
to the Romans

Brothers and sisters:
Are you unaware that we who were baptized
　into Christ Jesus
were baptized into his death?
We were indeed buried with him through baptism
　into death,
　so that, just as Christ was raised from the dead
　by the glory of the Father,
　we too might live in newness of life.

For if we have grown into union with him through a
　death like his,
　we shall also be united with him in the resurrec-
　tion.
We know that our old self was crucified with him,
　so that our sinful body might be done away with,
　that we might no longer be in slavery to sin.
For a dead person has been absolved from sin.
If, then, we have died with Christ,
　we believe that we shall also live with him.

This means that we have to continue to live as if we are dead to sin. Saying yes to God also means saying no to those things that keep us from union with him. When we are weak and feel ourselves slipping back into our old ways, we must reach out to the one who has died so that we might live in him, Jesus our Lord.

We know that Christ, raised from the dead, dies no more;
    death no longer has power over him.
As to his death, he died to sin once and for all;
    as to his life, he lives for God.
Consequently, you too must think of yourselves as being dead to sin
    and living for God in Christ Jesus.

The word of the Lord.

Lect. No. 41

RESPONSORIAL PSALM: Ps 118:1-2, 16-17, 22-23

How could we possibly express our gratitude to someone who was willing to die for us? Words fail, and yet we cannot but try to thank God for his incredible mercy.

Therefore, we live to praise God. Every moment of our lives must be lived as a response to God's gift of life. Furthermore, God does not just give us life: God gives us life filled with meaning and love.

The third section of our Responsorial Psalm speaks of a stone rejected by the builders becoming the cornerstone. This reminds us of the stone that held the cross (for it was a stone left by the builders in a quarry) and also that we ourselves were once rejected but have now become part of God's building, the Church.

℞. **Alleluia, alleluia, alleluia.**

Give thanks to the LORD, for he is good,
    for his mercy endures forever.
Let the house of Israel say,
    "His mercy endures forever."

℞. **Alleluia, alleluia, alleluia.**

"The right hand of the LORD has struck with power;
    the right hand of the LORD is exalted.
I shall not die, but live,
    and declare the works of the LORD."

℞. **Alleluia, alleluia, alleluia.**

The stone which the builders rejected
    has become the cornerstone.
By the LORD has this been done;
    it is wonderful in our eyes.

℞. **Alleluia, alleluia, alleluia.**

Lect.
No. 41

Like the other Gospel accounts of the resurrection, this one begins with the women going to the tomb very early on Sunday morning (just before one would see the sun at the horizon).

No one actually sees Jesus leave the tomb. The women only hear from the young man that Jesus has already risen.

This account was written for a community that was suffering martyrdom. They wanted Jesus to come with a fiery chariot to rescue them. Saint Mark was saying in this account that we, too, will hear about the resurrection but will not see the risen Jesus until we have died and risen with him.

The young man might be a baptismal symbol. There was a young man in the garden who lost his clothes when Jesus was arrested, and there is a young man here. When we are baptized we die with Christ (losing our clothes), and when we rise with him we are clothed in the power of the resurrection.

GOSPEL: Mark 16:1-7

A reading from the holy Gospel according to Mark

When the sabbath was over,
Mary Magdalene, Mary, the mother of James, and Salome
bought spices so that they might go and anoint him.
Very early when the sun had risen,
on the first day of the week, they came to the tomb.
They were saying to one another,
"Who will roll back the stone for us
from the entrance to the tomb?"
When they looked up,
they saw that the stone had been rolled back;
it was very large.
On entering the tomb they saw a young man
sitting on the right side, clothed in a white robe,
and they were utterly amazed.
He said to them, "Do not be amazed!
You seek Jesus of Nazareth, the crucified.
He has been raised; he is not here.
Behold the place where they laid him.
But go and tell his disciples and Peter,
'He is going before you to Galilee;
there you will see him, as he told you.'"

The Gospel of the Lord.

PASTORAL REFLECTIONS

After many weeks of penitential preparation, this evening we celebrate the defeat of sin and death and the victory of love. We use the word "Alleluia" ("Praise Yahweh") for the first time since Lent began in order to celebrate and participate in that victory.

April 1, 2018

EASTER SUNDAY OF
THE RESURRECTION OF THE LORD

Lect.
No. 42 **FIRST READING: Acts 10:34a, 37-43**

Our First Reading is taken from the speech that Saint Peter gave when he was summoned to the house of Cornelius, a Roman centurion whom God had led to conversion.

The speech is a form of the "kerygma," the first preaching that the apostles would proclaim concerning the life and mission of Jesus. Unlike Saint Paul's version, which often centered exclusively on the death and resurrection of Jesus, this one includes many of the elements of Jesus' earthly mission.

This is what one would expect, given the fact that Paul only knew the resurrected Jesus while Peter followed Jesus throughout his public ministry.

In proclaiming this kerygma, Peter is fulfilling his mission, which we hear outlined in this reading: Jesus commissioned the apostles to be his witnesses and to preach the good news to the nations. They were to continue the work of the prophets to proclaim the word of the Lord.

A reading from the Acts of the Apostles

Peter proceeded to speak and said:
"You know what has happened all over Judea,
   beginning in Galilee after the baptism
   that John preached,
   how God anointed Jesus of Nazareth
   with the Holy Spirit and power.
He went about doing good
   and healing all those oppressed by the devil,
   for God was with him.
We are witnesses of all that he did
   both in the country of the Jews and in Jerusalem.
They put him to death by hanging him on a tree.
This man God raised on the third day and granted
      that he be visible,
   not to all the people, but to us,
   the witnesses chosen by God in advance,
   who ate and drank with him after he rose from
      the dead.
He commissioned us to preach to the people
   and testify that he is the one appointed by God
   as judge of the living and the dead.
To him all the prophets bear witness,
   that everyone who believes in him
   will receive forgiveness of sins through his name."

The word of the Lord.

RESPONSORIAL PSALM: Ps 118:1-2, 16-17, 22-23 (℞.: 24)

Psalm 118 speaks about power and mercy. These are not two ideas that we would naturally associate, but it gives us an important insight into what mercy really is.

We often think of mercy as something that is gentle and even weak, but true mercy is a strong and courageous virtue.

Mercy does not avoid the truth. It fully recognizes that there are difficulties and yet forgives. It loves the other into healing. Mercy always ends up upon the cross.

This is Gospel truth. The world tells us that we can force others to do what we want them to do. Therefore, we sometimes try to use force to bring them to conversion.

God, on the other hand, realizes that you cannot force love. The only way to bring people to true love is by loving them over and over again. They do not deserve that love, but they need it. This is true mercy.

The Lord Jesus, through his cross and resurrection, has destroyed the power of sin and death and brought us into his life. He has taken what the world would consider a defeat and turned it into a powerful victory. This is truly the day the Lord has made, and we cannot but rejoice.

℞. **This is the day the Lord has made; let us rejoice and be glad.**

or:

℞. **Alleluia.**

Give thanks to the LORD, for he is good,
  for his mercy endures forever.
Let the house of Israel say,
  "His mercy endures forever."

℞. **This is the day the Lord has made; let us rejoice and be glad.**

or:

℞. **Alleluia.**

"The right hand of the LORD has struck with power;
  the right hand of the LORD is exalted.
I shall not die, but live,
  and declare the works of the LORD."

℞. **This is the day the Lord has made; let us rejoice and be glad.**

or:

℞. **Alleluia.**

The stone which the builders rejected
  has become the cornerstone.
By the LORD has this been done;
  it is wonderful in our eyes.

℞. **This is the day the Lord has made; let us rejoice and be glad.**

or:

℞. **Alleluia.**

SECOND READING

Lect. No. 42

In this passage from the Letter to the Colossians, we are reminded of the consequences of the Baptismal commitment that we renew today.

If we have died with Christ in order to rise with him, then we must live in a manner that is consistent with that choice. Our heart should be set on heaven.

The reward we will receive is that when Jesus returns at the end of time, we will share in his glory. We will live with him and in him for all eternity.

A Colossians 3:1-4

A reading from the Letter of Saint Paul
to the Colossians

Brothers and sisters:
    If then you were raised with Christ, seek what is
        above,
    where Christ is seated at the right hand of God.
Think of what is above, not of what is on earth.
For you have died, and your life is hidden with
        Christ in God.
When Christ your life appears,
    then you too will appear with him in glory.

The word of the Lord.

OR: B 1 Corinthians 5:6b-8

Saint Paul uses Passover symbolism to talk about the choices that we must make as Christians. Part of the Passover ceremony is to throw out all traces of leavened products at the beginning of the festival of unleavened bread.

We have experienced a new Passover: the death and resurrection of Jesus. We have passed over from death to life. We must reject all the traces of death that can still be found in our conduct. We must live for and in Jesus, our Lord and our all.

A reading from the first Letter of Saint Paul
to the Corinthians

Brothers and sisters:
    Do you not know that a little yeast leavens all
        the dough?
Clear out the old yeast,
    so that you may become a fresh batch of dough,
    inasmuch as you are unleavened.
For our paschal lamb, Christ, has been sacrificed.
Therefore, let us celebrate the feast,
    not with the old yeast, the yeast of malice and
        wickedness,
    but with the unleavened bread of sincerity and
        truth.

The word of the Lord.

Lect.
No. 42

SEQUENCE: *Victimae paschali laudes*

Sequences are ancient poems written to celebrate some of the major feasts of the liturgical year. This particular Sequence is filled with Easter symbolism. Jesus the Paschal Lamb is also the shepherd. (Many ancient churches in Europe have mosaics that depict a lamb in the center of a flock.)

Jesus the sinless one redeems us from our sin. Life and death collide on the cross. Death thinks itself victorious, but it has been defeated by love that gives life eternal.

The second part of the Sequence creates a dialogue between the Sequence's narrator and Mary of Magdala. She is encouraged to give witness to what she had seen at the tomb.

We call upon the risen Christ, our victorious King, to have mercy on us.

Christians, to the Paschal Victim
  Offer your thankful praises!
A Lamb the sheep redeems;
  Christ, who only is sinless,
  Reconciles sinners to the Father.
Death and life have contended in that combat stupendous:
  The Prince of life, who died, reigns immortal.
Speak, Mary, declaring
  What you saw, wayfaring.
"The tomb of Christ, who is living,
  The glory of Jesus' resurrection;
Bright angels attesting,
  The shroud and napkin resting.
Yes, Christ my hope is arisen;
  To Galilee he goes before you."
Christ indeed from death is risen, our new life obtaining.
  Have mercy, victor King, ever reigning!
  Amen. Alleluia.

Lect.
No. 42

ALLELUIA: cf. 1 Corinthians 5:7b-8a

For the first time in many weeks we proclaim the Alleluia Verse. We celebrate Jesus who is our Paschal Lamb and who died out of love for us.

℟. **Alleluia, alleluia.**

Christ, our paschal lamb, has been sacrificed;
let us then feast with joy in the Lord.

℟. **Alleluia, alleluia.**

At an afternoon or evening Mass, another Gospel may be read: Luke 24:13-35, pp. 203-204.

The Gospel from the Easter Vigil, p. 197, may also be read in place of the following Gospel at any time of the day.

Lect. No. 42

In the Gospel of John only one woman goes to the tomb on the morning of the resurrection: Mary of Magdala. She represents the Church who is seeking her savior. She is the first to give witness to the resurrection and is often called the proto-apostle.

She runs to Peter and the beloved disciple and announces that Jesus is no longer in the tomb. (She has not yet encountered the risen Jesus and therefore does not understand what has happened.)

Peter and the beloved disciple run to the tomb. The latter arrives first, but waits at the entrance until Peter can arrive. The beloved disciple arrived first because he was running with his heart, for he deeply loved the savior. He waited to enter because love bows to authority (represented by Peter).

Peter enters and sees, while the beloved disciple enters, sees, and believes because his heart leads him to faith.

The beloved disciple is not named for, at one level, he represents all of us. Today we all run to the tomb to give witness to the resurrection of Jesus, our Lord and our God.

GOSPEL: John 20:1-9

A reading from the holy Gospel according to John

On the first day of the week,
Mary of Magdala came to the tomb early in the morning,
while it was still dark,
and saw the stone removed from the tomb.
So she ran and went to Simon Peter
and to the other disciple whom Jesus loved, and told them,
"They have taken the Lord from the tomb,
and we don't know where they put him."
So Peter and the other disciple went out and came to the tomb.
They both ran, but the other disciple ran faster than Peter
and arrived at the tomb first;
he bent down and saw the burial cloths there, but did not go in.
When Simon Peter arrived after him,
he went into the tomb and saw the burial cloths there,
and the cloth that had covered his head,
not with the burial cloths but rolled up in a separate place.
Then the other disciple also went in,
the one who had arrived at the tomb first,
and he saw and believed.
For they did not yet understand the Scripture
that he had to rise from the dead.

The Gospel of the Lord.

Lect. No. 46

The Gospel of Luke is the most artistic Gospel in presenting the life and mission of Jesus. It often has symbolic scenes that are both incredibly beautiful and powerfully meaningful. This is especially true of the account of the resurrection.

Luke presents three resurrection narratives to speak of what happened when Jesus rose and what it means to us.

In the first scene, the women go to the tomb and see the empty grave and speak with the two angels ("men in dazzling garments"), but they do not see the risen Jesus.

Today we hear the second scene, the road to Emmaus. Here the two disciples encounter Jesus in the breaking of the bread (a symbol for the celebration of the Eucharist) and the explanation of the word (for the disciples' hearts burned within them when he explained the Scriptures to them).

The third scene presents Jesus who appears to his disciples in the flesh.

These three scenes are a paradigm of the Christian life. At first we hear about Jesus from others. Then we come to meet him in word and sacrament. Finally, as our faith grows, we meet him face to face.

Typical of Luke, all three accounts include an explanation of how all that happened to Jesus was in fulfillment of God's plan and had been foretold in the law and prophets.

GOSPEL: Luke 24:13-35

A reading from the holy Gospel according to Luke

That very day, the first day of the week,
two of Jesus' disciples were going
  to a village seven miles from Jerusalem called Emmaus,
  and they were conversing about all the things that
    had occurred.
And it happened that while they were conversing and
    debating,
  Jesus himself drew near and walked with them,
  but their eyes were prevented from recognizing him.
He asked them,
  "What are you discussing as you walk along?"
They stopped, looking downcast.
One of them, named Cleopas, said to him in reply,
  "Are you the only visitor to Jerusalem
  who does not know of the things
  that have taken place there in these days?"
And he replied to them, "What sort of things?"
They said to him,
  "The things that happened to Jesus the Nazarene,
  who was a prophet mighty in deed and word
  before God and all the people,
  how our chief priests and rulers both handed him
    over
  to a sentence of death and crucified him.
But we were hoping that he would be the one to
    redeem Israel;
  and besides all this,
  it is now the third day since this took place.
Some women from our group, however, have astounded us:
  they were at the tomb early in the morning
  and did not find his body;
  they came back and reported
  that they had indeed seen a vision of angels
  who announced that he was alive.

The phrase, "the breaking of the bread," was a liturgical phrase in use at the end of the first century A.D. Thus, when early Christians would read this phrase, they immediately would have associated it with the celebration of the Eucharist.

We should notice in this account that Jesus seems to appear in two different places at the same time (for while he was speaking with the disciples on the road to Emmaus, he was also appearing to Simon Peter in Jerusalem). Our glorified body will not be subject to the limitations of this earthly body. We will not be limited by time and space. We will not suffer from illness or death. Even our emotions will be purified. Our love will never be tinged by jealousy or confusion. We will be able to love as God himself loves.

We should also notice that the disciples do not recognize Jesus until late in the story. In some resurrection narratives, the disciples immediately recognize Jesus. In others, he is not recognized (Emmaus, Mary of Magdala in the garden, and by the sea in John 21). Jesus' risen body (and ours) is a continuity of this earthly body, but it is also changed and glorified.

The disciples speak of how their hearts burned within them while Jesus explained the Scriptures along the way. Even before Jesus broke bread with them, he was present to them in the word of God.

As we celebrate the Eucharist today, we meet Jesus in both of these moments: the breaking of the word and the breaking of the bread.

Then some of those with us went to the tomb
 and found things just as the women had described,
 but him they did not see."
And he said to them, "Oh, how foolish you are!
How slow of heart to believe all that the prophets
 spoke!
Was it not necessary that the Christ should suffer
 these things
 and enter into his glory?"
Then beginning with Moses and all the prophets,
 he interpreted to them what referred to him
 in all the Scriptures.
As they approached the village to which they were
 going,
 he gave the impression that he was going on farther.
But they urged him, "Stay with us,
 for it is nearly evening and the day is almost over."
So he went in to stay with them.
And it happened that, while he was with them at
 table,
 he took bread, said the blessing,
 broke it, and gave it to them.
With that their eyes were opened and they recognized
 him,
 but he vanished from their sight.
Then they said to each other,
 "Were not our hearts burning within us
 while he spoke to us on the way and opened the
 Scriptures to us?"
So they set out at once and returned to Jerusalem
 where they found gathered together
 the eleven and those with them who were saying,
 "The Lord has truly been raised and has appeared
 to Simon!"
Then the two recounted
 what had taken place on the way
 and how he was made known to them in the breaking of bread.

The Gospel of the Lord.

SECOND SUNDAY OF EASTER (OR OF DIVINE MERCY)

Lect. No. 44

FIRST READING: Acts 4:32-35

The First Reading is Saint Luke's idealized vision of life in the early Christian community. He wrote his Gospel and Acts for pagans who were considering conversion. He wanted to show them that Christians lived truly virtuous lives.

The community is described as living in perfect social order. They practice a communal distribution of goods so that none in the community was lacking anything. The apostles served as focal points of unity.

While the peacefulness of the community is probably exaggerated, this reading does remind us that we Christians should practice great charity and generosity in the way we treat each other.

A reading from the Acts of the Apostles

The community of believers was of one heart and mind,
   and no one claimed that any of his possessions was his own,
but they had everything in common.
With great power the apostles bore witness
   to the resurrection of the Lord Jesus,
   and great favor was accorded them all.
There was no needy person among them,
   for those who owned property or houses would sell them,
   bring the proceeds of the sale,
   and put them at the feet of the apostles,
   and they were distributed to each according to need.

The word of the Lord.

PASTORAL REFLECTIONS

This First Reading serves as an excellent example of taking Scripture out of context. All too often Christian communities (parishes, associations, etc.) have beaten themselves up because they are not as intimate and charitable as this first community. Yet, given Luke's tendency to exaggerate the unity of the Christian community in his writings, it is probably true that even the first Christian community was not as unified as he describes.

Lect. No. 44 **RESPONSORIAL PSALM: Ps 118:2-4, 13-15, 22-24 (℟.: 1)**

The Easter Season is filled with a sense of wonder and gratitude. We sing along with the psalmist that the mercy of God endures forever. We have experienced that mercy in our celebrations over this past week. We have commemorated the death and resurrection of the Lord Jesus. We have renewed our commitment to our baptismal promises.

One of our responses to these wondrous events is fear—not the fear in which we do not trust God's mercy (for we sing that the mercy of God endures forever). Rather, it is the sense of awe that we feel when we recognize how good and merciful God is.

When we think of how difficult it is to forgive others, we have a small glimpse into the mercy of God. Yet we cannot even begin to understand how profound that mercy is. God loves us all and destroys the power of sin by responding to us with ever greater mercy.

As we continue to sing our Easter songs and alleluias, we join in the joyful shouts of victory in the tents of the just.

This Easter joy does not mean that we have to ignore problems that we face in life. When we confront them, we know that nothing can separate us from God's love. If God died for us, then how much more will he lead us through our present difficulties into his peace.

℟. **Give thanks to the Lord for he is good, his love is everlasting.**

or:

℟. **Alleluia.**

Let the house of Israel say,
　"His mercy endures forever."
Let the house of Aaron say,
　"His mercy endures forever."
Let those who fear the LORD say,
　"His mercy endures forever."

℟. **Give thanks to the Lord for he is good, his love is everlasting.**

or:

℟. **Alleluia.**

I was hard pressed and was falling,
　but the LORD helped me.
My strength and my courage is the LORD,
　and he has been my savior.
The joyful shout of victory
　in the tents of the just.

℟. **Give thanks to the Lord for he is good, his love is everlasting.**

or:

℟. **Alleluia.**

The stone which the builders rejected
　has become the cornerstone.
By the LORD has this been done;
　it is wonderful in our eyes.
This is the day the LORD has made;
　let us be glad and rejoice in it.

℟. **Give thanks to the Lord for he is good, his love is everlasting.**

or:

℟. **Alleluia.**

Lect.
No. 44

SECOND READING: 1 John 5:1-6

The First Letter of John was most probably a treatise (not really a letter) written at the beginning of the second century A.D. to combat a heresy called Docetism.

The proponents of this heresy denied that Jesus was the Son of God. They felt that God could never take on human form and certainly never die on the cross.

They also seemed to have lacked in charity toward their brothers and sisters, and to have practiced immorality. Hence, we see the insistence in this passage upon loving all of the children of God and also upon observing the commandments.

The author of this treatise argues that his position is proven by the witness of three things: the water (Baptism), the blood (the Eucharist), and the Spirit (which gives witness in their hearts that what he was saying is the truth).

A reading from the first Letter of Saint John

Beloved:
Everyone who believes that Jesus is the Christ is
    begotten by God,
and everyone who loves the Father
loves also the one begotten by him.
In this way we know that we love the children of
    God
when we love God and obey his commandments.
For the love of God is this,
    that we keep his commandments.
And his commandments are not burdensome,
    for whoever is begotten by God conquers the
    world.
And the victory that conquers the world is our faith.
Who indeed is the victor over the world
    but the one who believes that Jesus is the Son of
    God?

This is the one who came through water and blood,
    Jesus Christ,
    not by water alone, but by water and blood.
The Spirit is the one that testifies,
    and the Spirit is truth.

The word of the Lord.

PASTORAL REFLECTIONS

Our image of God can strongly influence how we treat our sisters and brothers and vice versa. The vertical and the horizontal dimensions of our faith are closely related.

Lect. No. 44

The Alleluia Verse recalls Jesus' words to Thomas the apostle. We are the community that believed because we have heard and not because we have seen.

ALLELUIA: John 20:29

℟. **Alleluia, alleluia.**

You believe in me, Thomas, because you have seen me, says the Lord;
blessed are those who have not seen me, but still believe!

℟. **Alleluia, alleluia.**

Lect. No. 44

The first part of today's Gospel speaks of Jesus' first appearance to the disciples. They were filled with fear, but Jesus greets them with the words, "Peace be with you." There are no recriminations or accusations. Rather, there is total acceptance.

Jesus then breathes upon his disciples. Through this gesture, Jesus is breathing his Holy Spirit into the disciples. It recalls the Genesis creation story in which Adam was made into a living being through the breath of God's Spirit. Now, we are made into a new creation.

In the Gospel of Luke and Acts, the giving of the Spirit occurs on Pentecost Sunday. Here it occurs the evening of Easter. This is typical of John's Gospel, which tends to present the death and resurrection of Jesus as events that ended history as we know it. Time is not important for us any more, for we are now living in Jesus.

GOSPEL: John 20:19-31

A reading from the holy Gospel according to John

On the evening of that first day of the week,
when the doors were locked, where the disciples were,
for fear of the Jews,
Jesus came and stood in their midst
and said to them, "Peace be with you."
When he had said this, he showed them his hands and his side.
The disciples rejoiced when they saw the Lord.
Jesus said to them again, "Peace be with you.
As the Father has sent me, so I send you."
And when he had said this, he breathed on them and said to them,
"Receive the Holy Spirit.
Whose sins you forgive are forgiven them,
and whose sins you retain are retained."

Thomas, called Didymus, one of the Twelve,
was not with them when Jesus came.
So the other disciples said to him, "We have seen the Lord."

The handing on of the Holy Spirit is associated with the forgiveness of sins. The Spirit is the Father's love for Jesus and his love for the Father and their love for us. It is only through a powerful outpouring of love that our sins can be forgiven.

The second half of this story concerns Thomas. He did not want to believe in the resurrection until he had concrete evidence. We cannot always have absolute proof for our faith. We often must trust and take a risk (a leap of faith).

Thomas says to Jesus, "My Lord and my God!" This is one of the few times that Jesus is called "God" in the New Testament.

We also see that Jesus is truly risen in the flesh (for Thomas could touch his wounds). This was a rejection of an early heresy called Docetism, which denied the reality of the incarnation and suffering of Jesus.

Finally, those who believe without seeing (those of us in the generations after that of the eyewitnesses) are commended for believing.

But he said to them,
"Unless I see the mark of the nails in his hands
and put my finger into the nailmarks
and put my hand into his side, I will not believe."

Now a week later his disciples were again inside
and Thomas was with them.
Jesus came, although the doors were locked,
and stood in their midst and said, "Peace be with you."
Then he said to Thomas, "Put your finger here and see my hands,
and bring your hand and put it into my side,
and do not be unbelieving, but believe."
Thomas answered and said to him, "My Lord and my God!"
Jesus said to him, "Have you come to believe because you have seen me?
Blessed are those who have not seen and have believed."

Now, Jesus did many other signs in the presence of his disciples
that are not written in this book.
But these are written that you may come to believe
that Jesus is the Christ, the Son of God,
and that through this belief you may have life in his name.

The Gospel of the Lord.

PASTORAL REFLECTIONS

There are resurrection accounts in which Jesus is clearly recognized, and others in which he is not. This is a reminder that when we rise, we, too, will be the same but changed. Our bodies will be recognizable, but they will not suffer from the limitations of our earthly bodies.

April 15, 2018

THIRD SUNDAY OF EASTER

Lect. No. 47 **FIRST READING: Acts 3:13-15, 17-19**

Today's First Reading records the speech that Saint Peter gave to the crowd that had gathered in the temple when Peter healed a man crippled from birth.

The speech is a form of the kerygma, the first preaching of the good news. Notice how Jewish the discourse is. This is logical, for Peter was speaking to a Jewish audience.

Whenever we share the good news, we must make sure that we phrase it in a way that our audience can understand it (e.g., different ways for the elderly, teenagers, etc.).

Peter clearly states the guilt of the Jewish people and their leaders in putting Jesus to death; he just as clearly states that God does not want to punish them. God wants to invite them into new life in Christ.

Hence, he calls them to conversion so that their sins might be forgiven.

A reading from the Acts of the Apostles

Peter said to the people:
"The God of Abraham,
the God of Isaac, and the God of Jacob,
the God of our fathers, has glorified his servant Jesus,
whom you handed over and denied in Pilate's presence
when he had decided to release him.
You denied the Holy and Righteous One
and asked that a murderer be released to you.
The author of life you put to death,
but God raised him from the dead; of this we are witnesses.
Now I know, brothers,
that you acted out of ignorance, just as your leaders did;
but God has thus brought to fulfillment
what he had announced beforehand
through the mouth of all the prophets,
that his Christ would suffer.
Repent, therefore, and be converted, that your sins may be wiped away."

The word of the Lord.

Lect.
No. 47

RESPONSORIAL PSALM: Ps 4:2, 4, 7-8, 9 (℟.: 7a)

This psalm is actually an individual lament, but the verses chosen for today's Responsorial Psalm are hardly negative in character.

They strongly emphasize the trust that the psalmist places in the LORD. He is absolutely sure that God will deliver him from all his adversities.

The Psalmist is sure that as soon as the LORD hears his appeals, he will surely respond. He will intervene and rescue him.

Does God always intervene in our lives and make everything better? There is a saying that God always answers our prayers—only sometimes the answer is "no."

The one thing that is clear is that whether God answers "yes" or "no," he promises to accompany us in our good times and in our difficulties so that we will never be alone again.

Like the Psalmist, we are so filled with peace because we know that God is with us. No matter what happens, he will always be there for us. We can sleep like babies in the arms of a loving parent.

℟. **Lord, let your face shine on us.**

or:

℟. **Alleluia.**

When I call, answer me, O my just God,
    you who relieve me when I am in distress;
    have pity on me, and hear my prayer!

℟. **Lord, let your face shine on us.**

or:

℟. **Alleluia.**

Know that the LORD does wonders for his faithful
        one;
    the LORD will hear me when I call upon him.

℟. **Lord, let your face shine on us.**

or:

℟. **Alleluia.**

O LORD, let the light of your countenance shine
        upon us!
    You put gladness into my heart.

℟. **Lord, let your face shine on us.**

or:

℟. **Alleluia.**

As soon as I lie down, I fall peacefully asleep,
    for you alone, O LORD,
    bring security to my dwelling.

℟. **Lord, let your face shine on us.**

or:

℟. **Alleluia.**

Lect.
No. 47

SECOND READING: 1 John 2:1-5a

In the early days of the Church, there was a certain ambiguity toward the idea of Christians committing sins. If we belonged to Jesus and were washed free of our sins in the sacrament of Baptism, then we should abandon our inclinations to sin and live in the freedom of the children of God.

Yet, experience teaches us that we still are tempted, and once in a while we still fall. What can we say to this?

This reading tries to strike a balance. It tells us that we should not sin, for that negates our love for God. However, if we are weak and do sin, Jesus will be our advocate and intercede for us before the Father.

A reading from the first Letter of Saint John

My children, I am writing this to you
    so that you may not commit sin.
But if anyone does sin, we have an Advocate with
    the Father,
    Jesus Christ the righteous one.
He is expiation for our sins,
    and not for our sins only but for those of the
    whole world.
The way we may be sure that we know him is to
    keep
    his commandments.
Those who say, "I know him," but do not keep his
    commandments
    are liars, and the truth is not in them.
But whoever keeps his word,
    the love of God is truly perfected in him.

The word of the Lord.

Lect.
No. 47

ALLELUIA: cf. Luke 24:32

In this Alleluia Verse we, like the disciples on the road to Emmaus, recognize the presence of the Word of God in the Scriptures that we hear proclaimed.

℟. **Alleluia, alleluia.**

Lord Jesus, open the Scriptures to us;
make our hearts burn while you speak to us.

℟. **Alleluia, alleluia.**

Lect.
No. 47

This is the third of the resurrection narratives in the Gospel of Luke.

In the first, the women heard about the resurrection of Jesus but did not see him themselves. In the second, the two disciples encountered Jesus on the road to Emmaus in the breaking of the bread and the sharing of the Scriptures. In this third account, the disciples see Jesus face to face.

These three accounts give an outline of our life as Christians.

We first come to the faith because we have heard about Jesus from others (our parents, teachers, etc.). We then come to know Jesus in reading about him in the Gospels and in the celebration of the sacraments. Finally, we see him face to face, for we come to recognize his presence in our lives.

This particular account emphasizes the corporeal reality of the risen Jesus. There was a heresy called Docetism in the early Church that denied that Jesus had truly become flesh, and especially that he had suffered on the cross and risen.

This reading allows the disciples to see that Jesus had flesh and bones, even showing him eating some fish.

GOSPEL: Luke 24:35-48

A reading from the holy Gospel according to Luke

The two disciples recounted what had taken place on the way,
  and how Jesus was made known to them
in the breaking of bread.

While they were still speaking about this,
  he stood in their midst and said to them,
  "Peace be with you."
But they were startled and terrified
  and thought that they were seeing a ghost.
Then he said to them, "Why are you troubled?
And why do questions arise in your hearts?
Look at my hands and my feet, that it is I myself.
Touch me and see, because a ghost does not have flesh and bones
  as you can see I have."
And as he said this,
  he showed them his hands and his feet.
While they were still incredulous for joy and were amazed,
  he asked them, "Have you anything here to eat?"
They gave him a piece of baked fish;
  he took it and ate it in front of them.

He said to them,
  "These are my words that I spoke to you while I was still with you,
  that everything written about me in the law of Moses
  and in the prophets and psalms must be fulfilled."
Then he opened their minds to understand the Scriptures.
And he said to them,
  "Thus it is written that the Christ would suffer

The reading concludes with one of Luke's favorite themes: that Jesus had to fulfill all that had been written about him. Luke believed that God has a plan for each of us, and that our only true joy lies in being obedient to God's plan for us.

and rise from the dead on the third day
and that repentance, for the forgiveness of sins,
would be preached in his name
to all the nations, beginning from Jerusalem.
You are witnesses of these things."

The Gospel of the Lord.

PASTORAL REFLECTIONS

Some recent books have questioned the truth of the resurrection of Jesus. This is the very core of our faith. There are a few things we could consider when we reflect upon the resurrection.

First of all, how likely would it have been that these mostly uneducated men would have had the courage to preach the resurrection if it had not occurred?

Second, even in the accounts, the disciples are not pictured as being perfect (e.g., Thomas doubts, Peter enters the tomb and sees but is not said to believe, etc.). If the disciples were making it up, would they not have emphasized the success of their own witness?

Finally, in 1 Corinthians 15, Paul says that over 500 people witnessed the resurrected Jesus, some of whom were still alive when he was writing to the Corinthians. This is a fact that the people could check. He would not have dared to say it if it were not true.

FOURTH SUNDAY OF EASTER

Lect. No. 50

FIRST READING: Acts 4:8-12

Today's First Reading comes from the speech that Saint Peter makes to the Sanhedrin concerning the healing that he performed on the cripple. Although this is technically a simple justification of his actions, it is actually a type of kerygma (for in it he proclaims the truth of the events surrounding the death of Jesus).

He is telling the Jewish leaders that by their actions they have rejected the source of salvation whom Yahweh had sent to Israel.

The implied message is that, if they do not change their ways and stop inhibiting the proclamation of the Word of the Lord, then they will be rejected (even as they will have rejected Jesus by their actions).

A reading from the Acts of the Apostles

Peter, filled with the Holy Spirit, said:
"Leaders of the people and elders:
If we are being examined today
about a good deed done to a cripple,
namely, by what means he was saved,
then all of you and all the people of Israel should know
that it was in the name of Jesus Christ the Nazorean
whom you crucified, whom God raised from the dead;
in his name this man stands before you healed.
He is *the stone rejected by you, the builders,*
which has become the cornerstone.
There is no salvation through anyone else,
nor is there any other name under heaven
given to the human race by which we are to be saved."

The word of the Lord.

PASTORAL REFLECTIONS

One must always be cautious in reading these texts out of context. They have sometimes been used as a rationale for anti-Semitism. Paul considered himself to be a Jew until the day he died. The "Jews" did not cause Jesus' death; we did by our sins.

Lect. No. 50 **RESPONSORIAL PSALM: Ps 118:1, 8-9, 21-23, 26, 28, 29 (℟.: 22)**

The response for the Responsorial Psalm concerns the stone that the builders had rejected.

When Jesus was crucified, the soldiers fixed his cross into a cleft in the rock. Golgotha was a used-out quarry, and that particular stone had been left where it was because it was flawed (hence, rejected by the builders).

This saying (and Psalm 118, in which it is found) became so important to the early Church because they had seen it fulfilled before their very eyes.

The first section of Psalm 118 speaks of the choice between trusting in God or trusting in human beings.

Jesus trusted totally in the Father, and for this he was vindicated. Every human judgment said that he was defeated, but through love he conquered hate and sin.

The second part of the psalm speaks of the reversal of fortune just described (that one whom the world had rejected became the very source of our salvation).

The last part of the psalm is one of intense gratitude for all that God has done for us, for God truly is our savior.

℟. **The stone rejected by the builders has become the cornerstone.**

or:

℟. **Alleluia.**

Give thanks to the LORD, for he is good,
    for his mercy endures forever.
It is better to take refuge in the LORD
    than to trust in man.
It is better to take refuge in the LORD
    than to trust in princes.

℟. **The stone rejected by the builders has become the cornerstone.**

or:

℟. **Alleluia.**

I will give thanks to you, for you have answered me
    and have been my savior.
The stone which the builders rejected
    has become the cornerstone.
By the LORD has this been done;
    it is wonderful in our eyes.

℟. **The stone rejected by the builders has become the cornerstone.**

or:

℟. **Alleluia.**

Blessed is he who comes in the name of the LORD;
    we bless you from the house of the LORD.
I will give thanks to you, for you have answered me
    and have been my savior.
Give thanks to the LORD, for he is good;
    for his kindness endures forever.

℟. **The stone rejected by the builders has become the cornerstone.**

or:

℟. **Alleluia.**

Although the third section does not speak of the afterlife, the fourth section speaks of the closest concept to the afterlife that Israel had at this time: that people in future generations would know their story and tell it to others.

One's name and one's story were the ways that one was thought to continue to live on even after one had died.

And to him my soul shall live;
> my descendants shall serve him.

Let the coming generation be told of the Lord
> that they may proclaim to a people yet to be born
> the justice he has shown.

℟. **I will praise you, Lord, in the assembly of your people.**

or:

℟. **Alleluia.**

Lect. No. 53

SECOND READING: 1 John 3:18-24

Once again the Second Reading is taken from the First Letter of John. This passage has a series of profound messages.

It starts by encouraging Christians to practice their faith in action and not just speak about it (an idea also found in the Letter of James).

The second message is that we should trust in God's goodness, for God is greater than we are. We should place our hearts in God and make him the center of all that we are.

How can we know that God is the center? We must believe in Jesus as the only-begotten Son of God, and we have to keep the commandments.

This means that we have to recognize that our faith has both a vertical and a horizontal dimension. We must love both God and our brothers and sisters.

A reading from the first Letter of Saint John

Children, let us love not in word or speech but in deed and truth.

Now this is how we shall know that we belong to the truth
> and reassure our hearts before him
> in whatever our hearts condemn,
> for God is greater than our hearts and knows everything.

Beloved, if our hearts do not condemn us,
> we have confidence in God
> and receive from him whatever we ask,
> because we keep his commandments and do what pleases him.

And his commandment is this:
> we should believe in the name of his Son, Jesus Christ,
> and love one another just as he commanded us.

Those who keep his commandments remain in him,
> and he in them,
> and the way we know that he remains in us
> is from the Spirit he gave us.

The word of the Lord.

Lect.
No. 53

The Alleluia Verse presents a wisdom literature message that those who live in the ways of the Lord will be blessed. Their lives will be fruitful and complete.

Lect.
No. 53

One of the major themes of the Gospel of John is that we must establish an intimate relationship with God and abide in him.

When we do this, we find the true meaning of our lives. When we try to exist outside of that relationship, we find only frustration and loneliness.

Jesus is the way to the Father. He is the way and the truth and the life. That is why Jesus uses the allegory of his being the vine and we being the branches. He is the source of our vitality (just as vines give life to the branches on the vine). In him we will bear fruit, but apart from him we cannot hope to flourish.

This Gospel speaks extensively of the relationship that the Sacrament of the Eucharist establishes (chs. 6, 13, and 21). This also could be said to be a eucharistic symbol, for it is the Sacrament that celebrates the communion between Jesus and ourselves, and also that nourishes us so that we may be fruitful in God's love.

ALLELUIA: John 15:4a, 5b

℟. **Alleluia, alleluia.**

Remain in me as I remain in you, says the Lord.
Whoever remains in me will bear much fruit.

℟. **Alleluia, alleluia.**

GOSPEL: John 15:1-8

A reading from the holy Gospel according to John

Jesus said to his disciples:
"I am the true vine, and my Father is the vine grower.
He takes away every branch in me that does not bear fruit,
   and every one that does he prunes so that it bears more fruit.
You are already pruned because of the word that I spoke to you.
Remain in me, as I remain in you.
Just as a branch cannot bear fruit on its own
   unless it remains on the vine,
   so neither can you unless you remain in me.
I am the vine, you are the branches.
Whoever remains in me and I in him will bear much fruit,
   because without me you can do nothing.
Anyone who does not remain in me
   will be thrown out like a branch and wither;
   people will gather them and throw them into a fire
   and they will be burned.
If you remain in me and my words remain in you,
   ask for whatever you want and it will be done for you.
By this is my Father glorified,
   that you bear much fruit and become my disciples."

The Gospel of the Lord.

When the Ascension of the Lord is celebrated the following Sunday, the Second Reading and Gospel from the Seventh Sunday of Easter, pp. 235-236, may be read on the Sixth Sunday of Easter.

May 6, 2018

SIXTH SUNDAY OF EASTER

Lect. No. 56 **FIRST READING: Acts 10:25-26, 34-35, 44-48**

This episode speaks of the action of the Holy Spirit in guiding the growth of the early Church. The apostles were not deciding who should be accepted into the Christian communion and who should not be; it was the Holy Spirit who was making that decision and giving clear signs of those choices.

Peter travels to Cornelius who wanted to become a Christian even though he was not a Jew. (He was a pagan who was sympathetic to Jewish ways, or, as this was technically called, he was a God-fearer.)

Peter had just had a vision in which he saw a sheet descending from the heavens with unclean animals upon it and heard a voice ordering him to partake of those things that he had previously considered to be unclean. This was a prelude to his encounter with Cornelius (who, being a pagan, was considered to be unclean).

The Holy Spirit comes upon Cornelius, showing Peter and the others that God had already chosen Cornelius and his family as part of his holy people.

A reading from the Acts of the Apostles

When Peter entered, Cornelius met him
and, falling at his feet, paid him homage.
Peter, however, raised him up, saying,
"Get up. I myself am also a human being."

Then Peter proceeded to speak and said,
"In truth, I see that God shows no partiality.
Rather, in every nation whoever fears him and acts uprightly
is acceptable to him."

While Peter was still speaking these things,
the Holy Spirit fell upon all who were listening to the word.
The circumcised believers who had accompanied Peter
were astounded that the gift of the Holy Spirit
should have been poured out on the Gentiles also,
for they could hear them speaking in tongues and glorifying God.
Then Peter responded,
"Can anyone withhold the water for baptizing these people,
who have received the Holy Spirit even as we have?"
He ordered them to be baptized in the name of Jesus Christ.

The word of the Lord.

Lect. No. 56

RESPONSORIAL PSALM: Ps 98:1, 2-3, 3-4 (℟.: cf. 2b)

In the Sundays after Easter, we celebrate the early days of the Church when God guided the apostles in their missionary efforts. While they first preached to the Jewish nation, they soon realized that God was sending them to preach the good news to the Gentiles as well.

The Responsorial Refrain celebrates that moment when God reached out with his loving hand to those who were not part of the old covenant.

We sing a new song to our God. In Biblical languages there are two different words for new.

One of these words simply means that which is not old. The other word means something radically new, totally different from what existed before. That is the sense of the word "new" in this psalm.

We could never have discovered or understood the extent of God's love and mercy if it had not been revealed to us in the death and resurrection of Jesus.

We break into song to celebrate that love. We invite everyone and everything to praise God.

℟. **The Lord has revealed to the nations his saving power.**

or:

℟. **Alleluia.**

Sing to the Lord a new song,
    for he has done wondrous deeds;
his right hand has won victory for him,
    his holy arm.

℟. **The Lord has revealed to the nations his saving power.**

or:

℟. **Alleluia.**

The Lord has made his salvation known:
    in the sight of the nations he has revealed his justice.
He has remembered his kindness and his faithfulness
    toward the house of Israel.

℟. **The Lord has revealed to the nations his saving power.**

or:

℟. **Alleluia.**

All the ends of the earth have seen
    the salvation by our God.
Sing joyfully to the Lord, all you lands;
    break into song; sing praise.

℟. **The Lord has revealed to the nations his saving power.**

or:

℟. **Alleluia.**

Lect. No. 56

SECOND READING: 1 John 4:7-10

We have still another reading from the First Letter of John, this one centering on the favorite concept in the letter: love.

This letter does not define love as an emotion, but rather as an outpouring of oneself in the service of the other. God did this when he invited Jesus to die out of love for us. This taught us the true meaning of love, which is a choice and not a feeling.

This is what we are called to show toward God and toward our neighbor (for our brothers and sisters are also children of God).

A reading from the first Letter of Saint John

Beloved, let us love one another,
because love is of God;
everyone who loves is begotten by God and knows God.
Whoever is without love does not know God, for God is love.
In this way the love of God was revealed to us:
God sent his only Son into the world
so that we might have life through him.
In this is love:
not that we have loved God, but that he loved us
and sent his Son as expiation for our sins.

The word of the Lord.

Lect. No. 56

How can we live in the love of God? We must observe the commandments. It does no good to say that one loves God if one does not then live out that love in a concrete, everyday way, in the way one treats God and one's neighbor.

ALLELUIA: John 14:23

℟. **Alleluia, alleluia.**

Whoever loves me will keep my word, says the Lord,
and my Father will love him and we will come to him.

℟. **Alleluia, alleluia.**

PASTORAL REFLECTIONS

On this final Sunday before the Ascension, we are invited to remember that the miracle of the Resurrection is ultimately one of love—a love that is so powerful that all forms of death are defeated by it.

Lect.
No. 56

While the reading from First John emphasized the necessity of loving one's brothers and sisters, this reading from the Gospel of John stresses the fact that we have learned love from God.

God first loved us through the ministry of Jesus. He was that person who loved us so much that he was willing to lay down his life for us.

Having received that love and having decided that we want to abide in it, we now must share that love with others.

Notice that although the reading uses the word commandments, it does not mean the ten commandments as such. It means to observe the will of the Father, which is to abide in God's love and to love one's brothers and sisters.

This passage also reminds us that we are God's friends and not his slaves. He has established an intimate relationship with us, one that transforms our reality. As his friends and children, we know what God wants of us and he has given us the strength to do it.

GOSPEL: John 15:9-17

A reading from the holy Gospel according to John

Jesus said to his disciples:
"As the Father loves me, so I also love you.
Remain in my love.
If you keep my commandments, you will remain in my love,
    just as I have kept my Father's commandments
and remain in his love.

"I have told you this so that my joy may be in you
    and your joy might be complete.
This is my commandment: love one another as I love you.
No one has greater love than this,
    to lay down one's life for one's friends.
You are my friends if you do what I command you.
I no longer call you slaves,
    because a slave does not know what his master is doing.
I have called you friends,
    because I have told you everything I have heard from my Father.
It was not you who chose me, but I who chose you
    and appointed you to go and bear fruit that will remain,
    so that whatever you ask the Father in my name he may give you.
This I command you: love one another."

The Gospel of the Lord.

In the dioceses of the United States where it has been approved, the following Mass of the Ascension of the Lord is celebrated on May 13, in place of the Mass of the Seventh Sunday of Easter that appears on p. 233. These readings are used at the Vigil Mass and at the Mass during the Day.

May 10, 2018

THE ASCENSION OF THE LORD

Lect. No. 58

FIRST READING: Acts 1:1-11

Our First Reading for the feast of the Ascension is the only full account of the Ascension that is found in the New Testament. (The account found in the Gospel of Luke is a very perfunctory version.)

The account begins with a dedication to Theophilus. We do not know who Theophilus is. Various theories suggest he may be a Roman official whom Luke was trying to bring to conversion, or a rich gentleman who was paying for the work of making copies of this Gospel, or else it may be a symbolic name. This third possibility is the most likely. "Theos" means God and "phileo" means to love, so this book (and the Gospel of Luke) may well be dedicated to lovers of God, that is, all Christians.

We hear an outline of the ministry, which began in Jerusalem, and then spread to Judea and Samaria, and then to the ends of the earth. This is the exact pattern that one finds throughout the pages of the Acts of the Apostles.

Jesus promises the disciples that they will receive the gift of the Holy Spirit. In the Gospel of John, the disciples received that gift on Easter. In Acts, the apostles and disciples will receive this gift on the day of Pentecost.

A reading from the beginning of the Acts of the Apostles

In the first book, Theophilus,
I dealt with all that Jesus did and taught
until the day he was taken up,
after giving instructions through the Holy Spirit
to the apostles whom he had chosen.
He presented himself alive to them
by many proofs after he had suffered,
appearing to them during forty days
and speaking about the kingdom of God.
While meeting with them,
he enjoined them not to depart from Jerusalem,
but to wait for "the promise of the Father
about which you have heard me speak;
for John baptized with water,
but in a few days you will be baptized with the Holy Spirit."

When they had gathered together they asked him,
"Lord, are you at this time going to restore the kingdom to Israel?"
He answered them, "It is not for you to know the times or seasons
that the Father has established by his own authority.
But you will receive power when the Holy Spirit comes upon you,
and you will be my witnesses in Jerusalem,
throughout Judea and Samaria,
and to the ends of the earth."

Jesus ascends into the heavens in a cloud. The Book of Daniel predicted that the Son of Man would descend upon the clouds. Thus, it was appropriate that he ascend to heaven the same way.

Heaven is not really up above us; it is a different dimension beyond our understanding. Jesus may have ascended in this manner, however, so that the apostles would better understand what was happening. Thus, when we die, we will be with Jesus in heaven (but not necessarily floating on the clouds).

When he had said this, as they were looking on,
he was lifted up, and a cloud took him from their sight.
While they were looking intently at the sky as he was going,
suddenly two men dressed in white garments stood beside them.
They said, "Men of Galilee,
why are you standing there looking at the sky?
This Jesus who has been taken up from you into heaven
will return in the same way as you have seen him going into heaven."

The word of the Lord.

Lect. No. 58

RESPONSORIAL PSALM: Ps 47:2-3, 6-7, 8-9 (℟.: 6)

In Psalm 47 we praise God who is the king of heaven and earth. He sits upon his holy throne and judges the nations.

On this feast of the Ascension, we remember the day that Jesus ascended into the heavens to be enthroned next to the Father. He has been exalted and proclaimed as Lord of the heavens and the earth. Every knee shall bend and every head bow at the mention of his name.

The Jewish hasidic tradition has a saying that if God is our king, then we are at fault, but if God is not our king, then we are at fault.

The meaning of the saying is that if God is our king, we are at fault because we often do not treat him like our king.

However, if God is not our king, we are at fault for we have not made him our king.

℟. **God mounts his throne to shouts of joy: a blare of trumpets for the Lord.**

or:

℟. **Alleluia.**

All you peoples, clap your hands,
shout to God with cries of gladness.
For the LORD, the Most High, the awesome,
is the great king over all the earth.

℟. **God mounts his throne to shouts of joy: a blare of trumpets for the Lord.**

or:

℟. **Alleluia.**

God mounts his throne amid shouts of joy;
the LORD, amid trumpet blasts.
Sing praise to God, sing praise;
sing praise to our king, sing praise.

℟. **God mounts his throne to shouts of joy: a blare of trumpets for the Lord.**

or:

℟. **Alleluia.**

By celebrating God as our Lord and king, we are committing ourselves to the task of living as if he were the Lord of our lives. We praise him, we celebrate his goodness, we observe his commandments, and we live for and in him. Saint Francis of Assisi often used the expression, "My God and my all." This is exactly what it means to make Jesus the king of our lives.

For king of all the earth is God;
     sing hymns of praise.
God reigns over the nations,
     God sits upon his holy throne.

     ℟. **God mounts his throne to shouts of joy: a blare of trumpets for the Lord.**

or:

℟. **Alleluia.**

Lect. No. 58

SECOND READING A : Ephesians 1:17-23

The Second Reading is a prayer asking that we might understand the mystery into which God has called us. If we could only understand that mystery, then we surely would not have a problem finding the courage to live the Christian call.

The key to understanding this mystery is to reflect upon our redemption. Jesus died for us, but the Father exalted him. The Father raised Jesus from the dead and welcomed him into the glory of heaven.

The Father also proclaimed Jesus to be Lord of everything that exists in the heavens and on the earth and under the earth.

Viewing the cross without the eyes of faith, we might conclude that Jesus had been humiliated. However, the Father considered Jesus to be most loving, for on the cross Jesus showed himself to be obedient even unto death. This was the hour of Jesus' glory, and it was because of this that the Father exalted Jesus in supreme glory.

A reading from the Letter of Saint Paul to the Ephesians

Brothers and sisters:
May the God of our Lord Jesus Christ, the Father of glory,
give you a Spirit of wisdom and revelation
resulting in knowledge of him.
May the eyes of your hearts be enlightened,
     that you may know what is the hope that belongs
         to his call,
     what are the riches of glory
     in his inheritance among the holy ones,
     and what is the surpassing greatness of his power
     for us who believe,
     in accord with the exercise of his great might,
     which he worked in Christ,
     raising him from the dead
     and seating him at his right hand in the heavens,
     far above every principality, authority, power, and
         dominion,
     and every name that is named
     not only in this age but also in the one to come.
And he put all things beneath his feet
     and gave him as head over all things to the
         church,

If we reflect upon this, we will realize that when we are obedient to the Father's will in our lives, we are not losing our dignity. We are expressing the deepest level of love possible.

which is his body,
the fullness of the one who fills all things in every way.

The word of the Lord.

Lect.
No. 58

OR: B : Longer Form: Ephesians 4:1-13

This reading from the Letter to the Ephesians speaks of the oneness in heart and mind that our Christian calling should produce. The foundation of our faith is one (one Lord, one faith, one Baptism, one God and Father of all).

We cannot believe whatever we want, and we certainly cannot act in a manner that betrays the unity to which the Lord calls us.

To live in this unity, we must learn to treat each other with humility and gentleness and patience. We should not consider ourselves to be superior to others. We have to respect them and always consider their true good.

That might even mean sacrificing what we want for the greater good of the community (or certain members of the community).

Jesus "descended" when he was born as a babe in Bethlehem; he "ascended" back into the heavens on Ascension Thursday. In other words, he was always God, but he took on human form in order to save us.

A reading from the Letter of Saint Paul
to the Ephesians

Brothers and sisters,
   I, a prisoner for the Lord,
urge you to live in a manner worthy of the call
   you have received,
with all humility and gentleness, with patience,
bearing with one another through love,
striving to preserve the unity of the spirit
through the bond of peace:
one body and one Spirit,
as you were also called to the one hope of your
   call;
one Lord, one faith, one baptism;
one God and Father of all,
who is over all and through all and in all.

But grace was given to each of us
according to the measure of Christ's gift.
Therefore, it says:
   He ascended on high and took prisoners captive;
   he gave gifts to men.
What does "he ascended" mean except that he also
   descended
   into the lower regions of the earth?
The one who descended is also the one who ascended
   far above all the heavens,
   that he might fill all things.

God has given members of the community various gifts (that are called charisms). Saint Paul gives a short list of these gifts, e.g., being an apostle, prophet, or teacher.

These gifts were given not for the advantage of the person who received them but rather for the good of the community. We use them to build up the body of Christ, which is the Church.

And he gave some as apostles, others as prophets,
    others as evangelists, others as pastors and teachers,
to equip the holy ones for the work of ministry,
for building up the body of Christ,
until we all attain to the unity of faith
and knowledge of the Son of God, to mature manhood,
to the extent of the full stature of Christ.

The word of the Lord.

Lect. No. 58

OR: **C** : Shorter Form: Ephesians 4:1-7, 11-13

This reading from the Letter to the Ephesians speaks of the oneness in heart and mind that our Christian calling should produce. The foundation of our faith is one (one Lord, one faith, one Baptism, one God and Father of all).

We cannot believe whatever we want, and we certainly cannot act in a manner that betrays the unity to which the Lord calls us.

To live in this unity, we must learn to treat each other with humility and gentleness and patience. We should not consider ourselves superior to others. We have to respect them and consider their true good.

God has given members of the community various gifts (that are called charisms). Saint Paul gives a short list of these gifts, e.g., being an apostle, prophet, or teacher.

A reading from the Letter of Saint Paul to the Ephesians

Brothers and sisters,
    I, a prisoner for the Lord,
urge you to live in a manner worthy of the call you have received,
with all humility and gentleness, with patience,
bearing with one another through love,
striving to preserve the unity of the Spirit
through the bond of peace:
one body and one Spirit,
as you were also called to the one hope of your calling;
one Lord, one faith, one baptism;
one God and Father of all,
who is over all and through all and in all.

But grace was given to each of us
    according to the measure of Christ's gift.

And he gave some as apostles, others as prophets,
    others as evangelists, others as pastors and teachers,
to equip the holy ones for the work of ministry,

These gifts were given not for the advantage of the person who received them but rather for the good of the community. We use them to build up the body of Christ which is the Church.

for building up the body of Christ,
until we all attain to the unity of faith
and knowledge of the Son of God, to mature manhood,
to the extent of the full stature of Christ.

The word of the Lord.

Lect.
No. 58

ALLELUIA: Matthew 28:19a, 20b

The Alleluia Verse presents the commission that Jesus gave to the apostles. They would never be alone in that mission, however, for Jesus would be with them until the end of time.

℟. **Alleluia, alleluia.**

Go and teach all nations, says the Lord;
I am with you always, until the end of the world.

℟. **Alleluia, alleluia.**

Lect.
No. 58

GOSPEL: Mark 16:15-20

These verses come from the longer ending of the Gospel of Mark. Verses 9 through 20 of this chapter were added to the rest of the Gospel and completed the story of the resurrection.

In this passage Jesus commissions his apostles and promises them that he will accompany them and grant them miraculous powers to give witness to the good news. Some of the accounts in the Acts of the Apostles are, in fact, a fulfillment of these predictions (e.g., when Saint Paul is bitten by a poisonous snake and is not affected by its venom). Do these miracles still occur today? There are many stories of great and small ways that God intervenes in the lives of people even today (e.g., visions, locutions, other powerful events, coincidences that must be from God, etc.).

A reading from the holy Gospel according to Mark

Jesus said to his disciples:
"Go into the whole world
and proclaim the gospel to every creature.
Whoever believes and is baptized will be saved;
whoever does not believe will be condemned.
These signs will accompany those who believe:
in my name they will drive out demons,
they will speak new languages.
They will pick up serpents with their hands,
and if they drink any deadly thing, it will not
harm them.
They will lay hands on the sick, and they will recover."

So then the Lord Jesus, after he spoke to them,
was taken up into heaven
and took his seat at the right hand of God.
But they went forth and preached everywhere,
while the Lord worked with them
and confirmed the word through accompanying
signs.

The Gospel of the Lord.

In the dioceses of the United States where it has been approved, the Mass of the Ascension of the Lord that appears on p. 227 is celebrated today in place of the following Mass of the Seventh Sunday of Easter.

May 13, 2018

SEVENTH SUNDAY OF EASTER

Lect. No. 60

FIRST READING: Acts 1:15-17, 20a, 20c-26

The First Reading gives the account of the naming of a twelfth apostle to replace Judas who had killed himself.

Saint Luke was a strong believer in the fact that God had a plan for his Church. Part of that plan was that there were to be twelve apostles just as there were twelve patriarchs in the Old Testament. Thus, when one of the apostles was lost because of his betrayal of Jesus, it was essential to replace him.

This definition of who apostles are is different from that used by Saint Paul. For Paul, an apostle was anyone who gave witness to the resurrection of Jesus.

For Luke, an apostle was one of the twelve. Furthermore, that person had to have followed Jesus from the time of his baptism by John the Baptist until the day of his Ascension.

The new apostle is chosen by lot. In the Old Testament, the High Priest carried a small sack with the Urim and Thummim under his breastplate. They were either pieces of bones or

A reading from the Acts of the Apostles

Peter stood up in the midst of the brothers
—there was a group of about one hundred and
    twenty persons
in the one place—.
He said, "My brothers,
    the Scripture had to be fulfilled
    which the Holy Spirit spoke beforehand
    through the mouth of David, concerning Judas,
    who was the guide for those who arrested Jesus.
He was numbered among us
    and was allotted a share in this ministry.
"For it is written in the Book of Psalms:
    May another take his office.

"Therefore, it is necessary that one of the men
    who accompanied us the whole time
    the Lord Jesus came and went among us,
    beginning from the baptism of John
    until the day on which he was taken up from us,
    become with us a witness to his resurrection."
So they proposed two, Judas called Barsabbas,
    who was also known as Justus, and Matthias.
Then they prayed,
    "You, Lord, who know the hearts of all,
    show which one of these two you have chosen
    to take the place in this apostolic ministry
    from which Judas turned away to go to his own
        place."

233

dice. When he wanted to discern God's will, he would toss them. In choosing Matthias by lot, Peter was continuing that tradition.

Then they gave lots to them, and the lot fell upon Matthias,
and he was counted with the eleven apostles.

The word of the Lord.

Lect. No. 60

RESPONSORIAL PSALM: Ps 103:1-2, 11-12, 19-20 (℞.: 19a)

The Responsorial Psalm praises the Lord who controls everything in the heavens, on the earth, and under the earth. This is an important theme to celebrate immediately after Ascension Thursday.

We commemorated the fact that Jesus ascended from this world to sit at the right hand of the Father. Was Jesus leaving us alone? Were we expected to do this all on our own?

This psalm answers that question. In it we praise the God whose actions reach to the very ends of the earth. God has not abandoned us.

Furthermore, we see that these are not the actions of an autocrat who ruthlessly organizes the world according to his whims. He is filled with kindness. He does not remember our transgressions.

It is not that God is incapable of remembering, but rather that he chooses to forget.

He uses his great power, a power that orders the universe and commands angels to do his will, for our benefit.

℞. **The Lord has set his throne in heaven.**

or:

℞. **Alleluia.**

Bless the Lord, O my soul;
   and all my being, bless his holy name.
Bless the Lord, O my soul,
   and forget not all his benefits.

℞. **The Lord has set his throne in heaven.**

or:

℞. **Alleluia.**

For as the heavens are high above the earth,
   so surpassing is his kindness toward those who
     fear him.
As far as the east is from the west,
   so far has he put our transgressions from us.

℞. **The Lord has set his throne in heaven.**

or:

℞. **Alleluia.**

The Lord has established his throne in heaven,
   and his kingdom rules over all.
Bless the Lord, all you his angels,
   you mighty in strength, who do his bidding.

℞. **The Lord has set his throne in heaven.**

or:

℞. **Alleluia.**

Lect.
No. 60

SECOND READING: 1 John 4:11-16

This reading from the First Letter of John presents a quick summary of the theology of the Letters and Gospel of John.

God sent his Son into the world to teach us how much God loves us. Jesus died for us and saved us from our sins. Then, when Jesus ascended into the heavens, he sent his Spirit into our hearts.

We remain in God's love when we allow that Spirit to guide us and to teach us how to love one another. This is, in fact, the clearest sign that we believe in God, that we live as God taught us to live.

God is, after all, love. Whoever remains in love, therefore, remains in God, and God remains in that person.

A reading from the first Letter of Saint John

Beloved, if God so loved us,
we also must love one another.
No one has ever seen God.
Yet, if we love one another, God remains in us,
and his love is brought to perfection in us.

This is how we know that we remain in him and he in us,
that he has given us of his Spirit.
Moreover, we have seen and testify
that the Father sent his Son as savior of the world.
Whoever acknowledges that Jesus is the Son of God,
God remains in him and he in God.
We have come to know and to believe in the love God has for us.

God is love, and whoever remains in love
remains in God and God in him.

The word of the Lord.

Lect.
No. 60

ALLELUIA: cf. John 14:18

The Alleluia Verse reminds us that Jesus will never abandon us. He sent the Paraclete, who teaches us, encourages us, and consoles us.

℞. **Alleluia, alleluia.**

I will not leave you orphans, says the Lord.
I will come back to you, and your hearts will rejoice.

℞. **Alleluia, alleluia.**

Lect.
No. 60

This passage is taken from Jesus' prayer for his followers, which is part of the Gospel of John's Last Supper Discourse.

Jesus speaks of how he taught his disciples about his relationship with the Father. He and the Father were always one. He had invited the disciples into that relationship. He protected them and guided them. None of them were lost except for Judas who betrayed Jesus.

The Gospel considers the question of why God would have allowed Judas to betray Jesus. Could Satan, in some way, have possessed him and controlled his actions?

Jesus was leaving this world, but he was not abandoning his disciples. He asked the Father to protect them. They would be in the world but not of the world. The Father would keep them in the truth (the truth of his love).

The world hated them because the world opposed truth and love. It preferred to live in misery, so it rejected both Jesus and anyone associated with him.

GOSPEL: John 17:11b-19

A reading from the holy Gospel according to John

Lifting up his eyes to heaven, Jesus prayed, saying:

"Holy Father, keep them in your name that you have given me,

so that they may be one just as we are one.

When I was with them I protected them in your name that you gave me,

and I guarded them, and none of them was lost except the son of destruction,

in order that the Scripture might be fulfilled.

But now I am coming to you.

I speak this in the world

so that they may share my joy completely.

I gave them your word, and the world hated them,

because they do not belong to the world

any more than I belong to the world.

I do not ask that you take them out of the world

but that you keep them from the evil one.

They do not belong to the world

any more than I belong to the world.

Consecrate them in the truth. Your word is truth.

As you sent me into the world,

so I sent them into the world.

And I consecrate myself for them,

so that they also may be consecrated in truth."

The Gospel of the Lord.

PASTORAL REFLECTIONS

Christians always face a dynamic tension as they attempt to live in and not of the world. We do not reject the world for God created it. Yet, we must use it carefully, for our hearts and our attitude toward it have been distorted by sin.

PENTECOST SUNDAY

AT THE VIGIL MASS

[Simple Form]

FIRST READING:

Ⓐ Genesis 11:1-9

Lect. No. 62

Saint Luke describes the day of Pentecost as being a new creation. On the first day of creation, the Spirit of the LORD was breathed into a clump of mud, making it into a living being: Adam. Now that same Spirit was being breathed into the disciples, and they were becoming a new creation in Christ.

This new act of creation involves a healing of all the damage that had been done to the human race through the effects of sin.

The First Reading today offers an example of some of the damage that sin produced. It presents a story of the early days of humanity that explains the origin of all of the different languages in the world.

The creation of many different languages was seen as a punishment for sin, for it prevented people from communicating with each other. People had tried to build a tower to the heavens in an attempt to bring God down to earth. God confounds their attempts and prevents them from ever attempting this again.

A reading from the Book of Genesis

The whole world spoke the same language, using the same words.
While the people were migrating in the east,
    they came upon a valley in the land of Shinar and
    settled there.
They said to one another,
    "Come, let us mold bricks and harden them with
    fire."
They used bricks for stone, and bitumen for mortar.
Then they said, "Come, let us build ourselves a city
    and a tower with its top in the sky,
    and so make a name for ourselves;
    otherwise we shall be scattered all over the earth."

The LORD came down to see the city and the tower
    that the people had built.
Then the LORD said: "If now, while they are one
    people,
    all speaking the same language,
    they have started to do this,
    nothing will later stop them from doing whatever
    they presume to do.
Let us then go down there and confuse their language,
    so that one will not understand what another
    says."
Thus the LORD scattered them from there all over
    the earth,
    and they stopped building the city.

As with all of the stories found in the early chapters of the Book of Genesis (1—11), this story is more of a parable than a historic account of the birth of the various languages on the earth. It was probably based upon a very ancient story that has now been lost.

That is why it was called Babel,
    because there the Lord confused the speech of all
        the world.
It was from that place that he scattered them all
    over the earth.

The word of the Lord.

Lect.
No. 62

OR: B Exodus 19:3-8a, 16-20b

In this reading we hear of a great theophany in which God encounters his people on Mount Sinai. The mountain was wrapped in smoke and fire. There was thunder and the mountain shook violently. (It is interesting to contrast this description with the story of how God appeared to Elijah the prophet in 1 Kings 19.)

This epiphany of the power of God occurred shortly after the people of Israel left Egypt. The Lord had delivered them from the hands of their enemies. The people knew that God had intervened in their history to make them his own beloved people.

Therefore, the Lord invited his people into this covenant. He would be their God and they would be his people for all time. He asked them only that they keep the commandments he was giving them so that they might be holy and set apart in his name.

The feast of Pentecost is also a time for setting apart a people for God. In this case, who is

A reading from the Book of Exodus

Moses went up the mountain to God.
    Then the Lord called to him and said,
    "Thus shall you say to the house of Jacob;
    tell the Israelites:
    You have seen for yourselves how I treated the
        Egyptians
    and how I bore you up on eagle wings
    and brought you here to myself.
Therefore, if you hearken to my voice and keep my
        covenant,
    you shall be my special possession,
    dearer to me than all other people,
    though all the earth is mine.
You shall be to me a kingdom of priests, a holy
        nation.
That is what you must tell the Israelites."
So Moses went and summoned the elders of the
        people.
When he set before them
    all that the Lord had ordered him to tell them,
    the people all answered together,
    "Everything the Lord has said, we will do."

On the morning of the third day
    there were peals of thunder and lightning,

being set apart is the Church, the Mystical Body of Christ. The commandment he hands on to them is that they are to love each other as Jesus has loved them.

Like the people of Israel, God now calls the people of the Church to be a kingdom of priests, a holy nation unto the Lord.

God does not always encounter his people on mountains that tremble or with great winds and tongues of fire. This does not mean that God is absent. It simply means that God acts in many different ways, some miraculous and some everyday, to set apart a holy people to be his own.

and a heavy cloud over the mountain,
and a very loud trumpet blast,
so that all the people in the camp trembled.
But Moses led the people out of the camp to meet God,
and they stationed themselves at the foot of the mountain.
Mount Sinai was all wrapped in smoke,
for the LORD came down upon it in fire.
The smoke rose from it as though from a furnace,
and the whole mountain trembled violently.
The trumpet blast grew louder and louder, while Moses was speaking,
and God answering him with thunder.

When the LORD came down to the top of Mount Sinai,
he summoned Moses to the top of the mountain.

The word of the Lord.

Lect.
No. 62

This passage was written by the Prophet Ezekiel while he was in exile in Babylon. This is one of the first passages that speaks of the resurrection of the dead.

It is probable that when the prophet spoke of these bones coming to life, he intended this as a prophecy of the resurrection of the people of Israel. They were a nation in exile and they were as good as dead. God would breathe his spirit back into them and would bring them back to life. He would heal the wounds caused by their sins.

OR: C Ezekiel 37:1-14

A reading from the Book of the Prophet Ezekiel

The hand of the LORD came upon me,
and he led me out in the spirit of the LORD
and set me in the center of the plain,
which was now filled with bones.
He made me walk among the bones in every direction
so that I saw how many they were on the surface of the plain.
How dry they were!
He asked me:
Son of man, can these bones come to life?
I answered, "Lord GOD, you alone know that."
Then he said to me:

Nevertheless, this passage makes sense only if the prophet also believed that God could bring individuals back to life. The experience of living in exile in Babylon had taught Ezekiel that there must be a reward after this life.

It is probable that this passage is based upon the beliefs of the Persian people. They were the nation to the east of Babylon. Many of the Persians practiced the cult of Zoroaster. In this religion, the dead were laid out in the fields until the birds of the air picked their bones dry. The people of this religion believed that these bones would be raised from the dead by a good god on the last day.

Thus, when Ezekiel spoke to these bones, he probably had this idea in mind. Of course, like many of the prophets of the Old Testament, he added his own particular Jewish ideas to the passage.

In the same way in which the LORD breathed his Spirit into these bones to make them living creatures, so also God sent his Spirit into us to allow us to become a living people. Before he sent his Spirit, we were as good as dead.

We were separated from each other by false divisions brought about by our sinfulness. We were not joined together like the bones of a living body; we were scattered like dried out bones.

Prophesy over these bones, and say to them:
Dry bones, hear the word of the LORD!
Thus says the Lord GOD to these bones:
See! I will bring spirit into you, that you may come to life.
I will put sinews upon you, make flesh grow over you,
cover you with skin, and put spirit in you
so that you may come to life and know that I am the LORD.
I, Ezekiel, prophesied as I had been told,
and even as I was prophesying I heard a noise;
it was a rattling as the bones came together, bone joining bone.
I saw the sinews and the flesh come upon them,
and the skin cover them, but there was no spirit in them.
Then the LORD said to me:
Prophesy to the spirit, prophesy, son of man,
and say to the spirit: Thus says the Lord GOD:
From the four winds come, O spirit,
and breathe into these slain that they may come to life.
I prophesied as he told me, and the spirit came into them;
they came alive and stood upright, a vast army.
Then he said to me:
Son of man, these bones are the whole house of Israel.
They have been saying,
"Our bones are dried up,
our hope is lost, and we are cut off."
Therefore, prophesy and say to them: Thus says the Lord GOD:
O my people, I will open your graves
and have you rise from them,
and bring you back to the land of Israel.

Now God has made us into a living body again. We are one in him. We are God's own people, and we will be his presence upon the earth.

However, we must choose to live in God's love. That means making decisions to reject selfishness, which only brings death, and choosing to live in the freedom of God's own children.

Then you shall know that I am the LORD,
    when I open your graves and have you rise from them,
    O my people!
I will put my spirit in you that you may live,
    and I will settle you upon your land;
    thus you shall know that I am the LORD.
I have promised, and I will do it, says the LORD.

The word of the Lord.

Lect.
No. 62

This reading from the Book of the Prophet Joel is probably one of the last parts of the Old Testament written. It belongs to the apocalyptic tradition of the Bible. In this tradition, authors speak of how bad things have become, and how only an intervention of the LORD can make it better. Most apocalyptic books also use imaginative imagery to convey the idea of the coming judgment.

The LORD's intervention would occur through an outpouring of the Holy Spirit of the LORD upon all peoples. The Spirit of God would give us a revelation of the hidden secrets of God.

The prophet speaks of the great marvels that would accompany this outpouring of the Spirit. The image of the Spirit appearing in tongues of fire is taken from this passage. Saint Peter, in fact, quoted this very passage in his discourse to the crowd on Pentecost Sunday.

OR: **D** Joel 3:1-5

A reading from the Book of the Prophet Joel

Thus says the LORD:
    I will pour out my spirit upon all flesh.
Your sons and daughters shall prophesy,
    your old men shall dream dreams,
    your young men shall see visions;
even upon the servants and the handmaids,
    in those days, I will pour out my spirit.
And I will work wonders in the heavens and on the earth,
    blood, fire, and columns of smoke;
the sun will be turned to darkness,
    and the moon to blood,
at the coming of the day of the LORD,
    the great and terrible day.
Then everyone shall be rescued
    who calls on the name of the LORD;
for on Mount Zion there shall be a remnant,
    as the LORD has said,
and in Jerusalem survivors
    whom the LORD shall call.

The word of the Lord.

Lect. No. 62 **RESPONSORIAL PSALM: Ps 104:1-2, 24, 35, 27-28, 29, 30 (℟.: cf. 30)**

This Responsorial Psalm is a hymn of praise to the God of all creation. The greatest reason we have to praise God is that when he created, he sent out his Spirit into the world. Then, after we sinned and damaged creation, God sent forth his Spirit again on the day of Pentecost to renew the face of the earth. We are now a new creation.

We are not subject to many of the destructive effects of sin for we have been rescued from them by grace. God has clothed us with majesty and glory and robed us in light.

This is not to say that the renewal is totally complete, for we do not live in the "not yet." We live in the "already." We have received the Holy Spirit, which is God's down payment of the glory that awaits us, but we are also still waiting for the total fulfillment of all the promises Jesus made. Still, the kingdom has dawned and, if we look at things through the eyes of God, we will see his power at work in our midst.

We are totally dependent upon the generosity of God. As with all living creatures, if God withholds his breath, we cannot hope to survive. Likewise, if God withholds his Spirit, our spiritual life will perish. We will suffocate spiritually.

℟. **Lord, send out your Spirit, and renew the face of the earth.**

or:

℟. **Alleluia.**

Bless the LORD, O my soul!
  O LORD, my God, you are great indeed!
You are clothed with majesty and glory,
  robed in light as with a cloak.

℟. **Lord, send out your Spirit, and renew the face of the earth.**

or:

℟. **Alleluia.**

How manifold are your works, O LORD!
  In wisdom you have wrought them all—
the earth is full of your creatures;
  bless the LORD, O my soul! Alleluia.

℟. **Lord, send out your Spirit, and renew the face of the earth.**

or:

℟. **Alleluia.**

Creatures all look to you
  to give them food in due time.
When you give it to them, they gather it;
  when you open your hand, they are filled with good things.

℟. **Lord, send out your Spirit, and renew the face of the earth.**

or:

℟. **Alleluia.**

If you take away their breath, they perish
  and return to their dust.

However, if we trust in God and find our refuge in him, then we will not have to fear. God will provide his Spirit to renew our hearts. He never refuses his gift of the Spirit to those who ask for it in his name.

When you send forth your spirit, they are created,
and you renew the face of the earth.

℟. **Lord, send out your Spirit, and renew the face of the earth.**

or:

℟. **Alleluia.**

Lect.
No. 62

SECOND READING: Romans 8:22-27

A reading from the Letter of Saint Paul to the Romans

When God created the world, he breathed his Spirit into Adam and made him a living creature, a human being. We are not simply animals; we have something of God within us.

Yet, when we sinned, we denied that presence. We chose to follow that which could not give life. Furthermore, our sinfulness alienated not only us, but also all of creation. All that exists was made to be good, but our sins have made creation ambiguous. That which should lead us to God all too often leads us to sin.

As one example, just think of how often we misuse food. God created it to be good and of service to us, but we frequently eat too little or too much or the wrong thing.

We recognize the emptiness within us, and unfortunately we try to fill the void with sin and bad habits, etc., but none of it works. We are left feeling lonelier. The Spirit that Jesus breathed into his disciples fills the void. It reminds us of who we are, beloved children of God.

Brothers and sisters:
We know that all creation is groaning in labor pains even until now;
and not only that, but we ourselves,
who have the firstfruits of the Spirit,
we also groan within ourselves
as we wait for adoption, the redemption of our bodies.
For in hope we were saved.
Now hope that sees is not hope.
For who hopes for what one sees?
But if we hope for what we do not see, we wait with endurance.

In the same way, the Spirit too comes to the aid of our weakness;
for we do not know how to pray as we ought,
but the Spirit himself intercedes with inexpressible groanings.
And the one who searches hearts
knows what is the intention of the Spirit,
because he intercedes for the holy ones
according to God's will.

The word of the Lord.

Lect.
No. 62

The Holy Spirit descended upon the apostles and Mary in the form of tongues of fire. We ask that same Spirit to inflame our hearts.

Lect.
No. 62

In this Gospel passage Jesus identifies himself as the source of living water. This is an image that was found in Ezekiel. The prophet was commanded to pass through a great river that flowed from the temple. The water became so deep that he could not pass through it. The river was a symbol for the acts of worship in the temple that were a source of grace.

Now Jesus identifies himself as the true source of all grace. This was the water he offered to the Samaritan woman, and this is the water he gives to us.

ALLELUIA

℟. **Alleluia, alleluia.**

Come, Holy Spirit, fill the hearts of the faithful and kindle in them the fire of your love.

℟. **Alleluia, alleluia.**

GOSPEL: John 7:37-39

A reading from the holy Gospel according to John

On the last and greatest day of the feast,
Jesus stood up and exclaimed,
"Let anyone who thirsts come to me and drink.
As Scripture says:
> *Rivers of living water will flow from within him*
> *who believes in me."*
He said this in reference to the Spirit
that those who came to believe in him were to receive.
There was, of course, no Spirit yet,
because Jesus had not yet been glorified.

The Gospel of the Lord.

PASTORAL REFLECTIONS

It is often difficult to picture the Holy Spirit as a person. Many of the ways that we speak about the Holy Spirit portray him as more of a force (e.g., fire, wind, a dove) than a person. Yet, revelation teaches us that the Holy Spirit is a person, even if we do not fully understand what that means. It is not quite the same thing as saying that a human being is a person, but at the very least it means that God is not some impersonal force (like fate or energy).

PENTECOST SUNDAY
AT THE VIGIL MASS
[Extended Form]

Lect. No. 62

FIRST READING: Genesis 11:1-9

See p. 237.

Lect. No. 62

RESPONSORIAL PSALM: Ps 33:10-11, 12-13, 14-15 (℟.: 12)

At first glance, this psalm might seem to be a condemnation of all the nations upon the earth except Israel, since it is the nation that the Lord has chosen to be his own. The designs of the nations, on the other hand, are brought to nought.

God fashioned each one's heart; he knows the plans of all. As God of all peoples, he excludes no one from his love.

This psalm also is a consolation in that it reminds us that God knows us inside and out. The Holy Spirit, whose descent we celebrate today, resides in our hearts. No hidden thoughts or actions are unknown to the Lord. God knows how much we are trying to do what is right, despite our weaknesses and failures. All God wants is to embrace us in his love.

℟. **Blessed the people the Lord has chosen to be his own.**

The LORD brings to nought the plans of nations;
    he foils the designs of peoples.
But the plan of the LORD stands forever;
    the design of his heart, through all generations.

℟. **Blessed the people the Lord has chosen to be his own.**

Blessed the nation whose God is the LORD,
    the people he has chosen for his own inheritance.
From heaven the LORD looks down;
    he sees all mankind.

℟. **Blessed the people the Lord has chosen to be his own.**

From his fixed throne he beholds
    all who dwell on the earth,
He who fashioned the heart of each,
    he who knows all their works.

℟. **Blessed the people the Lord has chosen to be his own.**

Lect. No. 62

SECOND READING: Exodus 19:3-8a, 16-20b

See p. 238.

Lect. No. 62

RESPONSORIAL PSALM: Daniel 3:52, 53, 54, 55, 56 (℟.: 52b)

This canticle serves as a hymn of praise to God, who is both the God who guides our history and the God who rules over the cosmos.

God's throne on the cherubim refers to the presence of God upon the wings of the angels that sit on top of the Ark of the Covenant. This was called the mercy seat, and it was that place where God would appear in glory to his people.

Praise is one of the four forms of prayer (praise, intercession, thanksgiving, and contrition) that we lift up to our Lord. While we either receive something or thank God for something we have received in the other three forms of prayer, praise is gratuitous. We praise God simply because God is worthy of praise. Praise draws us out of ourselves and our own interests and invites us to serve another (in this case God) simply for the joy of being able to serve.

℟. **Glory and praise for ever!**

"Blessed are you, O Lord, the God of our fathers,
    praiseworthy and exalted above all forever;
And blessed is your holy and glorious name,
    praiseworthy and exalted above all for all ages."

℟. **Glory and praise for ever!**

"Blessed are you in the temple of your holy glory,
    praiseworthy and glorious above all forever."

℟. **Glory and praise for ever!**

"Blessed are you on the throne of your Kingdom,
    praiseworthy and exalted above all forever."

℟. **Glory and praise for ever!**

"Blessed are you who look into the depths
    from your throne upon the cherubim,
    praiseworthy and exalted above all forever."

℟. **Glory and praise for ever!**

"Blessed are you in the firmament of heaven,
    praiseworthy and glorious forever."

℟. **Glory and praise for ever!**

OR:

Ps 19:8, 9, 10, 11 (℟.: Jn 6:68c)

This Responsorial Psalm comes from the second part of Psalm 19, in which the community praises God who gave the law. The Jewish people considered the law to be a special gift from God, for it was a guide on how they might live a proper life pleasing to him. Most other people at that time feared their gods; Israel did not because the people knew that God was guiding them in his ways.

℟. **Lord, you have the words of everlasting life.**

The law of the LORD is perfect,
    refreshing the soul;
The decree of the LORD is trustworthy,
    giving wisdom to the simple.

℟. **Lord, you have the words of everlasting life.**

The precepts of the LORD are right,
    rejoicing the heart;
The command of the LORD is clear,
    enlightening the eye.

Six synonyms in these verses praise the law. Six is not the perfect number in the Bible; seven is. The verses that follow this Responsorial Psalm speak of interiorizing the law. Hence, the law receives its seventh attribute, showing it to be perfect when the law is written in our hearts and guides our deeds. Until then, it is only theory.

℞. **Lord, you have the words of everlasting life.**

The fear of the LORD is pure,
    enduring forever;
The ordinances of the LORD are true,
    all of them just.

℞. **Lord, you have the words of everlasting life.**

They are more precious than gold,
    than a heap of purest gold;
Sweeter also than syrup
    or honey from the comb.

℞. **Lord, you have the words of everlasting life.**

THIRD READING: Ezekiel 37:1-14

See p. 239.

RESPONSORIAL PSALM: Ps 107:2-3, 4-5, 6-7, 8-9 (℞.: 1)

This Responsorial Psalm speaks of God as a redeemer, one who rescues his people from the lands to which they have been scattered and one who leads them through danger to a safe home. This psalm could easily be read as a historical psalm that celebrates both the Exodus of God's people from their slavery in Egypt and their exile in Babylon. It also could be spiritualized and applied to our own lives.

We often wander away from the safe path that God has laid out for us. We often get lost in the desert of our hearts. God's love is the only love that will satisfy our hunger and thirst. God's love will respond to the deepest needs of our hearts.

Today we celebrate the fact that the Holy Spirit has been breathed into our hearts. The Holy Spirit is the love between

℞. **Give thanks to the Lord; his love is everlasting.**

or:

℞. **Alleluia.**

Let the redeemed of the LORD say,
    those whom he has redeemed from the hand of the foe
And gathered from the lands,
    from the east and the west, from the north and the south.

℞. **Give thanks to the Lord; his love is everlasting.**

or:

℞. **Alleluia.**

They went astray in the desert wilderness;
    the way to an inhabited city they did not find.
Hungry and thirsty,
    their life was wasting away within them.

℞. **Give thanks to the Lord; his love is everlasting.**

or:

℞. **Alleluia.**

the Father and the Son and their love for us. Jesus breathed that love into the hearts of his disciples on Easter Sunday. The Holy Spirit who descended upon the disciples filled them with a love so profound that they had to go out and proclaim the Good News. We receive that Spirit in every Sacrament, every prayer, every surrender to God's love that is part of our lives.

Thus, God is our Redeemer as well. We don't have to wander here or there to find comfort and love. God has redeemed us from guilt and fear. He has redeemed us from loneliness and meaning-lessness. He has brought us home by making our hearts his own home.

They cried to the L ORD in their distress;
　　from their straits he rescued them.
And he led them by a direct way
　　to reach an inhabited city.

> ℟. **Give thanks to the Lord; his love is everlasting.**

or:

> ℟. **Alleluia.**

Let them give thanks to the L ORD for his mercy
　　and his wondrous deeds to the children of men,
Because he satisfied the longing soul
　　and filled the hungry soul with good things.

> ℟. **Give thanks to the Lord; his love is everlasting.**

or:

> ℟. **Alleluia.**

Lect. No. 62	

FOURTH READING: Joel 3:15

See p. 241.

Lect. No. 62	

RESPONSORIAL PSALM: Ps 104:1-2, 24 and 35, 27-28, 29-30 (℟.: cf. 30)

See p. 242.

Lect. No. 62	

EPISTLE: Romans 8:22-27

See p. 243.

Lect. No. 62	

ALLELUIA

See p. 244.

Lect. No. 62	

GOSPEL: John 7:37-39

See p. 244.

The account of the day of Pentecost in Acts is filled with symbolic meaning.

Pentecost was already a pilgrimage festival for the Jewish people. That would explain the large crowd of Jews from all over the world who were there when the Holy Spirit descended upon the apostles and Mary. The fact that they are from all the countries mentioned in the account is a foreshadowing of the fact that the Gospel would eventually spread to all those nations. This might, in fact, be a list of all the nations that had already received the Gospel when this book was written.

The strong wind is reminiscent of the Spirit of the Lord that hovered over the waters on the first day of creation. This was a new creation in which the people of God were being made into the Church, the Mystical Body of Christ.

The tongues of fire were a fulfillment of the prophecy of Joel that the Spirit would come upon God's people. We are no longer filled with loneliness and alienation and fear.

Lect. No. 63

FIRST READING: Acts 2:1-11

A reading from the Acts of the Apostles

When the time for Pentecost was fulfilled,
    they were all in one place together.
And suddenly there came from the sky
    a noise like a strong driving wind,
    and it filled the entire house in which they were.
Then there appeared to them tongues as of fire,
    which parted and came to rest on each one of
        them.
And they were all filled with the Holy Spirit
    and began to speak in different tongues,
    as the Spirit enabled them to proclaim.

Now there were devout Jews from every nation
        under heaven staying in Jerusalem.
At this sound, they gathered in a large crowd,
    but they were confused
    because each one heard them speaking in his own
        language.
They were astounded, and in amazement they
        asked,
    "Are not all these people who are speaking
        Galileans?
Then how does each of us hear them in his native
        language?
We are Parthians, Medes, and Elamites,
    inhabitants of Mesopotamia, Judea and Cappado-
        cia,
    Pontus and Asia, Phrygia and Pamphylia,

249

There was a healing of the confusion of languages in the fact that the apostles could speak in their own language and everyone could understand them. Although this is called the gift of tongues, it is different from the phenomenon described in 1 Corinthians 12—14.

Egypt and the districts of Libya near Cyrene,
as well as travelers from Rome,
both Jews and converts to Judaism, Cretans and
   Arabs,
yet we hear them speaking in our own tongues
of the mighty acts of God."

The word of the Lord.

Lect.
No. 63

RESPONSORIAL PSALM: Ps 104:1, 24, 29-30, 31, 34 (℟.: cf. 30)

This is a hymn of praise for the God of creation. We praise God for he sent out his Spirit to create the world. After we sinned and damaged creation, God sent forth his Spirit again to renew the face of the earth. We are a new creation, not subject to the destructive effects of sin.

This is not to say that the renewal is totally complete, for we do not live in the "not yet." We live in the "already." We have indeed received the Holy Spirit, which is God's down payment of the glory that awaits us, but we are also still awaiting the total fulfillment of the promises Jesus made. Still, the kingdom has dawned and, if we look at things through the eyes of Jesus, we will see God's power at work in our midst.

We are totally dependent upon the generosity of God. As with all living creatures, we cannot survive if he withholds his breath. Likewise, if God withholds his Spirit, our spiritual life will perish. We will suffocate spiritually.

℟. **Lord, send out your Spirit, and renew the face of the earth.**

or:

℟. **Alleluia.**

Bless the LORD, O my soul!
   O LORD, my God, you are great indeed!
How manifold are your works, O LORD!
   the earth is full of your creatures;

℟. **Lord, send out your Spirit, and renew the face of the earth.**

or:

℟. **Alleluia.**

May the glory of the LORD endure forever;
   may the LORD be glad in his works!
Pleasing to him be my theme;
   I will be glad in the LORD.

℟. **Lord, send out your Spirit, and renew the face of the earth.**

or:

℟. **Alleluia.**

If you take away their breath, they perish
   and return to their dust.

However, if we trust in Jesus and find all of our strength in God, then we will not have to fear. God will provide his Spirit to those who ask him for it in his name. God will give us life that is so profound that even death will not conquer it.

When you send forth your spirit, they are created,
  and you renew the face of the earth.

℟. **Lord, send out your Spirit, and renew the face of the earth.**

or:

℟. **Alleluia.**

Lect. No. 63

SECOND READING: ◼A 1 Corinthians 12:3b-7, 12-13

The community of Corinth suffered from some misunderstandings concerning the role of the Holy Spirit. They considered the gifts they had received to be signs of power that made them better than others.

Saint Paul attempts to correct their arrogance by teaching them that gifts are given for the common service. They are not for our own profit. Each person in the community has been given special gifts that complement the gifts given to others. We need each other to be complete.

Furthermore, the gifts of the Spirit should bring us closer together, not create divisions. Before our baptism, we were divided from each other and forced to live as competitors and even enemies. Now we are one body in Christ and we only seek to build up that body in love.

A reading from the first Letter of Saint Paul to the Corinthians

Brothers and sisters:
  No one can say, "Jesus is Lord," except by the Holy Spirit.

There are different kinds of spiritual gifts but the same Spirit;
  there are different forms of service but the same Lord;
  there are different workings but the same God
  who produces all of them in everyone.
To each individual the manifestation of the Spirit
  is given for some benefit.

As a body is one though it has many parts,
  and all the parts of the body, though many, are one body,
  so also Christ.
For in one Spirit we were all baptized into one body,
  whether Jews or Greeks, slaves or free persons,
  and we were all given to drink of one Spirit.

The word of the Lord.

Throughout the first part of the Letter to the Galatians, Saint Paul spoke of the necessity to live according to the Spirit and not according to the Law. He was rejecting the tendency in the community to follow the old Jewish laws as if they could bring one peace and love.

This reading comes from the latter part of the letter. Here Paul counsels the community not to misinterpret his message. Freedom from the Law does not mean lawlessness.

True freedom is not the capacity to hurt and be selfish (for that is nothing but another form of enslavement). True freedom is the ability to love.

Paul gives two lists, one of vices and one of virtues. The list of vices has no real organization, while the list of virtues is a list of three sets of three.

The implied message of these two lists is that if one lives a life of vice, then one's life will be disordered and confused. If one, on the other hand, lives a life of virtue, then one will live in an ordered and peaceful manner.

OR: **B** Galatians 5:16-25

A reading from the Letter of Saint Paul
to the Galatians

Brothers and sisters, live by the Spirit
and you will certainly not gratify the desire of
the flesh.
For the flesh has desires against the Spirit,
and the Spirit against the flesh;
these are opposed to each other,
so that you may not do what you want.
But if you are guided by the Spirit, you are not
under the law.
Now the works of the flesh are obvious:
immorality, impurity, lust, idolatry,
sorcery, hatreds, rivalry, jealousy,
outbursts of fury, acts of selfishness,
dissensions, factions, occasions of envy,
drinking bouts, orgies, and the like.
I warn you, as I warned you before,
that those who do such things will not inherit the
kingdom of God.
In contrast, the fruit of the Spirit is love, joy, peace,
patience, kindness, generosity,
faithfulness, gentleness, self-control.
Against such there is no law.
Now those who belong to Christ Jesus have crucified their flesh
with its passions and desires.
If we live in the Spirit, let us also follow the Spirit.

The word of the Lord.

Lect.
No. 63

SEQUENCE: *Veni, Sancte Spiritus*

This beautiful Sequence is a hymn that celebrates the Holy Spirit. It speaks of many of the attributes that we associate with the Spirit.

First of all, the Spirit is called a light divine. We do not know our way to God, but the Spirit illumines our thoughts and prayers.

The Spirit is a comforter. This is one of the meanings of the title "Paraclete."

We often need to experience the love that is communicated through the Spirit. The Spirit is the love between the Father and the Son and between them and us.

The Spirit fills up the void in our heart. We long for fulfillment, yet so often we seek it in things that do not bring true joy and peace. The Spirit responds to our deepest aspirations.

We receive healing, both spiritual and physical, through the action of the Holy Spirit.

We also speak of the seven gifts that the Spirit has given us. The gifts are symbolic of the incredible multiplicity of gifts that the Spirit pours out upon us. They allow us to continue the work of God in the world.

Come, Holy Spirit, come!
And from your celestial home
Shed a ray of light divine!
Come, Father of the poor!
Come, source of all our store!
Come, within our bosoms shine.
You, of comforters the best;
You, the soul's most welcome guest;
Sweet refreshment here below;
In our labor, rest most sweet;
Grateful coolness in the heat;
Solace in the midst of woe.
O most blessed Light divine,
Shine within these hearts of yours,
And our inmost being fill!
Where you are not, we have naught,
Nothing good in deed or thought,
Nothing free from taint of ill.
Heal our wounds, our strength renew;
On our dryness pour your dew;
Wash the stains of guilt away:
Bend the stubborn heart and will;
Melt the frozen, warm the chill;
Guide the steps that go astray.
On the faithful, who adore
And confess you, evermore
In your sevenfold gift descend;
Give them virtue's sure reward;
Give them your salvation, Lord;
Give them joys that never end. Amen.
Alleluia.

Lect.
No. 63

We invite the Holy Spirit into our lives and our hearts. Without the love that the Spirit imparts, we cannot hope to live in God's love.

ALLELUIA

℟. **Alleluia, alleluia.**

Come, Holy Spirit, fill the hearts of your faithful and kindle in them the fire of your love.

℟. **Alleluia, alleluia.**

Lect.
No. 63

Having heard the Acts version of the descent of the Holy Spirit, we now hear the version contained in the Gospel of John.

Jesus breathes upon the disciples to give them the gift of the Holy Spirit. This is in imitation of how God created Adam. God breathed his Spirit into Adam and he came to life. In this account, Jesus breathes his Holy Spirit into the disciples and they are given new life in him.

The gift of the Holy Spirit is also associated with the forgiveness of our sins. The Spirit is God's love and is so filled with mercy that it brings us pardon. The sin against the Spirit is to believe that our sins are unforgivable or to presume upon God's mercy by only pretending to be sorry for what we have done.

GOSPEL: 🅐 John 20:19-23

A reading from the holy Gospel according to John

On the evening of that first day of the week,
   when the doors were locked, where the disciples were,
   for fear of the Jews,
   Jesus came and stood in their midst
   and said to them, "Peace be with you."
When he had said this, he showed them his hands
   and his side.
The disciples rejoiced when they saw the Lord.
Jesus said to them again, "Peace be with you.
As the Father has sent me, so I send you."
And when he had said this, he breathed on them
   and said to them,
   "Receive the Holy Spirit.
Whose sins you forgive are forgiven them,
   and whose sins you retain are retained."

The Gospel of the Lord.

Lect.
No. 63

OR: **B** John 15:26-27; 16:12-15

Scattered throughout the Last Supper Discourse in the Gospel of John are a series of statements concerning the Paraclete whom the Father and Jesus would send. The word Paraclete can be translated as Advocate, Counselor, Consoler, etc.

In this passage we hear how the Paraclete will reveal the truth to the disciples. Jesus speaks of how they were incapable of understanding everything that he could have told them.

Jesus' primary mission in this Gospel is to reveal to us how much God loves us, but the disciples failed to comprehend this revelation. The Spirit gave them (and us) the ability to know and love God.

While Jesus is the definitive revelation of who God is, we continue to understand that revelation better and better through the work of the Holy Spirit in our minds and hearts.

A reading from the holy Gospel according to John

Jesus said to his disciples:
"When the Advocate comes whom I will send you
    from the Father,
the Spirit of truth that proceeds from the Father,
he will testify to me.
And you also testify,
    because you have been with me from the begin-
        ning.

"I have much more to tell you, but you cannot bear it
        now.
But when he comes, the Spirit of truth,
    he will guide you to all truth.
He will not speak on his own,
    but he will speak what he hears,
    and will declare to you the things that are coming.
He will glorify me,
    because he will take from what is mine and de-
        clare it to you.
Everything that the Father has is mine;
    for this reason I told you that he will take from
        what is mine
    and declare it to you."

The Gospel of the Lord.

PASTORAL REFLECTIONS

John, who was a mystic, presents Pentecost as occurring on Easter Sunday. Being a mystic, time was not important for him, for with the Resurrection of Jesus from the dead, we have entered into eternity.

Luke, on the other hand, presents Pentecost as occurring fifty days after Easter. Luke is a historian and time is important, for it is in time that God reveals his love for us.

May 27, 2018

THE MOST HOLY TRINITY

FIRST READING:

Deuteronomy 4:32-34, 39-40

The First Reading comes from the Book of Deuteronomy. This was a book of the law that was found in the temple during the reforms of King Josiah (c. 622 B.C.).

This passage presents a renewal of the covenant that God made with Israel. One of the elements of every covenant formula is a recitation of the history of the relationship between the two parties. Thus, we hear an overview of the things that God had done for Israel. This list is filled with a sense of awe, for God had done things for Israel that had never even been heard of for any other nation.

Given everything that God had done for Israel, there was only one possible response: they must know and serve the LORD.

There is a strong emphasis both on the fact that Israel should serve God alone and on the fact that the LORD is the only God who exists. If Israel dedicates itself to the service of the LORD, then the people will find peace and joy. If not, they will not prosper.

A reading from the Book of Deuteronomy

Moses said to the people:
"Ask now of the days of old, before your time,
   ever since God created man upon the earth;
   ask from one end of the sky to the other:
   Did anything so great ever happen before?
Was it ever heard of?
Did a people ever hear the voice of God
   speaking from the midst of fire, as you did, and
      live?
Or did any god venture to go and take a nation for
      himself
   from the midst of another nation,
   by testings, by signs and wonders, by war,
   with strong hand and outstretched arm, and by
      great terrors,
   all of which the LORD, your God,
   did for you in Egypt before your very eyes?
This is why you must now know,
   and fix in your heart, that the LORD is God
   in the heavens above and on earth below,
   and that there is no other.
You must keep his statutes and commandments that
   I enjoin on you today,
   that you and your children after you may prosper,
   and that you may have long life on the land
   which the LORD, your God, is giving you forever."

The word of the Lord.

Lect. No. 165 **RESPONSORIAL PSALM: Ps 33:4-5, 6, 9, 18-19, 20, 22 (℟.: 12b)**

The Responsorial Psalm today is taken from a hymn of praise. It first praises God who created everything that exists with the word of his mouth. It then praises God who controls the destiny of all of the nations upon the earth.

The first part of the section quoted today speaks of the fact that God is upright, trustworthy, just, righteous, and kind. God, whose power extends to the very ends of the earth, nevertheless is good and kind and gentle.

God is the paradigm of virtue, and he infuses this virtue into everything that he created.

Because all of this is true, we can trust in God. He will always rescue us from our enemies (whether they be people or situations of danger) because our hope is in him.

The Responsorial Psalm repeats the reason for the source of our hope. God has chosen us to be his own possession. We do not deserve God's intervention because of something that we have done. We trust that God will save us because God has proven himself to be so good and loving and faithful to all his promises.

℟. **Blessed the people the Lord has chosen to be his own.**

Upright is the word of the LORD,
and all his works are trustworthy.
He loves justice and right;
of the kindness of the LORD the earth is full.

℟. **Blessed the people the Lord has chosen to be his own.**

By the word of the LORD the heavens were made;
by the breath of his mouth all their host.
For he spoke, and it was made;
he commanded, and it stood forth.

℟. **Blessed the people the Lord has chosen to be his own.**

See, the eyes of the LORD are upon those who fear him,
upon those who hope for his kindness,
to deliver them from death
and preserve them in spite of famine.

℟. **Blessed the people the Lord has chosen to be his own.**

Our soul waits for the LORD,
who is our help and our shield.
May your kindness, O LORD, be upon us
who have put our hope in you.

℟. **Blessed the people the Lord has chosen to be his own.**

Lect.
No. 165

SECOND READING: Romans 8:14-17

This passage from the Letter to the Romans speaks of the relationship that Jesus has established. We are now adopted as children of God.

The Spirit of God was breathed into us when God created Adam. That same Spirit was breathed into the disciples on the day of the resurrection (Gospel of John) or Pentecost (Acts of the Apostles). This Spirit reminds us that we have God's own breath inside of us. That breath gives voice to the fact that God is our own Father and Jesus is our brother. We must share both his sufferings (when we carry our own crosses) and his glory.

A reading from the Letter of Saint Paul
to the Romans

Brothers and sisters:
  Those who are led by the Spirit of God are sons
    of God.
For you did not receive a spirit of slavery to fall
    back into fear,
  but you received a Spirit of adoption,
  through whom we cry, "Abba, Father!"
The Spirit himself bears witness with our spirit
  that we are children of God,
  and if children, then heirs,
  heirs of God and joint heirs with Christ,
  if only we suffer with him
  so that we may also be glorified with him.

The word of the Lord.

Lect.
No. 165

ALLELUIA: Revelation 1:8

The Alleluia Verse gives praise to God who is three persons in one God. This truth was revealed to us through the life and ministry of Jesus.

℟. **Alleluia, alleluia.**

Glory to the Father, the Son, and the Holy Spirit;
to God who is, who was, and who is to come.

℟. **Alleluia, alleluia.**

PASTORAL REFLECTIONS

A proof that the Spirit of God abides in our hearts is the fact that if we were to ask ourselves what we would most like God to tell us, chances are that we would respond, "I love you." We would not be able to create a God that good on our own if the Spirit of God were not in our hearts revealing who God is. God is the answer to our deepest hopes because it is the Spirit of God who places those hopes in our hearts.

Lect. No. 165

GOSPEL: Matthew 28:16-20

This passage is the conclusion to the Gospel of Matthew. It is a type of commissioning of the apostles to proclaim the good news to the ends of the earth.

There are several important themes found in these verses that are repeated throughout the Gospel (especially in the chapters of teaching, e.g., the Sermon on the Mount).

Jesus has the authority of God and hands it on to his disciples. He sends them out to every nation and they are to preach and bring people to conversion. They are to baptize in the name of the Holy Trinity. Christians are called to lives of obedience. Finally, Jesus will always be with them until the end of time.

A reading from the holy Gospel according to Matthew

The eleven disciples went to Galilee, to the mountain to which Jesus had ordered them.
When they all saw him, they worshiped, but they doubted.
Then Jesus approached and said to them,
    "All power in heaven and on earth has been given to me.
Go, therefore, and make disciples of all nations,
    baptizing them in the name of the Father,
    and of the Son, and of the Holy Spirit,
    teaching them to observe all that I have commanded you.
And behold, I am with you always, until the end of the age."

The Gospel of the Lord.

PASTORAL REFLECTIONS

There are certain religions that call themselves Christian but do not profess belief in the Trinity, nor do they baptize in the name of the Trinity. Since the earliest days of the Church, it has been recognized that one must believe in the Trinity to be a Christian. A very early formulation of that belief (4th century) is in the Nicene Creed. This was not the beginning of that belief (as some recent books have suggested), but it was the official proclamation of a formula of what the Church believed from its earliest days.

June 3, 2018

THE MOST HOLY BODY AND BLOOD OF CHRIST (CORPUS CHRISTI)

Lect. No. 168

FIRST READING: Exodus 24:3-8

This passage tells of the ritual that was performed by Moses to formally establish the covenant between God and the people of Israel in the Sinai.

A covenant was a type of treaty made between two people or nations. They could be equals or one could be superior to the other.

There would always be a ritual associated with the initiation of the covenant. It involved a sacrifice (for the official term was to "cut" a covenant, referring to the cutting of the animal).

Notice that Moses sprinkles blood upon the people. This was known as the blood of the covenant (a phrase that would be used by Jesus during the Last Supper to refer to the cup of wine transformed into his own blood).

Blood was symbolic of life, and by sprinkling blood on the people, Moses was committing his people totally to the LORD. They would henceforth live if they lived in the LORD, but they would find only death and loneliness if they chose any other path.

A reading from the Book of Exodus

When Moses came to the people
and related all the words and ordinances of the
LORD,
they all answered with one voice,
"We will do everything that the LORD has told us."
Moses then wrote down all the words of the LORD
and,
rising early the next day,
he erected at the foot of the mountain an altar
and twelve pillars for the twelve tribes of Israel.
Then, having sent certain young men of the Israelites
to offer holocausts and sacrifice young bulls
as peace offerings to the LORD,
Moses took half of the blood and put it in large
bowls;
the other half he splashed on the altar.
Taking the book of the covenant, he read it aloud to
the people,
who answered, "All that the LORD has said, we will
heed and do."
Then he took the blood and sprinkled it on the people, saying,
"This is the blood of the covenant
that the LORD has made with you
in accordance with all these words of his."

The word of the Lord.

Lect. No. 168 **RESPONSORIAL PSALM: Ps 116:12-13, 15-16, 17-18 (℟.: 13)**

Corpus Christi Sunday, the Sunday that celebrates the most holy body and blood of Jesus, is a feast of thanksgiving for this incredible gift from God. We call this sacrament the Eucharist.

The word Eucharist means thanksgiving. Thus, it is appropriate that the Responsorial Psalm for today be a psalm of thanksgiving that praises God for his bounty and goodness.

The cup of salvation is a cup of libation that would be poured out in order to celebrate an act of salvation. This is also why one would make vows to the LORD, to respond in gratitude for all that God had done to rescue one from one's enemies.

These vows were to be paid in the presence of all of God's people. When we receive the Eucharist, we experience God's salvation. We taste the love of God. Now we must give witness to God's love to all whom we meet.

When we leave our church, we must share the love that we have experienced. As Saint Augustine says in one of his Easter homilies, we must become that which we have eaten. We must become bread that is broken to satisfy the hunger of the world.

℟. **I will take the cup of salvation, and call on the name of the Lord.**

or:

℟. **Alleluia.**

How shall I make a return to the LORD
   for all the good he has done for me?
The cup of salvation I will take up,
   and I will call upon the name of the LORD.

℟. **I will take the cup of salvation, and call on the name of the Lord.**

or:

℟. **Alleluia.**

Precious in the eyes of the LORD
   is the death of his faithful ones.
I am your servant, the son of your handmaid;
   you have loosed my bonds.

℟. **I will take the cup of salvation, and call on the name of the Lord.**

or:

℟. **Alleluia.**

To you will I offer sacrifice of thanksgiving,
   and I will call upon the name of the LORD.
My vows to the LORD I will pay
   in the presence of all his people.

℟. **I will take the cup of salvation, and call on the name of the Lord.**

or:

℟. **Alleluia.**

Lect.
No. 168

SECOND READING: Hebrews 9:11-15

The Letter to the Hebrews uses a Jewish style of argumentation called Midrash. One form of Midrash is to argue from the lesser to the greater. If something is true of the king, for example, then it is even more true of God.

In the Old Testament, High Priests offered sacrifices in which they poured out the blood of animals. Blood signified life, and that life canceled the death that we had brought upon ourselves through sin.

Yet the blood that the priests poured out was the blood of animals, and that was insufficient. It could not produce the eternal cleansing that we truly needed.

This is why Jesus allowed his blood to be shed. He was both High Priest and victim. The life that he poured out canceled the power of our sins.

We are no longer subject to the spiritual death that those sins brought. Even physical death has been conquered by the life and love that Jesus has poured into our lives.

A reading from the Letter to the Hebrews

Brothers and sisters:
When Christ came as high priest
of the good things that have come to be,
passing through the greater and more perfect tabernacle
not made by hands, that is, not belonging to this creation,
he entered once for all into the sanctuary,
not with the blood of goats and calves
but with his own blood, thus obtaining eternal redemption.
For if the blood of goats and bulls
and the sprinkling of a heifer's ashes
can sanctify those who are defiled
so that their flesh is cleansed,
how much more will the blood of Christ,
who through the eternal Spirit offered himself unblemished to God,
cleanse our consciences from dead works
to worship the living God.

For this reason he is mediator of a new covenant:
since a death has taken place for deliverance
from transgressions under the first covenant,
those who are called may receive the promised eternal inheritance.

The word of the Lord.

Lect. No. 168

Sequences are ancient hymns that were written to celebrate important feasts of the Church Year. This one celebrates the Sacrament of the Holy Eucharist.

This Sacrament and the love that Jesus has expressed to us through his life and his death are so incredibly profound that even if we were to praise him all of our lives, we could not begin to pay him the praise that he is due. Our act of praising him, in fact, is actually his greatest gift to us, for when we praise and thank him, we are fulfilling our greatest destiny.

Today we are especially grateful for his gift of the Sacrament of his body and blood. Jesus, on Holy Thursday evening, took the bread and wine that were used as part of the Passover supper ritual, and he called them his body and his blood. In this act, he transformed the significance of these actions. We are not only celebrating the passing over of the Israelites during their Exodus; we are also celebrating the passing over of Jesus from death into life.

Jesus, at the Last Supper, also commanded us to continue to do what he was doing. He said to do this in his memory. That is what we do when we take the bread and wine and call them the body and the blood of Christ. This is not simply a symbolic action; it is

SEQUENCE: *Lauda Sion*

The sequence Laud, O Zion (Lauda Sion), *or the shorter form beginning with the verse* Lo! the angel's food is given, *may be sung optionally before the Alleluia.*

Laud, O Zion, your salvation,
　Laud with hymns of exultation,
　　Christ, your king and shepherd true:

Bring him all the praise you know,
He is more than you bestow.
　　Never can you reach his due.

Special theme for glad thanksgiving
Is the quick'ning and the living
　　Bread today before you set:

From his hands of old partaken,
As we know, by faith unshaken,
　　Where the Twelve at supper met.

Full and clear ring out your chanting,
Joy nor sweetest grace be wanting,
　　From your heart let praises burst:

For today the feast is holden,
When the institution olden
　　Of that supper was rehearsed.

Here the new law's new oblation,
By the new king's revelation,
　　Ends the form of ancient rite:

Now the new the old effaces,
Truth away the shadow chases,
　　Light dispels the gloom of night.

What he did at supper seated,
Christ ordained to be repeated,
　　His memorial ne'er to cease:

And his rule for guidance taking,
Bread and wine we hallow, making
　　Thus our sacrifice of peace.

an action that truly accomplishes what it says. The bread truly becomes the body of Christ and the wine truly becomes the blood of Christ.

This is not something that our senses can detect. We believe by faith, for we trust fully in the fidelity of God's words.

Yet, this miracle is even greater than this. Even though many people consume the bread that has become the body of Jesus, Christ is not divided or diminished by this action.

Furthermore, Jesus' presence in this holy Sacrament does not depend upon our worthiness. Whether we are good or bad, Jesus still presents himself to us.

If we are good, then this Sacrament serves to enhance our sanctification. If we have chosen to be evil, however, then participating in the Eucharist would be a horrible lie. We would be committing a sin against the Sacrament of God's love.

The Sequence closes by reiterating that no matter how many times the host is broken, it is still the body of Christ. Jesus is still present in this holy Sacrament and he is still offering himself to us.

Sequences are ancient hymns that were written to celebrate important feasts of the

This the truth each Christian learns,
Bread into his flesh he turns,
　To his precious blood the wine:

Sight has fail'd, nor thought conceives,
But a dauntless faith believes,
　Resting on a pow'r divine.

Here beneath these signs are hidden
Priceless things to sense forbidden;
　Signs, not things are all we see:

Blood is poured and flesh is broken,
Yet in either wondrous token
　Christ entire we know to be.

Whoso of this food partakes,
Does not rend the Lord nor breaks;
　Christ is whole to all that taste:

Thousands are, as one, receivers,
One, as thousands of believers,
　Eats of him who cannot waste.

Bad and good the feast are sharing,
Of what divers dooms preparing,
　Endless death, or endless life.

Life to these, to those damnation,
See how like participation
　Is with unlike issues rife.

When the sacrament is broken,
Doubt not, but believe 'tis spoken,
　That each sever'd outward token
　　doth the very whole contain.

Nought the precious gift divides,
Breaking but the sign betides
　Jesus still the same abides,
　　still unbroken does remain.

The shorter form of the sequence begins here.

L o! the angel's food is given
To the pilgrim who has striven;

Church Year. This one cele-brates the Sacrament of the Holy Eucharist using a series of images of the Blessed Sacra-ment.

The first is of Isaac who was an only-beloved son who was almost sacrificed (like Jesus, the only-begotten Son of God who was sacrificed on the cross).

Jesus is also the new Paschal Lamb. He died the very hour that the Paschal lambs were being slaughtered in the temple. Like those lambs, none of his bones were broken.

He is also manna, bread from heaven to satisfy the deepest hunger of his people.

> **Lect. No. 168**

The Alleluia Verse quotes the Discourse on the Bread of Life from the Gospel of John. Jesus speaks of himself as being the bread that will nourish us and satisfy our most profound need.

See the children's bread from heaven,
   which on dogs may not be spent.

Truth the ancient types fulfilling,
Isaac bound, a victim willing,
   Paschal lamb, its lifeblood spilling,
   manna to the fathers sent.

Very bread, good shepherd, tend us,
Jesu, of your love befriend us,
   You refresh us, you defend us,
   Your eternal goodness send us
In the land of life to see.

You who all things can and know,
Who on earth such food bestow,
   Grant us with your saints, though lowest,
   Where the heav'nly feast you show,
Fellow heirs and guests to be. Amen. Alleluia.

ALLELUIA: John 6:51

℟. **Alleluia, alleluia.**

I am the living bread that came down from heaven, says the Lord; whoever eats this bread will live for-ever.

℟. **Alleluia, alleluia.**

PASTORAL REFLECTIONS

No matter how much we speak about the Eucharist, we never could exhaust the topic. Eucharist is a gift. (We give ourselves to God, and God gives himself to us.) It is a meal (representing the meal of the Last Supper). It is a sacrifice (an unbloody representation of the cross). It is the real presence of Jesus in his body and blood. It is also a promise of even more intimate union in the future.

Lect.
No. 168

GOSPEL: Mark 14:12-16, 22-26

Jesus gives instructions to his disciples concerning the preparations they were to make for the Passover meal. From the way that the passage is phrased, we do not have to interpret it as implying that Jesus knew of the room through a supernatural revelation. He might have simply made arrangements beforehand and told the man to await his disciples with a water jar. It could possibly indicate the Essene quarter of Jerusalem for Essene men carried their own water jars.

In the course of the meal we hear the words of consecration over the bread and the wine that become the body and blood of Jesus.

This version of the words is very close to that found in the Gospel of Matthew, and probably represents a more primitive tradition than the words found in the Gospel of Luke and First Corinthians.

The blood of the covenant (a phrase implying the initiation of a new covenant) is shed for the many. This is an Aramaic way of saying "for everyone."

The Passover meal traditionally ended with the singing of the Hallel hymns praising the Lord. Jesus and the disciples walked to the Mount of Olives where he prayed in the garden of Gethsemane.

A reading from the holy Gospel according to Mark

On the first day of the Feast of Unleavened Bread,
   when they sacrificed the Passover lamb,
Jesus' disciples said to him,
   "Where do you want us to go
   and prepare for you to eat the Passover?"
He sent two of his disciples and said to them,
   "Go into the city and a man will meet you,
   carrying a jar of water.
Follow him.
Wherever he enters, say to the master of the house,
   'The Teacher says, "Where is my guest room
   where I may eat the Passover with my disciples?"'
Then he will show you a large upper room furnished
      and ready.
Make the preparations for us there."
The disciples then went off, entered the city,
   and found it just as he had told them;
   and they prepared the Passover.

While they were eating,
   he took bread, said the blessing,
   broke it, gave it to them, and said,
   "Take it; this is my body."
Then he took a cup, gave thanks, and gave it to them,
   and they all drank from it.
He said to them,
   "This is my blood of the covenant,
   which will be shed for many.
Amen, I say to you,
   I shall not drink again the fruit of the vine
   until the day when I drink it new in the kingdom
      of God."
Then, after singing a hymn,
   they went out to the Mount of Olives.

The Gospel of the Lord.

TENTH SUNDAY IN ORDINARY TIME

Lect. No. 89 | **FIRST READING: Genesis 3:9-15**

Today, we read about the entrance of sin into the world and the punishment that we received because of it.

The first effect of sin is alienation: from God, from each other, and even from nature.

Before they sinned, Adam and Eve were naked, but they felt no shame. They had been living in a state of pure innocence. After their sin they felt only shame. They hid themselves and ran away from God, the one who loved them most. They blamed each other and even the snake for their fall.

God punished the man, the woman, and the snake. The man's punishment, which we do not hear in this passage, was to work hard for a living but never to receive a just recompense. The woman suffers childbirth pains. The snake loses its legs and crawls on its belly.

We should not interpret these punishments in a scientific manner. They are etiologies, simple explanations for situations that go beyond our understanding (e.g., why a woman suffers when she gives birth, why the snake has no legs).

A reading from the Book of Genesis

After the man, Adam, had eaten of the tree,
the LORD God called to the man and asked him,
"Where are you?"
He answered, "I heard you in the garden;
but I was afraid, because I was naked,
so I hid myself."
Then he asked, "Who told you that you were naked?
You have eaten, then,
from the tree of which I had forbidden you to eat!"
The man replied, "The woman whom you put here
with me—
she gave me fruit from the tree, and so I ate it."
The LORD God then asked the woman,
"Why did you do such a thing?"
The woman answered, "The serpent tricked me into
it, so I ate it."

Then the LORD God said to the serpent:
"Because you have done this, you shall be banned
from all the animals
and from all the wild creatures;
on your belly shall you crawl,
and dirt shall you eat
all the days of your life.
I will put enmity between you and the woman,
and between your offspring and hers;
he will strike at your head,
while you strike at his heel."

The word of the Lord.

Lect. No. 89

RESPONSORIAL PSALM: Ps 130: 1-2, 3-4, 5-6, 7-8 (℟.: 7bc)

Psalm 130 is an individual lament. It begins with an almost desperate appeal to the LORD for an intervention. Then there is a series of verses which speak of the things tormenting the psalmist. Finally, there is a todah. This is a thanksgiving for the deliverance that the psalmist is sure Yahweh will deliver.

There is a sense of urgency in this psalm, as if things had gone so far that there were only moments of life left. The image of the sentinel waiting for the dawn is especially appropriate. The dark is filled with danger and confusion, but with the dawn comes a restoration of hope. Throughout the Old Testament, the dawn was considered to be the hour of the day when God would intervene to save us from our enemies.

The psalmist readily admits that the disasters that had befallen him were probably due to his own sins. He even states that if the LORD were to mark his iniquities, he would have no chance of standing. He and Israel deserve everything that they were getting. Nevertheless, he is filled with hope that the LORD will deliver them from their dangers, for the LORD is truly merciful and gracious.

℟. **With the Lord there is mercy and fullness of redemption.**

Out of the depths I cry to you, O LORD;
    LORD, hear my voice!
Let your ears be attentive
    to my voice in supplication.

℟. **With the Lord there is mercy and fullness of redemption.**

If you, O LORD, mark iniquities,
    Lord, who can stand?
But with you is forgiveness,
    that you may be revered.

℟. **With the Lord there is mercy and fullness of redemption.**

I trust in the LORD;
    my soul trusts in his word.
More than sentinels wait for the dawn,
    let Israel wait for the LORD.

℟. **With the Lord there is mercy and fullness of redemption.**

For with the LORD is kindness
    and with him is plenteous redemption;
and he will redeem Israel
    from all their iniquities.

℟. **With the Lord there is mercy and fullness of redemption.**

Lect.
No. 89

SECOND READING: 2 Corinthians 4:13—5:1

St. Paul speaks of the fact that Jesus has risen from the dead, and he has thus destroyed the power of death over us. This is the source of our hope. We do not have to live in despair any longer.

We hold on to this truth even when we are suffering or dying. (Paul seems to be referring to some difficulties that he was experiencing during that period of time.)

Superficially, these things seem to be a disastrous defeat. But when we judge reality from a spiritual viewpoint, then we can see them as all but insignificant in light of the glory to which God is calling us.

Paul compares our earthly body to a tent. A tent is a temporary dwelling in which one lives for a time, but it is not one's permanent abode. God has prepared that other abode for us— our heavenly, glorified body that will no longer suffer from the limitations of this earthly condition.

We are not sure exactly what that glorified body will be like. St. Paul says that the seed planted in the ground does not look like the plant that springs from it, but there is a continuity.

A reading from the second Letter of Saint Paul to the Corinthians

Brothers and sisters:
Since we have the same spirit of faith,
   according to what is written, *I believed, therefore I spoke,*
   we too believe and therefore we speak,
   knowing that the one who raised the Lord Jesus
   will raise us also with Jesus
   and place us with you in his presence.
Everything indeed is for you,
   so that the grace bestowed in abundance on more and more people
   may cause the thanksgiving to overflow for the glory of God.
Therefore, we are not discouraged;
   rather, although our outer self is wasting away,
   our inner self is being renewed day by day.
For this momentary light affliction
   is producing for us an eternal weight of glory beyond all comparison,
   as we look not to what is seen but to what is unseen;
   for what is seen is transitory, but what is unseen is eternal.
For we know that if our earthly dwelling, a tent,
   should be destroyed,
   we have a building from God,
   a dwelling not made with hands, eternal in heaven.

The word of the Lord.

Lect.
No. 89

The ruler of this world is Satan. With Jesus' death upon the cross, love has conquered hate, life has conquered death.

Lect.
No. 89

In the first part of this passage, we hear an odd episode concerning the family of Jesus. They come to take him home because they (it is not clear if it is the family or others) think he is out of his mind. The family must have known that he was the Messiah. But Jesus was speaking about his death and resurrection. That made no sense to them. They were confused about who Jesus really was and especially what his mission was.

This is typical of the Gospel of Mark, wherein the family of Jesus and the disciples have a difficult time understanding who Jesus truly is. It is only at the cross and resurrection that they fully understand.

This misunderstanding on the part of the family of Jesus is contrasted with the outright rejection of Jesus by the scribes. They accuse Jesus of being demonic, of being possessed by Beelzebul (the name they used to identify the prince of the demons).

ALLELUIA: John 12:31b-32

℟. **Alleluia, alleluia.**

Now the ruler of this world will be driven out, says the Lord;
and when I am lifted up from the earth, I will draw everyone to myself.

℟. **Alleluia, alleluia.**

GOSPEL: Mark 3:20-35

A reading from the holy Gospel according to Mark

Jesus came home with his disciples.
Again the crowd gathered,
  making it impossible for them even to eat.
When his relatives heard of this they set out to seize him,
  for they said, "He is out of his mind."
The scribes who had come from Jerusalem said,
  "He is possessed by Beelzebul,"
  and "By the prince of demons he drives out demons."

Summoning them, he began to speak to them in parables,
  "How can Satan drive out Satan?
If a kingdom is divided against itself,
  that kingdom cannot stand.
And if a house is divided against itself,
  that house will not be able to stand.
And if Satan has risen up against himself
  and is divided, he cannot stand;
  that is the end of him.
But no one can enter a strong man's house to plunder his property
  unless he first ties up the strong man.

Jesus points out the illogic of their accusation. Why would Satan oppose demons? If anything, he would want more people to be possessed.

Jesus also speaks of the sin against the Holy Spirit. Many people have tried to identify that sin with one fault or another. Pope St. John Paul II said that one form of it is denying that God's mercy is greater than our sinfulness. The Holy Spirit is the love between the Father and the Son and the gift of their love for us. It is a sin against that love to believe that our guilt is greater than God's capacity to forgive.

The Gospel closes with another scene involving the family of Jesus. In parallel to the opening scene of this Gospel passage, they are seen as not quite measuring up. Jesus seems to favor those who surround him and who are doing God's will.

Then he can plunder the house.
Amen, I say to you,
all sins and all blasphemies that people utter
will be forgiven them.
But whoever blasphemes against the Holy Spirit
will never have forgiveness,
but is guilty of an everlasting sin."
For they had said, "He has an unclean spirit."

His mother and his brothers arrived.
Standing outside they sent word to him and called him.
A crowd seated around him told him,
"Your mother and your brothers and your sisters
are outside asking for you."
But he said to them in reply,
"Who are my mother and my brothers?"
And looking around at those seated in the circle he said,
"Here are my mother and my brothers.
For whoever does the will of God
is my brother and sister and mother."

The Gospel of the Lord.

June 17, 2018

ELEVENTH SUNDAY IN ORDINARY TIME

Lect. No. 92 **FIRST READING: Ezekiel 17:22-24**

The first reading presents the image of the growth of plants. It is God who regulates what will prosper and what will not. This image will be used in the Gospel where Jesus applies it to the question of how faith grows.

God will bring down the mighty and arrogant and will lift up the lowly and humble. This is a theme we hear in the hymn sung by the Blessed Virgin Mary, the Magnificat.

In Ezekiel's day, the mighty and arrogant were represented both by those who refused to repent their evil ways in Judah and by the nation of Babylon, which had conquered the kingdom of Judah and exiled its leading citizens.

A reading from the Book of the Prophet Ezekiel

Thus says the Lord GOD:
I, too, will take from the crest of the cedar,
   from its topmost branches tear off a tender shoot,
and plant it on a high and lofty mountain;
   on the mountain heights of Israel I will plant it.
It shall put forth branches and bear fruit,
   and become a majestic cedar.
Birds of every kind shall dwell beneath it,
   every winged thing in the shade of its boughs.
And all the trees of the field shall know
   that I, the LORD,
bring low the high tree,
   lift high the lowly tree,
wither up the green tree,
   and make the withered tree bloom.
As I, the LORD, have spoken, so will I do.

The word of the Lord.

Lect. No. 92 **RESPONSORIAL PSALM: Ps 92: 2-3, 13-14, 15-16 (℟.: cf. 2a)**

These verses form a hymn of thanksgiving to praise God as the guarantor of justice. There is never a time that the psalmist would cease giving thanks to the Lord because God is always just.

℟. **Lord, it is good to give thanks to you.**

It is good to give thanks to the LORD,
   to sing praise to your name, Most High,
to proclaim your kindness at dawn
   and your faithfulness throughout the night.

℟. **Lord, it is good to give thanks to you.**

According to the teaching of Wisdom Literature, if we do what is right and keep to God's ways, then we shall be blessed abundantly.

Yet, as Christians, we realize that our reward does not always come in this life. Sometimes we have to wait until the final judgment to see how God is the true measure of truth and justice and love.

Lect.
No. 92

Life in this world is good, but this is not our ultimate home. God created us so that we might share in his glory in heaven.

It is important to keep this in mind, for if we live only in and for this world, then we are bound to fall into patterns of behavior that are selfish and even self-destructive.

If, however, we keep our minds on eternity, then we will be able to live lives that are filled with the fruits of the Spirit. Every once in a while it is good to remind ourselves that we will someday face a final judgment for what we did in this life.

Lect.
No. 92

God sows his word within our hearts. If we have prepared our hearts well, that word will flourish and bear fruit.

The just one shall flourish like the palm tree,
    like a cedar of Lebanon shall he grow.
They that are planted in the house of the Lord
    shall flourish in the courts of our God.

℟. **Lord, it is good to give thanks to you.**

They shall bear fruit even in old age;
    vigorous and sturdy shall they be,
declaring how just is the Lord,
    my rock, in whom there is no wrong.

℟. **Lord, it is good to give thanks to you.**

SECOND READING: 2 Corinthians 5:6-10

A reading from the second Letter of Saint Paul to the Corinthians

Brothers and sisters:
  We are always courageous,
    although we know that while we are at home in the body
  we are away from the Lord,
    for we walk by faith, not by sight.
Yet we are courageous,
    and we would rather leave the body and go home to the Lord.
Therefore, we aspire to please him,
    whether we are at home or away.
For we must all appear before the judgment seat of Christ,
    so that each may receive recompense,
    according to what he did in the body, whether good or evil.

The word of the Lord.

ALLELUIA

℟. **Alleluia, alleluia.**

The seed is the word of God, Christ is the sower.
All who come to him will live for ever.

℟. **Alleluia, alleluia.**

Lect. No. 92

Whenever Jesus wanted to communicate God's word in a way that simple people could understand, he would use examples from everyday life. Since many of his listeners were farmers, many of his parables involved agricultural imagery.

Today we hear two parables that speak about the growth of seeds.

In the first parable, Jesus speaks about the mystery of the seed's growth. The farmer might plant the seed, but it is God who causes it to grow.

Likewise, we might preach the Word of God to others, but it is God who causes faith to grow in their hearts. Faith is a gift from God to which we respond. We can pray to receive a greater measure of faith, but God gives us faith when and how it is most useful to us.

The second parable reminds us that the kingdom of God often begins in small, almost insignificant ways. Only rarely do we see the great miracles. Most often we witness small miracles of grace: when one person forgives another; when a person dies to self to serve others; when a person rejects temptation to live in God's grace.

This parable also reminds us that when we join a faith community, we should not expect it to be perfect. We must commit ourselves to the gradual process of furthering the growth of the kingdom in our midst.

GOSPEL: Mark 4:26-34

A reading from the holy Gospel according to Mark

Jesus said to the crowds:
"This is how it is with the kingdom of God;
   it is as if a man were to scatter seed on the land
   and would sleep and rise night and day
   and through it all the seed would sprout and grow,
he knows not how.
Of its own accord the land yields fruit,
   first the blade, then the ear, then the full grain in
     the ear.
And when the grain is ripe, he wields the sickle at
     once,
   for the harvest has come."

He said,
   "To what shall we compare the kingdom of God,
   or what parable can we use for it?
It is like a mustard seed that, when it is sown in the
     ground,
   is the smallest of all the seeds on the earth.
But once it is sown, it springs up and becomes the
     largest of plants
   and puts forth large branches,
   so that the birds of the sky can dwell in its shade."
With many such parables
   he spoke the word to them as they were able to
     understand it.
Without parables he did not speak to them,
   but to his own disciples he explained everything
     in private.

The Gospel of the Lord.

THE NATIVITY OF ST. JOHN THE BAPTIST AT THE VIGIL MASS

Lect. No. 586

FIRST READING: Jeremiah 1:4-10

The First Reading sets the theme of this celebration: God had a plan that he fulfilled through his chosen ones. Even before the Prophet Jeremiah was born, he had already been chosen by the LORD to proclaim the word of God to Israel (just as John the Baptist had been chosen to prepare the way before Jesus).

Jeremiah objects that he is not capable of fulfilling the important mission to which the LORD is calling him. He complains that he is too young. He is inexperienced, and he fears that the elders will not listen to him. The LORD responds that he is certainly not capable of this mission on his own, but he will not be doing it on his own. The LORD would work through him to accomplish his purpose.

This is important to remember when we find ourselves in situations in which we feel inadequate. God will use our talents, but will also supply that which we do not have in order to give witness to God's love.

A reading from the Book of the Prophet Jeremiah

In the days of King Josiah, the word of the LORD came to me, saying:

Before I formed you in the womb I knew you,
    before you were born I dedicated you,
    a prophet to the nations I appointed you.

"Ah, Lord GOD!" I said,
    "I know not how to speak; I am too young."
But the LORD answered me,
Say not, "I am too young."
    To whomever I send you, you shall go;
    whatever I command you, you shall speak.
Have no fear before them,
    because I am with you to deliver you, says the
        LORD.

Then the LORD extended his hand and touched my
    mouth, saying,

See, I place my words in your mouth!
    This day I set you
    over nations and over kingdoms,
to root up and to tear down,
    to destroy and to demolish,
    to build and to plant.

The word of the Lord.

Lect. No. 586 **RESPONSORIAL PSALM: Ps 71:1-2, 3-4a, 5-6ab, 15ab and 17 (℟.: 6b)**

The Responsorial Psalm continues the theme found in the First Reading, i.e., that God has chosen us from before the time we were born and we must trust in him.

God is a refuge. Often we find it difficult to do the right thing when we are called upon to give witness to God's love. It can be painful to put aside hurts and resentments. Yet, if God really is the source of strength, then we will find the courage that we need to risk loving even those people who have hurt us.

The psalm also reminds us that we must not only trust God in our hearts. We also have to proclaim God's goodness to others. Sometimes we do that in words (telling others how God rescued us from our difficulties). Sometimes we do it by giving good example, e.g., remaining calm and trusting in the midst of serious troubles.

(Remember, we are celebrating the birth of a man who died as a martyr to give witness to God's justice and righteousness.)

℟. **Since my mother's womb, you have been my strength.**

In you, O Lord, I take refuge;
  let me never be put to shame.
In your justice rescue me, and deliver me;
  incline your ear to me, and save me.

℟. **Since my mother's womb, you have been my strength.**

Be my rock of refuge,
  a stronghold to give me safety,
  for you are my rock and my fortress.
O my God, rescue me from the hand of the wicked.

℟. **Since my mother's womb, you have been my strength.**

For you are my hope, O Lord;
  my trust, O Lord, from my youth.
On you I depend from birth;
  from my mother's womb you are my strength.

℟. **Since my mother's womb, you have been my strength.**

My mouth shall declare your justice,
  day by day your salvation.
O God, you have taught me from my youth,
  and till the present I proclaim your wondrous deeds.

℟. **Since my mother's womb, you have been my strength.**

Lect. No. 586 **SECOND READING: 1 Peter 1:8-12**

The Second Reading continues the theme of God having established a plan for our salvation, which he has accomplished through the mediation of first his messengers and then

A reading from the first Letter of Saint Peter

Beloved:
Although you have not seen Jesus Christ you love him;

the death and resurrection of his only Son.

These messengers (such as John the Baptist) were not proclaiming their message on their own authority. They were not serving themselves. They were being guided by the action of the Holy Spirit.

Saint Peter speaks of how this message of salvation was now available to the Christians to whom he was writing. They had not seen Jesus as he had, and yet they believed. This was all part of God's plan, and it was now being fulfilled in their midst.

This reading reminds us that God has a plan for our faith life as well. Things that occur in our life are not just coincidences; they are God's way of calling us to his life and his love.

even though you do not see him now yet believe in him,
you rejoice with an indescribable and glorious joy,
as you attain the goal of your faith, the salvation of your souls.

Concerning this salvation,
prophets who prophesied about the grace that was to be yours
searched and investigated it,
investigating the time and circumstances
that the Spirit of Christ within them indicated
when he testified in advance
to the sufferings destined for Christ
and the glories to follow them.
It was revealed to them that they were serving not themselves but you
with regard to the things that have now been announced to you
by those who preached the Good News to you
through the Holy Spirit sent from heaven,
things into which angels longed to look.

The word of the Lord.

| Lect. |
| No. 586 |

ALLELUIA: cf. John 1:7; Lk 1:17

The words of the Alleluia Verse are taken from the Prologue of John's Gospel. They remind us of the role of the Baptist: to give witness to Jesus, the true light of the world.

℟. **Alleluia, alleluia.**

He came to testify to the light,
to prepare a people fit for the Lord.
℟. **Alleluia, alleluia.**

| Lect. |
| No. 586 |

GOSPEL: Luke 1:5-17

The Gospel reading speaks of the annunciation given to Zechariah that Elizabeth, his wife, would bear a son.

A reading from the holy Gospel according to Luke

In the days of Herod, King of Judea,
there was a priest named Zechariah
of the priestly division of Abijah;

We hear that Elizabeth was elderly and barren. The way that this passage is phrased reminds us of the story of Sarah and Abraham, how they were elderly and without children and yet God intervened on their behalf.

Zechariah was a priest in the clan of Abijah. There were so many priests that they would come to worship in the temple only once every twenty-four weeks.

Then, while they were there, they would toss dice to see which of them was to perform the actual morning or evening sacrifice.

Zechariah had entered a portion of the temple that was intended only for the priests and levites. It was not easily visible to the crowd praying in the next courtyard.

The angel appears to him and announces that his wife would have a son. Zechariah was to name him John (a name that means "Yahweh is merciful") and was to make sure that he would not drink wine or other strong drinks (a sign that he was to be a Nazirite, one totally dedicated to the service of the Lord).

The child was also to be filled with the power of Elijah, for he would be the fulfillment of the prophecy that Elijah would come back to bring the people of Israel back to the Lord.

his wife was from the daughters of Aaron,
and her name was Elizabeth.
Both were righteous in the eyes of God,
observing all the commandments
and ordinances of the Lord blamelessly.
But they had no child, because Elizabeth was barren
and both were advanced in years.
Once when he was serving
as priest in his division's turn before God,
according to the practice of the priestly service,
he was chosen by lot
to enter the sanctuary of the Lord to burn incense.
Then, when the whole assembly of the people was
praying outside
at the hour of the incense offering,
the angel of the Lord appeared to him,
standing at the right of the altar of incense.
Zechariah was troubled by what he saw, and fear
came upon him.
But the angel said to him, "Do not be afraid, Zechariah,
because your prayer has been heard.
Your wife Elizabeth will bear you a son,
and you shall name him John.
And you will have joy and gladness,
and many will rejoice at his birth,
for he will be great in the sight of the Lord.
John will drink neither wine nor strong drink.
He will be filled with the Holy Spirit even from his
mother's womb,
and he will turn many of the children of Israel
to the Lord their God.
He will go before him in the spirit and power of Elijah
to turn their hearts toward their children
and the disobedient to the understanding of the
righteous,
to prepare a people fit for the Lord."

The Gospel of the Lord.

June 24, 2018
THE NATIVITY OF ST. JOHN THE BAPTIST AT THE MASS DURING THE DAY

Lect. No. 587

FIRST READING: Isaiah 49:1-6

Today is one of those rare occasions when the feast day of a saint replaces the normal Sunday readings and prayers.

The First Reading is taken from the second part of the Book of the Prophet Isaiah (the part written by an anonymous prophet during the Babylonian exile, 587-539 B.C.).

It is one of the songs of the Suffering Servant. It was not clear who that servant was intended to be, but Jesus applied these prophecies to himself.

Today they are applied to John the Baptist, for as a predecessor of Jesus, he mirrored many of the qualities of Jesus.

In this reading we hear of how the servant was chosen from before his birth (remember the story of the annunciation made to Zechariah in the temple).

He brings Israel back to the LORD (a good description of John's ministry). At the end of the reading we even hear that his ministry would extend beyond Israel.

A reading from the Book of the Prophet Isaiah

Hear me, O coastlands
    listen, O distant peoples.
The LORD called me from birth,
    from my mother's womb he gave me my name.
He made of me a sharp-edged sword
    and concealed me in the shadow of his arm.
He made me a polished arrow,
    in his quiver he hid me.
You are my servant, he said to me,
    Israel, through whom I show my glory.

Though I thought I had toiled in vain,
    and for nothing, uselessly, spent my strength,
yet my reward is with the LORD,
    my recompense is with my God.
For now the LORD has spoken
    who formed me as his servant from the womb,
that Jacob may be brought back to him
    and Israel gathered to him;
and I am made glorious in the sight of the LORD,
    and my God is now my strength!
It is too little, he says, for you to be my servant,
    to raise up the tribes of Jacob,
    and restore the survivors of Israel;
I will make you a light to the nations,
    that my salvation may reach to the ends of the earth.

The word of the Lord.

Lect. No. 587 **RESPONSORIAL PSALM: Ps 139:1-3, 13-14, 14-15 (℟.: 14a)**

The Responsorial Psalm continues the theme begun in the First Reading, that John the Baptist was chosen by God from before his birth.

God has a plan for each of us. In various passages of the New Testament, we hear that our names were written in the book of life even before we were conceived.

In Romans Paul speaks of how God brings that choice to completion.

We will only find true joy when we discern God's will and embrace it with our whole will.

Furthermore, we must remember that there is no part of our life that is unknown to God. All that we have and all that we are must be lived in him.

℟. **I praise you for I am wonderfully made.**

O LORD, you have probed me and you know me;
    you know when I sit and when I stand;
    you understand my thoughts from afar.
My journeys and my rest you scrutinize,
    with all my ways you are familiar.

℟. **I praise you for I am wonderfully made.**

Truly you have formed my inmost being;
    you knit me in my mother's womb.
I give you thanks that I am fearfully, wonderfully
        made;
    wonderful are your works.

℟. **I praise you for I am wonderfully made.**

My soul also you knew full well;
    nor was my frame unknown to you
when I was made in secret,
    when I was fashioned in the depths of the earth.

℟. **I praise you for I am wonderfully made.**

PASTORAL REFLECTIONS

There is a certain difficulty in saying that Jesus was a cousin of John the Baptist. Jesus came from the tribe of Judah, while John's father was a priest and he therefore belonged to the tribe of Levi. We do not believe that there was intermarriage between tribes.

Luke is the only Gospel that speaks of this familial relationship. In John's Gospel, the Baptist says that he did not know Jesus (or recognize him). We cannot fully resolve this difficulty; we have to admit that we do not know everything.

Lect. No. 587

SECOND READING: Acts 13:22-26

In this reading, we hear a proclamation of the kerygma (the teachings of the early Church) made to a mostly Jewish audience. This would explain the reference to David and Jesse and Israel throughout the passage.

John the Baptist, the last of the prophets, is also mentioned. It speaks of how John proclaimed a baptism of repentance.

Remember, the difference between John's baptism and Christian Baptism is that John's baptism was one of repentance, while Christian Baptism is one of repentance and reception of the Holy Spirit that makes us children of God.

Furthermore, even John the Baptist gave witness that he was not the Messiah. He spoke of Jesus as the Lamb of God who takes away the sins of the world, while he gave witness that he was not even worthy to untie his sandals.

A reading from the Acts of the Apostles

In those days, Paul said:
"God raised up David as their king;
of him he testified,
I have found David, son of Jesse, a man after my own heart;
he will carry out my every wish.
From this man's descendants God, according to his promise,
has brought to Israel a savior, Jesus.
John heralded his coming by proclaiming a baptism of repentance
to all the people of Israel;
and as John was completing his course, he would say,
'What do you suppose that I am? I am not he.
Behold, one is coming after me;
I am not worthy to unfasten the sandals of his feet.'

"My brothers, children of the family of Abraham,
and those others among you who are God-fearing,
to us this word of salvation has been sent."

The word of the Lord.

Lect. No. 587

ALLELUIA: cf. Luke 1:76

The Alleluia Verse is taken from the Benedictus, the hymn that Zechariah sang when he celebrated the birth of his son, John the Baptist.

℟. **Alleluia, alleluia.**

You, child, will be called prophet of the Most High, for you will go before the Lord to prepare his way.

℟. **Alleluia, alleluia.**

Lect.
No. 587

The Gospel tells of the birth of John the Baptist. Many of the elements that one would expect to find in the Gospel of Luke are found throughout this account (e.g., emphasis upon the mercy of God, a response of joy, the fulfillment of all of God's promises, etc.).

The family intends to name the baby after his father, Zechariah. Elizabeth, on the other hand, insists that the child be named John ("Yohanan" in Hebrew), the name revealed by the angel Gabriel.

This name means that Yahweh is merciful, and John's entire ministry will proclaim this truth. He expresses that mercy by calling Israel back to her Lord.

Although Zechariah is unable to speak, he insists on giving the child the name John by writing it on a tablet. The period of his silence comes to an end at that very moment.

Although it is not contained in today's passage, Zechariah immediately praises God for his faithfulness to his promises in the hymn called the Benedictus, which begins with the words, "Blessed be the Lord, the God of Israel, for he has come to his people and set them free."

GOSPEL: Luke 1:57-66, 80

A reading from the holy Gospel according to Luke

When the time arrived for Elizabeth to have her child
    she gave birth to a son.
Her neighbors and relatives heard
    that the Lord had shown his great mercy toward her,
    and they rejoiced with her.
When they came on the eighth day to circumcise the child,
    they were going to call him Zechariah after his father,
    but his mother said in reply,
    "No. He will be called John."
But they answered her,
    "There is no one among your relatives who has this name."
So they made signs, asking his father what he wished him to be called.
He asked for a tablet and wrote, "John is his name,"
    and all were amazed.
Immediately his mouth was opened, his tongue freed,
    and he spoke blessing God.
Then fear came upon all their neighbors,
    and all these matters were discussed
    throughout the hill country of Judea.
All who heard these things took them to heart, saying,
    "What, then, will this child be?"
For surely the hand of the Lord was with him.

The child grew and became strong in spirit,
    and he was in the desert until the day
    of his manifestation to Israel.

The Gospel of the Lord.

July 1, 2018

THIRTEENTH SUNDAY IN ORDINARY TIME

Lect. No. 98 **FIRST READING: Wisdom 1:13-15; 2:23-24**

The Book of Wisdom addresses one of the most difficult questions that has troubled philosophers: How could a good God allow suffering and death?

The answer given here is that God did not send these things into the world. They are the result of sin.

There is a rabbinic saying that "as the sin, so the punishment." Sin is a participation in death, for it is a choice against life. Therefore, the appropriate punishment for sin is to taste the consequences of what one has chosen when one sins: suffering and death.

What is true in one's own soul is seen to be true in one's body as well.

A reading from the Book of Wisdom

God did not make death,
nor does he rejoice in the destruction of the living.
For he fashioned all things that they might have being;
and the creatures of the world are wholesome,
and there is not a destructive drug among them
nor any domain of the netherworld on earth,
for justice is undying.
For God formed man to be imperishable;
the image of his own nature he made him.
But by the envy of the devil, death entered the world,
and they who belong to his company experience it.

The word of the Lord.

Lect. No. 98 **RESPONSORIAL PSALM: Ps 30:2, 4, 5-6, 11, 12, 13 (℟.: 2a)**

The First Reading and the Gospel speak of the gift of life that God gave to his beloved creatures. The first passage of this psalm expresses that same theme. God protected us from our enemies and preserved us from death, from going down into the netherworld.

℟. **I will praise you, Lord, for you have rescued me.**

I will extol you, O LORD, for you drew me clear
and did not let my enemies rejoice over me.
O LORD, you brought me up from the netherworld;
you preserved me from among those going down into the pit.

℟. **I will praise you, Lord, for you have rescued me.**

The second part of the psalm again praises the LORD, but this time for the fact that his anger does not last forever. Can we truly say that God becomes angry at us if we sin? A more accurate way of saying it would be to say that God becomes angry for us. He hates the poison that is destroying the life and love of his beloved children. That poison is sin and the loneliness that it brings, but God's ultimate purpose is always to bring us joy and life to the fullest.

Sing praise to the LORD, you his faithful ones,
　　and give thanks to his holy name.
For his anger lasts but a moment;
　　a lifetime, his good will.
At nightfall, weeping enters in,
　　but with the dawn, rejoicing.

℟. **I will praise you, Lord, for you have rescued me.**

Hear, O LORD, and have pity on me;
　　O LORD, be my helper.
You changed my mourning into dancing;
　　O LORD, my God, forever will I give you thanks.

℟. **I will praise you, Lord, for you have rescued me.**

Lect.
No. 98

SECOND READING: 2 Corinthians 8:7, 9, 13-15

This chapter in the Second Letter to the Corinthians deals with the collection that Saint Paul was organizing to assist the poor in the Church of Jerusalem. This Christian community was much poorer than other Christian communities. He collected funds from all over Asia Minor and Greece. In a sense, this was a continuation of the temple tax, that is, the money that Jews would send to the temple from wherever they lived.

In taking up this collection, he was reminding the members of the community of the example of Jesus. Although Jesus was God and therefore had every right to exercise his divine prerogatives, he became poor for our sake. Should we not be willing to share some of what we have in excess with those who do not have enough?

A reading from the second Letter of Saint Paul to the Corinthians

Brothers and sisters:
As you excel in every respect, in faith, discourse, knowledge, all earnestness, and in the love we have for you,
may you excel in this gracious act also.

For you know the gracious act of our Lord Jesus Christ,
　　that though he was rich, for your sake he became poor,
　　so that by his poverty you might become rich.
Not that others should have relief while you are burdened,
　　but that as a matter of equality
　　your abundance at the present time should supply their needs,
　　so that their abundance may also supply your needs,
　　that there may be equality.

Tertullian, one of the early Church Fathers, taught that those things that we have in excess should be considered to have been robbed from the poor.

As it is written:
Whoever had much did not have more,
*   and whoever had little did not have less.*

The word of the Lord.

Lect.
No. 98

ALLELUIA: cf. 2 Timothy 1:10

The Alleluia Verse continues the theme that Jesus has conquered death and restored life. Through his death he has destroyed spiritual and physical death forever.

℟. **Alleluia, alleluia.**

Our Savior Jesus Christ destroyed death
and brought life to light through the Gospel.

℟. **Alleluia, alleluia.**

Lect.
No. 98

GOSPEL: A Longer Form: Mark 5:21-43

In the ancient world, there were three different types of miracles: nature miracles, exorcisms, and healings. At the end of chapter 4, there was an account of Jesus calming the storm at sea. This would be considered a nature miracle. At the beginning of chapter 5, there is an account of a great exorcism (for the man had been possessed by Legion, a name that implies many demons). Finally, at the end of chapter 5 we hear the healing story.

There are, in fact, two healings. The smaller healing is that of the woman with the hemorrhage, and the larger one the raising of the daughter of Jairus from the dead.

Illness was considered to be a foretaste of death, so we could say that Jesus saved

A reading from the holy Gospel according to Mark

When Jesus had crossed again in the boat
    to the other side,
a large crowd gathered around him, and he stayed
    close to the sea.
One of the synagogue officials, named Jairus, came
    forward.
Seeing him he fell at his feet and pleaded earnestly
    with him, saying,
"My daughter is at the point of death.
Please, come lay your hands on her
    that she may get well and live."
He went off with him,
    and a large crowd followed him and pressed upon
    him.

There was a woman afflicted with hemorrhages for
    twelve years.
She had suffered greatly at the hands of many doctors
and had spent all that she had.

this woman and girl from the smaller and the larger deaths.

Mark put these miracles together to show us that Jesus had the power to do all things. This was to show how strange the reaction to him was by the people in Nazareth. (We will hear that Gospel next Sunday.)

This account begins with Jairus approaching Jesus and asking him for a favor. His daughter was dying, and he asked Jesus to intervene and heal her.

While Jesus was on his way, he passed a woman who had been ill with a hemorrhage for twelve years. This is most probably a reference to the menstrual flow.

This was something that would have made her unclean according to Jewish law. She was thus excluded from full participation in the life of the community.

The woman takes the initiative and touches the hem of Jesus' clothes. She is immediately healed.

The miracle is described in rather primitive terms, almost as if the power going out of Jesus was some sort of static electricity. The dialogue that follows makes it clear that it is not so much Jesus who healed her as her faith in Jesus.

On the way to Jairus' house, Jesus is told that the girl has already died. He nevertheless continues his pursuit. When he

Yet she was not helped but only grew worse.

She had heard about Jesus and came up behind him in the crowd
  and touched his cloak.

She said, "If I but touch his clothes, I shall be cured."

Immediately her flow of blood dried up.

She felt in her body that she was healed of her affliction.

Jesus, aware at once that power had gone out from him,
  turned around in the crowd and asked, "Who has touched my clothes?"

But his disciples said to Jesus,
  "You see how the crowd is pressing upon you,
  and yet you ask, 'Who touched me?'"

And he looked around to see who had done it.

The woman, realizing what had happened to her,
  approached in fear and trembling.

She fell down before Jesus and told him the whole truth.

He said to her, "Daughter, your faith has saved you.

Go in peace and be cured of your affliction."

While he was still speaking,
  people from the synagogue official's house arrived and said,
  "Your daughter has died; why trouble the teacher any longer?"

Disregarding the message that was reported,
  Jesus said to the synagogue official,
  "Do not be afraid; just have faith."

He did not allow anyone to accompany him inside
  except Peter, James, and John, the brother of James.

When they arrived at the house of the synagogue official,
  he caught sight of a commotion,
  people weeping and wailing loudly.

arrives, he encounters people ritually weeping for the dead girl.

One can discern the depth of their emotional involvement by the fact that they burst out laughing when Jesus says that the child is only sleeping.

There is a true simplicity to Jesus' comment, almost as if he sees something that the others cannot even understand. He raises the child from the dead and orders that she be given something to eat.

The crowd responds with awe. Jesus then orders them not to tell anyone (which he consistently does in this Gospel, for he is always trying to conceal his being the Messiah).

So he went in and said to them,
    "Why this commotion and weeping?
The child is not dead but asleep."
And they ridiculed him.
Then he put them all out.
He took along the child's father and mother
    and those who were with him
    and entered the room where the child was.
He took the child by the hand and said to her, *"Talitha koum,"*
    which means, "Little girl, I say to you, arise!"
The girl, a child of twelve, arose immediately and
    walked around.
At that they were utterly astounded.
He gave strict orders that no one should know this
    and said that she should be given something to
    eat.
The Gospel of the Lord.

<table><tr><td>Lect.
No. 98</td></tr></table>

GOSPEL: B Shorter Form: Mark 5:21-24, 35b-43

In the ancient world, there were three different types of miracles: nature miracles, exorcisms, and healings. At the end of chapter 4, there was an account of Jesus calming the storm at sea. This would be considered a nature miracle. At the beginning of chapter 5, there is an account of a great exorcism (for the man had been possessed by Legion, a name that implies many demons). Finally, at the end of chapter 5 we hear the healing story.

Mark put these miracles together to show us that Jesus had the power to do all things. This was to show how strange

A reading from the holy Gospel according to Mark

When Jesus had crossed again in the boat
    to the other side,
    a large crowd gathered around him, and he stayed
    close to the sea.
One of the synagogue officials, named Jairus, came
    forward.
Seeing him he fell at his feet and pleaded earnestly
    with him, saying,
    "My daughter is at the point of death.
Please, come lay your hands on her
    that she may get well and live."
He went off with him,
    and a large crowd followed him and pressed upon
    him.

the reaction to him was by the people in Nazareth. (We will hear that Gospel next Sunday.)

This account begins with Jairus approaching Jesus and asking him for a favor. His daughter was dying, and he asked Jesus to intervene and heal her.

On the way to Jairus' house, Jesus is told that the girl has already died. He nevertheless continues his pursuit. When he arrives, he encounters people ritually weeping for the dead girl.

One can discern the depth of their emotional involvement by the fact that they burst out laughing when Jesus says that the child is only sleeping.

There is a true simplicity to Jesus' comment, almost as if he sees something that the others cannot even understand. He raises the child from the dead and orders that she be given something to eat.

The crowd responds with awe. Jesus then orders them not to tell anyone (which he consistently does in this Gospel, for he is always trying to conceal the fact that he is the Messiah).

While he was still speaking,
　people from the synagogue official's house arrived and said,
　"Your daughter has died; why trouble the teacher any longer?"
Disregarding the message that was reported,
　Jesus said to the synagogue official,
　"Do not be afraid; just have faith."
He did not allow anyone to accompany him inside
　except Peter, James, and John, the brother of James.
When they arrived at the house of the synagogue official,
　he caught sight of a commotion,
　people weeping and wailing loudly.
So he went in and said to them,
　"Why this commotion and weeping?
The child is not dead but asleep."
And they ridiculed him.
Then he put them all out.
He took along the child's father and mother
　and those who were with him
　and entered the room where the child was.
He took the child by the hand and said to her, *"Talitha koum,"*
　which means, "Little girl, I say to you, arise!"
The girl, a child of twelve, arose immediately and walked around.
At that they were utterly astounded.
He gave strict orders that no one should know this
　and said that she should be given something to eat.

The Gospel of the Lord.

July 8, 2018

FOURTEENTH SUNDAY IN ORDINARY TIME

Lect. No. 101 **FIRST READING: Ezekiel 2:2-5**

The First Reading begins this Sunday's theme: that God has sent his Word to Israel (in the Old Testament through the prophets and in the New Testament through the person of Jesus), but his own people did not want to listen. They were obstinate, and they preferred to live in their ignorance.

This was certainly not innocent ignorance. They were not ignorant because they did not know any better, but because they had chosen to ignore what they should have seen and understood.

They had received a prophet, but they had decided to dismiss him and his message as irrelevant.

A reading from the Book of the Prophet Ezekiel

As the Lord spoke to me, the spirit entered into me
and set me on my feet,
and I heard the one who was speaking say to me:
Son of man, I am sending you to the Israelites,
rebels who have rebelled against me;
they and their ancestors have revolted against me
   to this very day.
Hard of face and obstinate of heart
   are they to whom I am sending you.
But you shall say to them: Thus says the Lord God!
And whether they heed or resist—for they are a rebellious house—
   they shall know that a prophet has been among
   them.

The word of the Lord.

Lect. No. 101 **RESPONSORIAL PSALM: Ps 123:1-2, 2, 3-4 (℟.: 2cd)**

The verses found in the Responsorial Psalm contrast with the attitude found in the First Reading and the Gospel. In those two readings we encounter an attitude of obstinacy and arrogance. In this psalm, we find an attitude of hopeful expectation and humble submission.

We beg for pity from God. We cannot demand our rights or

℟. **Our eyes are fixed on the Lord, pleading for his mercy.**

To you I lift up my eyes
   who are enthroned in heaven—
as the eyes of servants
   are on the hands of their masters.

℟. **Our eyes are fixed on the Lord, pleading for his mercy.**

argue that we have somehow been unjustly condemned. We are sinners, and we deserve to be condemned. Yet God has been merciful to us and does not hold our guilt against us.

This should produce a willingness to approach God with tremendous humility. We should be ready to hear God's voice when he calls to us and see the signs of his presence in our midst (whether these signs be mighty signs of power or humble everyday events).

As the eyes of a maid
     are on the hands of her mistress,
so are our eyes on the Lord, our God,
     till he have pity on us.

    ℟. **Our eyes are fixed on the Lord, pleading for his mercy.**

Have pity on us, O Lord, have pity on us,
     for we are more than sated with contempt;
our souls are more than sated
     with the mockery of the arrogant,
     with the contempt of the proud.

    ℟. **Our eyes are fixed on the Lord, pleading for his mercy.**

Lect. No. 101

SECOND READING: 2 Corinthians 12:7-10

In this passage from the latter part of the Second Letter to the Corinthians, we hear of how Saint Paul was tormented by a "thorn in the flesh." It is not clear whether this was a physical or a spiritual difficulty. Whichever, it was not taken away even though Paul requested this of God. Paul would have to rely upon God's strength and not his own efforts.

There are times that the Lord allows us to remain in our weakness to remind us that we must always rely upon him. This is troubling, for we would all like to be as perfect as possible. Yet, God sometimes leads us to a greater holiness by teaching us to surrender to God's will (and therefore our constant need of God's strength).

A reading from the second Letter of Saint Paul to the Corinthians

Brothers and sisters:
   That I, Paul, might not become too elated,
     because of the abundance of the revelations,
     a thorn in the flesh was given to me, an angel of Satan,
     to beat me, to keep me from being too elated.
Three times I begged the Lord about this, that it
     might leave me,
     but he said to me, "My grace is sufficient for you,
     for power is made perfect in weakness."
I will rather boast most gladly of my weaknesses,
     in order that the power of Christ may dwell with me.
Therefore, I am content with weaknesses, insults,
     hardships, persecutions, and constraints,
     for the sake of Christ;
     for when I am weak, then I am strong.

The word of the Lord.

Lect.
No. 101

ALLELUIA: cf. Luke 4:18

The Alleluia Verse repeats the proclamation that Jesus made in the Gospel of Luke when he entered the synagogue of Nazareth to preach.

℟. **Alleluia, alleluia.**

The Spirit of the Lord is upon me
for he sent me to bring glad tidings to the poor.

℟. **Alleluia, alleluia.**

Lect.
No. 101

GOSPEL: Mark 6:1-6

As we saw last week, Saint Mark established a pattern in chapters 4 and 5 to show that Jesus could perform any type of miracle (nature, exorcism, and healing). Jesus could "do it all."

Then, at the beginning of chapter 6, Jesus enters the synagogue in his hometown. One would have expected the townspeople to be filled with joy and pride. Instead, they are unwilling to accept him.

They knew him too well and refused to believe that he could be more than what they expected him to be. They were guilty of choosing to be obtuse and lacking in faith.

The phrase "brothers and sisters of Jesus" probably refers to his cousins.

There is another theory, though, that Joseph had been married and widowed before he was betrothed to Mary (and thus the brothers and sisters might be half-brothers and sisters).

A reading from the holy Gospel according to Mark

Jesus departed from there and came to his native place, accompanied by his disciples.
When the sabbath came he began to teach in the synagogue,
and many who heard him were astonished.
They said, "Where did this man get all this?
What kind of wisdom has been given him?
What mighty deeds are wrought by his hands!
Is he not the carpenter, the son of Mary,
and the brother of James and Joses and Judas and Simon?
And are not his sisters here with us?"
And they took offense at him.
Jesus said to them,
"A prophet is not without honor except in his native place
and among his own kin and in his own house."
So he was not able to perform any mighty deed there,
apart from curing a few sick people by laying his hands on them.
He was amazed at their lack of faith.

The Gospel of the Lord.

July 15, 2018

FIFTEENTH SUNDAY IN ORDINARY TIME

Lect.
No. 104 **FIRST READING: Amos 7:12-15**

Amaziah was a priest at the northern shrine of Bethel. He was offended by the idea that Amos, a southerner, would come to his shrine and proclaim a condemnation against his people. He called Amos a "visionary" and told him to go back home.

Amos responded that he was not a professional prophet. He had received most of his material from simply watching life go by and seeing that something was seriously wrong when the poor and defenseless were being exploited by the rich and the powerful.

A reading from the Book of the Prophet Amos

Amaziah, priest of Bethel, said to Amos,
    "Off with you, visionary, flee to the land of
    Judah!
There earn your bread by prophesying,
    but never again prophesy in Bethel;
    for it is the king's sanctuary and a royal temple."
Amos answered Amaziah, "I was no prophet,
    nor have I belonged to a company of prophets;
    I was a shepherd and a dresser of sycamores.
The LORD took me from following the flock, and
        said to me,
Go, prophesy to my people Israel."

The word of the Lord.

Lect.
No. 104 **RESPONSORIAL PSALM: Ps 85:9-10, 11-12, 13-14 (R.: 8)**

The Gospel will speak of how the disciples were sent off to proclaim the Good News to all who would hear. The Responsorial Psalm speaks of what that Good News is and what it produces.

It is a proclamation that God delivers us and saves us. God saves us from all of our enemies. While the psalm speaks of human enemies, our greatest enemies are really those from which Jesus saved us: sin, death, and alienation.

R. **Lord, let us see your kindness, and grant us your salvation.**

I will hear what God proclaims;
    the LORD—for he proclaims peace.
Near indeed is his salvation to those who fear him,
    glory dwelling in our land.

R. **Lord, let us see your kindness, and grant us your salvation.**

Kindness and truth shall meet;
    justice and peace shall kiss.
Truth shall spring out of the earth,
    and justice shall look down from heaven.

When we are liberated from these enemies, we find ourselves in a state of peace. The word peace ("Shalom" in Hebrew) means more than simply a cessation of war.

It means a state of profound goodness and righteousness in which we no longer live in fear or confusion. We find ourselves at home in our God.

℟. **Lord, let us see your kindness, and grant us your salvation.**

The LORD himself will give his benefits;
    our land shall yield its increase.
Justice shall walk before him,
    and prepare the way of his steps.

℟. **Lord, let us see your kindness, and grant us your salvation.**

Lect. No. 104

SECOND READING: 🅰 Longer Form: Ephesians 1:3-14

The Second Reading speaks of the fact that we have been chosen by the Lord to be his own. This is the Christian idea of predestination.

We sometimes misunderstand what this concept means. People often think that it means that everything is preordained and that we somehow lose our free will. This is not the case. Predestination means that God always wanted to invite us into his love.

The reading speaks of us having been chosen by the Lord before the foundation of the world. Even before we existed, God had chosen us by name.

Yet, we can always refuse the invitation. We can choose to sin and thereby choose hate instead of love.

Predestination does not mean that we must choose God—only that we can choose God and his ways because God chose us first.

A reading from the Letter of Saint Paul
to the Ephesians

Blessed be the God and Father of our Lord Jesus Christ,
    who has blessed us in Christ
    with every spiritual blessing in the heavens,
    as he chose us in him, before the foundation of the world,
    to be holy and without blemish before him.
In love he destined us for adoption to himself through Jesus Christ,
    in accord with the favor of his will,
    for the praise of the glory of his grace
    that he granted us in the beloved.

In him we have redemption by his blood,
    the forgiveness of transgressions,
    in accord with the riches of his grace that he lavished upon us.
In all wisdom and insight, he has made known to us
    the mystery of his will in accord with his favor
    that he set forth in him as a plan for the fullness of times,
    to sum up all things in Christ, in heaven and on earth.

God's plan is that all be placed under Christ's headship. Jesus is the fullest expression of what God intends for us, for he is the most complete expression of God's love and of obedience to God's will. Thus, when we live in love and obedience, we are one with Christ.

The Holy Spirit is God's down payment on his promises. The Holy Spirit tells us that we are God's chosen ones. Even before we arrive in heaven, we are already experiencing some of its joys through this revelation.

In him we were also chosen,
    destined in accord with the purpose of the One
    who accomplishes all things according to the intention of his will,
    so that we might exist for the praise of his glory,
    we who first hoped in Christ.
In him you also, who have heard the word of truth,
    the gospel of your salvation, and have believed in him,
    were sealed with the promised Holy Spirit,
    which is the first installment of our inheritance
    toward redemption as God's possession, to the praise of his glory.

The word of the Lord.

Lect. No. 104

SECOND READING: B Shorter Form: Ephesians 1:3-10

The Second Reading speaks of the fact that we have been chosen by the Lord to be his own. This is predestination.

People often think that predestination means that everything is preordained and that we lose our free will. This is not the case. Predestination means that God always wanted to invite us into his love.

The reading speaks of us having been chosen by the Lord before the foundation of the world. Even before we existed, God had chosen us.

Yet, we can always refuse the invitation. We can always choose to sin and thereby choose hate instead of love.

A reading from the Letter of Saint Paul to the Ephesians

Blessed be the God and Father of our Lord Jesus Christ,
    who has blessed us in Christ
    with every spiritual blessing in the heavens,
    as he chose us in him, before the foundation of the world,
    to be holy and without blemish before him.
In love he destined us for adoption to himself through Jesus Christ,
    in accord with the favor of his will,
    for the praise of the glory of God's grace
    that he granted us in the beloved.

In him we have redemption by his blood,
    the forgiveness of transgressions,
    in accord with the riches of his grace that he lavished upon us.

God's plan is that all be placed under Christ's headship. Jesus is the fullest expression of what God intends for us, for he is the most complete expression of God's love and of obedience to God's will. Thus, when we live in love and obedience, we are one with Christ.

In all wisdom and insight, he has made known to us
    the mystery of his will in accord with his favor
    that he set forth in him as a plan for the fullness
        of times,
    to sum up all things in Christ, in heaven and on
        earth.

The word of the Lord.

Lect.
No. 104

ALLELUIA: cf. Ephesians 1:17-18

God has predestined us to share in his love and glory. We ask the Father to reveal this truth to our hearts so that we may respond to his call with generosity. We ask the Holy Spirit to speak those truths to us in the depths of our soul.

℟. **Alleluia, alleluia.**

May the Father of our Lord Jesus Christ
enlighten the eyes of our hearts,
that we may know what is the hope
that belongs to our call.

℟. **Alleluia, alleluia.**

Lect.
No. 104

GOSPEL: Mark 6:7-13

In the past few chapters of the Gospel of Mark we have seen that Jesus had the authority to perform any type of miracle. In this passage we see Jesus pass that authority on to his disciples and send them out to proclaim the good news.

The disciples were not to take much with them. They were to trust in the providence of the Lord, for he would care for them.

If they were welcomed, a blessing would be visited upon those who welcomed them. If those to whom they were preaching rejected them, they

A reading from the holy Gospel according to Mark

Jesus summoned the Twelve and began to send them out two by two
and gave them authority over unclean spirits.
He instructed them to take nothing for the journey
    but a walking stick—
    no food, no sack, no money in their belts.
They were, however, to wear sandals
    but not a second tunic.
He said to them,
    "Wherever you enter a house, stay there until you
        leave.
Whatever place does not welcome you or listen to
        you,
    leave there and shake the dust off your feet
    in testimony against them."

would be cursed (for they would have called a curse upon themselves).

The curse was that they would have chosen not to hear the Good News that the disciples were proclaiming to them.

So they went off and preached repentance.

The Twelve drove out many demons,
   and they anointed with oil many who were sick
   and cured them.

The Gospel of the Lord.

PASTORAL REFLECTIONS

In practical terms, what does trust in God's providence mean for us? Should we sell the house and beg for a living each day? Some people are called to that heroic form of witness, but not everyone. It is prudent to plan for the future. We must feed our families. We should be able to enjoy the good things of this earth.

Yet, at the same time, we have to be careful not to let our possessions possess us. We have to use our blessings to help the poor. We have to recognize that all that we have comes from God. All of us are called to bear witness to our trust in God's providence, but each of us is called to do it in our own way.

July 22, 2018

SIXTEENTH SUNDAY IN ORDINARY TIME

Lect. No. 107 **FIRST READING: Jeremiah 23:1-6**

The major theme we hear in the First Reading today, that God is Israel's shepherd, was a very popular theme just before and during the time of the Babylonian Exile (587-539 B.C.).

The basic idea was that God had given leaders to the people of Israel. They were supposed to have cared for God's people as a shepherd guards his flock, but they had not done this. They had misled them into sinful ways. They had so misguided them that they had led them into ruin.

Now God was going to intervene and rescue his flock from the disaster into which they had fallen. In some of the prophetic passages that have this shepherd imagery, God would gather up the remnant of his people and become their shepherd himself.

In other passages such as today's reading, he would send a chosen one, an anointed one (Messiah), who would lead his flock along the paths of righteousness.

A reading from the Book of the Prophet Jeremiah

Woe to the shepherds
who mislead and scatter the flock of my pasture,
says the LORD.
Therefore, thus says the LORD, the God of Israel,
against the shepherds who shepherd my people:
You have scattered my sheep and driven them
away.
You have not cared for them,
but I will take care to punish your evil deeds.
I myself will gather the remnant of my flock
from all the lands to which I have driven them
and bring them back to their meadow;
there they shall increase and multiply.
I will appoint shepherds for them who will shepherd
them
so that they need no longer fear and tremble;
and none shall be missing, says the LORD.

Behold, the days are coming, says the LORD,
when I will raise up a righteous shoot to David;
as king he shall reign and govern wisely,
he shall do what is just and right in the land.
In his days Judah shall be saved,
Israel shall dwell in security.
This is the name they give him:
"The LORD, our justice."

The word of the Lord.

Lect.
No. 107

RESPONSORIAL PSALM: Ps 23:1-3, 3-4, 5, 6 (℟.: 1)

This beautiful hymn of trust was probably written around the time of the Babylonian Exile (for it uses the same symbolism as found in the First Reading).

It proclaims that God is a shepherd who guides his people carefully and protects them from all dangers. We hear words such as "repose," "restful," and "refreshes." It is obvious that these words are intended to portray a situation that could be described with the Hebrew word "Shalom."

The dark valley in this psalm is actually a valley that is as dark as death. This is a situation that should provoke fear, but God is tapping us with his rod and staff to assure us that he is still there and protecting us from all dangers.

We are so safe that we can sit down and eat a meal in the sight of our foes. Normally, seeing our enemies would cause anxiety and leave us without appetite. With God at our side, we have nothing to fear. When we surrender our fears and anxieties and trust in the providence of God, then we find true peace. When we give up control, we no longer have to worry about how we will get out of our difficulties.

℟. **The Lord is my shepherd; there is nothing I shall want.**

The LORD is my shepherd; I shall not want.
In verdant pastures he gives me repose;
beside restful waters he leads me;
he refreshes my soul.

℟. **The Lord is my shepherd; there is nothing I shall want.**

He guides me in right paths
for his name's sake.
Even though I walk in the dark valley
I fear no evil; for you are at my side
with your rod and your staff
that give me courage.

℟. **The Lord is my shepherd; there is nothing I shall want.**

You spread the table before me
in the sight of my foes;
you anoint my head with oil;
my cup overflows.

℟. **The Lord is my shepherd; there is nothing I shall want.**

Only goodness and kindness follow me
all the days of my life;
and I shall dwell in the house of the LORD
for years to come.

℟. **The Lord is my shepherd; there is nothing I shall want.**

Lect. No. 107

SECOND READING: Ephesians 2:13-18

The Second Reading celebrates the fact that Jesus' death and resurrection have destroyed all of the divisions that separate us from one another.

When God established a covenant with the Jewish people, he was making a choice in their favor. This naturally excluded those who were not Jews.

One group observed the law of God; the other did not even know that law. One group lived in peace with the Lord; the other did not even know his name.

When Jesus died and put to death the alienation caused by our sins, he destroyed every boundary that separated one person from another. We are now one in Christ.

All nations have been chosen and now participate in the peace that Jesus' cross has established.

A reading from the Letter of Saint Paul to the Ephesians

Brothers and sisters:
In Christ Jesus you who once were far off
have become near by the blood of Christ.

For he is our peace, he who made both one
    and broke down the dividing wall of enmity,
        through his flesh,
    abolishing the law with its commandments and
        legal claims,
    that he might create in himself one new person in
        place of the two,
    thus establishing peace,
    and might reconcile both with God,
    in one body, through the cross,
    putting that enmity to death by it.
He came and preached peace to you who were far
        off
    and peace to those who were near,
    for through him we both have access in one Spirit
        to the Father.

The word of the Lord.

Lect. No. 107

ALLELUIA: John 10:27

The Alleluia Verse continues the shepherd theme found in the First Reading and the Gospel. Jesus, our Good Shepherd, knows each of us by name and calls each one of us into his glory.

℟. **Alleluia, alleluia.**

My sheep hear my voice, says the Lord;
I know them, and they follow me.

℟. **Alleluia, alleluia.**

Lect. No. 107

GOSPEL: Mark 6:30-34

Last week we heard how Jesus sent his apostles to proclaim the Good News. They had now returned, and Jesus invited them to go to a deserted spot to rest. Yet the crowd did not let them do this. They desperately needed him.

Jesus could see that they hungered for the truth (that they were like sheep without a shepherd).

This Gospel passage displays the tensions of ministry. While it is good and even necessary to take time out to recharge our batteries, there are situations in which this is impossible. Still, we always have to remember that it is Jesus who is the shepherd (the humility to recognize that we are not the saviors of the world).

A reading from the holy Gospel according to Mark

The apostles gathered together with Jesus
and reported all they had done and taught.
He said to them,
    "Come away by yourselves to a deserted place
      and rest a while."
People were coming and going in great numbers,
    and they had no opportunity even to eat.
So they went off in the boat by themselves to a deserted place.
People saw them leaving and many came to know
    about it.
They hastened there on foot from all the towns
    and arrived at the place before them.

When he disembarked and saw the vast crowd,
    his heart was moved with pity for them,
    for they were like sheep without a shepherd;
    and he began to teach them many things.

The Gospel of the Lord.

PASTORAL REFLECTIONS

Finding the balance in our lives is always difficult. This is true of finding the balance between work and rest, between obligations to our family and those to people outside of our families, between God and those around us, between serving others and preserving a bit of time for recharging our own batteries.

None of us does this perfectly. Just as soon as we think that we have the right balance, something happens to throw it out of balance again (as we saw in today's Gospel). Finding a balance is a lifetime task that needs constant attention and will never be complete.

July 29, 2018

SEVENTEENTH SUNDAY IN ORDINARY TIME

Lect. No. 110 **FIRST READING: 2 Kings 4:42-44**

Elisha the prophet is seen as something of a miracle worker in the accounts of his ministry found in the Second Book of Kings (as opposed to Elijah whose accounts seem more realistic and down to earth). Here he is responsible for a miraculous multiplication of loaves that supplies the need of the one hundred people who were with him.

This is seen as a prefiguring of what Jesus does in the Gospels when he multiplies the loaves and fish to feed over five thousand people who had followed him to listen to his teaching.

A reading from the second Book of Kings

A man came from Baal-shalishah bringing to Elisha, the man of God,
twenty barley loaves made from the firstfruits,
    and fresh grain in the ear.
Elisha said, "Give it to the people to eat."
But his servant objected,
    "How can I set this before a hundred people?"
Elisha insisted, "Give it to the people to eat.
For thus says the LORD,
    'They shall eat and there shall be some left over.'"
And when they had eaten, there was some left over,
    as the LORD had said.

The word of the Lord.

Lect. No. 110 **RESPONSORIAL PSALM: Ps 145:10-11, 15-16, 17-18 (℟.: cf. 16)**

The Responsorial Psalm is a series of verses taken from Psalm 145, a hymn that praises the majesty and bounty of the LORD. This particular psalm is an alphabetic psalm (a psalm in which each verse begins with successive letters of the alphabet).

The reason why we are using this psalm today is obvious. We are celebrating the bounty of our God as seen in the miracle of the multiplication of loaves

℟. **The hand of the Lord feeds us; he answers all our needs.**

Let all your works give you thanks, O LORD,
    and let your faithful ones bless you.
Let them discourse of the glory of your kingdom
    and speak of your might.

℟. **The hand of the Lord feeds us; he answers all our needs.**

The eyes of all look hopefully to you,
    and you give them their food in due season;

301

and fish. This miracle should be understood as symbolic of the many ways in which God cares for us every day of our lives. He cares for us, body and soul, and never withholds his compassion.

This is why the psalm can express such an attitude of profound trust. The Psalmist was sure that the LORD would provide for all of his needs as soon as he would ask.

you open your hand
    and satisfy the desire of every living thing.

℞. **The hand of the Lord feeds us; he answers all our needs.**

The LORD is just in all his ways
    and holy in all his works.
The LORD is near to all who call upon him,
    to all who call upon him in truth.

℞. **The hand of the Lord feeds us; he answers all our needs.**

Lect.
No. 110

SECOND READING: Ephesians 4:1-6

God has invited us to a great dignity in being called his beloved children. He has forgiven our sins and healed our brokenness. Now we must live as if we are saved. We must respond to the love of God and live in that love.

This means that we must adopt a lifestyle that proclaims the mercy of God. We must live with humility and gentleness and patience. We cannot allow superficial differences to create divisions among us.

The Spirit of God is a spirit of unity that binds us together as a family of faith. As with the early Church, people who observe us must be able to remark, "See how Christians love one another."

A reading from the Letter of Saint Paul
to the Ephesians

Brothers and sisters:
I, a prisoner for the Lord,
    urge you to live in a manner worthy of the call
      you have received,
with all humility and gentleness, with patience,
bearing with one another through love,
striving to preserve the unity of the spirit through
      the bond of peace:
one body and one Spirit,
as you were also called to the one hope of your
      call;
one Lord, one faith, one baptism;
one God and Father of all,
    who is over all and through all and in all.

The word of the Lord.

**Lect.
No. 110**

The Alleluia Verse presents Jesus as a great prophet. He truly proclaims in word and deed the greatness of the mercy and love of God.

ALLELUIA: Luke 7:16

℟. **Alleluia, alleluia.**

A great prophet has risen in our midst.
God has visited his people.

℟. **Alleluia, alleluia.**

**Lect.
No. 110**

This Sunday we begin an interruption of the normal pattern of having Gospel passages taken from the Gospel of Mark.

For the next several weeks, the Sundays of Ordinary Time will have their Gospels chosen from the Gospel of John, specifically from chapter 6, which is the Multiplication of Loaves and Fish and then the Discourse on the Bread of Life.

Note that this multiplication takes place around the time of the Passover. It is one of three Passovers found in this Gospel.

John includes this detail to remind us that what is happening in this miracle is connected with what would happen during the next Passover: the Last Supper and the death and resurrection of Christ.

There is a boy who brings Jesus five barley loaves and two fish. Barley is the food of the poor, so this is probably all that the boy possessed. He gives it all to Jesus in an act of great generosity and trust, and

GOSPEL: John 6:1-15

A reading from the holy Gospel according to John

Jesus went across the Sea of Galilee.
A large crowd followed him,
    because they saw the signs he was performing on
        the sick.
Jesus went up on the mountain,
    and there he sat down with his disciples.
The Jewish feast of Passover was near.
When Jesus raised his eyes
    and saw that a large crowd was coming to him,
    he said to Philip,
    "Where can we buy enough food for them to eat?"
He said this to test him,
    because he himself knew what he was going to
        do.
Philip answered him,
    "Two hundred days' wages worth of food would
        not be enough
    for each of them to have a little."
One of his disciples,
    Andrew, the brother of Simon Peter, said to him,
    "There is a boy here who has five barley loaves
        and two fish;
    but what good are these for so many?"
Jesus said, "Have the people recline."
Now there was a great deal of grass in that place.

Jesus transforms it into something even greater.

There is much grass in this place, for Jesus is our Good Shepherd who leads us to verdant pastures where he gives us repose.

Jesus gives thanks ("eucharistein" in Greek to remind us of the Eucharist). The fragments are also gathered. (This phrase was used in the liturgy of the Eucharist in those days.)

This Gospel strongly emphasizes the fact that this is a prefiguring of the Sacrament of the Eucharist.

There are twelve baskets with fragments, enough to feed all of the tribes of Israel, just as the Eucharist nourishes all the tribes of the new Israel, the Church.

So the men reclined, about five thousand in number.
Then Jesus took the loaves, gave thanks,
    and distributed them to those who were reclining,
    and also as much of the fish as they wanted.
When they had had their fill, he said to his disciples,
    "Gather the fragments left over,
    so that nothing will be wasted."
So they collected them,
    and filled twelve wicker baskets with fragments
    from the five barley loaves
    that had been more than they could eat.
When the people saw the sign he had done, they said,
    "This is truly the Prophet, the one who is to come into the world."
Since Jesus knew that they were going to come and carry him off
    to make him king,
    he withdrew again to the mountain alone.

The Gospel of the Lord.

PASTORAL REFLECTIONS

The multiplication of loaves and fish has sometimes been described as being a social miracle: that Jesus shared all the food that he had and people were impressed by his generosity and they shared all the food that they had. This is a beautiful story, but it is not what is found in this Gospel account.

This is a nature miracle—one in which Jesus changes the rules of nature. This idea is reinforced by the fact that Jesus goes out for a walk on the Sea of Galilee in the next passage of the Gospel and he then calms a storm—both of which are also nature miracles. Miracles can and do happen, both in Jesus' day and our own.

Lect. No. 113 **FIRST READING: Exodus 16:2-4, 12-15**

The Israelite community shows a remarkable lack of gratitude toward the Lord who saved them from their slavery in Egypt. No matter how many times they were rescued from their dangers, they refused to trust in God. Yet, in spite of their ingratitude, God continued to bless them with signs of his love.

When they did not have anything to eat, God gave them bread in the desert in the form of manna and quail from the skies for meat.

The manna was not exactly bread. The way that the text describes it, it seems as if it was something that resembled a small seed. The Israelites would gather it and grind it to make a flour from which they would make bread.

The Israelites would gather only enough of it for the next day (with the exception of the Sabbath before which they would gather double the amount so that they would not have to work on the Sabbath).

In spite of this further sign of God's goodness, the Israelites continued to respond with ingratitude, for they eventually

A reading from the Book of Exodus

The whole Israelite community grumbled against Moses and Aaron.
The Israelites said to them,
"Would that we had died at the LORD's hand in the land of Egypt,
as we sat by our fleshpots and ate our fill of bread!
But you had to lead us into this desert
to make the whole community die of famine!"

Then the LORD said to Moses,
"I will now rain down bread from heaven for you.
Each day the people are to go out and gather their daily portion;
thus will I test them,
to see whether they follow my instructions or not.

"I have heard the grumbling of the Israelites.
Tell them: In the evening twilight you shall eat flesh,
and in the morning you shall have your fill of bread,
so that you may know that I, the LORD, am your God."

In the evening quail came up and covered the camp.
In the morning a dew lay all about the camp,
and when the dew evaporated, there on the surface of the desert
were fine flakes like hoarfrost on the ground.
On seeing it, the Israelites asked one another, "What is this?"
for they did not know what it was.

tired of this food and murmured against God.

But Moses told them,
  "This is the bread that the LORD has given you to eat."

The word of the Lord.

Lect. No. 113

RESPONSORIAL PSALM: Ps 78:3-4, 23-24, 25, 54 (℟.: 24b)

There is a tremendous sense of gratitude in this psalm, which contrasts well with the lack of gratitude expressed by the Israelites in the desert. The psalmist takes upon himself the responsibility of recounting the wonderful things that God did for our ancestors, and giving thanks to God for those wonderful deeds.

God is still working in our midst today. We see God's fingerprints in the many ways that God has guided us in the past. We still see God acting through the events of our everyday lives. Sometimes God intervenes in a powerful way, but most often God's interventions are subtle (but no less loving).

℟. **The Lord gave them bread from heaven.**

What we have heard and know,
  and what our fathers have declared to us,
we will declare to the generation to come,
  the glorious deeds of the LORD and his strength
  and the wonders that he wrought.

℟. **The Lord gave them bread from heaven.**

He commanded the skies above
  and opened the doors of heaven;
he rained manna upon them for food
  and gave them heavenly bread.

℟. **The Lord gave them bread from heaven.**

Man ate the bread of angels,
  food he sent them in abundance.
And he brought them to his holy land,
  to the mountains his right hand had won.

℟. **The Lord gave them bread from heaven.**

Lect. No. 113

SECOND READING: Ephesians 4:17, 20-24

Being a Christian means that we have to put aside the "old way" of acting. We have accepted a certain way of looking at things, a way that was taught by Christ. We cannot selfishly think just of ourselves, nor can

A reading from the Letter of Saint Paul to the Ephesians

Brothers and sisters:
  I declare and testify in the Lord
that you must no longer live as the Gentiles do,
in the futility of their minds;

we treat others with a lack of respect. We must try to see the world through God's eyes.

In order to do this, we must be willing to practice a certain amount of discipline. The pagans were famous for giving in to their most carnal desires. This did not free them; it simply made them slaves to their passions. True freedom is only possible when one lives in God's righteousness and holiness.

that is not how you learned Christ,

assuming that you have heard of him and were taught in him,

as truth is in Jesus,

that you should put away the old self of your former way of life,

corrupted through deceitful desires,

and be renewed in the spirit of your minds,

and put on the new self,

created in God's way in righteousness and holiness of truth.

The word of the Lord.

Lect. No. 113

Today's Alleluia Verse reminds us that the physical nourishment that God provides is not as important as the spiritual nourishment of his Word.

ALLELUIA: Matthew 4:4b

℟. **Alleluia, alleluia.**

One does not live on bread alone,

but on every word that comes forth from the mouth of God.

℟. **Alleluia, alleluia.**

Lect. No. 113

Last week we heard about the miraculous multiplication of five loaves of barley bread and two fish into enough food to nourish over five thousand people. After the five thousand had eaten their fill, the disciples gathered up the fragments that were left over, filling twelve baskets (enough for the twelve tribes of Israel).

The disciples got into their boats and were crossing the lake when Jesus came to them, walking on the water.

GOSPEL: John 6:24-35

A reading from the holy Gospel according to John

When the crowd saw that neither Jesus nor his disciples were there,

they themselves got into boats

and came to Capernaum looking for Jesus.

And when they found him across the sea they said to him,

"Rabbi, when did you get here?"

Jesus answered them and said,

"Amen, amen, I say to you,

you are looking for me not because you saw signs

but because you ate the loaves and were filled.

The next day those who were following Jesus crossed to the other side to see where he had gone.

Jesus accuses them of not truly seeking him, but rather seeking signs (miracles). They just wanted to see him do marvelous deeds, but they did not want to change their lives.

The account speaks of bread that comes down from heaven. During the exodus from Egypt to Israel, that bread was manna.

However, Jesus is the new bread from heaven. He is the true source of spiritual nourishment that will satisfy the deepest hunger of our hearts. In this part of the discourse, Jesus is presenting himself as the wisdom of God.

In the Old Testament, Wisdom was said to have prepared a meal for those who needed instruction. Those who would eat her bread and drink her wine would have life eternal. Jesus instructed the people; he was and is the source of eternal life.

Do not work for food that perishes
    but for the food that endures for eternal life,
    which the Son of Man will give you.
For on him the Father, God, has set his seal."
So they said to him,
    "What can we do to accomplish the works of God?"
Jesus answered and said to them,
    "This is the work of God, that you believe in the one
        he sent."
So they said to him,
    "What sign can you do, that we may see and believe
        in you?
What can you do?
Our ancestors ate manna in the desert, as it is written:
    He gave them bread from heaven to eat."
So Jesus said to them,
    "Amen, amen, I say to you,
    it was not Moses who gave the bread from heaven;
    my Father gives you the true bread from heaven.
For the bread of God is that which comes down from
        heaven
    and gives life to the world."

So they said to him,
    "Sir, give us this bread always."
Jesus said to them,
    "I am the bread of life;
    whoever comes to me will never hunger,
    and whoever believes in me will never thirst."

The Gospel of the Lord.

NINETEENTH SUNDAY IN ORDINARY TIME

Lect. No. 116

FIRST READING: 1 Kings 19:4-8

The First Reading and the Gospel continue the Bread of Life theme begun two weeks ago.

Elijah had just had his most successful encounter with the enemies of the LORD. He had challenged the priests of Baal to a contest on Mount Carmel and defeated them. This should have been the most joyful moment of Elijah's ministry.

Yet, almost immediately, the queen (Jezebel) sent Elijah a letter proclaiming that she would have him put to death. Elijah's reaction is powerful. He becomes severely depressed and goes off into the desert to die.

God sent an angel to nourish him and guide him on his journey to the mountain where Moses had met God and where Elijah would now encounter God in the whispering of the breeze.

A reading from the first Book of Kings

Elijah went a day's journey into the desert,
until he came to a broom tree and sat beneath it.
He prayed for death, saying:
"This is enough, O LORD!
Take my life, for I am no better than my fathers."
He lay down and fell asleep under the broom tree,
but then an angel touched him and ordered him to
get up and eat.
Elijah looked and there at his head was a hearth cake
and a jug of water.
After he ate and drank, he lay down again,
but the angel of the LORD came back a second time,
touched him, and ordered,
"Get up and eat, else the journey will be too long
for you!"
He got up, ate, and drank;
then strengthened by that food,
he walked forty days and forty nights to the
mountain of God, Horeb.

The word of the Lord.

Lect. No. 116

RESPONSORIAL PSALM: Ps 34:2-3, 4-5, 6-7, 8-9 (℟.: 9a)

This psalm has a dual intention. It is a thanksgiving hymn to express one's gratitude to the LORD for the ways that he had intervened to protect those who called out to him. Likewise, it is a wisdom psalm to teach those who read it that gratitude is the proper attitude to have toward the LORD at all times.

In the second and third sections we hear that when we call out to the LORD, he will deliver us from our fears and save us from all our distress. God is not indifferent to our plight. He intervenes and rescues us when we most need him.

The last section contains ideas that are found in the First Reading and the Gospel. We heard of an angel of the LORD in the First Reading, for it was an angel who saved Elijah from his hunger and depression. In the Gospel we hear how one can taste the goodness of God, for Jesus presents himself as the bread of life that nourishes and satisfies our deepest hunger.

℟. **Taste and see the goodness of the Lord.**

I will bless the LORD at all times;
  his praise shall be ever in my mouth.
Let my soul glory in the LORD;
  the lowly will hear me and be glad.

℟. **Taste and see the goodness of the Lord.**

Glorify the LORD with me,
  let us together extol his name.
I sought the LORD, and he answered me
  and delivered me from all my fears.

℟. **Taste and see the goodness of the Lord.**

Look to him that you may be radiant with joy,
  and your faces may not blush with shame.
When the afflicted man called out, the LORD heard,
  and from all his distress he saved him.

℟. **Taste and see the goodness of the Lord.**

The angel of the LORD encamps
  around those who fear him and delivers them.
Taste and see how good the LORD is;
  blessed the man who takes refuge in him.

℟. **Taste and see the goodness of the Lord.**

PASTORAL REFLECTIONS

The deliverance promised in this psalm does not always mean that God solves our problems. God rescues Elijah from his depression but then gives him further challenges. God delivers us by being with us and promising that he will never abandon us. He does not always make it all better, but he makes all the difference.

Lect.
No. 116

SECOND READING: Ephesians 4:30—5:2

We continue our readings from the Letter to the Ephesians with an appeal to live as true Christians. We were sealed by the Holy Spirit on the day of our Baptism. We should share that love in our dealings with each other.

We have seen the example of Christ who died for us. We should be willing to love and even die for our brothers and sisters.

This reading is a wonderful reminder that our Christian calling must be lived in our everyday events. We must be different in the way we treat people: compassionate and loving.

A reading from the Letter of Saint Paul
to the Ephesians

Brothers and sisters:
Do not grieve the Holy Spirit of God,
 with which you were sealed for the day of redemption.
All bitterness, fury, anger, shouting, and reviling
 must be removed from you, along with all malice.
And be kind to one another, compassionate,
 forgiving one another as God has forgiven you in Christ.

So be imitators of God, as beloved children, and live in love,
 as Christ loved us and handed himself over for us
 as a sacrificial offering to God for a fragrant aroma.

The word of the Lord.

Lect.
No. 116

ALLELUIA: John 6:51

The Alleluia Verse contains the major point of the Gospel reading today: that Jesus is the bread of life that has come down from heaven and that satisfies our most profound hunger.

℟. **Alleluia, alleluia.**

I am the living bread that came down from heaven,
 says the Lord;
whoever eats this bread will live forever.

℟. **Alleluia, alleluia.**

PASTORAL REFLECTIONS

St. Augustine teaches that we must become that which we eat: the body of Christ. Just as the Holy Spirit hallows the loaves on the altar to become the body of Christ, so also that same Holy Spirit hallows us (as we heard in the Second Reading) to become the Mystical Body of Christ.

Lect.
No. 116

Today's Gospel comes from the latter part of the first half of the Bread of Life Discourse. Jesus identifies himself as the bread of life that has descended from the heavens.

In this part of the discourse, the symbolism is primarily sapiential and secondarily eucharistic. Sapiential literature (wisdom literature) spoke of Lady Wisdom who would nourish the foolish with her bread and wine and instruct them in the ways of the Lord.

Jesus is saying that he is the fulfillment of that promise. He has come into the world to instruct us as to who God is and what he wants of us. If we allow ourselves to be nourished by his instruction, then we will have eternal life.

Only in the last verse of this section does the symbolism become primarily eucharistic, for Jesus says that the bread that he will give us is his flesh for the life of the world.

The Jews who heard this discourse were confused, for they thought they knew who Jesus was, i.e., the son of Joseph. They did not know his true identity, that he is the only-begotten Son of God.

GOSPEL: John 6:41-51

A reading from the holy Gospel according to John

The Jews murmured about Jesus because he said, "I am the bread that came down from heaven," and they said,
"Is this not Jesus, the son of Joseph?
Do we not know his father and mother?
Then how can he say,
'I have come down from heaven'?"
Jesus answered and said to them,
"Stop murmuring among yourselves.
No one can come to me unless the Father who sent me draw him,
and I will raise him on the last day.
It is written in the prophets:
They shall all be taught by God.
Everyone who listens to my Father and learns from him comes to me.
Not that anyone has seen the Father
except the one who is from God;
he has seen the Father.
Amen, amen, I say to you,
whoever believes has eternal life.
I am the bread of life.
Your ancestors ate the manna in the desert, but they died;
this is the bread that comes down from heaven
so that one may eat it and not die.
I am the living bread that came down from heaven;
whoever eats this bread will live forever;
and the bread that I will give is my flesh for the life of the world."

The Gospel of the Lord.

August 14, 2018

THE ASSUMPTION OF THE BLESSED VIRGIN MARY

AT THE VIGIL MASS

Lect.
No. 621

FIRST READING:

1 Chronicles 15:3-4, 15-16; 16:1-2

The First Reading speaks of the day that King David brought the Ark of the Covenant into Jerusalem. He had recently conquered the city, and now he wanted to make it a focal point of the faith.

The first attempt to bring the Ark into the city ended in failure. One of the soldiers accompanying the Ark touched it. He was immediately struck dead, for he had touched a sacred object.

The Ark was left where it was until David saw that the Ark brought blessing to the owner of the property where it had been placed.

Notice that David performs sacrifices and gives blessings. In ancient Israel, the king was also considered to be a priest.

The reason that this reading was chosen for this feast is that Mary is the Ark of the New Covenant. She held the presence of the living God within her womb, even as the Ark was the place where God manifested his presence.

A reading from the first Book of Chronicles

David assembled all Israel in Jerusalem to bring the ark of the LORD
   to the place that he had prepared for it.
David also called together the sons of Aaron and the
   Levites.

The Levites bore the ark of God on their shoulders
   with poles,
   as Moses had ordained according to the word of
   the LORD.

David commanded the chiefs of the Levites
   to appoint their kinsmen as chanters,
   to play on musical instruments, harps, lyres, and
   cymbals,
   to make a loud sound of rejoicing.

They brought in the ark of God and set it within the
   tent
   which David had pitched for it.
Then they offered up burnt offerings and peace offerings to God.
When David had finished offering up the burnt offerings and peace offerings,
   he blessed the people in the name of the LORD.

The word of the Lord.

Lect.
No. 621

RESPONSORIAL PSALM: Ps 132:6-7, 9-10, 13-14 (℞.: 8)

This psalm seems to have been written for a liturgical feast. It celebrates the kingship of David and the day that he brought the Ark of the Covenant into Jerusalem.

The conquest of Jerusalem was a question of power politics. David saw that the city lay between the northern and the southern tribes. He conquered the city and made it his capital because he wanted to unite the tribes. He moved the Ark into the city so that pilgrims would be forced to enter the city periodically and see the grandeur of the palace that he had built. His political machinations were brilliant.

Yet, the LORD used David's base political motives to reveal his mercy. He chose Zion (the mountain associated with the city of Jerusalem) to be his dwelling place upon the earth.

℞. **Lord, go up to the place of your rest, you and the ark of your holiness.**

Behold, we heard of it in Ephrathah;
  we found it in the fields of Jaar.
Let us enter into his dwelling,
  let us worship at his footstool.

℞. **Lord, go up to the place of your rest, you and the ark of your holiness.**

May your priests be clothed with justice;
  let your faithful ones shout merrily for joy.
For the sake of David your servant,
  reject not the plea of your anointed.

℞. **Lord, go up to the place of your rest, you and the ark of your holiness.**

For the LORD has chosen Zion;
  he prefers her for his dwelling.
"Zion is my resting place forever;
  in her will I dwell, for I prefer her."

℞. **Lord, go up to the place of your rest, you and the ark of your holiness.**

Lect.
No. 621

SECOND READING: 1 Corinthians 15:54b-57

This passage is taken from the end of a consideration on the resurrection of the dead. Saint Paul wants the Corinthians to understand that we will all rise on the last day. Death is no longer victorious, for Christ has conquered death and sin.

Paul speaks of the power of sin being the law. Sin had entered the world and it was terrible, but the law made sin even more horrific. We thought that

A reading from the first Letter of Saint Paul to the Corinthians

Brothers and sisters:
    When that which is mortal clothes itself with immortality,
then the word that is written shall come about:
  Death is swallowed up in victory.
  Where, O death, is your victory?
  Where, O death, is your sting?

the law would liberate us from sin, but the best that it could do was point out how much we are sinners. It left us more frustrated than before, and therefore ready to accept Christ as our only true liberation from the slavery of sin.

The sting of death is sin,
and the power of sin is the law.
But thanks be to God who gives us the victory
through our Lord Jesus Christ.

The word of the Lord.

Lect.
No. 621

This Beatitude speaks of those who listen to the word of God and make it part of their lives. Of all who ever lived, Mary did this most fully, for in her the word truly became incarnate.

ALLELUIA: Luke 11:28

℟. **Alleluia, alleluia.**

Blessed are they who hear the word of God
and observe it.

℟. **Alleluia, alleluia.**

Lect.
No. 621

When a woman cried out that Mary was blessed for she was the mother of Jesus, Jesus responded that the person is blessed who hears the word of God and observes it.

This is not an insult to Mary, for of all people who ever lived, she most successfully heard the word of God (e.g., in the invitation from the Archangel Gabriel to be the mother of the Son of God) and observed it.

GOSPEL: Luke 11:27-28

A reading from the holy Gospel according to Luke

While Jesus was speaking,
a woman from the crowd called out and said to him,
"Blessed is the womb that carried you
and the breasts at which you nursed."
He replied,
"Rather, blessed are those
who hear the word of God and observe it."

The Gospel of the Lord.

PASTORAL REFLECTIONS

One way to understand the Assumption of Mary into heaven is to think of how much she desired to be reunited with her Son after the Ascension. She knew him in spirit and sacrament, but as a mother she longed to wrap her arms around him. This longing one day became so strong that the bonds of gravity and this world could no longer hold her down.

August 15, 2018

THE ASSUMPTION OF THE BLESSED VIRGIN MARY

AT THE MASS DURING THE DAY

Lect. No. 622

FIRST READING:
Revelation 11:19a; 12:1-6a, 10ab

The First Reading is taken from the Book of Revelation. On one level, it speaks of the birth of Jesus upon the earth. On another level, it presents an image of the Church making Christ present again each day.

Like the woman in this passage, Mary gave birth to a child who was immediately endangered by the evil one who wanted to devour him. (This is probably a reference to the plot of King Herod to put the child to death.) God protected the child and destroyed the power of the serpent. The image of this woman clothed with the sun, with the moon under her feet and wearing a crown of twelve stars, has become an image of the Immaculate Conception.

But in this account the woman also represents the Church. Despite constantly being attacked by the forces of evil, she makes Christ present in the world. This is especially true when she suffers for the sake of the Gospel.

It is appropriate that the image would stand both for Mary and for the Church. Mary is the model of the Church. She is the example of what the Church should be, for she made the Word of God incarnate.

A reading from the Book of Revelation

God's temple in heaven was opened,
and the ark of his covenant could be seen in the temple.

A great sign appeared in the sky, a woman clothed with the sun,
with the moon beneath her feet,
and on her head a crown of twelve stars.
She was with child and wailed aloud in pain as she labored to give birth.
Then another sign appeared in the sky;
it was a huge red dragon, with seven heads and ten horns,
and on its heads were seven diadems.
Its tail swept away a third of the stars in the sky
and hurled them down to the earth.
Then the dragon stood before the woman about to give birth,
to devour her child when she gave birth.
She gave birth to a son, a male child,
destined to rule all the nations with an iron rod.
Her child was caught up to God and his throne.
The woman herself fled into the desert
where she had a place prepared by God.

Then I heard a loud voice in heaven say:
"Now have salvation and power come,
and the Kingdom of our God
and the authority of his Anointed One."

The word of the Lord.

Lect. No. 622

RESPONSORIAL PSALM: Ps 45:10, 11, 12, 16 (℞.: 10bc)

The Responsorial Psalm is taken from Psalm 45, a psalm written to celebrate the wedding feast of a king of Israel to his bride.

The queen stands at the right hand of the king in gold of Ophir. Gold of Ophir is a very precious form of gold. The queen at the right of the king is not his bride. His bride is the princess borne in before him. The queen is actually the queen mother.

Kings of Israel had many wives and none of them was the queen. The queen was the queen mother. One of her most important responsibilities was to prepare the wedding feast for her son. This is what she is doing at the right hand of the king.

The presence of Mary at the wedding feast of Cana is based upon this image. She is the queen mother who invites her Son to his wedding, the cross.

℞. **The queen stands at your right hand, arrayed in gold.**

The queen takes her place at your right hand in gold of Ophir.

℞. **The queen stands at your right hand, arrayed in gold.**

Hear, O daughter, and see; turn your ear,
forget your people and your father's house.

℞. **The queen stands at your right hand, arrayed in gold.**

So shall the king desire your beauty;
for he is your lord.

℞. **The queen stands at your right hand, arrayed in gold.**

They are borne in with gladness and joy;
they enter the palace of the king.

℞. **The queen stands at your right hand, arrayed in gold.**

Lect. No. 622

SECOND READING: 1 Corinthians 15:20-27

Jesus is described as being the firstfruits of those who have fallen asleep. The firstfruits are generally known for two things. First of all, they are known as being the best. Second, they are the promise of more that will shortly arrive. Jesus is the best of those who have risen from the dead, and he is also a promise to us that we will one day rise from the dead to live with him in heaven.

A reading from the first Letter of Saint Paul to the Corinthians

Brothers and sisters:
Christ has been raised from the dead,
the firstfruits of those who have fallen asleep.
For since death came through man,
the resurrection of the dead came also through man.
For just as in Adam all die,
so too in Christ shall all be brought to life,
but each one in proper order:

Adam's sin brought death into the world. We are not sure if Paul means physical death or spiritual death. Whichever, we were left hopeless due to the power of sin.

With Jesus having risen from the dead, sin and death no longer have any power over us. Jesus has already risen, and on the last day we will all rise with him to share in his glory. That is when Jesus' defeat of his last enemy, death, will be made manifest, for we will live forever with him to share in his glory.

Christ the firstfruits;

then, at his coming, those who belong to Christ;

then comes the end,

when he hands over the Kingdom to his God and
  Father,

when he has destroyed every sovereignty

and every authority and power.

For he must reign until he has put all his enemies
  under his feet.

The last enemy to be destroyed is death,

  for "he subjected everything under his feet."

The word of the Lord.

Lect.
No. 622

Our Alleluia Verse celebrates the reason for this feast: that our Blessed Mother was taken up into heaven body and soul to share in God's glory forever.

ALLELUIA

℟. **Alleluia, alleluia.**

Mary is taken up to heaven;
a chorus of angels exults.

℟. **Alleluia, alleluia.**

Lect.
No. 622

The Gospel presents the story of the Visitation of Mary to her cousin Elizabeth. The traditional site of Elizabeth's and Zechariah's house is Ein Karim, a small village not far outside of Jerusalem.

The child that Elizabeth is carrying gives witness to the presence of Jesus in their midst. The first person who ever recognized the presence of Jesus in the world was an unborn child. Typically, it is those whom society would evaluate as insignificant who are able to respond to God's call.

GOSPEL: Luke 1:39-56

A reading from the holy Gospel according to Luke

Mary set out
and traveled to the hill country in haste
to a town of Judah,
where she entered the house of Zechariah
and greeted Elizabeth.
When Elizabeth heard Mary's greeting,
  the infant leaped in her womb,
  and Elizabeth, filled with the Holy Spirit,
  cried out in a loud voice and said,
  "Blessed are you among women,
  and blessed is the fruit of your womb.

Elizabeth is filled with the Holy Spirit and thus is able to greet Mary with the phrase that we still use in the "Hail Mary." The Holy Spirit is important throughout the writings of Saint Luke.

Mary is especially blessed for her trust in the words of the Lord. She was generous and willing to place herself at the disposition of God.

Mary responds to this remarkable greeting with the hymn that we call the "Magnificat." This hymn is largely based upon the hymn of Hannah in 1 Samuel 2 (with the verses of various psalms added).

This beautiful hymn expresses the feelings of the "anawim," the poor ones of Yahweh. In the time of Jesus, the poor were despised by the powers that be. Jesus portrayed the exact opposite judgment of the poor. He considered them to be the chosen of the Father.

The reference to Mary remaining with Elizabeth for three months is probably an allusion to the fact that the Ark of the Covenant that King David brought into Jerusalem stayed in a nearby village for three months. Mary is the new Ark of the Covenant.

And how does this happen to me,
   that the mother of my Lord should come to me?
For at the moment the sound of your greeting
   reached my ears,
the infant in my womb leaped for joy.
Blessed are you who believed
   that what was spoken to you by the Lord
would be fulfilled."

And Mary said:
"My soul proclaims the greatness of the Lord;
   my spirit rejoices in God my Savior
   for he has looked with favor on his lowly servant.
From this day all generations will call me blessed:
   the Almighty has done great things for me,
   and holy is his Name.
He has mercy on those who fear him
   in every generation.
He has shown the strength of his arm,
   and has scattered the proud in their conceit.
He has cast down the mighty from their thrones,
   and has lifted up the lowly.
He has filled the hungry with good things,
   and the rich he has sent away empty.
He has come to the help of his servant Israel
   for he has remembered his promise of mercy,
   the promise he made to our fathers,
   to Abraham and his children for ever."

Mary remained with her about three months
   and then returned to her home.

The Gospel of the Lord.

PASTORAL REFLECTIONS

All of us are sooner or later the "anawim." We are defeated by sin, by loneliness, by physical problems, etc. Mary's example reminds us that God will always be there for us to raise us up (even from the dead).

August 19, 2018

TWENTIETH SUNDAY IN ORDINARY TIME

Lect. No. 119 **FIRST READING: Proverbs 9:1-6**

Today's First Reading from the Book of Proverbs is an exposition of the theme that was implied in last week's Gospel reading: that of wisdom nourishing those who seek her.

Wisdom is personified as a noble lady who calls to the foolish of the city and asks them to turn aside and sup with her so that they might forsake foolishness and learn the wisdom of the LORD.

Wisdom is an attribute of God that reaches out to the chosen people to instruct them in the ways of the LORD.

A reading from the Book of Proverbs

Wisdom has built her house,
    she has set up her seven columns;
she has dressed her meat, mixed her wine,
    yes, she has spread her table.
She has sent out her maidens; she calls
    from the heights out over the city:
"Let whoever is simple turn in here";
    to the one who lacks understanding, she says,
"Come, eat of my food,
    and drink of the wine I have mixed!
Forsake foolishness that you may live;
    advance in the way of understanding."

The word of the Lord.

Lect. No. 119 **RESPONSORIAL PSALM: Ps 34:2-3, 4-5, 6-7 (℟.: 9a)**

This psalm has a dual intention. It is a thanksgiving hymn to render one's gratitude to the LORD for the ways that he had intervened to protect those who called out to him. LIkewise, it is a wisdom psalm to teach those who read it that gratitude is the proper attitude toward the LORD at all times.

In the second and third sections, we hear that when we call out to the LORD, God will deliver us from our fears and save us from all our distress. God is not

℟. **Taste and see the goodness of the Lord.**

I will bless the LORD at all times;
    his praise shall be ever in my mouth.
Let my soul glory in the LORD;
    the lowly will hear me and be glad.

℟. **Taste and see the goodness of the Lord.**

Glorify the LORD with me,
    let us together extol his name.
I sought the LORD, and he answered me
    and delivered me from all my fears.

℟. **Taste and see the goodness of the Lord.**

320

indifferent to our plight. He intervenes and rescues us.

The responsory verse reminds us that we experience this goodness in the sacrament that we are now celebrating, the Eucharist.

Look to him that you may be radiant with joy,
  and your faces may not blush with shame.
When the poor one called out, the LORD heard,
  and from all his distress he saved him.

℟. **Taste and see the goodness of the Lord.**

Lect. No. 119

SECOND READING: Ephesians 5:15-20

Over the past weeks we have read passages from Ephesians that encouraged us to live charitably toward one another, especially toward fellow Christians.

This week's passage from Ephesians makes a distinction between the ways of the world and the ways of those who are servants of the Lord. The ways of the world are foolishness, drunkenness, and ignorance.

We have rejected these ways to live in the Spirit of God. This is expressed in the way that we treat each other and in our attitude toward God.

We should be acting and speaking in a holy manner that does not give scandal and that edifies those who see or hear us.

A reading from the Letter of Saint Paul
to the Ephesians

Brothers and sisters:
Watch carefully how you live,
  not as foolish persons but as wise,
  making the most of the opportunity,
  because the days are evil.
Therefore, do not continue in ignorance,
  but try to understand what is the will of the Lord.
And do not get drunk on wine, in which lies debauchery,
  but be filled with the Spirit,
  addressing one another in psalms and hymns and
    spiritual songs,
  singing and playing to the Lord in your hearts,
  giving thanks always and for everything
  in the name of our Lord Jesus Christ to God the
    Father.

The word of the Lord.

Lect. No. 119

The Alleluia Verse repeats Jesus' words through which he invites us to partake of his flesh and blood in the sacrament of the Eucharist and so to remain in him.

ALLELUIA: John 6:56

℟. **Alleluia, alleluia.**

Whoever eats my flesh and drinks my blood
remains in me and I in him, says the Lord.

℟. **Alleluia, alleluia.**

Lect.
No. 119

The Gospel continues the Discourse on the Bread of Life. Today's first verse proclaims that the bread that Jesus gives us is his flesh.

It is difficult for us to understand how scandalous this would have been at the time of Jesus. The Jews who were listening understood this as cannibalism. Jesus did not better the situation when he then told them that they would have to drink his blood.

Blood was sacred to the Jews and it belonged to God alone. This is why in kosher butchering the animal is completely bled. Blood signifies life, and life is God's prerogative. Thus, for Jesus to offer his blood would have been incredibly horrific.

This passage was included in the Gospel of John to teach believers that the Eucharist was not simply a symbolic action that was nothing more than a commemoration. It is truly the sacrament of the body and blood of Jesus.

Even if we cannot understand this (just as the Jews could not understand), we must trust and believe and eat and drink to have life in Jesus.

GOSPEL: John 6:51-58

A reading from the holy Gospel according to John

Jesus said to the crowds:
"I am the living bread that came down from heaven;
   whoever eats this bread will live forever;
   and the bread that I will give
   is my flesh for the life of the world."

The Jews quarreled among themselves, saying,
   "How can this man give us his flesh to eat?"
Jesus said to them,
   "Amen, amen, I say to you,
   unless you eat the flesh of the Son of Man and
      drink his blood,
   you do not have life within you.
Whoever eats my flesh and drinks my blood
   has eternal life,
   and I will raise him on the last day.
For my flesh is true food,
   and my blood is true drink.
Whoever eats my flesh and drinks my blood
   remains in me and I in him.
Just as the living Father sent me
   and I have life because of the Father,
   so also the one who feeds on me
   will have life because of me.
This is the bread that came down from heaven.
Unlike your ancestors who ate and still died,
   whoever eats this bread will live forever."

The Gospel of the Lord.

August 26, 2018

TWENTY-FIRST SUNDAY IN ORDINARY TIME

Lect. No. 122

FIRST READING: Joshua 24:1-2a, 15-17, 18b

Today's readings conclude the cycle of readings based upon the Miracle of the Multiplication of Loaves and Fish and the Discourse on the Bread of Life.

The First Reading comes from the Book of Joshua. This is a historic book produced by the Deuteronomist authors.

They based their works on the concept that they should retell Israel's history as it should have happened (and not as it actually happened).

This passage speaks of the renewal of the covenant at Shechem. Joshua asks the people to choose between Yahweh and the gods of the nations.

The necessity of choosing is also found in the Gospel today.

Joshua mentions that many of their ancestors previously served other gods. It is believed that many of those who left Egypt with Moses were not Israelites, but were pagan slaves who saw an opportunity to escape, and who then allowed themselves to be incorporated into Israel.

A reading from the Book of Joshua

Joshua gathered together all the tribes of Israel at Shechem,
   summoning their elders, their leaders,
   their judges, and their officers.
When they stood in ranks before God,
   Joshua addressed all the people:
   "If it does not please you to serve the LORD,
   decide today whom you will serve,
   the gods your fathers served beyond the River
   or the gods of the Amorites in whose country you
      are now dwelling.
As for me and my household, we will serve the
   LORD."

But the people answered,
   "Far be it from us to forsake the LORD
   for the service of other gods.
For it was the LORD, our God,
   who brought us and our fathers up out of the land
      of Egypt,
   out of a state of slavery.
He performed those great miracles before our very
   eyes
   and protected us along our entire journey
   and among the peoples through whom we passed.
Therefore we also will serve the LORD, for he is our
   God."

The word of the Lord.

Lect. No. 122 — RESPONSORIAL PSALM: Ps 34:2-3, 16-17, 18-19, 20-21 (℟.: 9a)

This is the third time in recent weeks that we are using this particular psalm for the Responsorial Psalm. As in previous weeks, we are using verses 2 and 3, but the rest of the verses being used are new.

They emphasize the humility of those who are calling upon the LORD to rescue them from their adversity. Those who follow God must make themselves humble and vulnerable in order to be able to follow wherever God will lead them.

This is both a hymn of thanksgiving and a wisdom psalm. The author gives thanks to the LORD for all the ways in which he was delivered from his enemies. This very act is an example to the people of Israel that they should always live in gratitude.

This is a proper attitude toward God who is always showering his blessings upon us (both for the Psalmist and for us).

℟. **Taste and see the goodness of the Lord.**

I will bless the LORD at all times;
   his praise shall be ever in my mouth.
Let my soul glory in the LORD;
   the lowly will hear me and be glad.

℟. **Taste and see the goodness of the Lord.**

The LORD has eyes for the just,
   and ears for their cry.
The LORD confronts the evildoers,
   to destroy remembrance of them from the earth.

℟. **Taste and see the goodness of the Lord.**

When the just cry out, the LORD hears them,
   and from all their distress he rescues them.
The LORD is close to the brokenhearted;
   and those who are crushed in spirit he saves.

℟. **Taste and see the goodness of the Lord.**

Many are the troubles of the just one,
   but out of them all the LORD delivers him;
he watches over all his bones;
   not one of them shall be broken.

℟. **Taste and see the goodness of the Lord.**

PASTORAL REFLECTIONS

Today's readings remind us that the Eucharist is not a right but a privilege, and one that requires a certain degree of consistency. If we want to be one with the Lord, then we must give witness to that relationship in our everyday lives.

Lect. No. 122

SECOND READING: A Longer Form: Ephesians 5:21-32

This reading has two major themes. The first presents the attitude that husbands and wives should have toward each other.

The second speaks of the bond between husbands and wives as being analogous to the bond between Christ and the Church.

The first teaching is based upon the teachings of Stoic philosophy. Stoics believed that there was a proper order for all things, and that we would only find peace if we observed that order.

Unlike most Stoic teachings, however, this passage also teaches about the obligation of a husband to love his wife. There are mutual obligations to honor and support each other.

We could ask whether the author of this letter would phrase his teaching the same way today. Was this (the teaching that women should be subordinate) an eternal teaching of truth, or was it simply a teaching based upon cultural understandings of what God wants?

The teaching on marriage is very positive. Unlike Saint Paul's teaching in 1 Corinthians that one should marry to avoid temptation, this letter teaches that marriage is a foreshadowing of the union between Christ and the Church.

A reading from the Letter of Saint Paul to the Ephesians

Brothers and sisters:
Be subordinate to one another out of reverence for Christ.
Wives should be subordinate to their husbands as to the Lord.
For the husband is head of his wife
    just as Christ is head of the church,
    he himself the savior of the body.
As the church is subordinate to Christ,
    so wives should be subordinate to their husbands
    in everything.
Husbands, love your wives,
    even as Christ loved the church
    and handed himself over for her to sanctify her,
    cleansing her by the bath of water with the word,
    that he might present to himself the church in splendor,
    without spot or wrinkle or any such thing,
    that she might be holy and without blemish.
So also husbands should love their wives as their own bodies.
He who loves his wife loves himself.
For no one hates his own flesh
    but rather nourishes and cherishes it,
    even as Christ does the church,
    because we are members of his body.
For this reason a man shall leave his father and his mother
    and be joined to his wife,
    and the two shall become one flesh.
This is a great mystery,
    but I speak in reference to Christ and the church.

The word of the Lord.

Lect. No. 122

SECOND READING: B Shorter Form: Ephesians 5:2a, 25-32

This reading has two major themes. The first teaching is based upon Stoic philosophy. Stoics believed that there was a proper order for all things.

Unlike most Stoic teachings, however, this passage also speaks about the obligation of husbands to love their wives. There are mutual obligations to honor and support each other.

Would the author of this letter phrase his teaching the same way today? Was the teaching that women should be subordinate an eternal truth, or was it based upon cultural understandings of what God wanted?

The teaching on marriage is very positive. Unlike Saint Paul's teaching in 1 Corinthians that one should marry to avoid temptation, this letter teaches that marriage is a foreshadowing of the union between Christ and the Church.

It is so much more positive, in fact, that many scholars wonder whether Paul actually wrote this letter.

A reading from the Letter of Saint Paul to the Ephesians

Brothers and sisters:
Live in love, as Christ loved us.
Husbands, love your wives,
    even as Christ loved the church
    and handed himself over for her to sanctify her,
    cleansing her by the bath of water with the word,
    that he might present to himself the church in splendor,
    without spot or wrinkle or any such thing,
    that she might be holy and without blemish.
So also husbands should love their wives as their own bodies.
He who loves his wife loves himself.
For no one hates his own flesh
    but rather nourishes and cherishes it,
    even as Christ does the church,
    because we are members of his body.
For this reason a man shall leave his father and his mother
    and be joined to his wife,
    and the two shall become one flesh.
This is a great mystery,
    but I speak in reference to Christ and the church.

The word of the Lord.

Lect. No. 122

ALLELUIA: John 6:63c, 68c

The Alleluia Verse repeats Saint Peter's profession of faith in Jesus at the end of the Discourse on the Bread of Life.

℟. **Alleluia, alleluia.**

Your words, Lord, are Spirit and life;
you have the words of everlasting life.

℟. **Alleluia, alleluia.**

Lect.
No. 122

As we saw in last week's Gospel, the proclamation that Jesus would give his flesh and blood for the people to devour was a statement that would have been scandalous to those who heard it.

It required an act of total faith to believe that this was possible and that it was what God wanted.

Some of those who were listening to Jesus decided not to believe in him after this. Like the Jews in the desert after the exodus, they murmured at what Jesus told them.

They then separated themselves from his disciples and went their own way.

Jesus asked the twelve whether they were also planning to abandon him. Peter responded that there was nowhere that they could possibly go. They recognized that Jesus was the Holy One of God and that he spoke words of eternal life.

This is one of the few times in the Gospel of John where Peter and the twelve are given a very positive opportunity to profess their faith. (Usually, they are negatively contrasted with the profound love of the Beloved Disciple.)

GOSPEL: John 6:60-69

A reading from the holy Gospel according to John

Many of Jesus' disciples who were listening said, "This saying is hard; who can accept it?"
Since Jesus knew that his disciples were murmuring about this,
he said to them, "Does this shock you?
What if you were to see the Son of Man ascending to where he was before?
It is the spirit that gives life,
while the flesh is of no avail.
The words I have spoken to you are Spirit and life.
But there are some of you who do not believe."
Jesus knew from the beginning the ones who would not believe
and the one who would betray him.
And he said,
"For this reason I have told you that no one can come to me
unless it is granted him by my Father."

As a result of this,
many of his disciples returned to their former way of life
and no longer accompanied him.
Jesus then said to the Twelve, "Do you also want to leave?"
Simon Peter answered him, "Master, to whom shall we go?
You have the words of eternal life.
We have come to believe
and are convinced that you are the Holy One of God."

The Gospel of the Lord.

September 2, 2018

TWENTY-SECOND SUNDAY IN ORDINARY TIME

Lect. No. 125 **FIRST READING: Deuteronomy 4:1-2, 6-8**

Today's Gospel reading returns to the cycle of passages taken from Mark (with the First Reading and the Responsorial Psalm reinforcing the main topic found in the Gospel).

The First Reading today is taken from the Book of Deuteronomy. The name of this book is derived from two Greek words: "Deutero," which means "second," and "nomos," which means "law." This book was found in the temple by King Josiah (c. 622 B.C.).

It is not known when it was written, but it became the basis of a great reform that permanently transformed the religion of Israel (e.g., henceforth one could only worship the LORD with sacrifices at the temple in Jerusalem).

This passage speaks of the goodness of the law that God was giving to his people. They would no longer have to wonder what God wanted of them.

He was revealing his will to them in a very clear manner so that they might observe it and always be blessed.

A reading from the Book of Deuteronomy

Moses said to the people:
"Now, Israel, hear the statutes and decrees
which I am teaching you to observe,
that you may live, and may enter in and take possession of the land
which the LORD, the God of your fathers, is giving you.
In your observance of the commandments of the LORD, your God,
which I enjoin upon you,
you shall not add to what I command you nor subtract from it.
Observe them carefully,
for thus will you give evidence
of your wisdom and intelligence to the nations,
who will hear of all these statutes and say,
'This great nation is truly a wise and intelligent people.'
For what great nation is there
that has gods so close to it as the LORD, our God,
is to us
whenever we call upon him?
Or what great nation has statutes and decrees
that are as just as this whole law
which I am setting before you today?"

The word of the Lord.

Lect.
No. 125

RESPONSORIAL Psalm: Ps 15:2-3, 3-4, 4-5 (℟.: 1a)

The Responsorial Psalm continues the theme found in the First Reading that those who follow the law of the LORD would be blessed.

It is a wisdom psalm that was intended as a teaching for the young of Israel to instruct them on how to live the good life.

This particular psalm goes beyond the letter of the law to the spirit behind it. It speaks of teaching others through justice and respect.

Furthermore, it is obvious from several phrases (e.g., "thinks the truth in his heart," "honors those who fear the LORD") that one is asked to observe the law in more than an external manner. Rather, one must interiorize it and make it the guide of one's thoughts and actions.

℟. **The one who does justice will live in the presence of the Lord.**

Whoever walks blamelessly and does justice;
    who thinks the truth in his heart
    and slanders not with his tongue.

℟. **The one who does justice will live in the presence of the Lord.**

Who harms not his fellow man,
    nor takes up a reproach against his neighbor;
by whom the reprobate is despised,
    while he honors those who fear the LORD.

℟. **The one who does justice will live in the presence of the Lord.**

Who lends not his money at usury
    and accepts no bribe against the innocent.
Whoever does these things
    shall never be disturbed.

℟. **The one who does justice will live in the presence of the Lord.**

Lect.
No. 125

SECOND READING: James 1:17-18, 21b-22, 27

This is the first of a series of readings taken from the Letter of James that we will see over the next several weeks.

The first part of this reading reminds us that everything we possess comes from the Lord. Therefore, we should be grateful for what we have received, and we should also be willing to share it with those who do not have enough.

A reading from the Letter of Saint James

Dearest brothers and sisters:
    All good giving and every perfect gift is from above,
coming down from the Father of lights,
    with whom there is no alteration or shadow caused by change.
He willed to give us birth by the word of truth
    that we may be a kind of firstfruits of his creatures.

The second half of the reading introduces a theme that will be repeated all throughout this letter: that our faith must be expressed in action.

It is not enough to believe in one's heart without expressing that faith in the way one treats one's sisters and brothers (and especially those who are weakest in our society, i.e., the widows and the orphans).

Humbly welcome the word that has been planted in you
and is able to save your souls.

Be doers of the word and not hearers only, deluding yourselves.

Religion that is pure and undefiled before God and the Father is this:
to care for orphans and widows in their affliction
and to keep oneself unstained by the world.

The word of the Lord.

Lect.
No. 125

The Alleluia Verse speaks of what God intended us to be: creatures filled with the dignity of God's own truth. This contrasts well with what we could easily become if we are not careful: slaves to the law.

ALLELUIA: James 1:18

℟. **Alleluia, alleluia.**

The Father willed to give us birth by the word of truth
that we may be a kind of firstfruits of his creatures.

℟. **Alleluia, alleluia.**

Lect.
No. 125

In this passage from the Gospel of Mark, we hear of an encounter between Jesus and the Pharisees.

Pharisees were dedicated laymen who attempted to live the law of the Lord to the greatest possible extent. They would normally work all day long at their occupations, and then they would study the law.

They wanted to build a fence around the law, i.e., take the law to its widest possible extent to be sure that they were not breaking the least important of the laws and their prescriptions.

GOSPEL: Mark 7:1-8, 14-15, 21-23

A reading from the holy Gospel according to Mark

When the Pharisees with some scribes who had come from Jerusalem
gathered around Jesus,
they observed that some of his disciples ate their meals
with unclean, that is, unwashed, hands.
—For the Pharisees and, in fact, all Jews,
do not eat without carefully washing their hands,
keeping the tradition of the elders.
And on coming from the marketplace
they do not eat without purifying themselves.
And there are many other things that they have traditionally observed,

They gathered in schools to determine what the law intended. These interpretations often extended the law far beyond what it was originally intended to address.

Because the Pharisees were so idealistic, they easily fell into the trap of judgmentalism. This is how they treated Jesus and the disciples in this passage.

Jesus responds with a certain vehemence. He felt that their dedication to minute prescriptions of the law while they failed to respect the people they were serving was hypocritical.

He also felt that they took their legal discussions much too seriously ("teaching as doctrines human precepts"). He calls upon them to adopt the proper interior disposition, one of charity and gentleness.

If one's heart is filled with rancor and judgmentalism, then no matter what that person does externally, he or she would be sinning against God's love and still be trapped in sin and hate.

the purification of cups and jugs and kettles and
  beds.—
So the Pharisees and scribes questioned him,
  "Why do your disciples not follow the tradition of
    the elders
  but instead eat a meal with unclean hands?"
He responded,
  "Well did Isaiah prophesy about you hypocrites,
    as it is written:
    This people honors me with their lips,
      but their hearts are far from me;
    in vain do they worship me,
      teaching as doctrines human precepts.
You disregard God's commandment but cling to
  human tradition."
He summoned the crowd again and said to them,
  "Hear me, all of you, and understand.
Nothing that enters one from outside can defile that
    person;
  but the things that come out from within are what
    defile.

"From within people, from their hearts,
  come evil thoughts, unchastity, theft, murder,
  adultery, greed, malice, deceit,
  licentiousness, envy, blasphemy, arrogance, folly.
All these evils come from within and they defile."

The Gospel of the Lord.

PASTORAL REFLECTIONS

It is all too easy to fall into judgmentalism, especially when we see things that are objectively wrong. Yet, sitting in judgment of others does not do them or us any good.

Since there are times that we cannot help but have these thoughts, then maybe we can use the thoughts as an opportunity for good. Every time that we find ourselves judging others, we can use that temptation as an opportunity to pray for them.

September 9, 2018
TWENTY-THIRD SUNDAY IN ORDINARY TIME

Lect. No. 128

FIRST READING: Isaiah 35:4-7a

The First Reading comes from a section toward the end of the first part of the Book of the Prophet Isaiah (the part actually written by the Prophet around 700 B.C.).

Typical of many prophetic books, this section ends with a hymn that promises a time of restoration. After Israel had been chastised for all of its sins, it would be blessed by the LORD and be made fruitful again.

This idea is presented in terms of the blind being able to see and the deaf able to hear and the mute able to speak. This theme is also found in the Gospel today where we will see Jesus heal the man who was deaf and mute.

A reading from the Book of the Prophet Isaiah

Thus says the LORD:
Say to those whose hearts are frightened:
 Be strong, fear not!
Here is your God,
 he comes with vindication;
with divine recompense
 he comes to save you.
Then will the eyes of the blind be opened,
 the ears of the deaf be cleared;
then will the lame leap like a stag,
 then the tongue of the mute will sing.
Streams will burst forth in the desert,
 and rivers in the steppe.
The burning sands will become pools,
 and the thirsty ground, springs of water.

The word of the Lord.

Lect. No. 128

RESPONSORIAL PSALM: Ps 146:6-7, 8-9, 9-10 (℟.: 1b)

This thanksgiving hymn praises God who would liberate all of those who were oppressed in any way (whether from difficulties caused by human foes or by illnesses or other physical problems).

God is seen as our Savior who feeds the hungry and sets captives free. We could easily spiritualize this idea, for Jesus

℟. **Praise the Lord, my soul!**

or:

℟. **Alleluia.**

The God of Jacob keeps faith forever,
 secures justice for the oppressed,
 gives food to the hungry.
The LORD sets captives free.

has set us free from all those things that hold us in bondage, i.e., sin and fear, loneliness and resentment, etc.

As we pray this psalm, we could ask ourselves to name those ways in which God has liberated us. There might have been bad habits that we could not break, or relationships that were not healthy and life-giving, or situations in which we were blind or deaf to what our actions were doing to others.

It is the LORD who gives us perspective as to what the consequences are of the things we are doing, and also grants us the strength and love to break out of the prisons that we have made for ourselves.

℟. **Praise the Lord, my soul!**

or:

℟. **Alleluia.**

The LORD gives sight to the blind;
　the LORD raises up those who were bowed down.
The LORD loves the just;
　the LORD protects strangers.

℟. **Praise the Lord, my soul!**

or:

℟. **Alleluia.**

The fatherless and the widow the LORD sustains,
　but the way of the wicked he thwarts.
The LORD shall reign forever;
　your God, O Zion, through all generations. Alleluia.

℟. **Praise the Lord, my soul!**

or:

℟. **Alleluia.**

Lect.
No. 128

SECOND READING: James 2:1-5

The Second Reading is a continuation of the Letter of James. This particular passage is scathing in its attack on favoritism within the community toward those who are rich.

It reminds its readers that Jesus did not judge people this way. Jesus, in fact, saw the poor as those who are truly blessed, while he condemned the rich as self-satisfied and arrogant.

The rich are not ready to listen to the good news because they feel as if they do not need it, while the poor realize that they have nothing to lose.

A reading from the Letter of Saint James

My brothers and sisters, show no partiality
　as you adhere to the faith in our glorious Lord
　　Jesus Christ.
For if a man with gold rings and fine clothes
　comes into your assembly,
　and a poor person in shabby clothes also comes in,
　and you pay attention to the one wearing the fine
　　clothes
　and say, "Sit here, please,"
　while you say to the poor one, "Stand there," or "Sit
　　at my feet,"
　have you not made distinctions among yourselves
　and become judges with evil designs?
Listen, my beloved brothers and sisters.

In fact, they recognize that they desperately need Jesus' saving message because they have nowhere else to turn.

Did not God choose those who are poor in the world
to be rich in faith and heirs of the kingdom
that he promised to those who love him?

The word of the Lord.

**Lect.
No. 128**

The Alleluia Verse reminds us that the kingdom Jesus established through his deeds and preaching heals both our hearts and our bodies.

ALLELUIA: cf. Matthew 4:23

℟. **Alleluia, alleluia.**

Jesus proclaimed the Gospel of the kingdom
and cured every disease among the people.

℟. **Alleluia, alleluia.**

**Lect.
No. 128**

This passage in which Jesus heals the man who was deaf and mute is in stark contrast to the Gospel that we heard last week.

That Gospel spoke of the Pharisees who could physically hear and speak, but they chose to make themselves spiritually blind and deaf and mute. This man, however, was physically deaf and mute, and Jesus gives him the freedom to hear and speak freely.

Typical of Mark's Gospel, after Jesus heals the man, he tells him not to spread word of what had happened (lest people misinterpret his mission in terms of power). Yet the people are filled with awe and spread the news everywhere.

In our Baptism ceremonies, we still use this idea of opening ears to hear God's words and mouths to speak them.

GOSPEL: Mark 7:31-37

A reading from the holy Gospel according to Mark

Again Jesus left the district of Tyre
and went by way of Sidon to the Sea of Galilee,
into the district of the Decapolis.
And people brought to him a deaf man who had a
speech impediment
and begged him to lay his hand on him.
He took him off by himself away from the crowd.
He put his finger into the man's ears
and, spitting, touched his tongue;
then he looked up to heaven and groaned, and
said to him,
"Ephphatha!"—that is, "Be opened!"—
And immediately the man's ears were opened,
his speech impediment was removed,
and he spoke plainly.
He ordered them not to tell anyone.
But the more he ordered them not to,
the more they proclaimed it.
They were exceedingly astonished and they said,
"He has done all things well.
He makes the deaf hear and the mute speak."

The Gospel of the Lord.

TWENTY-FOURTH SUNDAY IN ORDINARY TIME

Lect. No. 131

FIRST READING: Isaiah 50:4c-9a

The First Reading comes from the third song of the Suffering Servant of Yahweh. These four hymns are found in the second part of the Book of the Prophet Isaiah.

They speak of a mysterious figure who would bring salvation to his people through his suffering. He would be gentle and humble and extend the promise of salvation to all the nations of the earth.

Jesus considered himself to be the fulfillment of this prophecy. This is obvious from a number of the terms that he applied to himself and his future suffering (which we hear predicted in today's Gospel).

His idea of being the Messiah was not one of power but rather one of service and even suffering for the sake of his people.

A reading from the Book of the Prophet Isaiah

The Lord GOD opens my ear that I may hear;
    and I have not rebelled,
    have not turned back.
I gave my back to those who beat me,
    my cheeks to those who plucked my beard;
my face I did not shield
    from buffets and spitting.

The Lord GOD is my help,
    therefore I am not disgraced;
I have set my face like flint,
    knowing that I shall not be put to shame.
He is near who upholds my right;
    if anyone wishes to oppose me,
    let us appear together.
Who disputes my right?
    Let that man confront me.
See, the Lord GOD is my help;
    who will prove me wrong?

The word of the Lord.

PASTORAL REFLECTIONS

As we hear Christ ask the disciples, "Who do you say that I am?" we should remember that the question is also addressed to us. Do we want a powerful miracle-worker who will solve all of our problems, or do we want someone who challenges us to love and serve and die to ourselves so that we might live in him?

Lect.
No. 131

RESPONSORIAL PSALM: Ps 116:1-2, 3-4, 5-6, 8-9 (℟.: 9)

The Responsorial Psalm is taken from a thanksgiving psalm that celebrates the fact that the LORD had delivered the Psalmist from impending doom. The seriousness of the danger is obvious from the multiple mentions of the fact that the Psalmist was facing death and the LORD rescued him from that fate.

Even the refrain is a reminder of this idea, for the Psalmist would be able to walk in the land of the living (and not be consigned to the underworld).

It is interesting to read this psalm in connection with our First Reading and today's Gospel. In both of these we hear of the suffering of the just one. In neither would the just one be delivered from the fate of dying for his people.

Only after death would the LORD then raise him from the dead (seen in the Gospel and the fourth song of the Suffering Servant).

This certainly makes us ask what it means to be rescued by God. Does it always mean that we escape the dangers that we face, or does it sometimes mean that we must face them (only not alone, for God would always be there with us)?

Does God make it all better all of the time, or does he make all the difference to us no matter what might happen?

℟. **I will walk before the Lord, in the land of the living.**

or:

℟. **Alleluia.**

I love the LORD because he has heard
   my voice in supplication,
because he has inclined his ear to me
   the day I called.

℟. **I will walk before the Lord, in the land of the living.**

or:

℟. **Alleluia.**

The cords of death encompassed me;
   the snares of the netherworld seized upon me;
   I fell into distress and sorrow,
and I called upon the name of the LORD,
   "O LORD, save my life!"

℟. **I will walk before the Lord, in the land of the living.**

or:

℟. **Alleluia.**

Gracious is the LORD and just;
   yes, our God is merciful.
The LORD keeps the little ones;
   I was brought low, and he saved me.

℟. **I will walk before the Lord, in the land of the living.**

or:

℟. **Alleluia.**

For he has freed my soul from death,
   my eyes from tears, my feet from stumbling.
I shall walk before the LORD
   in the land of the living.

This psalm certainly makes us question what we want of the LORD. Do we want someone who will solve all of our problems like magic?

℟. **I will walk before the Lord, in the land of the living.**

or:

℟. **Alleluia.**

Lect. No. 131

SECOND READING: James 2:14-18

Today we read the central idea of the Letter of James: that a theoretical faith without action does no good. James uses the absurd example of telling people who are cold and starving that they should keep warm and well fed while not doing anything to help them. Our good works must be performed to give expression to our faith. Words are cheap; it is actions that count.

This is not really opposed to the writings of Paul. He opposed works of the law, by which he meant doing things that would make God love us more.

He felt that God's love was gratuitous, and we could never earn it. Yet even Paul spoke of the fact that once we experienced God's love, we must respond to it through works of faith-filled love.

A reading from the Letter of Saint James

What good is it, my brothers and sisters,
   if someone says he has faith but does not have works?
Can that faith save him?
If a brother or sister has nothing to wear
   and has no food for the day,
   and one of you says to them,
   "Go in peace, keep warm, and eat well,"
   but you do not give them the necessities of the body,
   what good is it?
So also faith of itself,
   if it does not have works, is dead.

Indeed someone might say,
   "You have faith and I have works."
Demonstrate your faith to me without works,
   and I will demonstrate my faith to you from my works.

The word of the Lord.

Lect. No. 131

ALLELUIA: Galatians 6:14

The Alleluia Verse quotes a passage from Saint Paul's Letter to the Galatians in which he speaks of his rejection of all those things that could separate him from the Lord.

℟. **Alleluia, alleluia.**

May I never boast except in the cross of our Lord
through which the world has been crucified to me
   and I to the world.

℟. **Alleluia, alleluia.**

Lect.
No. 131

In this Gospel we hear Saint Peter's profession of faith. He proclaims that he believes that Jesus is the Messiah. It is obvious from this reading that Peter interpreted this in terms of power. He wanted Jesus to be a conquering hero so that he might share in his glory.

However, this is not what Jesus came to do. He was here to liberate us from sin and alienation, not from the occupying Roman army.

This is why we hear throughout this Gospel that Jesus did not accept the title Messiah, for he realized that those who followed him did not really understand his mission.

He speaks of his role in terms of being the Son of Man who would suffer and die, and then rise after three days. In saying this, he was applying the songs of the Suffering Servant to himself.

Peter rejects that message and rebukes Jesus. Jesus then tells him that he is not acting in a godly manner, but rather like Satan (for he was tempting Jesus).

Jesus speaks of the necessity for all of his followers to take up their cross and follow him. To be a Christian is to be willing to die on the cross with him.

GOSPEL: Mark 8:27-35

A reading from the holy Gospel according to Mark

Jesus and his disciples set out
　　for the villages of Caesarea Philippi.
Along the way he asked his disciples,
　　"Who do people say that I am?"
They said in reply,
　　"John the Baptist, others Elijah,
　　still others one of the prophets."
And he asked them,
　　"But who do you say that I am?"
Peter said to him in reply,
　　"You are the Christ."
Then he warned them not to tell anyone about him.

He began to teach them
　　that the Son of Man must suffer greatly
　　and be rejected by the elders, the chief priests,
　　　　and the scribes,
　　and be killed, and rise after three days.
He spoke this openly.
Then Peter took him aside and began to rebuke him.
At this he turned around and, looking at his disciples,
　　rebuked Peter and said, "Get behind me, Satan.
You are thinking not as God does, but as human
　　beings do."

He summoned the crowd with his disciples and said
　　to them,
　　"Whoever wishes to come after me must deny
　　　　himself,
　　take up his cross, and follow me.
For whoever wishes to save his life will lose it,
　　but whoever loses his life for my sake
　　and that of the gospel will save it."

The Gospel of the Lord.

TWENTY-FIFTH SUNDAY IN ORDINARY TIME

Lect. No. 134 FIRST READING: Wisdom 2:12, 17-20

The First Reading comes from the Book of Wisdom, a late addition to the Old Testament (probably written in the last century before the birth of Jesus).

The theme of this reading and the Gospel is the suffering of the just one at the hands of evil people.

The Gospel contains Jesus' second prediction of his passion. This reading speaks of how the evil conspire to attack the just one because they cannot stand his goodness.

If we try to live Christian lives, if we choose the good and reject evil, we, too, will suffer for the Good News. There are people who will resent us for our choices and they will oppose us.

A reading from the Book of Wisdom

The wicked say:
Let us beset the just one, because he is obnoxious
    to us;
he sets himself against our doings,
reproaches us for transgressions of the law
    and charges us with violations of our training.
Let us see whether his words be true;
    let us find out what will happen to him.
For if the just one be the son of God, God will de-
    fend him
    and deliver him from the hand of his foes.
With revilement and torture let us put the just one
    to the test
    that we may have proof of his gentleness
    and try his patience.
Let us condemn him to a shameful death;
    for according to his own words, God will take
    care of him.

The word of the Lord.

Lect. No. 134 RESPONSORIAL PSALM: Ps 54:3-4, 5, 6-8 (℟.: 6b)

The Responsorial Psalm is an individual lament, the cry of a Psalmist who is oppressed by the difficulties that surround him. He calls upon the LORD, knowing that God will listen to his appeal.

℟. **The Lord upholds my life.**

O God, by your name save me,
    and by your might defend my cause.
O God, hear my prayer;
    hearken to the words of my mouth.

Once again we must ask how the LORD will respond to our prayers. At times, God intervenes in powerful ways and rights the wrongs. Miracles can and do happen. Other times, God asks us to trust in the midst of suffering. Rather than making it all better, he tells us that he will meet us on the cross.

In either case, he will answer our appeal in the most loving way possible.

℞. **The Lord upholds my life.**

For the haughty have risen up against me,
  the ruthless seek my life;
  they set not God before their eyes.

℞. **The Lord upholds my life.**

Behold, God is my helper;
  the Lord sustains my life.
Freely will I offer you sacrifice;
  I will praise your name, O LORD, for its goodness.

℞. **The Lord upholds my life.**

Lect. No. 134

SECOND READING: James 3:16—4:3

The Second Reading continues the cycle of readings taken from the Letter of James. This one warns against the danger of allowing one's passions to guide one's actions.

Saint James says that bad things happen when we allow our passions to run amok. We end up using others as objects for our own gratification.

We end up living miserable lives of jealousy and resentment.

If, on the other hand, we live with a spirit of peace, gentleness, mercy, etc., then we will be able to live with others as God intended us to do.

We will not be worried that we are somehow missing out on something, but rather we will be willing to share everything that we have with those who need our help.

A reading from the Letter of Saint James

Beloved:
Where jealousy and selfish ambition exist,
  there is disorder and every foul practice.
But the wisdom from above is first of all pure,
  then peaceable, gentle, compliant,
  full of mercy and good fruits,
  without inconstancy or insincerity.
And the fruit of righteousness is sown in peace
  for those who cultivate peace.

Where do the wars
  and where do the conflicts among you come from?
Is it not from your passions
  that make war within your members?
You covet but do not possess.
You kill and envy but you cannot obtain;
  you fight and wage war.
You do not possess because you do not ask.
You ask but do not receive,
  because you ask wrongly, to spend it on your
  passions.

The word of the Lord.

Lect.
No. 134

God has not called us to be condemned or to be slaves; he has invited us into the dignity of the children of a loving Father who share in his glory.

Lect.
No. 134

Today we hear the second prediction of the passion in the Gospel of Mark. As with the first, Jesus does not use the word "Messiah" when he speaks about himself in the third person singular. Rather, he calls himself the "Son of Man."

This title is drawn from the Book of Daniel where the Son of Man receives power and authority, but it is also derived from the songs of the Suffering Servant in the Book of the Prophet Isaiah.

The disciples, who did not understand the first prediction of the passion, do not understand what Jesus is saying. They are clinging to power. This is why Jesus tells them that whoever serves a child is doing his will. (This is not the passage in which Jesus tells his disciples to become like little children.)

Children cannot pay us back for what we are doing for them, so serving a child (or those who are powerless and who have no influence in society) is to serve Christ himself.

ALLELUIA: cf. 2 Thessalonians 2:14

℟. **Alleluia, alleluia.**

God has called us through the Gospel
to possess the glory of our Lord Jesus Christ.

℟. **Alleluia, alleluia.**

GOSPEL: Mark 9:30-37

A reading from the holy Gospel according to Mark

Jesus and his disciples left from there and began a
    journey through Galilee,
but he did not wish anyone to know about it.
He was teaching his disciples and telling them,
    "The Son of Man is to be handed over to men
    and they will kill him,
    and three days after his death the Son of Man will
      rise."
But they did not understand the saying,
    and they were afraid to question him.

They came to Capernaum and, once inside the house,
    he began to ask them,
    "What were you arguing about on the way?"
But they remained silent.
They had been discussing among themselves on the
    way
    who was the greatest.
Then he sat down, called the Twelve, and said to them,
    "If anyone wishes to be first,
    he shall be the last of all and the servant of all."
Taking a child, he placed it in their midst,
    and putting his arms around it, he said to them,
    "Whoever receives one child such as this in my
      name, receives me;
    and whoever receives me,
    receives not me but the One who sent me."

The Gospel of the Lord.

September 30, 2018

TWENTY-SIXTH SUNDAY IN ORDINARY TIME

Lect. No. 137 **FIRST READING: Numbers 11:25-29**

This passage from the Book of Numbers tells the latter part of an episode that occurred while the people of Israel were wandering in the desert after leaving Egypt.

Moses was overwhelmed with the responsibility of caring for this often difficult people, so God anointed seventy elders with his Spirit so that they could help lead the people.

Two of the elders were not present in front of the tent of sanctuary when the Spirit descended upon the seventy, but they nevertheless received the Spirit where they were standing in camp.

A young man reported this to Moses in the belief that they were doing something wrong (as if they were stealing some power that did not belong to them).

Moses responded to the young man that they were not doing anything wrong, for this was a gift of God that he wished everyone had.

A reading from the Book of Numbers

The LORD came down in the cloud and spoke to Moses.
Taking some of the spirit that was on Moses,
    the LORD bestowed it on the seventy elders;
    and as the spirit came to rest on them, they
        prophesied.

Now two men, one named Eldad and the other
        Medad,
    were not in the gathering but had been left in the
        camp.
They too had been on the list, but had not gone out
        to the tent;
    yet the spirit came to rest on them also,
    and they prophesied in the camp.
So, when a young man quickly told Moses,
    "Eldad and Medad are prophesying in the camp,"
    Joshua, son of Nun, who from his youth had been
        Moses' aide, said,
    "Moses, my lord, stop them."
But Moses answered him,
    "Are you jealous for my sake?
Would that all the people of the LORD were prophets!
Would that the LORD might bestow his spirit on
        them all!"

The word of the Lord.

Lect. No. 137

RESPONSORIAL PSALM: Ps 19:8, 10, 12-13, 14 (℟.: 9a)

The Responsorial Psalm is taken from a hymn that praises the goodness of the law of the LORD. The law was a special gift from God to teach us how to live godly lives.

It is not a series of impersonal regulations, but a revelation of God's own will for us.

In Psalm 19, there are six references to the law of the LORD. This is unusual, for seven is the perfect number in the Bible (for the ancients believed that there were seven planets, and the number seven thus signified the whole universe or perfection).

Yet, there is a seventh reference to the law at the end of the psalm when the Psalmist speaks of how the law must be in his words and in his heart.

The law only becomes perfect when it is interiorized and becomes second nature to us.

℟. **The precepts of the Lord give joy to the heart.**

The law of the LORD is perfect,
    refreshing the soul;
the decree of the LORD is trustworthy,
    giving wisdom to the simple.

℟. **The precepts of the Lord give joy to the heart.**

The fear of the LORD is pure,
    enduring forever;
the ordinances of the LORD are true,
    all of them just.

℟. **The precepts of the Lord give joy to the heart.**

Though your servant is careful of them,
    very diligent in keeping them,
yet who can detect failings?
    Cleanse me from my unknown faults!

℟. **The precepts of the Lord give joy to the heart.**

From wanton sin especially, restrain your servant;
    let it not rule over me.
Then shall I be blameless and innocent
    of serious sin.

℟. **The precepts of the Lord give joy to the heart.**

PASTORAL REFLECTIONS

The Gospels use an exaggerated form of discourse that was common in the times of Jesus. He did not intend for people to cut off body parts, but rather to make clear choices. When we read the Sacred Scriptures, we must remember to interpret them within their cultural context lest we make them say something that Jesus never intended.

Lect.
No. 137

SECOND READING: James 5:1-6

This is the last of a series of readings from the Letter of James that we have seen over the past several weeks. One of the major themes of the letter is social justice.

Today's reading is an attack on the unjust practices of the rich who exploit the poor.

Saint James reminds us that our earthly wealth cannot endure. It will eventually end up on the trash heap along with everything else that we possess. The only things that are truly eternal are love and virtue and faith in God.

We are reminded by this reading that we have a solemn obligation to work for justice in this world. God expects us to help the poor with the blessings that he has bestowed upon us. That is why he gave us those blessings in the first place.

A reading from the Letter of Saint James

Come now, you rich, weep and wail over your impending miseries.

Your wealth has rotted away, your clothes have become moth-eaten,

     your gold and silver have corroded,

     and that corrosion will be a testimony against you;

     it will devour your flesh like a fire.

You have stored up treasure for the last days.

Behold, the wages you withheld from the workers

     who harvested your fields are crying aloud;

     and the cries of the harvesters

     have reached the ears of the Lord of hosts.

You have lived on earth in luxury and pleasure;

     you have fattened your hearts for the day of slaughter.

You have condemned;

     you have murdered the righteous one;

     he offers you no resistance.

The word of the Lord.

Lect.
No. 137

ALLELUIA: cf. John 17:17b, 17a

In a world filled with temporary and partial truths, it is important to remember that God's Word is an eternal truth that never goes out of fashion.

℟. **Alleluia, alleluia.**

Your word, O Lord, is truth;
consecrate us in the truth.

℟. **Alleluia, alleluia.**

| Lect. |
| No. 137 |

GOSPEL: Mark 9:38-43, 45, 47-48

Over the past couple of weeks, we have heard Jesus predict his passion and we have also heard the inappropriate responses of his disciples. They did not understand that Jesus' mission was not about power, it was about service.

This is seen again at the beginning of this reading. John tries to convince Jesus to prevent others from casting out demons in Jesus' name.

It is as if John considers this to be a monopoly that they alone should possess. Jesus rejects that notion and tells the disciples not to do anything.

There are then a series of sayings. The first speaks of the blessing that one would receive for serving the disciples in Jesus' name.

Jesus then speaks of the horror of giving scandal to God's little ones.

Finally, he speaks of cutting off that which causes one to sin. This is a very Jewish way of speaking. Jesus does not intend us to cut off body parts.

Yet it is true that we often have to make choices against things and activities that might lead us into sin (avoiding the near occasion of sin).

A reading from the holy Gospel according to Mark

At that time, John said to Jesus,
   "Teacher, we saw someone driving out demons
     in your name,
  and we tried to prevent him because he does not
     follow us."
Jesus replied, "Do not prevent him.
There is no one who performs a mighty deed in my
     name
  who can at the same time speak ill of me.
For whoever is not against us is for us.
Anyone who gives you a cup of water to drink
  because you belong to Christ,
  amen, I say to you, will surely not lose his reward.

"Whoever causes one of these little ones who believe in me to sin,
  it would be better for him if a great millstone
  were put around his neck
  and he were thrown into the sea.
If your hand causes you to sin, cut it off.
It is better for you to enter into life maimed
  than with two hands to go into Gehenna,
  into the unquenchable fire.
And if your foot causes you to sin, cut if off.
It is better for you to enter into life crippled
  than with two feet to be thrown into Gehenna.
And if your eye causes you to sin, pluck it out.
Better for you to enter into the kingdom of God with
     one eye
  than with two eyes to be thrown into Gehenna,
  where 'their worm does not die, and the fire is not
     quenched.'"

The Gospel of the Lord.

October 7, 2018

TWENTY-SEVENTH SUNDAY IN ORDINARY TIME

Lect. No. 140 FIRST READING: Genesis 2:18-24

This First Reading was chosen because the Gospel speaks of divorce and how it violates God's intention that man and woman be joined in marriage.

This is a very ancient account, and it is more of a parable than a historic account of creation.

The naming of the animals was an act of dominion. When one knew the name of something, then one had power over it.

God forms Eve out of Adam's rib. Why a rib? Possibly because the Sumerian word for "rib" was the same as the word for "life."

There is a sense of intimacy in the choice of the title "woman." Men and women were intended for each other and they complete each other.

Although when this story was written, women left their homes and lived with a man's family, this account speaks of the opposite occurring (probably a vestige of a very old version of this story when Hebrew society was matriarchal).

A reading from the Book of Genesis

The LORD God said: "It is not good for the man to be alone.
I will make a suitable partner for him."
So the LORD God formed out of the ground
various wild animals and various birds of the air,
and he brought them to the man to see what he would call them;
whatever the man called each of them would be its name.
The man gave names to all the cattle,
all the birds of the air, and all wild animals;
but none proved to be the suitable partner for the man.

So the LORD God cast a deep sleep on the man,
and while he was asleep,
he took out one of his ribs and closed up its place with flesh.
The LORD God then built up into a woman the rib
that he had taken from the man.
When he brought her to the man, the man said:
"This one, at last, is bone of my bones
and flesh of my flesh;
this one shall be called 'woman,'
for out of 'her man' this one has been taken."
That is why a man leaves his father and mother
and clings to his wife,
and the two of them become one flesh.

The word of the Lord.

Lect.
No. 140

RESPONSORIAL PSALM: Ps 128:1-2, 3, 4-5, 6 (℟.: cf. 5)

The Responsorial Psalm is a wisdom psalm that speaks of the blessings received by those who walk in the way of the LORD.

The images used in this psalm are societal. The first has to do with the blessing that one would receive in one's work. One would eat the fruit of one's handiwork.

Remember how, when Adam was punished for his sin, he was told that he would work hard but only receive a scanty recompense. Here the curse would be reversed, and one would no longer be frustrated.

The second image is the blessing of a happy family life. Typically, the blessing is seen in terms of many children.

Finally, one's larger society would also be blessed, for Zion and Jerusalem would prosper.

℟. **May the Lord bless us all the days of our lives.**

Blessed are you who fear the LORD,
　who walk in his ways!
For you shall eat the fruit of your handiwork;
　blessed shall you be, and favored.

℟. **May the Lord bless us all the days of our lives.**

Your wife shall be like a fruitful vine
　in the recesses of your home,
your children like olive plants
　around your table.

℟. **May the Lord bless us all the days of our lives.**

Behold, thus is the man blessed
　who fears the LORD.
The LORD bless you from Zion:
　may you see the prosperity of Jerusalem
all the days of your life.

℟. **May the Lord bless us all the days of our lives.**

May you see your children's children.
　Peace be upon Israel!

℟. **May the Lord bless us all the days of our lives.**

Lect.
No. 140

SECOND READING: Hebrews 2:9-11

Today's Second Reading from the Letter to the Hebrews is part of a series that will continue for seven Sundays before the Solemnity of Our Lord Jesus Christ, King of the Universe. There is much Hebrew and Greek symbolism in this work. It is not quite a letter, but actually more of a treatise. Today's reading uses Hebrew imagery to make a point.

A reading from the Letter to the Hebrews

Brothers and sisters:
He "for a little while" was made "lower than the angels,"
　that by the grace of God he might taste death for everyone.

For it was fitting that he,
　for whom and through whom all things exist,

While Psalm 8 says that man was made little less than the angels, this author reads the verse as saying he was made less than the angels for a little while (thus making it refer to the incarnation).

This celebrates the fact that Jesus was born one like us to save us.

Lect.
No. 140

The Alleluia Verse reminds us that the question of divorce heard in the Gospel is not one of law, but rather one of love of God and love of one's brothers and sisters.

in bringing many children to glory,
    should make the leader to their salvation perfect
        through suffering.
He who consecrates and those who are being conse-
    crated
    all have one origin.
Therefore, he is not ashamed to call them "brothers."

The word of the Lord.

ALLELUIA: 1 John 4:12

℟. **Alleluia, alleluia.**

If we love one another, God remains in us
and his love is brought to perfection in us.

℟. **Alleluia, alleluia.**

Lect.
No. 140

GOSPEL: ◼A Longer Form: Mark 10:2-16

The Gospel begins with the question of divorce. Many of the rabbis at the time of Jesus were interpreting the law to make it as easy as possible for a man to divorce his wife. (Wives were not permitted to divorce their husbands.) They could be divorced for something as trivial as burning a meal.

Jesus rejected this tendency as an abuse. He was trying to protect women from exploitation, but, as we see in this reading, he was also trying to protect the sanctity of the bonds of marriage.

He taught that God intended man and woman to become one flesh. Given that this is

A reading from the holy Gospel according to Mark

The Pharisees approached Jesus and asked,
"Is it lawful for a husband to divorce his wife?"
They were testing him.
He said to them in reply, "What did Moses command
    you?"
They replied,
    "Moses permitted a husband to write a bill of di-
        vorce
    and dismiss her."
But Jesus told them,
    "Because of the hardness of your hearts
    he wrote you this commandment.
But from the beginning of creation, *God made them
    male and female.*
*For this reason a man shall leave his father and
    mother*

true, how could they, a man and woman, separate from each other and divorce?

It is absolutely clear that Jesus condemned divorce. We see his condemnation in the Synoptic Gospels (twice in Matthew and also in First Corinthians).

This is not something that the Church made up later, as some would argue, but rather something about which Jesus was adamant.

The second half of this reading speaks of the children who were being brought to Jesus to be blessed. From the tenor of the passage, it would appear that the parents of these children were insistent and they were bothering Jesus. (At least this is how the disciples interpreted it.)

Jesus rejected their evaluation based upon power and prestige. He welcomed and blessed the little ones and he also told his disciples that they must learn from and become like those children (filled with simplicity and innocence and not with the hunger for power that they were so often exhibiting in this Gospel).

and be joined to his wife,
and the two shall become one flesh.
So they are no longer two but one flesh.
Therefore what God has joined together,
  no human being must separate."
In the house the disciples again questioned Jesus
  about this.
He said to them,
  "Whoever divorces his wife and marries another
  commits adultery against her;
  and if she divorces her husband and marries another,
  she commits adultery."

And people were bringing children to him that he
  might touch them,
  but the disciples rebuked them.
When Jesus saw this he became indignant and said
  to them,
  "Let the children come to me;
  do not prevent them, for the kingdom of God belongs to such as these.
Amen, I say to you,
  whoever does not accept the kingdom of God like
  a child
  will not enter it."
Then he embraced them and blessed them,
  placing his hands on them.

The Gospel of the Lord.

PASTORAL REFLECTIONS

While Jesus clearly condemned divorce, he also called upon us to love the broken. It is a great pastoral challenge to be faithful to both of these values.

Lect.
No. 140

GOSPEL: B Shorter Form: Mark 10:2-12

The Gospel deals with the question of divorce. Many of the rabbis at the time of Jesus were interpreting the law to make it as easy as possible for a man to divorce his wife. (Wives were not permitted to divorce their husbands.)

They could be divorced for something as trivial as burning a meal.

Jesus rejected this tendency as an abuse. He was trying to protect women from exploitation, but, as we see in this reading, he was also trying to protect the sanctity of the bonds of marriage.

He taught that God intended man and woman to become one flesh. Given this, how could they possibly separate from each other and divorce?

It is absolutely clear that Jesus condemned divorce. We see this condemnation in the Synoptic Gospels (twice in Matthew and also in Paul's First Letter to the Corinthians).

This is not something that the Church made up later, as some would argue, but something about which Jesus was adamant.

A reading from the holy Gospel according to Mark

The Pharisees approached Jesus and asked,
"Is it lawful for a husband to divorce his wife?"
They were testing him.
He said to them in reply, "What did Moses command
    you?"
They replied,
  "Moses permitted a husband to write a bill of divorce
  and dismiss her."
But Jesus told them,
  "Because of the hardness of your hearts
  he wrote you this commandment.
But from the beginning of creation, *God made them
    male and female.*
*For this reason a man shall leave his father and
    mother*
  and be joined to his wife,
  and the two shall become one flesh.
So they are no longer two but one flesh.
Therefore what God has joined together,
  no human being must separate."
In the house the disciples again questioned Jesus
    about this.
He said to them,
  "Whoever divorces his wife and marries another
  commits adultery against her;
  and if she divorces her husband and marries another,
  she commits adultery."

The Gospel of the Lord.

October 14, 2018
TWENTY-EIGHTH SUNDAY IN ORDINARY TIME

Lect. No. 143

FIRST READING: Wisdom 7:7-11

The oldest concept of wisdom was that it was folk knowledge concerning how one might live the good life. The Book of Wisdom was written later in the Old Testament period, and in it wisdom is seen as God's revelation of his loving will and the mystery of his person.

This reading matches well the theme of the Gospel where we hear that we should love God and love those who are our neighbors.

This is truly God's will, and this is the most assured way of living lives that are anchored in God.

A reading from the Book of Wisdom

I prayed, and prudence was given me;
I pleaded, and the spirit of wisdom came to me.
I preferred her to scepter and throne,
and deemed riches nothing in comparison with her,
    nor did I liken any priceless gem to her;
because all gold, in view of her, is a little sand,
    and before her, silver is to be accounted mire.
Beyond health and comeliness I loved her,
and I chose to have her rather than the light,
    because the splendor of her never yields to sleep.
Yet all good things together came to me in her company,
and countless riches at her hands.

The word of the Lord.

Lect. No. 143

RESPONSORIAL PSALM: Ps 90:12-13, 14-15, 16-17 (℟.: 14)

The Responsorial Psalm reminds us that we cannot hope to please God without God first revealing to us what that means. We are fundamentally incapable of discerning God's will on our own. This is why we pray for wisdom.

We ask the LORD to send his Spirit into our hearts so that we might know his ways. We ask that same Spirit to give us the courage to do that which God has revealed to us.

℟. **Fill us with your love, O Lord, and we will sing for joy!**

Teach us to number our days aright,
    that we may gain wisdom of heart.
Return, O LORD! How long?
    Have pity on your servants!

℟. **Fill us with your love, O Lord, and we will sing for joy!**

Fill us at daybreak with your kindness,
    that we may shout for joy and gladness all our days.

351

We ask God to bless the work of our hands. This psalm reminds us that God is not only involved in things that we consider to be religious, but he is also present in every dimension of our lives.

No matter what occupation we have, we should ask God to bless our work. Otherwise, something will be missing.

We might even be accomplishing great things according to the standards of the world, but if God is not a part of it, it will have no heart or soul.

Make us glad, for the days when you afflicted us,
for the years when we saw evil.

℟. **Fill us with your love, O Lord, and we will sing for joy!**

Let your work be seen by your servants
and your glory by their children;
and may the gracious care of the Lord our God be ours;
prosper the work of our hands for us!
Prosper the work of our hands!

℟. **Fill us with your love, O Lord, and we will sing for joy!**

Lect. No. 143

SECOND READING: Hebrews 4:12-13

This passage speaks of the word of God being a two-edged sword. God's word is not something that can be ignored or discounted. It cuts right to our heart. This image is used in the Book of Revelation where a sword comes from the mouth of Jesus (his word) and the Gospel of Luke where Mary is told a sword would pierce her heart. (In the Bible, the heart is where one thinks.)

God's word would pierce her thoughts to help her believe what was impossible: that her Son was the Son of God.

A reading from the Letter to the Hebrews

Brothers and sisters:
Indeed the word of God is living and effective,
sharper than any two-edged sword,
penetrating even between soul and spirit, joints and marrow,
and able to discern reflections and thoughts of the heart.
No creature is concealed from him,
but everything is naked and exposed to the eyes of him
to whom we must render an account.

The word of the Lord.

PASTORAL REFLECTIONS

It has been said that if the word of God does not in some way challenge us, then we probably have missed its point.

Lect.
No. 143

ALLELUIA: Matthew 5:3

The Alleluia Verse calls the poor in spirit blessed. The poor in spirit are those who are not arrogant or presumptuous, but rather docile to God's will.

℟. **Alleluia, alleluia.**

Blessed are the poor in spirit,
for theirs is the kingdom of heaven.

℟. **Alleluia, alleluia.**

Lect.
No. 143

GOSPEL: ◼A Longer Form: Mark 10:17-30

In the beginning of this Gospel, Jesus challenges a man for calling him good. This is what a rabbi in his time would do, for the term "good" was reserved for God (as Jesus states).

Jesus then recites a number of the commandments as an explanation of what one should do. The commandments are stated as the minimum that one must do to remain in the grace of God.

The man who came to Jesus responds that he has always observed the commandments.

Jesus, loving the man, then challenges him and asks him to sell what he has and give it to the poor and follow him.

Jesus was calling the man to be the most that he could possibly be. He knew that this sacrifice would not be easy, but it is the same sacrifice that each Christian must face at some point in life.

A reading from the holy Gospel according to Mark

As Jesus was setting out on a journey, a man ran up,
knelt down before him, and asked him,
"Good teacher, what must I do to inherit eternal life?"
Jesus answered him, "Why do you call me good?
No one is good but God alone.
You know the commandments: *You shall not kill;*
  you shall not commit adultery;
  you shall not steal;
  you shall not bear false witness;
  you shall not defraud;
  honor your father and your mother."
He replied and said to him,
  "Teacher, all of these I have observed from my youth."
Jesus, looking at him, loved him and said to him,
  "You are lacking in one thing.
Go, sell what you have, and give to the poor
  and you will have treasure in heaven; then come, follow me."
At that statement his face fell,
  and he went away sad, for he had many possessions.

We must decide what is really important, what is worth living and dying for, and be willing to pay that price.

The man cannot give up the security of his many possessions and he goes away sad.

His hands were already filled with what he owned, and he could not embrace Jesus and his call.

Jesus then speaks of the difficulty of the rich entering the kingdom of God.

The apostles were astonished, for the rich were considered to be blessed at the time of Jesus. The apostles, in fact, were hoping that they would become rich.

Yet, Jesus tells them it is easier for a camel to pass through the eye of a needle than for a rich person to enter the kingdom.

There are two theories on this saying. The first is that one of the gates of Jerusalem, an especially low gate, was known as the eye of the needle.

The other theory is that Jesus really meant a needle's eye (i.e., it was really that difficult for a rich man to enter the kingdom).

The passage ends with the consoling words that all who follow Christ will be amply rewarded.

Jesus looked around and said to his disciples,
"How hard it is for those who have wealth
to enter the kingdom of God!"
The disciples were amazed at his words.
So Jesus again said to them in reply,
"Children, how hard it is to enter the kingdom of God!
It is easier for a camel to pass through the eye of a needle
than for one who is rich to enter the kingdom of God."
They were exceedingly astonished and said among themselves,
"Then who can be saved?"
Jesus looked at them and said,
"For human beings it is impossible, but not for God.
All things are possible for God."
Peter began to say to him,
"We have given up everything and followed you."
Jesus said, "Amen, I say to you,
there is no one who has given up house or brothers or sisters
or mother or father or children or lands
for my sake and for the sake of the gospel
who will not receive a hundred times more now in this present age:
houses and brothers and sisters
and mothers and children and lands,
with persecutions, and eternal life in the age to come."
The Gospel of the Lord.

Lect.
No. 143

GOSPEL: B Shorter Form: Mark 10:17-27

Jesus challenges the man who came to him for calling him good. This is what a rabbi in his time would do, for the term "good" was reserved for God (as Jesus states).

Jesus then recites the commandments as an explanation of what one should do. This man responds that he has always observed the commandments.

Jesus, loving the man, asks him to sell what he has and give it to the poor and follow him.

Jesus knew that this sacrifice would not be easy, but it is the same sacrifice that each Christian must face at some point in life.

We must decide what is really important, what is worth living and dying for, and we must be willing to pay that price.

The man cannot give up the security of his many possessions and he goes away sad.

His hands were already filled with what he owned, and he could not therefore embrace Jesus and his call.

Jesus then speaks of the difficulty of the rich entering the kingdom of God.

The apostles were astonished, for the rich were consid-

A reading from the holy Gospel according to Mark

As Jesus was setting out on a journey, a man ran up,
  knelt down before him, and asked him,
  "Good teacher, what must I do to inherit eternal life?"
Jesus answered him, "Why do you call me good?
No one is good but God alone.
You know the commandments: *You shall not kill;*
  you shall not commit adultery;
  you shall not steal;
  you shall not bear false witness;
  you shall not defraud;
  honor your father and your mother."
He replied and said to him,
  "Teacher, all of these I have observed from my youth."
Jesus, looking at him, loved him and said to him,
  "You are lacking in one thing.
Go, sell what you have, and give to the poor
  and you will have treasure in heaven; then come, follow me."
At that statement his face fell,
  and he went away sad, for he had many possessions.

Jesus looked around and said to his disciples,
  "How hard it is for those who have wealth
  to enter the kingdom of God!"
The disciples were amazed at his words.
So Jesus again said to them in reply,
  "Children, how hard it is to enter the kingdom of God!
It is easier for a camel to pass through the eye of a needle

ered to be blessed. The apostles, in fact, were hoping that they would become rich (as we saw in the Gospels of the past few weeks).

Yet, Jesus tells them it is easier for a camel to pass through the eye of a needle (either a very low gate in Jerusalem or an absurd example to signify something utterly impossible) than for a rich person to enter the kingdom.

than for one who is rich to enter the kingdom of God."
They were exceedingly astonished and said among themselves,
"Then who can be saved?"
Jesus looked at them and said,
"For human beings it is impossible, but not for God.
All things are possible for God."

The Gospel of the Lord.

PASTORAL REFLECTIONS

This discourse between Jesus and the rich young man does not quite seem fair, but it is. The young man wanted easy answers. He was willing to go only so far in his faith life. He wanted to keep the rules, but not to pay the ultimate price.

God challenges us in the same way that Jesus challenged the rich young man. He invites us to go beyond the rules with a faith that is unconditional. This means letting go of what is comfortable. It involves saying "no" to some things so that we might say "yes" to that which is more important.

In other words, what would we be willing to give up if we could not have both it and God—money? prestige? Our health? Our family? Our life?

No wonder the rich young man's face fell. No wonder that he thought that Jesus was asking the impossible of him. Yet, the irony is that no matter how much we hold on to of what we think is precious, we will sooner or later have to give it up as well.

October 21, 2018

TWENTY-NINTH SUNDAY IN ORDINARY TIME

Lect. No. 146 **FIRST READING: Isaiah 53:10-11**

This passage comes from the fourth of the songs of the Suffering Servant in Isaiah. It presents the idea that the servant will suffer for the sake of his people. Through his suffering and death, their sins will be forgiven.

Furthermore, God will reward the servant for the fact that he gave up his life by raising him from the dead. (This is how he will see fullness of days even though he dies for the sake of our sins.)

A reading from the Book of the Prophet Isaiah

The LORD was pleased
to crush him in infirmity.

If he gives his life as an offering for sin,
he shall see his descendants in a long life,
and the will of the LORD shall be accomplished
through him.

Because of his affliction
he shall see the light in fullness of days;
through his suffering, my servant shall justify
many,
and their guilt he shall bear.

The word of the Lord.

Lect. No. 146 **RESPONSORIAL PSALM: Ps 33:4-5, 18-19, 20, 22 (℟.: 22)**

The Responsorial Psalm comes from a hymn of praise. It glorifies the LORD whose word is upright and just.

Because God is so good, we can turn to him and entrust our plea into his hands. He will surely reply to our entreaty with great generosity, for we have placed our trust in him.

This psalm was normally sung as a response to an intervention in which God rescued those who had called upon him, but it can also be used as a

℟. **Lord, let your mercy be on us, as we place our trust in you.**

Upright is the word of the LORD,
and all his works are trustworthy.
He loves justice and right;
of the kindness of the LORD the earth is full.

℟. **Lord, let your mercy be on us, as we place our trust in you.**

See, the eyes of the LORD are upon those who fear him,
upon those who hope for his kindness,
to deliver them from death
and preserve them in spite of famine.

hymn of trust by those who have not yet seen that intervention.

That is when it is especially difficult to trust in God, for we cannot yet see the evidence of his concern. Still, it is then that we show that we truly trust in God (when trust seems all but impossible).

℟. **Lord, let your mercy be on us, as we place our trust in you.**

Our soul waits for the LORD,
　who is our help and our shield.
May your kindness, O LORD, be upon us
　who have put our hope in you.

℟. **Lord, let your mercy be on us, as we place our trust in you.**

Lect.
No. 146

SECOND READING: Hebrews 4:14-16

One of the central images of the Letter to the Hebrews is that Jesus is our High Priest.

He offered up the sacrifice of his own life. (He was, therefore, both the priest lifting up the offering and the offering itself.)

We are filled with confidence, for although Jesus exercised this great office, he nevertheless was able to identify with our weakness.

He experienced everything we do except sin, so he understands us and can empathize with our need.

A reading from the Letter to the Hebrews

Brothers and sisters:
Since we have a great high priest who has passed
　through the heavens,
Jesus, the Son of God,
let us hold fast to our confession.
For we do not have a high priest
　who is unable to sympathize with our weaknesses,
　but one who has similarly been tested in every
　way,
　yet without sin.
So let us confidently approach the throne of grace
　to receive mercy and to find grace for timely help.

The word of the Lord.

Lect.
No. 146

ALLELUIA: Mark 10:45

The Alleluia Verse reminds us of the true meaning of Jesus' ministry: he gave his life in order to set us free from sin and whatever holds us captive.

℟. **Alleluia, alleluia.**

The Son of Man came to serve
and to give his life as a ransom for many.

℟. **Alleluia, alleluia.**

Lect.
No. 146

GOSPEL: **A** Longer Form: Mark 10:35-45

Over these past several weeks we have seen two predictions of the passion and the numerous examples of how the disciples misinterpreted what Jesus was saying.

Jesus spoke of giving up his life in service, while the disciples thought in terms of power and prestige.

In today's Gospel, we hear one more example of their incomprehension.

Immediately before this passage Jesus has predicted his passion a third time. James and John respond to this prediction by asking for the favor of sitting on Jesus' right and left.

This is comparable to telling your best friend that you are dying, and hearing that person say that it is a shame but could they have your car when you are gone.

Jesus speaks of the fate of suffering and dying for others in terms of being baptized and drinking the cup of which he is to drink.

This reminds us that both of these sacraments (Baptism and Eucharist) are forms of dying to oneself in order to live for and in Christ.

He also tells them that the greatest in the kingdom is not the one who is served by others, but rather the one who serves.

A reading from the holy Gospel according to Mark

James and John, the sons of Zebedee, came to Jesus and said to him,
"Teacher, we want you to do for us whatever we ask of you."
He replied, "What do you wish me to do for you?"
They answered him, "Grant that in your glory
we may sit one at your right and the other at your left."
Jesus said to them, "You do not know what you are asking.
Can you drink the cup that I drink
or be baptized with the baptism with which I am baptized?"
They said to him, "We can."
Jesus said to them, "The cup that I drink, you will drink,
and with the baptism with which I am baptized, you will be baptized;
but to sit at my right or at my left is not mine to give
but is for those for whom it has been prepared."
When the ten heard this, they became indignant at James and John.
Jesus summoned them and said to them,
"You know that those who are recognized as rulers over the Gentiles
lord it over them,
and their great ones make their authority over them felt.
But it shall not be so among you.
Rather, whoever wishes to be great among you will be your servant;
whoever wishes to be first among you will be the slave of all.

This is a Gospel logic that is contrary to the values of the world.

For the Son of Man did not come to be served
but to serve and to give his life as a ransom for many."

The Gospel of the Lord.

**Lect.
No. 146**

GOSPEL: 🅱 Shorter Form: Mark 10:42-45

Over these past several weeks we have seen two predictions of the passion and the numerous examples of how the disciples misinterpreted Jesus' mission.

Jesus spoke of giving up his life in the service of others, while the disciples thought in terms of power and prestige.

In today's Gospel, Jesus tells his disciples that the greatest in the kingdom is not the one who is served by others, but rather the one who serves.

This is a Gospel logic that is contrary to the values of the world.

A reading from the holy Gospel according to Mark

Jesus summoned the Twelve and said to them,
"You know that those who are recognized as rulers over the Gentiles
lord it over them,
and their great ones make their authority over them felt.
But it shall not be so among you.
Rather, whoever wishes to be great among you will be your servant;
whoever wishes to be first among you will be the slave of all.
For the Son of Man did not come to be served
but to serve and to give his life as a ransom for many."

The Gospel of the Lord.

PASTORAL REFLECTIONS

It is in the Gospel of Mark that we see most clearly how Jesus overturns the values of our society. Power, prestige, and wealth are no longer important. What is most important is our willingness to express our love in service of others.

These truths are called Gospel irony, for they make no sense in the logic of this world; there is a greater wisdom, however, that St. Paul calls the wisdom of the cross.

October 28, 2018

THIRTIETH SUNDAY IN ORDINARY TIME

Lect. No. 149 **FIRST READING: Jeremiah 31:7-9**

The First Reading speaks of the restoration that the LORD was going to establish for his people.

The earlier part of the Book of the Prophet Jeremiah was an almost continuous catalog of condemnations and threats. Israel was told that its sin was so profound that it would be annihilated.

Yet the LORD relented and promised that a remnant would remain and flourish. He would establish a new covenant that would be written upon their hearts.

Those who were exiles would be brought back to the promised land. Even those who were normally considered to be incapable of travel—the woman with small children, the blind, and the lame—would be led along ways that had been prepared for them.

A reading from the Book of the Prophet Jeremiah

Thus says the LORD:
  Shout with joy for Jacob,
    exult at the head of the nations;
    proclaim your praise and say:
The LORD has delivered his people,
    the remnant of Israel.
Behold, I will bring them back
    from the land of the north;
I will gather them from the ends of the world,
    with the blind and the lame in their midst,
the mothers and those with child;
    they shall return as an immense throng.
They departed in tears,
    but I will console them and guide them;
I will lead them to brooks of water,
    on a level road, so that none shall stumble.
For I am a father to Israel,
    Ephraim is my first-born.

The word of the Lord.

PASTORAL REFLECTIONS

At times it can seem all but impossible to believe that things will get better, but God does bring back the exiles (whether they be the exiles in Babylon or our exiled hearts that have been broken). The restoration does not always come in the way we had hoped, but it always comes in the way that we need.

Lect.
No. 149 **RESPONSORIAL PSALM: Ps 126: 1-2, 2-3, 4-5, 6 (℟.: 3)**

The Responsorial Psalm continues the theme of restoration found in the First Reading. It speaks of the experience of God's people who were brought back from exile.

They had been carried off to a foreign land weeping, but now they were being fully restored. Even the nations, the pagan peoples, could see what God was doing for them.

The third section of the psalm changes from what seems to be past events (even if they do not seem to be events of the distant past) to present entreaties. The Psalmist beseeches the LORD to continue his beneficence and restore the fortunes of his people.

If he had already done so much for them, bringing them back from all the lands to which they had been scattered, then certainly he could complete his work by blessing their enterprises with success.

We often pray to God this way, recalling how God has led us through difficulties in the past, and asking God to do so once again for we are in need.

℟. **The Lord has done great things for us; we are filled with joy.**

When the LORD brought back the captives of Zion,
  we were like men dreaming.
Then our mouth was filled with laughter,
  and our tongue with rejoicing.

℟. **The Lord has done great things for us; we are filled with joy.**

Then they said among the nations,
  "The LORD has done great things for them."
The LORD has done great things for us;
  we are glad indeed.

℟. **The Lord has done great things for us; we are filled with joy.**

Restore our fortunes, O LORD,
  like the torrents in the southern desert.
Those that sow in tears
  shall reap rejoicing.

℟. **The Lord has done great things for us; we are filled with joy.**

Although they go forth weeping,
  carrying the seed to be sown,
they shall come back rejoicing,
  carrying their sheaves.

℟. **The Lord has done great things for us; we are filled with joy.**

Lect. No. 149

SECOND READING: Hebrews 5:1-6

Today's Second Reading continues the theme seen last week i.e., Jesus is our High Priest.

Like Aaron, Jesus did not choose to be a priest; he was chosen. It was God the Father who decided that he should serve this role for the people of Israel and for all the other peoples. Jesus was to be the priest who offered up a sacrifice (which was the offering of his own life).

Jesus is a priest in the line of Melchizedek, a priest forever.

Melchizedek was a pagan priest whom Abraham encountered while returning from battle. Abraham gave him a tithe of the booty. Melchizedek then offered a sacrifice of bread and wine.

Like Melchizedek, Jesus was not a descendant of Aaron nor of the tribe of Levi. Like him, he offered bread and wine.

A reading from the Letter to the Hebrews

Brothers and sisters:
Every high priest is taken from among men
and made their representative before God,
to offer gifts and sacrifices for sins.
He is able to deal patiently with the ignorant and
erring,
for he himself is beset by weakness
and so, for this reason, must make sin offerings
for himself
as well as for the people.
No one takes this honor upon himself
but only when called by God,
just as Aaron was.
In the same way,
it was not Christ who glorified himself in becoming high priest,
but rather the one who said to him:
You are my son:
this day I have begotten you;
just as he says in another place:
You are a priest forever
according to the order of Melchizedek.

The word of the Lord.

Lect. No. 149

ALLELUIA: cf. 2 Timothy 1:10

The Alleluia Verse continues the restoration theme found in the First Reading and the Responsorial Psalm, introducing the idea of light (to hint at the Gospel healing of the blind man).

℟. **Alleluia, alleluia.**

Our Savior Jesus Christ destroyed death
and brought life to light through the Gospel.

℟. **Alleluia, alleluia.**

Lect.
No. 149

GOSPEL: Mark 10:46-52

Jesus and his disciples were leaving Jericho, a city situated on the road to Jerusalem. This is important to know, for the title that the blind man uses when he calls upon Jesus is "Son of David."

This proclamation is a preparation for the things that would shortly occur in Jerusalem when Jesus will be proclaimed Son of David on Palm Sunday and then crucified as king of the Jews on Good Friday.

Jesus heals Bartimaeus, the blind man, telling him that his faith had saved him. Throughout the Gospels, there is a certain inconsistency concerning the connection of faith and miracles.

At times, it is the faith of the people that produces the miracles (e.g., here, the woman with the hemorrhage); at other times Jesus performs the miracles and the people acquire faith through what has happened (e.g., the Wedding Feast of Cana).

A reading from the holy Gospel according to Mark

As Jesus was leaving Jericho with his disciples and a sizable crowd,
Bartimaeus, a blind man, the son of Timaeus,
sat by the roadside begging.
On hearing that it was Jesus of Nazareth,
he began to cry out and say,
"Jesus, son of David, have pity on me."
And many rebuked him, telling him to be silent.
But he kept calling out all the more,
"Son of David, have pity on me."
Jesus stopped and said, "Call him."
So they called the blind man, saying to him,
"Take courage; get up, Jesus is calling you."
He threw aside his cloak, sprang up, and came to Jesus.
Jesus said to him in reply, "What do you want me to do for you?"
The blind man replied to him, "Master, I want to see."
Jesus told him, "Go your way; your faith has saved you."
Immediately he received his sight
and followed him on the way.

The Gospel of the Lord.

PASTORAL REFLECTIONS

The crowd wanted Bartimaeus to be quiet. They did not want him to rock the boat, but Bartimaeus refused to play their game. He insisted upon what he felt he needed. There are times in our lives when we must speak up and even shake things up for the sake of truth and love.

Lect. No. 667

FIRST READING: Revelation 7:2-4, 9-14

We hear about how the chosen ones were to be marked with the seal of the living God upon their foreheads. In the Book of the Prophet Ezekiel this mark was the Hebrew letter "tau," the first letter of the word Torah, which means "the law." All faithful Jews were to be observers of the law to the deepest part of their being.

In the New Testament, the elect are to be sealed with the Greek letter "tau," which looks like the modern "T." It is a symbol for the cross, for all of Christ's brothers and sisters are to be sealed with the sign of the cross.

We hear that there are one hundred and forty-four thousand to be sealed. Some Christian sects argue that this is the number of people who will be going to heaven.

This is a misunderstanding of the symbolism of the Book of Revelation. In this book, that which we see is the superficial meaning, while that which we hear is the spiritual significance.

John saw a crowd without number from every nation and race and people and tongue. These are the people who are going to heaven. They are numberless.

A reading from the Book of Revelation

I, John, saw another angel come up from the East,
, holding the seal of the living God.
He cried out in a loud voice to the four angels
    who were given power to damage the land and
    the sea,
    "Do not damage the land or the sea or the trees
    until we put the seal on the foreheads of the ser-
    vants of our God."
I heard the number of those who had been marked
    with the seal,
    one hundred and forty-four thousand marked
    from every tribe of the children of Israel.

After this I had a vision of a great multitude,
    which no one could count,
    from every nation, race, people, and tongue.
They stood before the throne and before the Lamb,
    wearing white robes and holding palm branches
    in their hands.
They cried out in a loud voice:
    "Salvation comes from our God, who is seated on
    the throne,
    and from the Lamb."
All the angels stood around the throne
    and around the elders and the four living creatures.
They prostrated themselves before the throne,
    worshiped God, and exclaimed:
    "Amen. Blessing and glory, wisdom and thanks-
    giving,

365

However, John also heard that they were one hundred and forty-four thousand. This number is twelve times twelve times one thousand. Twelve stands for the twelve patriarchs of the Old Testament. Twelve also stands for the twelve apostles. One thousand stands for a very large number.

Thus, one hundred and forty-four thousand means the Old and New Israel. The number is their spiritual identity, not the actual number of those going to heaven.

honor, power, and might
> be to our God forever and ever. Amen."

Then one of the elders spoke up and said to me,
> "Who are these wearing white robes, and where did they come from?"

I said to him, "My lord, you are the one who knows."
He said to me,
> "These are the ones who have survived the time of great distress;
> they have washed their robes
> and made them white in the Blood of the Lamb."

The word of the Lord.

Lect. No. 667

RESPONSORIAL PSALM: Ps 24:1bc-2, 3-4ab, 5–6 (℟.: 6)

Psalm 24 is a wisdom psalm that was probably used for pilgrimages to the temple. Wisdom literature speaks of how to live the good life, a life pleasing to the LORD.

This psalm asks who can ascend the mountain of the LORD, the mountain leading to Jerusalem and its temple. Only that person whose hands are sinless and whose heart is clean can participate in the worship of the LORD.

This does not mean that we must be perfect to belong to God's holy people. All of us are sinners, but we must make an effort to convert and change our ways. This is a lifetime project and we will not be totally perfect until the last day. Yet, in the meantime, we commit ourselves more and more to service of our God and our brothers and sisters. This is the way that we will be those who seek "the face of the God of Jacob."

℟. **Lord, this is the people that longs to see your face.**

The LORD's are the earth and its fullness;
> the world and those who dwell in it.
For he founded it upon the seas
> and established it upon the rivers.

℟. **Lord, this is the people that longs to see your face.**

Who can ascend the mountain of the LORD?
> or who may stand in his holy place?
One whose hands are sinless, whose heart is clean,
> who desires not what is vain.

℟. **Lord, this is the people that longs to see your face.**

He shall receive a blessing from the LORD,
> a reward from God his savior.
Such is the race that seeks for him,
> that seeks the face of the God of Jacob.

℟. **Lord, this is the people that longs to see your face.**

Lect. No. 667

The First Letter of John is a masterful treatise on the love of God. It is here, in fact, that we hear the phrase that God is love.

God has demonstrated how much he loves us by the fact that we are called children of God. God does not call us slaves; God calls us his friends and even his beloved children.

This does not mean that everyone will love us. The world hated Jesus because it could not embrace Jesus and his message. It wanted selfishness, and Jesus preached love and sacrifice.

We are already God's children. What we shall be in the future cannot even be imagined, for it will be a participation in the glory of God.

Lect. No. 667

The Lord Jesus offers to be our refuge when life becomes a burden to us. He is the source of peace for our hearts and our only true joy. Only in him will we find true rest.

Lect. No. 667

Today's Gospel presents the Beatitudes from the Gospel of Matthew. In Matthew's Gospel, Jesus is the new Moses. He is the founder of the New Israel, the Church. Like Moses who climbed Mount Sinai to receive the law, Jesus climbed a moun-

SECOND READING: 1 John 3:1-3

A reading from the first Letter of Saint John

Beloved:
See what love the Father has bestowed on us
that we may be called the children of God.
Yet so we are.
The reason the world does not know us
is that it did not know him.
Beloved, we are God's children now;
what we shall be has not yet been revealed.
We do know that when it is revealed we shall be like him,
for we shall see him as he is.
Everyone who has this hope based on him makes himself pure,
as he is pure.

The word of the Lord.

ALLELUIA: Matthew 11:28

℟. **Alleluia, alleluia.**

Come to me, all you who labor and are burdened,
and I will give you rest, says the Lord.

℟. **Alleluia, alleluia.**

GOSPEL: Matthew 5:1-12a

A reading from the holy Gospel according to Matthew

When Jesus saw the crowds, he went up the mountain,
and after he had sat down, his disciples came to him.

tain in order to give the new law to the New Israel (the Sermon on the Mount).

Unlike the ten commandments of the old law, the Beatitudes are not a series of dos and don'ts. They are a call to generosity. One no longer asks how much one can do before it becomes a sin. One must ask what one can do to become a better Christian.

The poor in spirit are those who are not proud (unlike the Pharisees). Those who hunger and thirst for righteousness are the Christians. They were unjustly thrown out of the synagogue for their profession of faith in Jesus. Likewise, they are persecuted for the sake of the kingdom.

Those who are clean of heart are those whose every thought is of God. If one's every thought is of God, then one will see signs of God everywhere (for creation is a gift from God). One will judge everything that one sees to be a sign of God's goodness and generosity.

He began to teach them, saying:
"Blessed are the poor in spirit,
    for theirs is the Kingdom of heaven.
Blessed are they who mourn,
    for they will be comforted.
Blessed are the meek,
    for they will inherit the land.
Blessed are they who hunger and thirst for righteousness,
    for they will be satisfied.
Blessed are the merciful,
    for they will be shown mercy.
Blessed are the clean of heart,
    for they will see God.
Blessed are the peacemakers,
    for they will be called children of God.
Blessed are they who are persecuted for the sake of righteousness,
    for theirs is the Kingdom of heaven.
Blessed are you when they insult you and persecute you
    and utter every kind of evil against you falsely because of me.
Rejoice and be glad,
    for your reward will be great in heaven."

The Gospel of the Lord.

PASTORAL REFLECTIONS

Today's feast offers an excellent opportunity to consider those people in our lives who taught us the meaning of sanctity. Very few of us will ever meet someone who will one day be canonized, but we all meet people who lovingly respond to God's call. This is why St. Paul called the members of the Christian communities "saints," for he realized that there are many saints all around us.

November 4, 2018

THIRTY-FIRST SUNDAY IN ORDINARY TIME

Lect. No. 152 **FIRST READING: Deuteronomy 6:2-6**

The Gospel today will speak of the two great commandments, i.e., to love the LORD with all one's heart and soul and strength and to love one's neighbor as one's self.

The First Reading thus gives the Old Testament citation of the first great law. This passage was prayed each day by devout Jews, for it is the "Shema Israel" (a Hebrew title that means "Hear, O Israel").

The rabbis said that to love the LORD with all one's heart meant to love the LORD with one's intellect (remember that in the Bible one thinks with one's heart). To love the LORD with one's soul meant to love the LORD even to the moment that they separate soul from body during persecution. To love the LORD with one's strength meant to love the LORD with all of one's material possessions.

A reading from the Book of Deuteronomy

Moses spoke to the people, saying:
"Fear the LORD, your God,
  and keep, throughout the days of your lives,
  all his statutes and commandments which I enjoin
    on you,
  and thus have long life.
Hear then, Israel, and be careful to observe them,
  that you may grow and prosper the more,
  in keeping with the promise of the LORD, the God
    of your fathers,
  to give you a land flowing with milk and honey.

"Hear, O Israel! The LORD is our God, the LORD
    alone!
Therefore, you shall love the LORD, your God,
  with all your heart,
  and with all your soul,
  and with all your strength.
Take to heart these words which I enjoin on you
    today."

The word of the Lord.

PASTORAL REFLECTIONS

Given that the main theme of today's Mass is to love God and to love one's neighbor, it is a good opportunity to remind ourselves that love is not an emotion—it is a choice. We do not always receive consolation for making that choice, but we find peace when we truly love with our heart, soul, and strength.

Lect. No. 152

RESPONSORIAL PSALM: Ps 18:2-3, 3-4, 47, 51 (℟.: 2)

This is a hymn of praise to God who delivered us from all our enemies. We hear that God is a rock, fortress, and deliverer (titles that give a sense of how safe we feel in his presence).

The First Reading and the Gospel speak of how we should love God with all our heart, soul, and strength. This love is an act of trust.

It is not easy to make this act of trust, especially when we have been hurt by so many things throughout our lives. But this psalm reminds us that God's love is the only love in our lives that will never go away and never make mistakes.

℟. **I love you, Lord, my strength.**

I love you, O Lᴏʀᴅ, my strength,
    O Lᴏʀᴅ, my rock, my fortress, my deliverer.

℟. **I love you, Lord, my strength.**

My God, my rock of refuge,
    my shield, the horn of my salvation, my stronghold!
Praised be the Lᴏʀᴅ, I exclaim,
    and I am safe from my enemies.

℟. **I love you, Lord, my strength.**

The Lᴏʀᴅ lives! And blessed be my rock!
    Extolled be God my savior,
you who gave great victories to your king
    and showed kindness to your anointed.

℟. **I love you, Lord, my strength.**

Lect. No. 152

SECOND READING: Hebrews 7:23-28

This reading contrasts the priesthood of Jesus to that of the priests of the Old Testament. Those priests did not live forever. There were many of them, one after another. Jesus, on the other hand, lives forever.

This letter was influenced by Greek philosophy. In Platonic philosophy, the one is better than the many. The one perfectly expresses the idea being communicated, but the many are many because each one of them fails to fully communicate what is intended.

A reading from the Letter to the Hebrews

Brothers and sisters:
The levitical priests were many
    because they were prevented by death from remaining in office,
    but Jesus, because he remains forever,
    has a priesthood that does not pass away.
Therefore, he is always able to save those who approach God through him,
    since he lives forever to make intercession for them.

It was fitting that we should have such a high priest:
    holy, innocent, undefiled, separated from sinners,
    higher than the heavens.

Thus, Jesus is the perfect High Priest while the priests of the Old Testament always fell short.

Furthermore, the priests of the Old Testament were sinners. Therefore, when they sacrificed they had to do so for themselves and for the people.

Jesus, being sinless, could offer sacrifices for us alone (for he did not need them for himself).

Lect. No. 152

The Alleluia Verse continues the idea that our goal is to love the Lord with all of our heart, soul, and strength. We do this by keeping God's commandments and by thus abiding in his love.

Lect. No. 152

All throughout the Gospel, the Pharisees and scribes had been trying to trap Jesus in order to have charges that they might bring against him. We can assume that this was what the scribe was trying to do when he approached Jesus with the question of which was the greatest of the commandments.

Jesus gives the scribe the simple answer that to love God and love neighbor are the two

He has no need, as did the high priests,
    to offer sacrifice day after day,
    first for his own sins and then for those of the
        people;
    he did that once for all when he offered himself.
For the law appoints men subject to weakness to be
        high priests,
    but the word of the oath, which was taken after
        the law,
    appoints a son,
    who has been made perfect forever.

The word of the Lord.

ALLELUIA: John 14:23

℟. **Alleluia, alleluia.**

Whoever loves me will keep my word,
    says the Lord; and my Father will love him
    and we will come to him.

℟. **Alleluia, alleluia.**

GOSPEL: Mark 12:28b-34

A reading from the holy Gospel according to Mark

One of the scribes came to Jesus and asked him, "Which is the first of all the commandments?"
Jesus replied, "The first is this:
    Hear, O Israel!
    The Lord our God is Lord alone!
    You shall love the Lord your God with all your
        heart,
    with all your soul,
    with all your mind,
    and with all your strength.

greatest of the commandments. What seems to have begun as a test ends in a form of mutual admiration, for the scribe acknowledges the wisdom of Jesus' answer, and Jesus acknowledges the honesty and integrity of the scribe's acknowledgment.

Note that the scribes and the Pharisees seem to have been a bit nonplussed by this response, for there was a simple wisdom to it and they did not dare ask other questions.

This interchange could give us a sense of how to respond to those who are trying to play games with us. Jesus refuses to play their game. He answers their questions with simple honesty, and they are disarmed.

The second is this:

You shall love your neighbor as yourself.

There is no other commandment greater than these."

The scribe said to him, "Well said, teacher.

You are right in saying,

'He is One and there is no other than he.'

And 'to love him with all your heart,

with all your understanding,

with all your strength,

and to love your neighbor as yourself'

is worth more than all burnt offerings and sacrifices."

And when Jesus saw that he answered with understanding,

he said to him,

"You are not far from the kingdom of God."

And no one dared to ask him any more questions.

The Gospel of the Lord.

PASTORAL REFLECTIONS

It is often difficult to balance love of God with love of neighbor. Should we spend our time praying or serving the poor? Should we dedicate our time to our family or to our church community? We will always be torn between these calls while we are upon this earth.

In November we remember the dead, and it is a good time to meditate upon the fact that in heaven we will no longer be torn between loving God and loving each other. In heaven we will be able to love both. In fact, we will be able to love everyone without it taking away from our love of each one.

November 11, 2018

THIRTY-SECOND SUNDAY IN ORDINARY TIME

Lect. No. 155 **FIRST READING: 1 Kings 17:10-16**

The First Reading tells the story of a poor widow of a town named Zarephath (which was about 9 miles to the south of Sidon, a territory outside of Israel). There was a great drought in the land.

The reason for this was that the Israelites were worshiping Baal, the pagan god of fertility. They believed that Baal would bring the rain to fertilize the land.

Yahweh withheld the rain to show them that he was the true God of the rain, the only true God.

The widow only had a small amount of food when Elijah, the man of God, asked her for something to eat. She responded that she was planning to prepare what little she had for herself and her son and then sit down and die.

Yet, Elijah reassured her and told her that she would not suffer from want. So she trusted and obeyed him and prepared a cake of bread for him to eat.

This is not unlike the Gospel story today in which the poor widow gives everything that she has, two small coins, to the temple.

A reading from the first Book of Kings

In those days, Elijah the prophet went to Zarephath.
  As he arrived at the entrance of the city,
    a widow was gathering sticks there; he called out to her,
  "Please bring me a small cupful of water to drink."
She left to get it, and he called out after her,
  "Please bring along a bit of bread."
She answered, "As the LORD, your God, lives,
  I have nothing baked; there is only a handful of flour in my jar
  and a little oil in my jug.
Just now I was collecting a couple of sticks,
  to go in and prepare something for myself and my son;
  when we have eaten it, we shall die."
Elijah said to her, "Do not be afraid.
Go and do as you propose.
But first make me a little cake and bring it to me.
Then you can prepare something for yourself and your son.
For the LORD, the God of Israel, says,
  'The jar of flour shall not go empty,
  nor the jug of oil run dry,
  until the day when the LORD sends rain upon the earth.'"
She left and did as Elijah had said.
She was able to eat for a year, and he and her son as well;

God miraculously fulfilled the promise that Elijah had made. The woman's jug of oil and jar of flour did not run out for the entire time of the drought.

the jar of flour did not go empty,
nor the jug of oil run dry,
as the LORD had foretold through Elijah.

The word of the Lord.

Lect.
No. 155

RESPONSORIAL PSALM: Ps 146:7, 8-9, 9-10 (℟.: 1b)

The Responsorial Psalm celebrates the fact that the LORD cares for those who have no one else to provide for their needs. It speaks of the widow and the orphan as well as the stranger (the foreigner).

All of these are traditional categories for people who need a defender to care for them. God will be that guardian and shield.

Our role as Christians is to continue the work of looking out for the most defenseless in our society. While we have many social institutions, there are still many people who for one reason or another fall through the cracks.

As in most societies, it is often the elderly and the young who suffer most. We are to be their advocates and protectors.

It is said that the moral worth of a society is judged by how the most defenseless of its citizens are treated. We should always try to reach out to those who have been left behind and to give them a helping hand.

℟. **Praise the Lord, my soul!**

or:

℟. **Alleluia.**

The LORD keeps faith forever,
    secures justice for the oppressed,
    gives food to the hungry.
The LORD sets captives free.

℟. **Praise the Lord, my soul!**

or:

℟. **Alleluia.**

The LORD gives sight to the blind;
    the LORD raises up those who were bowed down.
The LORD loves the just;
    the LORD protects strangers.

℟. **Praise the Lord, my soul!**

or:

℟. **Alleluia.**

The fatherless and the widow he sustains,
    but the way of the wicked he thwarts.
The LORD shall reign forever;
    your God, O Zion, through all generations. Alleluia.

℟. **Praise the Lord, my soul!**

or:

℟. **Alleluia.**

Lect.
No. 155

SECOND READING: Hebrews 9:24-28

We continue the theme seen in last week's reading from the Letter to the Hebrews: that Jesus is our High Priest and that he has offered himself as the perfect offering once and for all.

As in last week's reading, the many sacrifices of the Old Testament priests are contrasted with the one sacrifice of Christ.

The Old Testament priests had to offer many sacrifices because all of their sacrifices were imperfect. None of them fully accomplished that which was intended: to free us from our sins.

Jesus, on the other hand, offered the perfect sacrifice. He was sinless, and therefore his sacrifice was one of pure love.

Furthermore, he was God's only Son, and therefore his sacrifice of his own life was absolutely perfect and accomplished what it sought: the remission of our sins.

A reading from the Letter to the Hebrews

Christ did not enter into a sanctuary made by hands,
a copy of the true one, but heaven itself,
that he might now appear before God on our behalf.
Not that he might offer himself repeatedly,
as the high priest enters each year into the sanctuary
with blood that is not his own;
if that were so, he would have had to suffer repeatedly
from the foundation of the world.
But now once for all he has appeared at the end of the ages
to take away sin by his sacrifice.
Just as it is appointed that human beings die once,
and after this the judgment, so also Christ,
offered once to take away the sins of many,
will appear a second time, not to take away sin
but to bring salvation to those who eagerly await him.

The word of the Lord.

Lect.
No. 155

ALLELUIA: Matthew 5:3

The Alleluia Verse returns to the main theme found in the First Reading and the Gospel: blessed are the poor in spirit, those who place all their trust in the Lord.

℟. **Alleluia, alleluia.**

Blessed are the poor in spirit,
for theirs is the kingdom of heaven.

℟. **Alleluia, alleluia.**

Lect.
No. 155

GOSPEL: ▲ Longer Form: Mark 12:38-44

The Gospel provides a powerful contrast between the scribes who loved to be seen and given places of honor, and the poor widow who contributes everything she has to the temple.

The scribes are described as people who devour the savings of widows. They seek contributions for their religious work, but everything they do is for prestige and for show.

They are really arrogant in their practice of their religious duties. They use religion as a way to advance themselves at the cost of others.

The poor widow, on the other hand, demonstrated the true spirit of religious faith. Her small contribution was all that she had. She was placing herself totally in the hands of the Lord. She was not seeking power and prestige—she was simply performing an act of absolute trust.

She is what the Beatitudes call poor in spirit, for her only treasure was the love of God.

A reading from the holy Gospel according to Mark

In the course of his teaching Jesus said to the crowds,
   "Beware of the scribes, who like to go around in long robes
   and accept greetings in the marketplaces,
   seats of honor in synagogues,
   and places of honor at banquets.
They devour the houses of widows and, as a pretext, recite lengthy prayers.
They will receive a very severe condemnation."

He sat down opposite the treasury
   and observed how the crowd put money into the treasury.
Many rich people put in large sums.
A poor widow also came and put in two small coins worth a few cents.
Calling his disciples to himself, he said to them,
   "Amen, I say to you, this poor widow put in more than all the other contributors to the treasury.
For they have all contributed from their surplus wealth,
   but she, from her poverty, has contributed all she had,
   her whole livelihood."

The Gospel of the Lord.

PASTORAL REFLECTIONS

A good measure of our true motivation is our response when we are not thanked or even noticed for doing a good deed.

Lect.
No. 155

GOSPEL: B Shorter Form: Mark 12:41-44

The poor widow of this Gospel demonstrates the true spirit of religious faith. Her small contribution to the temple treasury was all that she had. She was placing herself totally in the hands of the Lord. She was not seeking power and prestige—she was simply performing an act of absolute trust.

She is what the Beatitudes call poor in spirit, for her only treasure was the love of God. In that sense, even though the amount of her actual offering was insignificant, its value was much greater than the offerings of those who had much more in surplus and who could afford to make great gestures of generosity.

A reading from the holy Gospel according to Mark

Jesus sat down opposite the treasury
and observed how the crowd put money into the treasury.
Many rich people put in large sums.
A poor widow also came and put in two small coins worth a few cents.
Calling his disciples to himself, he said to them,
"Amen, I say to you, this poor widow put in more than all the other contributors to the treasury.
For they have all contributed from their surplus wealth,
but she, from her poverty, has contributed all she had,
her whole livelihood."

The Gospel of the Lord.

PASTORAL REFLECTIONS

The poor widow had little, so she could only give a little. Yet, her gift was greater than that of those who gave more from their surplus.

What do we think of those who have not received as much in terms of family background, moral training, etc.? Maybe some of those who are doing much less than we are in moral terms are also giving what little they have, while we might only be giving from our surplus.

We never really know what moral gifts a person has or does not have. This is why it is so dangerous to judge them. We just don't know.

November 18, 2018

THIRTY-THIRD SUNDAY IN ORDINARY TIME

Lect. No. 158

FIRST READING: Daniel 12:1-3

The readings for the last week of Ordinary Time are always a bit apocalyptic in nature.

They are preparing us for the end of the Church Year and also for the end of the world.

The First Reading today is taken from the Book of Daniel. It speaks of Michael, the archangel, who will fight a great battle against the forces of evil. There will be a time of tribulation.

Apocalyptic books always spoke of this tribulation as a time when the good would be tested and the evil would be defeated.

Finally, those who have died will rise from the grave, some to receive their eternal reward and others to be condemned and suffer their eternal punishment.

A reading from the Book of the Prophet Daniel

In those days, I, Daniel,
heard this word of the Lord:
"At that time there shall arise
Michael, the great prince,
guardian of your people;
it shall be a time unsurpassed in distress
since nations began until that time.
At that time your people shall escape,
everyone who is found written in the book.

"Many of those who sleep in the dust of the earth
shall awake;
some shall live forever,
others shall be an everlasting horror and disgrace.

"But the wise shall shine brightly
like the splendor of the firmament,
and those who lead the many to justice
shall be like the stars forever."

The word of the Lord.

Lect. No. 158

RESPONSORIAL PSALM: Ps 16:5, 8, 9-10, 11 (℞.: 1)

The First Reading and the Gospel speak of the era of tribulation, that era in human history when the forces of good and the forces of evil will be locked in mortal combat.

At that time, God will send his protection upon those who have professed his cause.

℞. **You are my inheritance, O Lord!**

O LORD, my allotted portion and my cup,
you it is who hold fast my lot.
I set the LORD ever before me;
with him at my right hand I shall not be disturbed.

℞. **You are my inheritance, O Lord!**

This Responsorial Psalm is a profession of faith in that providence. We can always trust that God will protect us from all that would seek to lead us astray.

While apocalyptic books tend to speak of a great period of tribulation, one could argue that every era is a period of tribulation.

In every era we are called to give witness to our faith, something that always requires trust and surrender.

Therefore my heart is glad and my soul rejoices,
    my body, too, abides in confidence;
because you will not abandon my soul to the nether-
        world,
    nor will you suffer your faithful one to undergo
        corruption.

℟. **You are my inheritance, O Lord!**

You will show me the path to life,
    fullness of joys in your presence,
    the delights at your right hand forever.

℟. **You are my inheritance, O Lord!**

| Lect. |
| No. 158 |

SECOND READING: Hebrews 10:11-14, 18

Once again we hear the idea that Jesus was the perfect High Priest who offered the sacrifice of his life and love once and for all time. There was no need to repeat this sacrifice, for it was perfectly effective in obtaining the forgiveness of our sins.

When we celebrate the Eucharist, we are not repeating the sacrifice of Jesus one more time. At Mass, we pass outside of the normal understanding of time and place.

We are present again at the Last Supper and Mount Calvary. We are not repeating it; we are once again present at it.

A reading from the Letter to the Hebrews

Brothers and sisters:
Every priest stands daily at his ministry,
    offering frequently those same sacrifices
    that can never take away sins.
But this one offered one sacrifice for sins,
    and took his seat forever at the right hand of God;
    now he waits until his enemies are made his foot-
        stool.
For by one offering
    he has made perfect forever those who are being
        consecrated.

Where there is forgiveness of these,
    there is no longer offering for sin.

The word of the Lord.

Lect.
No. 158

The Alleluia Verse continues the apocalyptic theme found in the First Reading and the Gospel, that we must always be ready for the return of the Lord in glory, for we know neither the time nor the place.

Lect.
No. 158

In this passage Jesus speaks of the end of the world. He uses language that was in vogue during his time, e.g., tribulation, cosmic disturbances, etc.

It is not clear if Jesus intended this to be understood literally, or if it was a symbolic way of saying that the world would come to an end.

Jesus also speaks of the Son of Man descending upon a cloud. This is a citation from the Book of Daniel, which states that the Son of Man will appear before the Ancient One (Yahweh) to receive power and dominion.

Jesus is saying that he will rule over the heavens and the earth at the end of time.

Jesus tells his listeners to look for the signs, but he also tells them that no one knows when it will occur. We are always seeing signs of our own end (e.g., gray hair, pain, etc.). These are reminders that we will not last forever, and therefore should be ready for our end.

As for the end of the world, while we believe in it, we do not know when it will occur.

ALLELUIA: Luke 21:36

℟. **Alleluia, alleluia.**

Be vigilant at all times
and pray that you have the strength to stand before
the Son of Man.

℟. **Alleluia, alleluia.**

GOSPEL: Mark 13:24-32

A reading from the holy Gospel according to Mark

Jesus said to his disciples:
"In those days after that tribulation
the sun will be darkened,
and the moon will not give its light,
and the stars will be falling from the sky,
and the powers in the heavens will be shaken.

"And then they will see 'the Son of Man coming in the
clouds'
with great power and glory,
and then he will send out the angels
and gather his elect from the four winds,
from the end of the earth to the end of the sky.

"Learn a lesson from the fig tree.
When its branch becomes tender and sprouts leaves,
you know that summer is near.
In the same way, when you see these things happening,
know that he is near, at the gates.
Amen, I say to you,
this generation will not pass away
until all these things have taken place.
Heaven and earth will pass away,
but my words will not pass away.

"But of that day or hour, no one knows,
neither the angels in heaven, nor the Son, but
only the Father."

The Gospel of the Lord.

November 25, 2018
Last Sunday in Ordinary Time
OUR LORD JESUS CHRIST, KING OF THE UNIVERSE

Lect. No. 161 | **FIRST READING: Daniel 7:13-14**

The First Reading on this solemnity comes from the Book of Daniel. It speaks of the Son of Man standing before the Ancient One (Yahweh) to receive power and dominion over the nations.

When it was written, this passage was intended as a promise that Israel (the Son of Man) would eventually triumph over all of its enemies. At the time of Jesus, it was understood more in terms of the Messiah being given rule over all of the nations upon the earth (which is the way that we are using this reading today).

A reading from the Book of the Prophet Daniel

As the visions during the night continued, I saw
one like a Son of man coming,
   on the clouds of heaven;
when he reached the Ancient One
   and was presented before him,
the one like a Son of man received dominion,
   glory, and kingship;
   all peoples, nations, and languages serve him.
His dominion is an everlasting dominion
   that shall not be taken away,
   his kingship shall not be destroyed.

The word of the Lord.

Lect. No. 161

RESPONSORIAL PSALM: Ps 93:1, 1-2, 5 (℞.: 1a)

The Responsorial Psalm continues the theme of the royal dignity of Jesus. It uses verses from a psalm that spoke of Yahweh as king of all the earth.

It celebrates the fact that God created the world (and therefore has dominion over it). He also rules over all of the nations upon the earth.

God has shared that dignity with Jesus when he proclaimed him to be Lord of everything that is in the heavens, on the earth, and under the earth.

℞. **The Lord is king; he is robed in majesty.**

The LORD is king, in splendor robed;
   robed is the LORD and girt about with strength.

℞. **The Lord is king; he is robed in majesty.**

And he has made the world firm,
   not to be moved.
Your throne stands firm from of old;
   from everlasting you are, O LORD.

℞. **The Lord is king; he is robed in majesty.**

Your decrees are worthy of trust indeed;
   holiness befits your house,
   O LORD, for length of days.

℞. **The Lord is king; he is robed in majesty.**

Lect.
No. 161

SECOND READING: Revelation 1:5-8

Jesus is the first of those who will rise from the dead. The firstfruits are usually known as the best of the harvest and the promise that more fruit will follow.

Jesus is the best of those who will rise, but he is also the promise that we, too, will rise with him.

Jesus is also the king of kings. This was an important statement to be made during a time of persecution when it seemed as if the pagan kings ruled and controlled everything (and even in our days when it sometimes seems as if things happen with no rhyme or reason).

The author of this book is saying that this is an illusion. Jesus is the true king of kings and nothing can occur without his consent.

A reading from the Book of Revelation

Jesus Christ is the faithful witness,
  the firstborn of the dead and ruler of the kings of
    the earth.
To him who loves us and has freed us from our sins
    by his blood,
  who has made us into a kingdom, priests for his
    God and Father,
  to him be glory and power forever and ever.
  Amen.

Behold, he is coming amid the clouds,
  and every eye will see him,
    even those who pierced him.
All the peoples of the earth will lament him.
  Yes. Amen.

"I am the Alpha and the Omega," says the Lord God,
  "the one who is and who was and who is to come,
    the almighty."

The word of the Lord.

  ℟. **Alleluia, alleluia.**

Lect.
No. 161

ALLELUIA: Mark 11:9, 10

The Alleluia Verse repeats the words proclaimed by the crowd in Jerusalem on Palm Sunday. They acknowledge Jesus as one who is sent by God and who is to be king of the nation and of our hearts.

Blessed is he who comes in the name of the Lord!
Blessed is the kingdom of our father David that is to
    come!

  ℟. **Alleluia, alleluia.**

Lect. No. 161

GOSPEL: John 18:33b-37

The Gospel speaks of the kingship of Christ. It recounts the trial of Jesus before Pilate. Jesus explains to Pilate that his kingdom is not of this world. He did not come into this world to establish a political kingdom or to free the Jews from Roman dominion.

Jesus came to set us free from our greater bondage, the bondage to sin and death. He does this by proclaiming in word and deed how much the Father loves us.

Jesus is not a king who will reign upon a majestic throne and wear a crown of gold. He will reign upon a cross and wear a crown of thorns; in doing this, he showed what true authority is.

The authority of the rulers of this world is nothing but an illusion. They believe that they control events, but it is only love that can truly conquer. Jesus is the king of love upon the cross.

A reading from the holy Gospel according to John

Pilate said to Jesus,
"Are you the King of the Jews?"
Jesus answered, "Do you say this on your own
    or have others told you about me?"
Pilate answered, "I am not a Jew, am I?
Your own nation and the chief priests handed you
    over to me.
What have you done?"
Jesus answered, "My kingdom does not belong to
    this world.
If my kingdom did belong to this world,
    my attendants would be fighting
    to keep me from being handed over to the Jews.
But as it is, my kingdom is not here."
So Pilate said to him, "Then you are a king?"
Jesus answered, "You say I am a king.
For this I was born and for this I came into the
    world,
    to testify to the truth.
Everyone who belongs to the truth listens to my
    voice."

The Gospel of the Lord.

PASTORAL REFLECTIONS

As we reach the end of a liturgical year, the Church reminds us that we will not live forever (individually and collectively). The goal is that when God calls us home, there will be nothing left unsaid, nothing left undone.

APPENDIX 1: INTRODUCTION TO THE BOOKS OF THE BIBLE THAT ARE READ IN THE THREE-YEAR CYCLE

GENESIS

The first book of the Bible tells of the history of the world in its earliest stages (the Primordial History) and during the period of the Patriarchs up to the time that the people of Israel went down to Egypt to escape the great drought during the days of Joseph.

The first eleven chapters contain stories that are not strictly historical in the sense of being a day to day account of the early history of the world. These chapters nevertheless contain important truths about the early days of humanity.

God created us out of love and called us to live in obedience to his commands. We, in the person of Adam and Eve, sinned against God and were punished for our disobedience. Sin grew in the world until God sent his punishment in the form of a great flood.

Beginning with chapter 12, we hear of the history of Abraham and Sarah, Isaac and Rebekah, Jacob and his wives and children, especially Joseph. These stories seem to contain more historic information than the earlier chapters. Some of the customs mentioned in the stories, for example, have been dated back to the period in which the Patriarchs were said to have lived.

It is believed that the information contained in this book comes from three major sources.

The first source is the Yahwist source. It was written during the reigns of David and Solomon (c. 950 B.C.) in the southern part of Israel. It emphasizes the role of the monarchy and the importance of Judah and his tribe in salvation history. This source is called the Yahwist source because it often refers to God by the name Yahweh.

The second source is the Elohist source. This dates to around 850 B.C. and was written in the north of Israel. It emphasizes the importance of prophets and the Sinai covenant. Because the kings of the north were often unfaithful to the ways of the Lord, kings are not seen as laudable figures.

The third source is the Priestly source. It was written during the exile in Babylon (587-539 B.C.). It emphasizes the importance of law and tradition. This source tends to be very accurate in measurements of time and space.

The book achieved its present form sometime around the Babylonian exile (c. 587-539 B.C.).

EXODUS

This book tells of the miraculous events that surrounded the exodus of the people of Israel from their slavery in Egypt. It begins with the infancy of Moses and ends with a description of the construction of the objects of cult that Israel was to use when it worshiped the Lord.

The same sources that appear in the Book of Genesis are also found in this book. This would explain why certain events are sometimes described twice in slightly different circumstances (for the two versions were derived from different sources).

This book contains one version of the ten commandments (20:17). The other version is found in the Book of Deuteronomy 5:6-21. The law is seen as a gift from God, for it instructs Israel on how it can follow the ways of the Lord and be faithful to their covenant.

The hymn that the community sings to celebrate its escape from the forces of Pharaoh in Exodus 15 is actually a very ancient hymn. Scholars believe the grammar and vocabulary of the hymn show it to date to the actual time of the exodus. Thus, this is one of the earliest parts of the Bible to have been written.

It is also in this book that God reveals his name, YHWH (i.e., Yahweh), to Moses (3:14). It is said that this name means "I am who I am." It has been interpreted by some rabbis as meaning, "I am who I am for you, who I have always been for you, who I will always be for you." (In modern Bibles LORD in capital letters stands for the name of God, because the Jews never pronounced it.)

LEVITICUS

This is the third of the five books of the Pentateuch. Its name is derived from the word "Levite," for most of the material contained in the book is Levitical law. Unlike Genesis, Exodus, and Numbers, which are amalgamations of various sources, this book is almost entirely derived from the Priestly Source written during the Babylonian Exile (587-539 B.C.).

The people of Israel were living in exile, and the priestly authors felt that they needed to define the obligations of the law in a clear manner so that the Israelites would not lose their cultural identity while living in a foreign land. Among the topics presented are laws concerning sacrifice, the priesthood of Aaron and his descendants, cleanliness and uncleanness, the ritual for the day of atonement, votive offerings, and the law of holiness.

NUMBERS

The Book of Numbers continues the story of Israel during the period in which they dwelt in the desert for forty years while they were being purified by the Lord so that they might enter the promised land.

It is composed of the same sources that we saw in Genesis and Exodus.

It obtained its name from the fact that Israel took a census of those who were with them in the desert. The number of men who left Egypt is cited as being over 600,000, most probably an exaggerated number.

It also contains many instructions for worship and other community actions.

Important episodes include the first attempt to enter the promised land (which failed because of the fear of the people and their lack of trust in the providence of the Lord), Balaam's curse upon Israel (which actually turns out to be a blessing), the choice of the seventy-two elders to assist Moses in

governing the people of Israel, and instructions for the division of the promised land when Israel would conquer it.

DEUTERONOMY

Deuteronomy means "the second law." A scroll of the law was discovered by King Josiah when he was reforming the temple cult. It is not known whether the book is ancient and had been lost in the temple during a period of decline in the faith of Israel or whether it was placed in the temple to be found at that time.

Its teachings represent a reform of the way that Israel practiced its religion. Previous to its promulgation, there were shrines to the Lord upon most of the heights of the land. Many of these shrines were dedicated both to Yahweh and to Baal, the pagan god of fertility. The main reform of this book was that it established that one could only worship the Lord with sacrifices in the temple in Jerusalem.

There is an extensive series of legislation throughout the book, including another version of the Ten Commandments. (One version is found in Exodus.) Many of the laws are correctives of the pagan practices that had entered into the faith of Israel. The *She'ma Israel*, the profession of faith of the Jewish people, is contained in 6:4ff.

The book closes with Moses designating Joshua as his successor and then dying. He was buried by God on Mount Nebo. These chapters might have originally been in another of the books of the Pentateuch, and were then attached to the end of this particular book.

The school that produced this book is called the Deuteronomist school. They not only wrote this book of law but also edited many of the other books that had been written previous to this period. Their major tendency was to write history as it should have happened, and not as it necessarily happened. Thus, they describe the conquest of the holy land as a series of spectacular successes against pagan armies (e.g., Joshua) as opposed to a slow infiltration of tribes into a land where they faced bitter opposition (e.g., Judges).

JOSHUA

The Book of Joshua is the sixth Book of the Old Testament, named after the successor of Moses, who led the Israelites into Canaan. The book contains a systematic account of the conquest of the Promised Land. Its purpose is to demonstrate God's fidelity in giving the Israelites the land he had promised them for an inheritance. It includes: (1) the conquest of Canaan; (2) division of the land; and (3) return of the Trans-Jordanian tribes and Joshua's farewell. Like the first five Books of the Bible, Joshua was built up by a long and complex process of editing traditional materials.

Although the victories of Joshua are an action of God, they also call for the active collaboration and faith of his People.

FIRST SAMUEL

First Samuel describes the history of Israel from the end of the period of Judges until the time when Saul and his sons die in battle against the Philistines.

The book opens with the story of the birth of Samuel, the last and greatest of the judges. Judges were charismatic leaders who exercised executive, legislative, judicial, and even priestly power. Chapter 2 presents the hymn that Hannah chanted to celebrate the birth of her son Samuel. This hymn was used as the basis of Mary's hymn in the Gospel of Luke.

The early part of the book describes some of the disasters that Israel suffered in this period. The people became frightened and they asked for a king. God and Samuel chose Saul, a Benjaminite, as the king of Israel. There are two judgments concerning Israel's request. (Each judgment derives from a different source.) One judgment is that the request is understandable, but the other is that the people of Israel were subtly rejecting God, their true king, by requesting a human king.

Saul displeased God, and Samuel had to choose another king who was more pleasing to God. He chose David and anointed him. The latter chapters of this book speak of the growing enmity between Saul and David based upon Saul's jealousy.

SECOND SAMUEL

Second Samuel describes the history of Israel from the death of Samuel until the end of the reign of David. (His death is described at the beginning of First Kings.) The book begins with David's mourning for the death of King Saul and especially for his son and David's friend Jonathan.

David accedes to the throne of the southern tribes while Ishbaal, one of Saul's sons, becomes king of the ten northern tribes. At the end of a long civil war, David is proclaimed king of the united tribes. He conquers Jerusalem, makes it his capital, and moves the ark of the covenant there.

The rest of the book is a history of David's deeds and even misdeeds. While he is spectacularly successful in political terms, his personal and family life are another matter. He sins against the LORD by committing adultery with Bathsheba, the wife of Uriah the Hittite, and by conducting a census of the people of Israel, implying that they were his possession. He witnessed the death of his son Amnon who raped his daughter Tamar, and of another son Absalom, who rose up in rebellion against David.

FIRST KINGS

The First Book of Kings describes the period of history that began with the death of David and the succession of Solomon as king until the days of King Jehoshaphat of Judah and of King Ahaziah of Israel.

The book opens with the twelve tribes forming a united kingdom. After the death of Solomon, however, King Rehoboam acted foolishly and alienated the ten northern tribes, which seceded and formed their own kingdom, Israel. The southern kingdom was henceforth known as Judah.

The early chapters describe the successes of Solomon (e.g., his construction of the temple in Jerusalem and massive cities and fortifications throughout the land). They also speak of his sinfulness, for he built shrines to the pagan gods of his many wives.

The latter chapters speak of the prophetic career of Elijah. He led Israel away from syncretism to greater fidelity in the Lord. He condemned King Ahab and his wife Jezebel for their religious errors and their social conduct (e.g., stealing the field of Naboth the Jezreelite by having him killed).

In chapter 18 we hear about the contest on Mount Carmel between Elijah and the priests of Baal to determine who was the true God in Israel. In chapter 19 we hear of Elijah's encounter with God on Mount Sinai when he met him not in earthquake or fire or wind as Moses had when he received the law, but in the gentle breeze. The meaning of this passage is that God does not always act in a miraculous, spectacular fashion, but rather he often brings about his will in ordinary, everyday events.

SECOND KINGS

The Second Book of Kings tells the history of the kingdoms of Israel and Judah from the days of Elijah and Elisha until the time of the Babylonian exile.

The early chapters of the book speak of the ascent of Elijah into heaven on a fiery chariot and the ministry of Elisha. The account of Elisha resembles the story of a famous miracle worker.

Much of the book is a chronicle of the infidelity of the kings of both kingdoms and how God visited his judgment upon them through the hands of pagan kings.

In 722 B.C. the northern kingdom of Israel was annihilated and its nobility carried off into exile in Assyria. In 587 B.C. the same fate befell the citizens of the southern kingdom of Judah (although they, at least, returned from exile in Babylon).

One of the high points of the book is the accession of King Josiah to the throne of Judah and his reform of the religion of his people (during which the Book of Deuteronomy was discovered and promulgated).

The book also reports the reigns of Kings Ahaz and Hezekiah. These were two kings who reigned during much of the prophetic career of Isaiah.

FIRST CHRONICLES

The First Book of Chronicles outlines the history of Israel from the creation of Adam until the construction of the temple in Jerusalem. Much of the information contained in this book is also contained in the Books of Samuel and the Books of Kings. It was probably produced by the Deuteronomist school, which tended to tell history as it should have happened and not necessarily as it happened. Thus, its story of King David excludes all of the more scandalous material concerning his adultery, the scandals in his family, etc.

SECOND CHRONICLES

Like First Chronicles, this book is a Deuteronomist revision of the information contained in the First and Second Books of Kings. It begins with the accession of Solomon to the throne and closes with the decree of Cyrus permitting the Jewish people to return from exile in Babylon (c. 539 B.C.). Typical of this school of literature, an idealized view of Israel's history is presented. Solomon is portrayed as being one of the greatest kings of Israel, second only to David. His role in constructing the temple of God in Jerusalem is strongly emphasized.

The history of the kings of the north is all but ignored (for this school considered those kings to be faithless and deceitful), while that of the kings of Judah is presented in greater detail.

NEHEMIAH

Nehemiah was a Jewish official of the Persian emperor who was appointed governor of Judah around 445 B.C. The book named after him speaks of the actions of the prophet and Ezra (a priest). Nehemiah arrived in Jerusalem at a time when the Jewish nation was demoralized and drifting. He rebuilt the walls of the city. He reestablished Jewish law as the law of the land. He promoted social justice (e.g., giving loans with no interest). He ordered those who had married foreign wives to send them away. (In his days, this was seen as a purification of the religion of Israel.)

JOB

The Book of Job presents an extended reflection upon the problem of pain and suffering. Satan (who is presented as being God's district attorney) convinces God to withdraw his beneficence from Job to see whether Job would curse the LORD. No matter how much Job suffers, he refuses to curse God. Yet he acknowledges that what he was suffering was unjust.

The theory that sin is the cause of all suffering is strongly rejected. Job expresses his anger at the injustice that he was experiencing, even challenging God to explain why he would allow these things to happen.

The saying, "the patience of Job," is a bit misleading. He is patient for two chapters, and then rants and raves against God for more than thirty chapters. In the end, God appears and puts Job to the test. Job realizes that he does not understand all things, and that he must respond to all trials with trust in God.

PSALMS

The Book of Psalms is a collection of 150 psalms written during a period of almost 1,000 years, and it has become the Prayer Book of the Church. They are divided into five books of psalms, each ending with a doxology. The numbers assigned to the psalms are different in the original Hebrew version and the Greek translation. Although many of them are attributed to great historic figures such as David, they were actually dedicated to those people and not written by them.

The psalms are poetry and many demonstrate the most common attribute of Hebrew poetry (parallelism). A large number of the words used in the psalms are *hapax legomena* (words used only once in the Bible).

There are several identifiable literary genres in the psalms. A large number of the psalms are individual or communal lamentations. There are also hymns, royal psalms, hymns of trust, wisdom psalms, thanksgivings, historic psalms, penitential psalms, etc.

PROVERBS

The Book of Proverbs is really two different books written at very different periods of Israel's history.

The older portion of the book is that beginning with chapter 10 and running to the end of the book. It is a series of folk sayings on how to live the good life. It was written to instruct the young on how they could live in the ways of the Lord and receive God's blessings.

This portion is very similar to wisdom books of neighboring cultures (especially Egypt). Some of the sayings, in fact, seem to have been borrowed from those cultures.

The first nine chapters of the book are much more Greek in tone. They must have been written after the conquest of Alexander the Great, so they probably date to the third century B.C. or later. They speak of wisdom as a personalized attribute of God, Lady Wisdom. The reason for this presentation is that Jewish people adopted the Greek idea that God was totally removed from our experience, that he was the uncreated creator who never had anything to do with his creation. They thus spoke of some of God's attributes as mediators to communicate God's will to us. Among those attributes were God's glory, holiness, spirit, and wisdom.

Wisdom calls to the foolish to instruct them in the ways of the Lord. She offers to nourish them, giving them bread and wine. (This idea is used symbolically in the Discourse on the Bread of Life in John 6.) She tells them that if they embrace her knowledge, they will receive everlasting life.

ECCLESIASTES

In addition to its Greek name ("Ecclesiastes"), this book is also known by its

Hebrew name, Qoheleth. It is a wisdom book written late in the Old Testament period (c. 250 B.C.). The name of the author is uncertain, for the word Qoheleth could be symbolic since it means "the preacher." The book speaks of the impossibility of discerning God's will. God has a plan (for there is a season for everything), but we cannot adequately know it. Thus, it is best to live a reasonably virtuous life. Do not work too much or too little, nor eat too much or too little, etc. Everything else is a chasing after wind.

Rabbis argued about whether to accept this book into the canon or not for quite some time because of its cynicism. Yet this book serves as a good corrective for the overly optimistic attitude of other wisdom literature.

WISDOM

The Book of Wisdom is one of the younger books of the Old Testament. It displays many signs of having been written during the period in which Greek culture heavily influenced Judaism. Because it was only written in Greek, it was not accepted into the Hebrew Bible and is not found in Protestant Bibles as well.

Wisdom is personified as a spirit that is totally pure. King Solomon prayed for and received the gift of wisdom in order to rule the people of Israel in the ways of the Lord.

We hear how the evil would be punished for their iniquity and the good would receive an eternal reward. This is one of the few books of the Old Testament that speak about our destiny in the afterlife as being one that is filled with joy.

The latter part of the book gives a panorama of the history of Israel and explains how wisdom was present in each of those stages. One interesting teaching contained in this section is that the plagues of Egypt involved many animals because the people of Egypt had worshiped animals. There is a rabbinic teaching that as the sin, so the punishment.

SIRACH

The Book of Sirach is one of the wisdom books of literature of the Old Testament. It is included in Catholic Bibles but is not found in Protestant Bibles because until recently we only possessed the Greek version of this book (and Protestants follow the rabbis' definition of the Old Testament, that only those books written in Hebrew or Aramaic were acceptable).

The premise of the book is that it was written by Jesus Sirach and translated into Greek by his grandson. Some manuscripts of portions of the original Hebrew text have been found in Qumran and Egypt.

Typical of wisdom literature, the book contains a series of instructions on how to live the good life. The reader is advised to follow the path of virtue. There are instructions for almost every dimension of individual, family, and community life.

The hymn to wisdom in chapter 24 shows heavy Greek influence. It speaks of Wisdom who was an architect helping God create the world. Wisdom visited the people of Israel and pitched her tent among them (an image used in the prologue of the Gospel of John when it speaks of the incarnation).

The book closes with a series of accounts of the deeds of the great men of Israel and a hymn of thanksgiving to the Lord.

ISAIAH

The Book of Isaiah is actually a combination of the prophecies of three different prophets (or schools of prophecy).

The first part of the book, from chapter 1 to 39, is attributed to Isaiah the prophet who ministered to the southern kingdom of Judah from around 740 B.C. until sometime after 700 B.C.

His major theme was that God was holy, and we were called to live in that holiness. That meant that we had to exhibit a way of life that was consistent with the holiness of God.

The first chapters of the book are similar to those of the Prophet Amos. Isaiah admonishes the people to live social justice and to care for the poor, for this is what the holiness of God demands.

From chapters 7 to 11 we hear various episodes and oracles that shaped Isaiah's understanding of the coming Messiah. At first Isaiah hoped for a new king who would be better than the old king. (Remember, all of the kings of Judah and Israel were considered to be the anointed of the Lord and thus each one of them was a messiah.) Eventually, he stopped hoping for a better king and he began to speak of a coming era in which God would intervene through one particular Messiah. This era would be filled with peace and justice. Even nature would experience this, for animals that were natural enemies such as the lion and the lamb could lie down together in peace.

Much of the rest of his prophecy is a series of oracles against nations that had attacked Judah or against his own people for their infidelity.

The second part of the book runs from chapter 40 to 55. This was written during the exile in Babylon (587-539 B.C.) and is attributed to an anonymous author called Deutero-Isaiah. It is a book of consolation. God promises Israel that it will be wondrously restored.

This section of the book also contains four poems called the songs of the suffering servant of Yahweh. They speak about a mysterious figure who will bring salvation to Israel and also to the Gentiles. He will be meek and gentle. He will suffer for our sins and die for us, but the Lord will raise him from the dead.

The third section of the book runs from chapter 56 to 66. It was written after the exile. The people thought that when they returned to Israel all would be well, but it did not turn out that way. This prophecy encourages them and admonishes them to convert their ways. Chapter 58 speaks of fasting, telling the people that God does not want us to get involved in empty rituals. He wants us to transform the way we live with him and each other.

JEREMIAH

Of all of the prophets of the Old Testament, Jeremiah is the one who is said to have best foreshadowed Jesus. The reason for this is his heroic suffering for the sake of the message that God had given him to share with his people. He called them to conversion and warned them of the consequences of their actions, but they refused to listen to him. Then, when they suffered the consequences of their own choices, they blamed Jeremiah for what was happening to them. He was beaten, saw his writings burned by the king, was thrown into a cistern to die, and eventually died while being dragged down to Egypt.

Jeremiah preached during one of the most turbulent periods of the history of the kingdom of Judah. One king was following another with fearful rapidity. The people of Judah and their kings were at one moment subjects of Egypt, at the next of Babylon.

Early in Jeremiah's career he witnessed the finding of the Book of Deuteronomy in the temple. This book contained a new law that outlawed all shrines of the Lord in the land with the exception of the temple in Jerusalem. His own family lost their livelihood for they were a family of priests at a shrine to the north of Jerusalem. Yet Jeremiah rejoiced and embraced the reform.

However, it brought him only trouble. He speaks in a series of poems of his feelings of abandonment by the Lord. (These are called his Confessions, e.g., 20:7-18.) Yet he felt that he could not run away from his responsibility to proclaim God's word, so he continued to preach.

In chapter 31 Jeremiah speaks of a new covenant that the Lord will make with the people of Israel. This covenant will not be written upon tablets of stone; it will be written upon their hearts.

Jeremiah also spoke of individual responsibility for sin. We will not be punished for the sins of our ancestors, but rather for our own sins.

Jeremiah's ministry ended shortly after the destruction of Jerusalem and the deportation of most of the nobility to Babylon. During the siege he had told the king and the people to surrender to the Babylonians and receive their punishment for God had sent this chastisement. Because he told the people to surrender and not fight, the princes of the land accused him of sedition and punished him. When the city was conquered, he was not mistreated by the Babylonians. Shortly after the conquest someone assassinated the Babylonian governor, and Jeremiah was forced to accompany those who were fleeing to Egypt to avoid the coming punishment. He died along the way.

BARUCH

The Book of Baruch was purported to have been written by Baruch, the secretary to Jeremiah, during the Babylonian exile. Because the only version of the book extant is written in Greek, it was not included in the Hebrew or Protestant Old Testaments.

It begins with an appeal for the people to turn back to wisdom, which would lead them to the Lord. The law of God is seen as wisdom incarnate.

There are also some songs of lamentation and a purported letter of Jeremiah to the exiles in Babylon.

EZEKIEL

Ezekiel was the only major prophet to prophesy outside of Israel (for he prophesied while he lived in exile in Babylon). Because of this, it was quite some time before his book was accepted by the elders of the Jewish community. His book is filled with extraordinary visions, oracles, and prophetic actions.

Ezekiel was a priest carried away into exile during the first partial exile of 597 B.C. For the next ten years he preached to the exiles and to the community that still resided in Jerusalem. After the second exile of 587 B.C., he continued his ministry addressing himself to the old and new exiles with whom he lived.

His book begins with the account of a theophany, the appearance of the Lord in the form of a fiery chariot.

He performed a number of symbolic actions to draw the attention of his audience to the serious nature of their situation. They refused to listen and change their ways.

In the latter part of the book, we hear of the restoration that the Lord will bring upon Israel. The temple would be rebuilt and purified. (He describes its dimensions in great detail toward the end of the book.) That which was dead in them would be filled with life (the meaning of the story of the valley filled with dry bones in chapter 37). The temple would become the source of a font of grace and divine love that will renew the land (the story of the river flowing from the altar in the temple and running out into the entire land in chapter 47). God would give his people hearts of flesh to replace their hearts of stone (chapter 36).

DANIEL

Although this book was attributed to a Prophet named Daniel during the period of the Babylonian Exile, it was actually written during the period of persecution at the time of the Maccabees (c. 175 B.C.). (We know this because many of the historic details contained in this book are incorrect.)

The first half of the book is a series of stories set during the Babylonian period that are intended to be parables concerning the need to give witness to the faith. The second half of the book is apocalyptic in style and speaks of the eventual triumph of the people of God over every adversity.

Chapters 13 and 14 (the story of Susanna and Bel and the Dragon) were written only in Greek (as well as part of chapter 3, the hymn of the three young men in the furnace). They are thus not accepted by Protestant churches, while they are part of the canon accepted by Catholic and Orthodox churches.

HOSEA

Hosea was a minor prophet from the northern kingdom of Israel (c. 750 B.C.). He was married to a woman named Gomer who was unfaithful. No matter how much she strayed, he continued to love her. He even allowed himself to be made a fool of in order to try to win her back.

Hosea realized that his relationship with Gomer paralleled God's relationship with Israel. God had made a covenant with Israel and had blessed his people with prosperity, but God's people had strayed and worshiped false gods. The Prophet also used the image of God being a loving parent and Israel being a disobedient child who refused to be corrected, or who even refused to be born when the time had come.

The book has suffered from a considerable amount of editorial reordering of material. This has made it difficult to understand the meaning of certain passages.

JOEL

The Book of Joel is one of the most apocalyptic books in the Old Testament. It speaks about the coming judgment of the Day of the Lord. The enemies of the Lord will be punished while those faithful to his covenant will be rewarded.

This book speaks about a coming outpouring of the Spirit of the Lord upon the whole nation. This passage is quoted by Peter on the day of Pentecost to explain what was happening to those who had received the gift of the Holy Spirit that day.

AMOS

Amos was one of the Minor Prophets (c. 750 B.C.). He was from the southern kingdom of Judah, but his mission was to the people of the north. Amos speaks of himself as being a herdsman and a dresser of sycamore trees (which probably indicates a relatively poor person).

He was not a professional Prophet, and most of his message seems to have come from his observations of the world rather than through special revelations. He calls Israel to task for allowing social injustice in which the poor were oppressed while the rich lived in luxury.

JONAH

While the Book of Jonah is said to be a prophetic book, it is most probably a parable written during the post-exilic period (after 539 B.C.). It speaks of a prophet named Jonah who is called by God to proclaim the destruction of the pagan city of Nineveh for its sins. Jonah at first refuses because he fears that the Ninevites might repent and thus avoid the punishment that they deserve.

He tries to flee on a ship, but it runs into a storm. He is eventually thrown overboard and swallowed by a large fish that spews him up on shore. He preaches repentance to the Ninevites, and they immediately begin a period of penance. God withholds his punishment, and Jonah is very depressed for what he feared had come true. God speaks to him of how all people are his own, and how he loves and cares for them all.

Many scholars believe that this was a parable written to speak of the fact that Yahweh was the God of all nations. Israel had been swallowed by a large fish (Babylon), and now they were being called to recognize the fact that God was concerned for everyone (for if there is only one God, then God is the God of all peoples).

MICAH

Micah was a minor prophet in the middle of the eighth century B.C. He came from the small town of Moresheth-Gath. He fostered small town values and fought the corruption of army officials and court officials from Jerusalem. He opposed social injustice and oppression. He, like Amos, condemned a formal liturgical life that did not result in a transformation of one's conduct. He speaks of the destruction of the dynasty ruling in Jerusalem and the rise of a new dynasty from the descendants of David living in Bethlehem. This prophecy would later be seen to foretell the birthplace of the Messiah.

HABAKKUK

Habakkuk was one of the minor prophets, and his book was written at the end of the seventh century B.C. The prophet questions why God allows his people to suffer. Why does God allow one pagan nation (Assyria) to be punished by another pagan nation (Babylon), for that second pagan nation only becomes arrogant? The prophet eventually concludes that God will right all things in God's own time. Chapter 3 of the book is a hymn of praise for God who will save his people.

ZEPHANIAH

The Book of Zephaniah is one of the books of the minor prophets. It gives a series of oracles against the people of the nations surrounding Israel and against the people of Israel itself. They will all be punished on the Day of the Lord. It describes that day as a day of woe and of distress.

Yet, the book closes with a hymn of praise of the Lord. Both the people of Israel and even the people of the nations would turn to the Lord and pray to him alone. All the dispersed will be gathered together and healed by the Lord.

ZECHARIAH

The Book of Zechariah was actually produced in two stages. The first part dates to the period shortly after the Jewish people had returned from their exile in Babylon. It is a series of warnings that they should walk in the ways of the Lord, but it also speaks of encouragement and hope. This continues through the first eight chapters of the book.

The second section of the book is a series of judgments and oracles that were written much later (some probably dating to the Greek period, after 330 B.C.). The most important passage for us is that which speaks of the entrance of the Messiah into the city of Jerusalem. He is described as riding a donkey, the colt of an ass (9:9). The humble manner in which he entered the city was intended to be in contrast with the arrogance of all of the kings and generals who had conquered Jerusalem and had entered it riding on great chargers. The Messiah would be a ruler who would restore peace to the land. This passage was fulfilled when Jesus en-

tered the city of Jerusalem on Palm Sunday riding on a donkey.

MALACHI

Malachi is believed to be the last of the prophets. He was a minor prophet. We are not sure whether this is actually the author's name, for the word Malachi means "my messenger," so it might be more of a title than a proper name.

He complains about the fact that the Jewish people have not been faithful to their covenant responsibilities. Their priests offer inferior sacrifices, men divorce the wives of their youth, etc. There will be a coming judgment when God will reward the good and punish the evil.

The book closes with a promise of the return of Elijah to prepare for the Day of the Lord. This was fulfilled in the ministry of John the Baptist, who performed Elijah's mission in New Testament times.

GOSPEL OF MATTHEW

Matthew is the longest and the most Jewish of the gospels. It has numerous quotations from the Old Testament to show how Jesus fulfilled the law and the prophets and numerous references to Jewish customs all throughout.

Ancient tradition speaks of it being the first gospel written. This is why it is always listed as the first gospel in the list of the four. This tradition also speaks of it having been written in Aramaic.

Modern scholarship calls this into question. It is obvious that Matthew copied much of his material from Mark and not vice versa (for Mark is short and ungrammatical and Matthew is longer and better organized). Furthermore, these same scholars have determined that the Greek version of the gospel that we now possess is not a translation from another language. Rather, the gospel was originally written in Greek.

We can still sustain the ancient tradition if we propose that Matthew, the tax collector, wrote part of today's Gospel of Matthew.

Then, some decades later, a second author took that book, combined it with material from Mark and other sources, and produced the Gospel of Matthew as we know it today. This second author kept the original name of the Gospel of Matthew, because this name showed that the gospel had apostolic authority.

This second author was probably a converted Pharisee (for there are so many quotes from the Old Testament throughout the gospel). He probably wrote around 80 A.D. as a response to a persecution that his community was suffering. It was about this time that Christians were definitively excluded from the synagogue.

This was a response to the destruction of the temple. Jewish authorities felt that without the binding force of the temple, they could no longer afford the luxury of allowing several different versions of their faith to co-exist. Christians were shunned, and sometimes murdered for their faith. They were told that they had rejected the God of Israel and would burn in hell forever.

This second Matthew told Christians that they were not cut off from Israel. They were, in fact, the true Israel, while the Jews who had not accepted Jesus were a false Israel for they had not accepted the Messiah whom Yahweh had sent.

Second Matthew combined the material of the gospel into sections of narrative (action) and discourse (teaching). He produced five major sections of teaching to mirror the first five books of the Old Testament that Jews called the Torah.

He presented Jesus as the new Moses for the new Israel. Like Moses, Jesus was endangered as a child by an evil king. Like him he fasted in the desert. Like him, he climbed a mountain where he presented a new law (the Sermon on the Mount).

Throughout the gospel there is a polemic against the leaders of the Jews, especially the Pharisees. This is because they were the ones who had excluded Christians from the synagogues. Furthermore, there are refutations of lies spread about Jesus by the leaders of the Jews, e.g., the resurrection scene. Jesus also uses the Pharisees as an example of what the apostles should not be in their exercise of authority.

This gospel contains more parables than Mark. Many of them speak about the coming judgment and how people must choose to live in the path of the Lord.

GOSPEL OF MARK

The Gospel of Mark is probably the first gospel written. It is believed that it was written in Rome around the year 70 A.D. It was written by John Mark, a disciple who accompanied Paul and Barnabas on one missionary journey (but departed from their company before the journey was finished). John Mark eventually traveled to Rome and became a disciple of Peter.

The gospel presents the story of Jesus in a straightforward manner with little embellishment. If one were to compare it to a modern medium, one might speak of it as the home movies of Jesus' ministry. The writing style is poor. Stories are often pasted together with little transition or connection.

Mark presents Jesus as the Messiah who is most of all the Son of Man. Every time that someone is prepared to proclaim Jesus as the Messiah, Jesus silences him. Rather, he says that he is the Son of Man. This title is derived from two Old Testament sources: Daniel 7 where the Son of Man would receive power and authority and dominion, and the Songs of the Suffering Servant in Isaiah where the servant of the Lord would suffer in order to expiate our sins.

The disciples of Jesus and his own family do not fully understand his mission until after the resurrection. Three times Jesus predicts his passion (chapters 8, 9, and 10), and three times the disciples respond inappropriately because they understand his role of being Messiah in terms of power and not in terms of service.

Even the resurrection scene presents this message. The shorter ending (ends at 16:8) speaks of the women hearing about the resurrection but not seeing Jesus themselves.

This was most probably the original ending to the gospel. Mark's message, especially to the Church of Rome that was undergoing persecution, was that one does not see the risen Jesus until one has died with him.

There are relatively few parables in the gospel. Chapter 13 speaks about the coming apocalyptic era when God will judge the earth.

Many of the expressions heard and the scenes portrayed show Jesus in an embarrassingly human stance. The other Synoptic Gospels, Matthew and Luke, tend to modify that material to show Jesus as more dignified and more divine.

GOSPEL OF LUKE

We believe that the Gospel of Luke was written around 80-85 A.D. Tradition holds that it was written by Luke, a Gentile convert and disciple of Paul. He is also traditionally said to have been a physician. All of this is credible considering the content and the style of the gospel.

Like the Gospel of Matthew, Luke begins with the story of the infancy of Jesus. There are actually a pair of annunciation and birth stories: that of John the Baptist, which is miraculous, and that of Jesus, which is even more astounding.

Throughout Luke's gospel Jesus reaches out to the poorest of the poor, the "anawim." This phrase means the poor ones of Yahweh. Jewish authorities at the time of Jesus looked with disdain upon the poor for they did not study or observe the law. Jesus, on the other hand, considered them the chosen of God. They could not rely upon their own resources, so they had to rely upon the grace of God to survive. This made them ready to accept the message of God whenever it was addressed to them, and especially when it came in the person of Jesus.

The poor in this gospel are those who are physically poor, but also those who are spiritually poor or excluded from society for any reason. Thus, Jesus reaches out to sinners, to foreigners, to women, etc. The first to hear of his birth were the shepherds (this was not an honorable occupation at the time of the birth of Jesus) and the last was the good thief on the cross.

Jesus invited these people to experience salvation. Salvation is a present reality, for the minute we meet Jesus and encounter his love, we are already saved.

Jesus speaks of how God reaches out to the sinner and rejoices when that person turns from sin. Many of the parables that are specific to this gospel are centered on that theme.

For Luke, the city of Jerusalem holds a special importance for it is the holy city where God's will would be manifested in the death and resurrection of Jesus. Thus, the gospel begins in Jerusalem, and Jesus is on the journey toward Jerusalem for most of the gospel (from 9:51). Then in the Acts of the Apostles, the gospel message spreads from Jerusalem (the spiritual center of the world) to Rome (the political center of the world).

This is also the gospel of prayer. The other Synoptic Gospels speak of Jesus praying a couple of times, but this gospel tells of eleven episodes in which he prayed. The purpose of Jesus' prayer was to discern the will of the Father so that he might be obedient to it. One of the ways that Jesus saves us is that he teaches how we can be obedient to the will of God so that the disobedience of the first sin might be repaired. Jesus also speaks of praying for those things that are needed with insistence (e.g., the parable of the widow who insists upon her rights from the judge).

GOSPEL OF JOHN

John is the only gospel that is not considered to be a Synoptic Gospel. The word synoptic means that one is seeing the story from one point of view. The Gospel of John sees the Jesus story from a very different point of view than the other gospels.

There are fewer miracles in this gospel and they are never called miracles. They are always signs that point to a greater reality, the depth of the Father's love for us.

This is why Jesus came to earth: to reveal to us how much God loves us. When we recognize this love, we can turn from our sins and experience the life of God, which is so profound that even death cannot diminish it.

There is only one sin in this gospel: not to believe Jesus is the Son of God. All other sins and commandments are derived from this.

Throughout the gospel we see the beloved disciple who most perfectly follows the will of the Father by loving Jesus with a profound love. The other disciples of Jesus, and especially the apostles, do not succeed as well. Peter often appears in the same scenes as the beloved disciple, but he always falls short of that disciple's faith response.

The prologue, the beginning of the gospel, is a beautiful poem that the author of this gospel borrowed and adapted to speak of Jesus as one who pre-existed even before he was born in Bethlehem. He is the word through whom the world was created, and the wisdom that instructed the people of Israel.

The Last Supper Discourse is an extended collection of teachings that instruct the community on the relationship between the Father and Jesus, between them and the disciples, and on who the Paraclete is, etc.

The beautiful bread of life discourse lies at the very heart of the gospel. It is not the midway point in terms of material, but it is the fourth of seven signs that appear in the gospel. The Eucharist was the central sacrament for this community and the very meaning of who they were as a community. In this discourse we hear that the bread of life is the very flesh of Jesus. The word flesh is the same word that is used in the prologue to say that the word became human. Thus, the author is stating that whatever Jesus became in the incarnation, that is what the Eucharist is.

At the Last Supper Jesus further instructs the disciples upon the meaning of the Eucharist when he washes their feet. Eucharist is also Jesus serving us and we being called to serve each other.

Many of the scenes throughout the gospel are written in symbolic language and can only be understood fully when one understands the key to the symbolic interpretation. For example, the abundance of wine at the wedding feast of Cana is due to the fact that Jesus was preparing his own messianic banquet where he would marry the Church.

There are a number of characters who appear only in this gospel, e.g., Nathanael and Nicodemus. There are also characters whom we know only by a title and not by their name (e.g., the Samaritan woman at the well, the man born blind, etc.).

This is the gospel that most emphasizes the divinity of Jesus. He knows all things. He is in control of everything from beginning to end. He is the pre-existent Word of God. When people ask him who he is, he often responds with a phrase that begins, "I am," in order to mirror the name Yahweh. Even when he is being arrested and he inquires whom his would-be captors are seeking and they respond, "Jesus of Nazareth," Jesus simply answers, "I am." This response causes them to fall on the ground, for they are in the presence of the living God.

ACTS OF THE APOSTLES

The Acts of the Apostles is the second volume of a two-volume work written by Luke. The first volume was the Gospel of Luke and this told of the ministry of Jesus while he resided in this world in the flesh. The second volume tells of the ministry of Jesus that the Spirit of God guided through the actions of the apostles.

The first part of the book emphasizes the actions of Peter and the other apostles who resided in Jerusalem, and the latter part of the book centers on the missionary journeys of Paul.

In the first chapter we hear Jesus tell the apostles that they must give witness to the gospel in Judea, and in Samaria, and to the ends of the earth. This list serves as a short table of contents for Acts. We hear how the gospel began in Jerusalem (the religious center of the world) and in the last chapters we hear how the gospel reaches the ends of the earth (Rome, the political center of the world).

It is absolutely clear that all missionary activities are guided by the Holy Spirit. It is the Spirit who gives the apostles the courage to first proclaim the gospel message on the day of Pentecost. It is the Spirit who leads them to accept Cornelius into the community. The Spirit guides Paul wherever he goes, etc.

The book does not close with the martyrdom of Paul in Rome. Many have asked why. The most obvious reason is that this book is not about Paul. It is about the spread of the gospel, and when the gospel reached Rome, the book was complete.

Some of the details of the book are historically questionable. We know this because they contradict what Paul says in his own letters. It is possible that Luke did not have a full account of all that happened, and whenever he ran short of material, he still provided a story. Nevertheless, the majority of details in the book are at least credible, and sometimes even affirmed by what is found in Paul's letters.

Luke shows a tremendous prejudice toward order and comradeship within the community. He deemphasizes difficulties and speaks of the harmony of the early Christian community (2:43-47 and 4:32-37). He was trying to win converts from among the Gentiles, and so he portrayed the community in its best light. Even he, though, cannot ignore the difficulties in chapter 6, which led to the naming of the seven Greek-speaking disciples to do the work of the diaconate, and the confusion over what obligations the Gentile converts had toward the law of Israel (chapter 15).

ROMANS

The Letter to the Romans is one of Paul's last, if not his last letter. He was writing to a community that he had not founded and that he had never visited.

Paul was planning to visit Jerusalem within the near future. He was carrying the proceeds of a collection that he had made in Greece and Asia Minor to help the poor of the mother Church. Yet he was worried, for many rumors had been spread about his teachings and especially about his attitude toward Judaism.

Therefore, he wrote to the community at Rome to explain his teaching concerning faith and salvation. The reasoning was that, since that community had been founded by missionaries from Jerusalem, they could communicate to that Church that Paul was really not teaching things contrary to the faith.

There is an overall Jewish tenor to the letter from its first words. Paul speaks of Jesus being a fulfillment of the promises of the prophets and having descended according to the flesh from King David.

Throughout the first chapters he argues that we are all worthy of God's condemnation, both Jew and Gentile. We have all sinned, and we are all subject to the wrath of God, but God has responded to our plight with incredible mercy. God, through the death and resurrection of his Son, has ransomed us from sin and called us into the liberty of the children of God.

Later in the letter he speaks of the fate of those Jews who had not yet converted. Paul says that they are subject to disobedience for a good reason, for they have been removed from the tree of the people of God for a while so that the Gentiles who believed in Jesus might be grafted on to that tree. His future hope was that the Jews would then become jealous and would themselves accept Jesus.

Paul also speaks of the proper attitude toward civil authorities. They have received their commission from the Lord, so they should be respected and obeyed.

The letter closes with a long list of people who are to be greeted. Scholars have often wondered where this list originated, for Paul did not know the members of this community. It is now believed that this might be part of a covering letter for a copy of the Letter to the Romans that Paul sent to another community (possibly Ephesus, for many of the people mentioned are associated with that region).

FIRST CORINTHIANS

The First Letter to the Corinthians was a letter written to a community that was deeply troubled by divisions and heretical tendencies.

When Paul arrived in Corinth, he was only one of many preachers proclaiming a new religion from the East. Most of the other religions had ecstatic tendencies in which the believer would seek to be possessed by the spirits of the gods. From the tenor of this letter, it would seem that some in the community interpreted Paul's message in this same manner.

They claimed that they had received a special revelation from the Holy Spirit that was superior to any human teaching. This led to factionalism in the community, for one group felt itself superior to the others. It led to problems of sexual immorality, for the adherents of this belief either practiced an attitude that they were spiritual creatures and it did not matter what they did in the flesh (licentiousness) or stated that they were spiritual creatures and they should never have anything to do with the flesh (absolute abstemiousness).

There were difficulties concerning the eating of meat offered to idols. Most meat sold in the markets had previously been offered to pagan idols. Could a Christian eat it? The response that the problem makers gave was that since the pagan god did not really exist, they could do whatever they wanted. Paul responded that while that was true, they might be giving poor example, especially to those whose consciences were weak.

There were problems in the celebration of the Lord's Supper. At this time the entire Passover meal was celebrated at the Eucharist, but some in the community had little to eat while others had too much. Paul spoke to them of the fact that the Eucharist is communion both with Jesus and with each other. By not practicing charity, they were sinning against the Eucharist.

There were problems with speaking in tongues, a practice in which one allows the Holy Spirit to speak through oneself. Unfortunately, some vaunted their ability to speak in tongues, even disrupting services in the community. Paul gave clear instructions on how this gift should be used.

Finally, there were some who denied the bodily resurrection. They wanted to be entirely spiritual, so they rejected the idea that they would regain their body at the resurrection. Paul responded that if Jesus did not rise from the dead, then we are the most pitiable of creatures.

Chapter 3, verses 10-15 is one of the few places in the New Testament where there is a teaching on the existence of Purgatory.

SECOND CORINTHIANS

The Second Letter to the Corinthians is a continuation of the discussion begun in First Corinthians. The first nine chapters are an attempt by Paul to reconcile with the community. He felt that the difficulties had gone on long enough, and those who had been responsible for the problems had repented from their evil ways.

The last four chapters are an angry denunciation of the troublemakers.

Scholars now believe that the last four chapters were actually a letter written before the first nine chapters. In those nine chapters, in fact, he refers to an earlier angry letter, which could well be the last chapters of what is now Second Corinthians. Because the letters were copied from papyri to scrolls, it is possible that a scribe simply made a mistake in the order of the chapters and inverted them. This makes even more sense when one considers the fact that toward the end of the first nine chapters Paul asks the Corinthians to be generous in a collection that he is gathering for the community in Jerusalem. It would be very odd to ask for money and then berate the community for four chapters.

There is even a fragment toward the end of chapter six and the beginning of chapter seven (6:14—7:1) that scholars believe might be from a letter that preceded the present First Letter to the Corinthians. In First Corinthians Paul speaks of an earlier correspondence in which he had given them rules concerning how they should interact with nonbelievers. The verses mentioned above do not fit in their present context and speak of the very things that Paul said he spoke of in that first letter.

This would mean that Second Corinthians is actually composed of fragments of at least three letters. It also means that Paul had to write at least four letters to this community to address their difficulties, an indication of how deeply ingrained they were. Saint Clement of Rome, the fourth Pope, wrote them again toward the end of the first century to discuss the exact same difficulties that Paul addressed all throughout his Corinthians correspondence.

The most beautiful image presented in this letter is that in which Paul speaks of the ministers of the gospel being earthen vessels that contain a great treasure, the gospel message they are sharing.

GALATIANS

The Letter to the Galatians was one of the most difficult letters Paul wrote. He was writing to a community that had fallen into error, and throughout the letter there is a sense of anger and frustration.

Galatians, unlike Paul's other letters, is not addressed to one community. Galatia was a region, and Paul was writing to all of the small Christian communities dispersed throughout that region.

He had preached the gospel to them, and many had converted to the faith. The vast majority of those who converted were pagans.

Sometime later, a group of Jewish-Christian missionaries arrived from Jerusalem. They undercut Paul's teaching by saying that Paul had preached an "easy" gospel to them. Paul had told them that it was not necessary to be circumcised or to follow Jewish law after they had been baptized. Remember that when one was baptized, one was really becoming a Jew who believed in the Messiah whom Yahweh had sent. They said that Paul had only tried to buy their favor.

Many in the community favored adopting Jewish ways. Paul wrote them to admonish them severely. He told them that they were liberated from their sins not by Jewish customs, but by the death and resurrection of Jesus. Their sins had already been washed away in their Baptism. If they adopted Jewish ways, it meant that they did not sufficiently trust in this message and that they did not have faith.

Paul adopted a very Jewish way of presenting this message. It is called Midrash, a type of rabbinic argumentation. In Midrash, one takes a verse from scripture and combines it with a similar verse from another place to produce a third meaning. This is not often used today, especially in Christian circles, but in Paul's day is was accepted as the proper way to argue Jewish questions.

Paul also gives an account of the "Council of Jerusalem," a meeting between Paul (and his disciples) and the apostles that occurred in Jerusalem sometime during the middle to the late 40's. At that meeting, they all reached the decision that pagans did not have to follow Jewish law if they converted to Christianity.

EPHESIANS

Colossians and Ephesians are two letters that are related (for they have many expressions in common). They are both attributed to Paul, but it is possible that he did not write either. There are expressions and situations described in the letters that cause some scholars to doubt their Pauline origin.

The author begins the letter with a hymn that praises Jesus and that proclaims that all existing things are to be put under Christ's headship in the fullness of time. As in Colossians, even heavenly powers are said to be subject to the authority of Jesus.

Paul's other letters speak of the fact that there is no importance if one is Jew or Gentile; this letter goes further and says that Jews and Gentiles have been made into one people through the death and resurrection of Christ.

Ephesians presents a developed theology of the Church as the body of Christ. In the course of his discussion on the Church, Paul speaks of the union of Christ and the Church in terms of something that is as intimate as the marriage union between a husband and a wife. This is a much more positive portrait of marriage than we find in Paul's other letters where marriage is something that must be done to avoid sin.

Much of the second part of the letter is an exhortation to live according to the values that give witness to the love of God in daily life. Christians are to combat vice and the powers of evil and live a totally blameless life. As in Colossians, there is an instruction on proper conduct within families and between slaves and masters, although this particular version is more elaborate.

PHILIPPIANS

The Letter to the Philippians is one of Paul's last and most intimate letters. He is writing from prison, and the fact that he faced possible death colors many of the thoughts he includes in this communication. He speaks of the necessity to make peace in the community. He tells the community that he does not know whether he will live or die, but that it does not make all that much difference because if he lives, he will preach and work for the Lord, but if he dies he will be with the Lord. He speaks about his conversion and how he changed his way of looking at things. The very things that he had previously considered most important were now considered to be rubbish in light of knowing and loving the Lord.

Chapter 2 contains a beautiful hymn that speaks of Jesus and his humility. Jesus, who was in the form of God (meaning that he was God), gave up the prerogatives of his divinity to serve us by dying on the cross. God responded to this sacrifice by proclaiming him Lord of all of creation.

COLOSSIANS

Colossians and Ephesians are two letters that are related (for many expressions are in common). They are both attributed to Paul, but it is possible that he did not write

either. There are expressions and situations described in the letters that cause some scholars to doubt their Pauline origin.

This letter's author speaks of Jesus in whom the fullness of divinity dwells. He is the visible likeness of the invisible God. All creatures, even those that are spiritual, are subject to him. This is important, for Greek philosophy taught that the more spiritual a creature was, the more it resembled God. Angels were totally spiritual creatures, while Jesus was incarnate. Some thought that this meant that the angels were superior to Jesus. This letter insists on Christians not worshiping angels, and on the fact that Jesus is far superior to them. Some types of behavior are condemned that seem to have originated in Jewish practices.

The letter closes with an instruction on how members of families and the community should treat one another and also with some information about Paul's travels and ministry. It is interesting that Mark is spoken of in positive terms, for Acts had spoken of a rift between Mark and Paul after he abandoned Paul on a missionary journey.

FIRST THESSALONIANS

The First Letter to the Thessalonians is most probably the first letter that Paul wrote. He was writing to a community that was very successful in turning from their previous errors to the truth of the gospel. Paul even speaks of the faith of the Thessalonians being famous throughout the entire world.

This is actually one of the problems that Paul had to address. They were so successful that they started to become boastful, thinking that they had arrived at success through their own efforts. He writes an extensive thanksgiving (the entire first three chapters of this letter) to remind them that their success is a gift from the Lord.

In these chapters he speaks of the rapport that exists among the missionaries, the community, and God. The relationship between the missionaries and the Thessalonians is critical, for they learned about their faith through them. Yet the missionaries could never have preached if the Lord had not called them and given them the courage to proclaim the gospel, and the Thessalonians could never have accepted their message if the Spirit of the Lord had not prompted their hearts to listen to the missionaries and interpret their message as the word of God. Our faith has both a horizontal and a vertical dimension.

The last chapters speak of the end times. Paul teaches in chapter 4 that on the last day those who have died will rise from the dead to be with the Lord, while those who are still alive will not have to die. They will be "caught up into the clouds." This particular expression should not be interpreted literally. It was simply Paul's way of expressing the fact that they would be with the Lord in heaven.

Finally, the last chapter talks about when the return of the Lord would occur without our knowing, how we should always be ready, and how we must combat against evil with the armor of the virtues.

SECOND THESSALONIANS

Second Thessalonians is one of the letters attributed to St. Paul. Many modern scholars doubt this attribution because of the dissimilarities in language and theology between it and First Thessalonians. Eschatology is one of the major themes of the letter. Paul warns the community not to be fooled by those who claim to foretell the end of the world. He also speaks of a mysterious figure whom he calls "the liar."

FIRST TIMOTHY

This is one of the Pastoral Epistles. The authorship is in doubt, for though it purports to have been written by St. Paul, its language and theology is different from that found in Paul's authentic letters.

This letter contains a warning concerning the false teachers who were troubling the community. There are a number of pastoral recommendations (e.g., presenting the attributes of bishops and deacons,

outlining proper relationships within families, etc.). Many of the teachings are based upon Stoic ideas concerning the proper ways to do things. The author of this letter was very concerned with giving good witness in whatever one did.

SECOND TIMOTHY

Second Timothy is one of the Pastoral Epistles. It is supposedly sent to Timothy, a convert whose father was pagan but whose mother was Jewish. Paul had him circumcised because he was technically Jewish since one obtained one's Jewishness through the mother.

This letter is purported to be Paul's last instruction to Timothy before he was martyred. (It is doubtful that Paul actually wrote this letter.) He wants to encourage him and instruct him that his own and Timothy's sufferings are a share in the suffering of Christ.

Paul speaks of the need to give witness, especially in what he calls the end times. He also warns Timothy concerning certain individuals who were spreading heresy.

This is one of the few writings in the Bible that speaks of inspiration of these sacred texts (3:14-17).

TITUS

The Letter to Titus is one of the three Pastoral Letters. It is attributed to Paul, although many scholars believe that it was probably written by one of his disciples. Titus, the recipient, was a pagan who was baptized by Paul. He accompanied Paul to the Council of Jerusalem. At the time he received this letter, he was a bishop and organizer of the Church in Crete.

The letter speaks of the qualifications that leaders of the Church should possess. It gives instructions on the proper way for Christians to act in family and in the community. It warns the reader not to become involved in silly arguments about questions of faith.

PHILEMON

This is the only undisputed letter of St. Paul to be written to an individual. Paul writes to Philemon, asking him to welcome his returning slave Onesimus. That slave had been with Paul in prison and had converted to the faith. Although Paul does not specifically ask for the release of the slave, he seems to imply this course of action.

HEBREWS

Paul's Letter to the Hebrews is not written by Paul, it is not a letter, and it is not intended for the Hebrews.

This treatise was written by an anonymous author in the middle of the first century A.D. The author is a Jewish-Christian who was trying to convince a community of Jewish-Christians that they could abandon many of their old Jewish ways because Jesus was their High Priest.

The argumentation is strange to us, and is based upon Greek philosophy and Jewish Midrash argumentation. The main theme drawn from Greek philosophy is that of form and matter. A form is the ideal representation of an object, while the matter is the concrete representation of that thing. The form is perfect, for it represents all exemplars of a particular thing, while matter is imperfect for it represents only the one thing that it is (e.g., the idea of a book versus a real book).

Jesus was the "form" while all the other priests of the Old Testament were the "matter." Jesus was one and perfect. The priests of the Old Testament were imperfect, and they therefore had to be many.

The Jewish Midrash argument is that if one can say something that is true about a lesser creature, then one can say that it is much more true about a greater creature. The rabbis often spoke of how kings were this or that, and how the king of kings, Yahweh, was so much greater. The author of this treatise speaks of the worship of the Old Testament and how it was this or that, while the worship inaugurated by Jesus was far superior.

The "letter" closes with an admonition to live with greater faith and obedience to God the Father. Faith is described as being assurance about the things hoped for and conviction about the things not seen.

JAMES

The Letter of James is attributed to James, the brother (cousin) of the Lord Jesus.

The central argument of the letter is that we must live our commitment of faith in the Lord in our everyday lives. We cannot say we have faith and then treat the poor with disdain or ignore their need.

The letter speaks of the blessedness of those who undergo trials and therefore whose faith is proven real.

James warns against using the tongue to create divisions within the community. He speaks of it as a small organ in the body, yet one that can cause the greatest of difficulties.

He condemns arrogance and boasting, presumption and avarice. Toward the end of the letter he speaks of those who are ill and who should seek an anointing from the elders of the community (the scriptural basis for the Sacrament of Anointing).

FIRST PETER

Some scholars question whether First Peter was written by the prince of the apostles, but there are no convincing arguments that would make us reject Peter's authorship.

The letter speaks of the dignity that has been conferred upon us Christians through the Sacrament of Baptism. We have been made a holy race chosen by the Lord, a royal priesthood. We must live that holiness by choosing a virtuous life.

We are to live an ordered life-style, obeying the proper authorities. Our families should be examples of virtue lived out on an everyday basis.

Peter exhorts the reader not to become discouraged by suffering, for Christ himself suffered. He also says that it would be better to suffer unjustly (when we do not deserve it) than to be punished for what we have done.

In chapter 3 Peter speaks of how Jesus preached to the souls of those who had died and invited them into heaven. This is the scriptural basis for our belief that Jesus descended into the underworld after his death to invite into heaven all of those who had never heard of him.

Peter closes the letter by charging the leaders of the Church to be honest and gentle in their care of the flock. He also encourages younger men to obey their elders with humility.

SECOND PETER

While the author of this letter claims to be Peter the Apostle, it is almost surely written by an anonymous author (most probably a Hellenistic Jew). The major theme of the letter is that the delay of the parousia does not mean that it will not occur. Some heretical movements proclaimed that there would be no final judgment. The author uses his claim of apostolic authority to show that both the second coming and the final judgment are revealed truth.

The letter was probably written at the end of the first century A.D. or the beginning of the second century. It was accepted into the canon at a relatively late date (the 4th century A.D.). Even in the earliest days of the Church its authorship was an open question.

FIRST JOHN

Ironically, the First Letter of John is not a letter. This becomes clear when one observes that it does not have the formal opening and closing that one would expect in a Greek letter, nor does it speak in the same manner that one would expect to see in a letter.

It is a treatise written sometime after the publication of the Gospel of John. Because that Gospel portrays Jesus as very divine, knowing and controlling everything all throughout his ministry, it was a bit suspect by the early Christian community. They were being assailed by a heresy called Docetism, which denied the humanity of Jesus. Some thought that this gospel was suspiciously similar to the Docetist teachings.

Thus, the author of this letter emphasizes the humanity of Jesus. The prologue to the letter mirrors the prologue to the Gospel of John, but while the gospel's prologue spoke of the Word that existed forever in the presence of God, the letter's prologue speaks of the word of God that became so incarnate that we observed it, spoke with it, touched it, etc.

The other major point that this letter makes is that one must observe the commandments if one wants to be called a disciple of Jesus. The Gospel of John taught that there was really only one commandment: to believe that Jesus was the only-begotten Son of God. The theory was that if one believed this, one would live a life compatible with that belief. It was what Saint Augustine said when he taught that we should love God and do what he would.

The problem was that some members of the community did what they wanted, which was not always moral. When they were questioned on it, they would proclaim that they were living in the freedom of the Sons of God and that they were anointed by the Holy Spirit, so no one should be questioning their conduct.

This letter calls them liars, for one cannot sin and still live in the light. By sinning, one has already chosen the darkness. Furthermore, if one loves God, one must love God's children, one's own brothers and sisters in the community.

The letter also defines God as love, and it states that if anyone wants to live in God, that person must live in love. It gives an important observation by stating that it is not that we have loved God first. God has loved us first and taught us the true meaning of love. We can only respond to this incredible generosity on the part of God.

BOOK OF REVELATION

The Book of Revelation is the only apocalyptic book to be part of the New Testament. Between 200 B.C. and 200 A.D., several apocalyptic books were written in Jewish and Christian communities. They all have certain things in common.

All apocalyptic books speak of two world eras: the present evil era and the coming age when God will reign upon the earth. This is their major difference with prophetic books. Prophetic books call people to conversion, for if they convert, God might remit their punishment. In apocalyptic books, things have progressed too far. There must be a cataclysmic change to purify the world from its perfidy.

Apocalyptic books also have extensive symbolism. Colors, numbers, animals, clothing, battles between angels and the forces of evil, etc. are all part of their symbolic matrix.

For example, numbers are important throughout most of these books. Ten stands for a fairly large amount, but seven stands for perfection (for ancient peoples believed that there were seven planets, and thus to say seven was to say the entire universe). Therefore, in their thinking, seven designated a number that was larger than ten. One thousand was considered an indefinite sum but a very large number.

Twelve symbolized both the number of the tribes of Israel and the number of the apostles. Thus, twelve times twelve times one thousand, or one hundred and forty-four thousand, stood for the Old and the New Israel, which the Lord had blessed with incredible fecundity (the meaning of the 1,000).

The Book of Revelation is not so much about when the end times will occur. Rather, it is a call to witness while one awaits the end times. (Remember the word witness in Greek is "martureo," for many will be called to martyrdom in order to give witness to the gospel.)

The forces of evil will combat the forces of good throughout history. Jesus defeated those forces on the cross, and we share in that victory every time we take up our cross in order to die with Jesus so that we might live with him forever.

APPENDIX 2: THE RESPONSORIAL PSALM*

In his final recorded appearance to the apostles before his Ascension, Jesus spoke of what was written about him in "the Law, the Prophets, and the Psalms" (Luke 24:44). Hence, the Church has always indicated, especially through the Liturgy, that there is a history of Christ in the Psalms.

Each Sunday in the Responsorial Psalm at Mass, the liturgical assembly is invited to read a page of this history. In doing so, every one of us can discern some aspect of Jesus and hear his voice on a matter of importance to us.

However, in order for this result to be attained we must participate fully, consciously, and actively in the Responsorial Psalm, which occurs after the First Reading in the Liturgy of the Word.

Liturgists tell us that the Responsorial Psalm together with the Alleluia Acclamation before the Gospel is the most important part of the people's responses in the Proper of the Mass for it functions as a kind of commentary on the Scriptures just proclaimed. It draws the soul to arrive at the interpretation of the Reading intended by the Church.

Indeed, the Responsorial Psalm is the only psalm used at Mass for its own sake rather than to accompany an action. It is the Word of God. That is why the Church insists that it may never be replaced by a nonbiblical text.

However, it is evident that in many cases, the people do not even know what is happening as the Responsorial Psalm goes flitting by during the celebration. This is even truer when the Responsorial Psalm is sung by the cantor with only a Refrain relegated to the people.

What is needed is to make information available to all about the function of this part of Mass, so that they will be able to take advantage of the music and the words to enter into the theme of response. The following observations may be of help in this respect.

CANTICLE OF THE COVENANT

Throughout the history of the Church, which is the people of God (in figure in the Old Testament and in fulfillment in the New), we find a pattern. God "speaks" to his people by accomplishing wondrous deeds for them. The people respond by celebrating these wondrous deeds.

God guides the people of the Exodus across the Red Sea. Miriam, following the lead of Moses her brother, celebrates the Lord who has cast horse and rider into the sea (Exodus 15:1, 21).

God delivers Hannah from her sterility by giving her a son, Samuel. Hannah responds by celebrating the Lord who enables a sterile woman to give birth (1 Samuel 2:5).

God delivers Tobit from blindness. Tobit responds by celebrating the Lord who lets his light rise over Jerusalem as well as in the hearts of his people (Tobit 13:11).

In New Testament times, God blesses Mary's virginity by letting her become the Mother of Jesus. Mary responds by glorifying the Lord and exulting in God her Savior, in Jesus whom she is bearing (Luke 1:46-55).

In accord with these examples, the Responsorial Psalm plays a similar role in the liturgical celebration. The Word proclaimed recalls God's wondrous deeds of old. The assembly celebrates these wondrous deeds and actualizes them in the celebration. It responds to the God of these wonders with the Responsorial Psalm.

The Word proclaimed is the word of the Covenant. The Responsorial Psalm is the canticle of the Covenant. It prepares for the Covenant, and asks God to keep us in it.

*Reprinted with permission from *Active Participation at Mass* by Anthony M. Buono, pp. 65-72, © 1994 by Alba House.

THE PSALTER:
THE CHRISTIAN PRAYER BOOK

In order to sing the Responsorial Psalm well, we should get to know something about the Book of Psalms or Psalter. It has become the book of Christian prayer, the compendium of the entire biblical message.

According to St. Thomas Aquinas, the Psalter—in contrast to the other biblical writings—"embraces in its universality the matter of all of theology. The reason why this biblical book is the one most used in the Church is that it contains in itself all Scripture. Its characteristic note is to restate, under the form of praise, all that the other biblical books express by way of narrative, exhortation, and discussion.

"The purpose of the Psalter is to make people pray, to elevate souls to God through contemplation of his infinite majesty, through meditation on the excellence of eternal happiness, and through communion in the holiness of God and the efficacious imitation of his perfection" *(Exposition on the Psalms of David)*.

The Psalms have been called with good reason "a school of Christian prayer." These sacred songs cover a wide range of human experiences; they bring out our strengths and weaknesses, faith and wonderment, joys and sorrows.

The Psalms also show forth the prophesied glory of Jesus: for it is only in Christ that their full significance is revealed. The noted Bible scholar Joseph Gelineau has written that Jesus "personally described himself as the Lord whom God seated at his right hand (Psalm 110 - Matthew 22:44); as the stone rejected by the builders which became the head of the corner (Psalm 118 - Matthew 21:42); as he who comes, blessed in the name of the Lord (Psalm 118 - Matthew 23:39); he personally applied to himself on the cross the appeal of the persecuted psalmist (Psalm 22 - Matthew 27:46) and his prayer of trust (Psalm 31 - Luke 23:46)."

Thus, the Psalms set forth Christ's lowly coming to earth, then his kingly and priestly power, and finally his beneficent labors and the shedding of his Blood for our redemption. So Christological are they that they have rightly been termed "the Gospel according to the Holy Spirit." It is the Holy Spirit who inserted in them indisputable references to the life of Christ.

POETIC QUALITIES OF THE PSALMS

The Psalms are among the world's best poetry. We all know "The Lord Is My Shepherd," but there are a host of others among the 150 Psalms that are just as classical.

The poetry of the Psalms contains rhythm, which is the recurrence of accented or unaccented syllables at regular intervals, but its outstanding trait is parallelism, which consists in the equal distribution or balance of thought in the various lines of each verse.

Synonymous parallelism is the repetition of the same thought with equivalent expressions:

"He who is throned in heaven laughs;
the Lord derides them."

Antithetic parallelism expresses a thought by contrast with an opposite:

"For the Lord watches over the way of the just,

but the way of the wicked vanishes."

Synthetic parallelism occurs when a second line completes the thought of the first by giving a comparison:

"When I call out to the Lord,
he answers me from his holy mountain,
when I lie down in sleep,
I wake again, for the Lord sustains me."

By paying attention to the poetic aspect of the Psalms, we will be able to recite or sing the Responsorial Psalm with more understanding and greater participation.

PRAYING THE RESPONSORIAL PSALM

The Psalms are not readings or prose prayers, even though on occasion they may be recited as readings. In Hebrew they were called "Songs of praise" and in Greek *Psalmoi,* that is, "Songs to be sung to the lyre." All the Psalms have a musical quality that dictates the correct way of delivering them.

Even when a Psalm is recited and not sung, its delivery must still be governed by its musical character. A Psalm presents a text to the minds of those singing it and listening to it, but it aims at moving their hearts.

In order to pray the Psalms with understanding, we must meditate on them verse by verse, with our hearts ready to respond in the way the Holy Spirit desires. As the one who inspired the Psalmists, the Holy Spirit is always present to those who in faith and love are ready to receive his grace.

Indeed, the singing of the Responsorial Psalm expresses the reverence that is due to God's majesty, but it should also be the expression of a joyful spirit and a loving heart, in keeping with its character as sacred poetry and inspired song and above all in keeping with the freedom of the children of God.

The Responsorial Psalm is a different prayer from one composed by the Church. The inspired Psalmist often addresses the people as he recalls the history of God's people; sometimes he addresses creation, and at other times he even introduces a dialogue between God and the people.

In praying the Psalm we should open our hearts to the different attitudes that may be expressed, which vary with the type of writing to which it belongs (Psalms of Grief or Trust or Gratitude and the like). Although the Psalms originated many centuries ago in the East, they express accurately the pain and hope, the unhappiness and trust, of every people and every age and country, and celebrate especially faith in God, revelation, and redemption.

In the words of another renowned Scripture scholar, Andre Choracqui, "We were born with this book [of Psalms] in our very bones. A small book; 150 poems; 150 steps between death and life; 150 mirrors of our rebellions and our loyalties, of our agonies and our resurrections."

The Psalms have great power to raise minds to God, to inspire devotion, to evoke gratitude in favorable times, and to bring consolation and strength in sad times. They constitute an inexhaustible treasury of prayers for every occasion and mood in a format that is true to the whole tradition of the History of Salvation.

Thus, we should strive to pray the Responsorial Psalm with the best of intentions both at home and at Mass. It will then become for us an opportunity to rediscover our own humanity, in its anguish, its rebellion, its violence, and its reconciliation as well.

It will become for us an opportunity to rediscover more broadly the whole of history, for example, those men and women who also struggle, who suffer, who cry out, who hope, and who pray in the four corners of the earth.

Finally, it will become for us an opportunity to encounter Christ mysteriously present in the heart of this humankind in which we find ourselves.

APPENDIX 3: GLOSSARY AND PRONUNCIATION GUIDE

For purposes of pronunciation, a simple system of phonetic spelling has been devised and included in parentheses for every entry defined. The **accented syllable** is indicated by **capital letters,** and the pronunciation for the letters is as follows.

uh = a, e, i, o, u unaccented (the Schwa)	**o** = odd (short)	**yoo** = use, unite (accented, long)
a = hat	**oh** = no	**uhr** = further
ah = father	**oi** = noise, joy	**ch** = church
ai = aisle, ice	**ow** = cow	**sh** = shame, wish
aw = awful, for	**oo** = boot	**zh** = vision
ay = ape, care	**u** = foot, book (accented, long)	**g** = get
e = get (short)	**uh** = culture, cut (accented, short)	**j** = judge
ee = eve	**yuh** = nature (unaccented, short)	**k** = cow, key
i = pit (short)		**kw** = quick
		w = witch

Aaron (AR-uhn; ER-uhn). Brother of Moses and the first high priest of Israel (Ex 6:20; 28:1ff).

Abba (AB-uh; ah-BAH). Aramaic word for "father" or "daddy" used by Jesus of his Father (Mk 14:36).

Abelmoholah (ay-buhl-mi-HOH-luh). A city on the Jordan River and the residence of Elisha the prophet (1 Kgs 19:16).

Abiathar (uh-BAI-uh-thuh). Son of the priest Ahimelech (1 Sm 22:20) and himself a priest of David (2 Sm 8:17). He is mentioned by Jesus in the discussion with the Pharisees concerning the apostles' picking grain on the sabbath (Mk 2:26).

Abijah (uh-BAI-juh). Son and successor of Rehoboam (1 Chr 3:10) and ancestor of Jesus (Mt 1:7).

Abilene (ab-uh-LEEN; -LEE-nee). A district ruled by Lysanias (Lk 3:1) at the time of Jesus that lay to the northwest of Damascus.

Abishai (uh-BAI-shi). A brother of Joab, he accompanied David during his flight from Saul (1 Sm 26:6ff) and from Absalom (2 Sm 16:9).

Abiud (uh-BAI-uhd). An ancestor of Jesus (Mt 1:13).

Abner (AB-nuhr). A commander of the army of Saul (1 Sm 17:55; 26:7). He first sided with a son of Saul, Ishbaal, after the death of Saul. He eventually betrayed him and furthered the cause of David among the tribes of the north.

Abraham (AY-bruh-ham). Founder of the Hebrew nation and father of the people of God (Gn 11:26ff; 17:4f, etc.). Originally called Abram (Gn 11:26), he received the name Abraham at the time of God's covenant with him (Gn 17:4).

Abram (AY-bruhm). *See* **Abraham.**

Achaia (uh-KAI-uh). Roman province comprising the central part of modern Greece (Acts 18:12, 27).

Achim (AY-kim). An ancestor of Jesus (Mt 1:14).

Acts of the Apostles (aks uhv thee uh-POS-uhlz). The book that continues the Gospel of Luke with a history of the primitive Church.

Adam (AD-uhm). The first man (Gn 2:8), who was placed in the garden of Eden (Gn 2:15) but disobeyed God and was expelled from the garden (Gn 3:23).

Advocate (AD-vuh-kut). See Paraclete.

Ahaz (AY-haz). Son and successor of King Jotham of Judah (2 Kgs 15:38) and father of Hezekiah (2 Kgs 16:20). It was to him that Isaiah prophesied that the Messiah would be Emmanuel, God with us (Is 7:14).

Alexander (al-ig-ZAN-duhr). Son of Simon of Cyrene and brother of Rufus (Mk 15:21).

Alpha (AL-fuh). First letter of the Greek alphabet. Used with "omega," the last letter, it signifies completeness, as "from A to Z." God is termed the Alpha and Omega, the First and the Last, the Beginning and the End (Rv 1:8), as is also Christ (Rv 22:13).

Alphaeus (al-FEE-uhs). Father of James the Less (Mt 10:3; Acts 1:13).

Amalek (AM-uh-lek). Eponymous founder of a nomadic tribe that dwelt in the Negeb (Gn 36:12). The Amalekites fought with the Israelites during their time in the Sinai (Ex 17:8ff). They also fought various battles against Israel, often in alliance with Israel's enemies.

Amaziah (am-uh-ZAI-uh). A priest at Bethel at the time of the Prophet Amos (Am 7:12).

Amminadab (uh-MIN-uh-dab). Father of Nahshon (Nm 1:7), father-in-law of Aaron (Ex 6:23), and an ancestor of Jesus (Mt 1:4).

Amos (AY-muhs). The third of the 12 Minor Prophets of the Old Testament, who proclaimed the need for social justice in people's relationships with each other. One of the ancestors of Jesus (Mt 1:10) bears the name Amos, but—as the NAB indicates in a footnote—a better reading is "Amon."

Amoz (AY-muhz). Father of the Prophet Isaiah (Is 2:1).

Ancient One (AYN-chuhnt won). A new translation for the more traditional "Ancient of Days," it is a name of God taken from apocalyptic writings that appears three times in Daniel (7:9, 13, 22).

Andrew (AN-droo). Brother of Peter (Jn 1:40) and one of the twelve apostles (Mt 10:2).

Anna (AN-uh). The aged prophetess who spoke of the coming redemption at Jesus' presentation in the temple (Lk 2:36ff).

Annas (AN-uhs). High priest of Jerusalem (6–15 A.D.), whose office passed to his sons and his son-in-law Caiaphas (Jn 18:13). He was involved in the trials of Jesus (Jn 18:13ff).

Antioch (AN-tee-ok). Name of two cities. Antioch on the Orontes River was the capital of Syria where the disciples of Jesus were first called "Christians" (Acts 11:19–26). Antioch in Pisidia on the border with Phrygia was one of the first cities in which Paul preached (Acts 13:14ff).

Apollos (uh-POL-uhs). An educated Christian Jew from Alexandria, who preached in Ephesus and in Corinth (Acts 18:24—19:1). Some scholars have proposed that he might be the author of the Letter to the Hebrews.

Arabia (uh-RAY-bee-uh). Northern part of the peninsula between the Red Sea and the Persian Gulf (Is 21:13) or the entire peninsula (Neh 2:19).

Arabs (AR-uhbz). Inhabitants of Arabia, some of whom were in Jerusalem on the day of Pentecost (Acts 2:11).

Aramean (ar-uh-MEE-uhn). A member of a nomadic people from northern Syria and southern Babylon.

Archelaus (ar-kuh-LAY-uhs). Son of Herod the Great, who became the ruler of Judea, Samaria, and Idumea upon his father's death in 4 B.C.–6 A.D. and was deposed in 6 A.D. (Mt 2:22).

Arimathea (ar-i-muh-THEE-uh). A town in Judah that was the birthplace of Joseph of Arimathea, who buried Jesus in his own tomb (Mk 15:43).

Asaph (AY-saf). A person's name, e.g., a cantor in the temple under David and Solomon to whom Psalms 50 and 73—83 are attributed.

Asher (ASH-uhr). Name of one of the twelve tribes of Israel and of its Patriarch, who was the eighth son of Jacob (Gn 49:20). Anna was from this tribe (Lk 2:36).

Asia (AY-zhuh). The Roman province of Asia, which included only the western third of what is now Asia Minor. Ephesus was its capital and it was evangelized by Paul on his 3rd missionary journey (Acts 18—21).

Attalia (at-uh-LAI-uh). A seaport on the coast of Pamphylia (Asia Minor).

Augustus (uh-GUS-tuhs). Emperor of Rome from 31 B.C. to 14 A.D., during whose reign Jesus was born (Lk 2:1).

Azor (AY-zawr). An ancestor of Jesus (Mt 1:13f).

Baal (BAY-uhl). The chief god of the Phoenicians and Canaanites, worshiped as the god of crops, flocks, and fertility—even by some Israelites (1 Kgs 16:31–33).

Baal-shalishah (BAY-uhl SHAHL-uh-shuh). A place in Ephraim from which bread and grain were brought to Elisha when he was at Gilgal (2 Kgs 3:42–44).

Babel (BAY-buhl). The place where the ancients built a tower to the heavens in arrogance before God (Gn 11:9).

Babylon (BAB-uh-luhn). A city on the Euphrates and the capital of the Babylonian Empire to which the Israelites were exiled in 597 and 587 B.C. (2 Chr 36:20; Ps 137:1). In the New Testament, the name was used as a synonym for Rome (1 Pt 5:13; Rv 14:8; 17:5). *See* **Babylonian Exile.**

Babylonian Exile (ba-buh-LOH-nee-uhn EK-sai-uhl). The period in Jewish history from the carrying away of the people to Babylon in 597 and 587 to their return in 538 B.C. (Mt 1:11).

Barabbas (buh-RAB-uhs). A prisoner whom Pilate released in place of Jesus (Mk 15:6–15).

Barsabbas (bahr-SAB-uhs). Name of two men: (1) Joseph Barsabbas, also called Justus, who was one of the candidates to succeed Judas Iscariot as an apostle (Acts 1:23). (2) The surname of Judas, the prophet, who was sent to Antioch together with Barnabas, Paul, and Silas to communicate the decisions of the Council of Jerusalem to the community there (Acts 15:22–32).

Bartholomew (bahr-THOL-uh-myoo). One of the twelve apostles (Mk 3:18).

Bartimaeus (bahr-tuh-MEE-uhs). A blind beggar from Jericho who was cured by Jesus (Mk 10:46–52).

Baruch (BA-ruhk; buh-ROOk). The prophet Jeremiah's secretary, to whom is ascribed the third of the 18 Prophetic Books of the Old Testament.

Beautiful Gate (bee-YOO-tuh-ful gayt). Possibly a gate on the eastern side of the temple where Peter and John healed a paralytic (Acts 3:1–11).

Beelzebul (bee-EL-zee-buhl). Name of the god of Canaan, who in the New Testament is referred to as the prince of demons (Mk 3:22). The name literally means "the Lord of the Flies."

Bethany (BETH-uh-nee). A village on the eastern slope of the Mount of Olives (Lk 10:38; Jn 11:1, 18).

Bethlehem (BETH-li-hem). The birthplace of Jesus, a village 4.5 miles south of Jerusalem (Lk 2:4–7).

Bethphage (BETH-fuh-jee). A village east of Bethany mentioned in connection with Jesus' triumphal entry into Jerusalem (Mk 11:1).

Bethsaida (beth-SAY-uh-duh; -SAI-duh). A town on the northern shore of the Sea of Galilee (later called Julia) that was the home of Andrew, Peter, and Philip (Jn 1:44; 12:21).

Boaz (BOH-az). Husband of Ruth (Ru 4:13) and ancestor of Jesus (Mt 1:5f).

Caesar (SEE-zuhr). Surname of Julius Caesar, given from the 1st century onward to the Roman emperors (Lk 2:1; 3:1).

Caesarea (sez-uh-REE-uh). Name of various cities. (1) Caesarea Philippi, a town where Jesus prepared his disciples for his approaching sufferings and death and Peter made his famous confession of Christ's divinity (Mk 8:27). (2) A town where the converted Paul was sent to escape the Hellenists who tried to kill him (Acts 9:30).

Caiaphas (KAY-uh-fuhs; KAI-yuh-fuhs). High priest (18—36 A.D.) and head of the Sanhedrin during the trial of Jesus (Mt 26:57).

Cana (KAY-nuh). Village of Galilee, located north of Nazareth, and site of Jesus' first miracle (Jn 2:1–11).

Canaan (Kay-nuhn). One of the old names for Palestine, the land of the Canaanites who were dispossessed by the Israelites.

Capernaum (kuh-PUHR-nay-uhm). A town on the northwestern shore of the Sea of Galilee where Jesus made his headquarters during his Galilean ministry (Mk 2:1).

Cappadocia (kap-uh-DO-shee-uh). A province in eastern Asia Minor (Acts 2:9).

Carbuncles (KAHR-bun-kuhlz). As used in the Bible, something bright and glittering, possibly rubies or emeralds (Is 54:12).

Carmel (KAHR-mel). A mountain chain and ancient site of worship, often lauded for its beauty (Is 35:2).

Carnelians (kahr-NEL-yuhnz). Hard sparkling reddish quartz used in jewelry (Is 54:11).

Cephas (SEE-fuhs). The name given by Jesus to the apostle Peter, Peter meaning "rock" (Jn 1:42).

Chaldeans (kal-DEE-uhnz). Members of an Eastern Aramean tribe that beginning in 1100 B.C. invaded Babylon. They are termed ancestors of the Israelites (Jdt 5:6) as a result of the tradition that Abraham came from Ur of the Chaldees (Gn 11:28). In exile the Israelites became servants of the "king of the Chaldeans" (2 Chr 36:20).

Cherubim (CHER-uh-bim). In the Old Testament, these were superhuman beings whose nature was not made explicit. They were regarded as the porters who carry God (Ps 18:11; 80:2) and were a sign of his power, for he was enthroned on the cherubim (1 Sm 4:4; 2 Kgs 19:15). In Christian tradition, they are identified as the second of the nine choirs of angels.

Chloe (KLOH-ee). A woman whose people informed Paul of factions in the Corinthian community (1 Cor 1:11).

Chronicles (KRON-i-kulz). Fifth and sixth of the 17 Historical Books of the Old Testament.

Cilicia (suh-LISH-ee-uh). A region that lay along the southeastern coast of Asia Minor.

Cleopas (KLEE-oh-puhs). One of the disciples with whom Jesus walked on the way to Emmaus and broke bread (Lk 24:18).

Clopas (KLOH-puhs). The husband of Mary of Clopas (Jn 19:25).

Colossians (kuh-LOSH-uhnz). People of Colossae in Phrygia to whom Paul wrote one of the Letters of the New Testament.

Corinth (KOR-inth). Capital of the province of Achaia, and an extremely commercial city, which Paul made the center of his activity in Greece (Acts 18:11).

Corinthians (kuh-RIN-thee-uhnz). Christians of Corinth to whom Paul wrote two of the Letters of the New Testament.

Cornelius (kawr-NEEL-yuhs). A Roman centurion from Caesarea who was baptized by Peter (Acts 10f), showing that the Church was open to pagans as well as Jews.

Cretans (KREE-tans). Inhabitants of Crete, an island in the Mediterranean forming a natural bridge between Europe and Asia Minor, some of whom were in Jerusalem on the day of Pentecost (Acts 2:11).

Cush (koosh). Ethiopia (modern day Sudan).

Cyrene (sai-REEN). A Greek colony in northern Africa, with a large population of Greek-speaking Jews. Many of them were in Jerusalem on the day of Pentecost (Acts 2:10).

Cyrus (SAI-ruhs). Founder of the Persian world empire, who in October 539 B.C. overthrew the Babylonian king, Nabonidus, and allowed the Jews to return from their exile (2 Chr 36:22f). He is termed God's anointed by Isaiah (Is 45:1).

Daniel (DAN-yuhl). An ancient figure of wisdom who is attributed to be the author of the Book of Daniel (which although placed in the time of the Babylonian Exile was actually written much later during the time of the Maccabees). He is called the last of the 4 Major Prophets of the Old Testament.

David (DAY-vid). Second and greatest King of Israel and an ancestor of Jesus (Mt 1:6).

Decapolis (di-KAP-uh-lis). A federation of 10 Greek cities in Palestine mostly east of the Jordan, through which Jesus passed during his public ministry (Mk 5:20; 7:31).

Deuteronomy (doo-tuh-RON-uh-mee). Fifth and last Book of the Pentateuch.

Diadem (DAI-uh-dem). A crown or royal headband (Is 62:3).

Didymus (DID-i-muhs). Greek form of the name Thomas (the apostle), which signifies "twin" (Jn 11:16; 20:24; 21:2).

Dromedaries (DROM-uh-der-eez). Camels with unusual speed and trained for riding (Is 60:6).

Ebed-melech (ee-bid-MEE-lik). An Ethiopian eunuch who saved Jeremiah the prophet from a cistern into which he had been thrown (Jer 38:7ff).

Ecclesiastes (i-klees-ee-AS-tees). Fourth of the 7 Wisdom Books of the Old Testament.

Eden (EE-duhn). Place where God planted a garden in which he put Adam and Eve (Gn 2:8).

Egypt (EE-juhpt). A country northeast of Africa often in contact with Israel. Egyptian Jews were in Jerusalem on the day of Pentecost (Acts 2:10).

Elamites (EE-luh-maits). Inhabitants of Elam, east of Babylon (Gn 10:22; 14:1ff), some of whom were in Jerusalem on the day of Pentecost (Acts 2:9).

Eldad (EL-dad). One who prophesied in the Israelite camp in the wilderness (Nm 11:26ff).

Eleazar (el-ee-AYZ-uhr). An ancestor of Joseph, the husband of Mary (Mt 1:15).

Eli (EE-lai). A priest of Shiloh (1 Sm 1:9) who judged Israel forty years (1 Sm 4:18). He spoke to Hannah (1 Sm 1:12ff), and it was to him that the child Samuel was brought (1 Sm 1:28; 2:11; 3:1–10).

Eli, Eli [or: Eloi, Eloi], Lema Sabachthani (AY-lee, AY-lee, LAY-muh, sa-BAK-thuh-nee). The English transliteration of a Greek phrase (Mt 27:46; Mk 15:34), which is in turn the transliteration of the Hebrew (or Aramaic) version of Ps 22:1: "My God, my God, why have you abandoned me?"

Eliab (i-LEE-uhb). Eldest son of Jesse and brother of David who presented a commanding appearance (1 Sm 16:6).

Eliakim (i-LAI-uh-kim). Son of Hilkiah and successor to Shebna as King Hezekiah's majordomo (Is 22:20ff).

Elijah (i-LAI-juh). A prophet during the reigns of Ahab and Jezebel in the Northern Kingdom (1 Kgs 17:1–16).

Elisha (i-LAI-shuh). A prophet in the Northern Kingdom in the second half of the 9th century B.C. (2 Kgs 4:8–16).

Eliud (i-LAI-uhd). An ancestor of Jesus (Mt 1:14f).

Elizabeth (i-LIZ-uh-buht). Wife of Zechariah, mother of John the Baptist, and relative of the Virgin Mary (Lk 1:5–57).

Emmanuel (i-MAN-yoo-uhl). Symbolic name meaning "God is with us" given by Isaiah to the child whose birth he foretold (Is 7:14) and which is applied to Jesus (Mt 1:23).

Emmaus (i-MAY-uhs). The town 7 miles from Jerusalem to which two disciples walked on the day of the resurrection accompanied by Jesus (Lk 24:13–35).

Ephah (EE-fuh). A measurement of weight (1 Sm 1:24); also the name of a son of Midian (Gn 25:4) and eponymous ancestor of a tribe (Is 60:6).

Ephesians (i-FEE-shuhnz). Inhabitants of Ephesus in Asia Minor to whom Paul wrote one of the Letters of the New Testament.

Ephphathah (EF-uh-thuh). An Aramaic word, meaning "Be opened," that was uttered by Jesus as he was healing a deaf man (Mk 7:34).

Ephraim (EE-free-uhm). One of the twelve tribes of Israel, which became the principal tribe of the Northern Kingdom (Jer 31:9; Zec 9:10).

Ephrathah (EF-ruh-thuh). Ancient name of Bethlehem or the district around it (Mi 5:1).

Esther (ES-tuhr). Eleventh of the 13 Historical Books of the Old Testament.

Euphrates (yoo-FRAY-teez). A large river that runs from Armenia to the Persian Gulf. It and the Tigris form the two boundaries of Mesopotamia. It also forms one of the boundaries of the widest extent of the borders of Israel.

Eve (EEV). The first woman whom God placed in the garden of Eden (Gn 2:22).

Exodus (EK-suh-duhs). The deliverance of the Israelites from Egypt by God's mighty hand; also, the second Book of the Pentateuch that narrates the story of this great event.

Expiation (ek-spee-AY-shuhn). A translation of the Hebrew word for pardon or suppression of sin. Jesus is called "an expiation" because he assumes pardon of all sins (Rom 3:25).

Ezekiel (i-ZEE-kee-uhl). Third of the 4 Major Prophets who prophesied in exile during the Babylonian Captivity in the 6th century B.C.

Ezra (EZ-ruh). Priest and scribe who is the main character of the seventh of the 13 Historical Books of the Old Testament.

Feast of Unleavened Bread (feest uhv uhn-LEV-uhnd bred). A feast of spring and renewal celebrating the founding event of the people of God: the deliverance from bondage by the Exodus from Egypt (Lv 23:4–8; Mk 14:1, 12). Each family reenacted the first Passover by eating the Passover meal.

Gabbatha (GAB-uh-thuh). A district in Jerusalem where Pilate's official residence was located (Jn 19:13).

Gabriel (GAY-bree-uhl). An angel who interpreted the vision of Daniel (Dn 8:15ff) and told him of the seventy weeks (Dn 9:22ff). He also announced the birth of John the Baptist to Zechariah (Lk 1:11ff) and that of Jesus to Mary (Lk 1:26ff). In Christian tradition he is known as an archangel, the eighth of the nine choirs of angels.

Galatians (guh-LAY-shuhnz). The inhabitants of Galatia, a Roman province in central Asia, to whom Paul addressed one of the Letters of the New Testament.

Galileans (gal-uh-LEE-uhnz). Inhabitants of Galilee (Lk 13:1).

Galilee (GAL-uh-lee). The region west of the Sea of Galilee and the Jordan, where Jesus was reared and began preaching (Mk 1:14).

Gehazi (gi-HAY-zee). Servant of the prophet Elisha (2 Kgs 4:8ff).

Gehenna (gi-HEN-uh). Place of punishment after death or after the Last Judgment (Mt 10:28).

Genesis (JEN-uh-sis). First Book of the Pentateuch.

Gennasaret (gi-NES-uh-ret). *See* **Sea of Galilee.**

Gentiles (JEN-tailz). Among the Jews it meant either foreign nations (Acts 7:45) or pagans, i.e., polytheists or idolaters who did not worship Yahweh (Mt 4:15; Lk 2:32).

Gethsemane (geth-SEM-uh-nee). A garden on the Mount of Olives, which was the scene of Christ's agony and betrayal (Mt 26:36–56).

Gibeon (GIB-ee-uhn). Hivite city north of Jerusalem that was a cult center and a royal shrine until Solomon's reign (1 Kgs 3:4–15).

Gilgal (GIL-gal). A site near Jericho associated with Joshua's renewal of the covenant (Jos 4:19f) and the site of Saul's installation as king (1 Sm 10:8).

Golgotha (GOL-guh-thuh). Aramaic name ("Place of the Skull") for a little hill northwest of Jerusalem where Jesus was crucified (Mt 27:33).

Gomorrah (guh-MAWR-uh). One of the cities destroyed by God because of its immorality (Gn 19:1ff). It became a symbol for God's judgment upon the sinful.

Greeks (greekz). Name that identified the inhabitants of Greece but also referred to a specific culture: Hellenism (cf. 1 Cor 1:22).

Habakkuk (HAB-uh-kuk). Eighth of the 12 Minor Prophets of the Old Testament.

Haggai (HAG-ai). Tenth of the 12 Minor Prophets of the Old Testament.

Hannah (HAN-uh). The mother of Samuel, the last judge of Israel (1 Sm 1—2).

Hebrews (HEE-brooz). Last of the Letters of the New Testament.

Hebron (HEE-bruhn). A city in the hill country of Judah, this was the city from which David reigned for seven years before he was made king of the united kingdom of the northern and southern tribes of Israel (2 Sm 2:11).

Hellenists (HEL-uh-nists). Jews from outside Palestine who took Greek as their primary language and adopted Greek ideas and practices (Acts 6:1).

Herod (HER-uhd). The Herodian family, which though Jewish in religion was Idumean in origin. Herod "the Great" was appointed by Rome as King of Judea in 40 B.C. He slaughtered the infants at Bethlehem (Mt 2:16).

Archelaus (ahr-kuh-LAY-uhs) was ethnarch of Judea 4 B.C. to 6 A.D. **Antipas (AN-tee-pahs)** was tetrarch of Galilee and Perea until 39 A.D. He married his brother's wife Herodias and beheaded John the Baptist. **Philip (FIL-uhp),** tetrarch of Trachonitis, was a mild man. His grandson, Herod **Agrippa (uh-GRIP-uh) I,** was king of all Palestine from 41 to 44 A.D. and put James to death (Acts 12:2). His son, **Agrippa II,** ruled in Trachonitis until 100 A.D. The latter heard Paul's defense (Acts 25:23ff).

Herodians (hi-ROH-dee-unz). Partisans and courtiers of the reigning dynasty of the Herods. They conspired with their enemies, the Pharisees, against Jesus (Mt 22:16).

Hezekiah (hez-uh-KAI-uh). Son and successor of Ahaz as King of Judah for 29 years (2 Kgs 18—20), who reformed the worship (2 Kgs 18:4ff) and was an ancestor of Jesus (Mt 1:9f).

Hezron (HEZ-ruhn). An ancestor of Jesus (Mt 1:3).

Hilkiah (hil-KAI-uh). The father of Eliakim (Is 22:20). Name of six other persons (mostly priests) in Israel.

Holocausts (HAHL-oh-kosts). In the ancient sacrifices only the blood and certain parts of the victim were offered to God; the rest was divided among the priest and faithful who had offered it (Lv 7:11–21). A holocaust (from the Greek "wholly burnt") was a sacrifice in which an entire animal except its hide was consumed in the fire on the altar, with the primary purpose of rendering glory to God (Lv 1:1ff).

Horeb (HAWR-eb). The mountain at which Moses received his commission (Ex 3:1) and to which Elijah fled (1 Kgs 19:9).

Hosanna (hoh-ZAH-nuh). Hebrew expression signifying "May God save," used in the course of Jewish feasts (Ps 118:25f). It served as an acclamation during Jesus' entrance into Jerusalem, in the sense of "Long live," and it is always chanted during the course of the Liturgy (Mt 21:9).

Hosea (hoh-ZAY-uh). Third of the 12 Minor Prophets of the Old Testament, who spoke of his difficult relationship with his wife as being parallel to the relationship between God and the people of Israel.

Hur (huhr). A contemporary of Moses who, along with Aaron, helped hold Moses' arms upright during Israel's battle with Amalek (Ex 17:10ff).

Iconium (i-KOH-nee-uhm). A city in Asia Minor visited by Paul (Acts 13:51—14:6, 21).

Isaac (AI-zik). Son of Abraham (Gn 17:19), whose immolation ordered by God, then prevented, prefigures the sacrifice of Christ (Gn 22).

Isaiah (ai-SAY-uh). First of the 4 Major Prophets of the Old Testament, who prophesied especially about the Passion of our Lord. Isaiah was a great prophet of Israel from 740 to 700 B.C. Chapters 40 to 55 of the Book named after him were probably written much later during the Babylonian Exile (587–539 B.C.) and chapters 56 to 66 after the Exile.

Iscariot (is KAR-ee-uht). Surname of Judas, the apostle who betrayed Jesus (Mt 26:14).

Isles (ailz). Dry land as opposed to water (Is 42:15), but its extended meaning was one of the farthest regions of the earth (Ps 72:10; Is 41:5).

Israel (IZ-ray-uhl). Name given by God to Jacob, the son of Isaac (Gn 32:29). Also used for his descendants, the twelve tribes of the Hebrews, and later the ten northern tribes led by Ephraim, as well as of the Church (the new Israel: Gal 6:16).

Israelites (IZ-ray-uh-laits). People of Israel (Acts 10:36).

Ituraea (i-TYOO-ree-uh). A region northwest of Palestine beyond the Jordan ruled by Herod Philip (Lk 3:1).

Jaar (JAY-uhr). Another name for Kiriath-jearim, one of the Canaanite towns and a center of Baal worship, where the Ark remained for a few generations (Ps 132:6).

Jacob (JAY-kuhb). Son of Isaac and Rebekah and twin brother of Esau, whose birthright he took (Gn 25). He was renamed Israel by God (Gn 32:29). The name also refers to the father of Joseph, foster father of Jesus (Mt 1:16).

Jairus (JAI-ruhs). The synagogue-ruler whose daughter Jesus raised from the dead (Mk 5:22; 8:41).

James (jaymz). Name of three persons: (1) the apostle James ("the less"), son of Alphaeus (Mt 10:3); (2) the apostle James ("the greater"), son of Zebedee and brother of John the apostle who died as a martyr during the persecution of Herod Agrippa (Acts 12:2); (3) James, the "brother of the Lord," probably the son of Mary of Clopas, who was the first bishop of Jerusalem, martyred in 62, and presumed author of one of the Letters of the New Testament (Gal 1:19; Mt 13:55).

Javan (JAY-vuhn). A name that stands for the cities on the west coast of Asia Minor (Is 66:19; Ez 27:13).

Jechoniah (jek-uh-NAI-uh). A variant of Jehoiachin, son of Jehoiakim, grandson of Josiah (1 Chr 3:15, 17), and ancestor of Jesus (Mt 1:11f).

Jehoshaphat (ji-HOSH-uh-fat). Son and successor of Asaph as King of Judah for 25 years (1 Kgs 22:42) and ancestor of Jesus (Mt 1:8).

Jeremiah (jer-uh-MAI-uh). Second of the 4 Major Prophets, who prefigures the Messiah mainly by his personal sufferings.

Jericho (JER-uh-koh). An ancient city at the southern end of the Jordan Valley, also called the City of Palms (Dt 34:3), which was miraculously captured by Joshua as the opening wedge of his battle to take Canaan (Jos 6). It was also the site of Jesus' healing of the blind Bartimaeus (Mk 10:46).

Jerusalem (ji-ROO-suh-luhm). Capital of Israel, conquered by David (also called City of David), known as the city of God (Heb 12:22; Rv 3:12) and the Holy City (Mt 4:5; 27:53). The Church is the new Jerusalem and the image of the Heavenly Jerusalem (Gal 4:26; Rv 21:1—22:5).

Jesse (JES-ee). The Father of David (Is 11:1) and an ancestor of Jesus (Mt 1:6).

Jesu (JAY-zoo). Diminutive and familiar form of Jesus.

Jesus (JEE-zuhs). The personal name of the Son of God made man, which means: "The Lord is salvation" or "Savior," and denotes his mission: to save humans from death and sin and make them once more children of God and heirs of heaven.

Jethro (JETH-roh). The father-in-law of Moses (Ex 3:1), he is also called

Reuel (Ex 2:18) and Hobab (Nm 10:29). He was a priest of Midian.

Joanna (joh-AN-uh). A woman who helped to support Jesus and his followers (Lk 8:2) and who went to the tomb on Easter Sunday (Lk 24:10).

Job (johb). First of the 7 Wisdom Books of the Old Testament.

Joel (JOH-uhl). Second of the 12 Minor Prophets of the Old Testament.

John (jon). Son of Zebedee and brother of James the Greater who became an apostle and wrote the last of the 4 gospels; three of the Catholic Letters are also attributed to him. Another John is the author of the Book of Revelation.

John the Baptist (jon thuh BAP-tist). Son of Zechariah and Elizabeth (Lk 1:5ff), who was Christ's precursor.

Jonah (JOH-nuh). Fifth of the 12 Minor Prophets of the Old Testament, whose book serves as a parable reminding Israel that God is Lord of all peoples upon the earth.

Joram (JAWR-uhm). Son and successor of Jehoshaphat as King of Judah (1 Kgs 22:51) and an ancestor of Jesus (Mt 1:8). Also called Jehoram.

Jordan (JAWR-duhn). The largest river in Palestine, which played a large part in the history of Israel and the early public life of Christ (Mt 3:13–17).

Joseph (JOH-sif). Son of Jacob and Rachel (Gn 30:24). He is regarded by the Church as a figure of Joseph, the "just man," who was the spouse of the Virgin Mary and foster father of Christ (Mt 1:18ff).

Joses (JOH-siz). Cousin of Jesus (Mk 6:3—called Joseph in Mt 13:55). Son of Mary (Mk 15:40, 47), wife of Clopas (Jn 19:25—called Joseph in Mt 27:56).

Joshua (JOSH-yoo-uh). First of the 3 Books that follow the Pentateuch.

Josiah (joh-SAI-uh). Son and successor of Amon as King of Judah (2 Kgs 21:24), who reformed religion and repaired the temple, and was an ancestor of Jesus (Mt 1:10f).

Jotham (JOH-thuhm). King of Judah in the time of Isaiah (2 Kgs 15:32) and an ancestor of Jesus (Mt 1:9).

Judah (JOO-duh). Son of Jacob (Gn 29:35) and ancestor of the tribe of Israel whose capital was Jerusalem. After the schism of the 10 northern tribes it became the Kingdom of Judah or Judea. He was an ancestor of Jesus (Mt 1:3).

Judas (JOO-duhs). Name of five persons: (1) Judas (Jude Thaddeus) the apostle (Lk 6:16; Mt 10:3); (2) Judas, a "brother of the Lord," and presumed author of the "Letter of Jude" (Mk 6:3); (3) Judas, surnamed Barsabbas, sent by the apostles to Antioch (Acts 15:22, 32); (4) Judas Iscariot, who betrayed Jesus (Mt 10:4); (5) Judas of Damascus at whose house Paul lodged after his conversion (Acts 9:11).

Jude (jood). See Judas: 2.

Judea (joo-DEE-uh). The most southern part of the three districts of Palestine west of the Jordan. Together with Samaria and Idumea it formed the Roman province of Judea with its capital at Jerusalem.

Judean (joo-DEE-uhn). Adjectival form of Judea.

Judges (JUHJ-iz). Second of the 3 Books that follow the Pentateuch.

Judith (JOO-dith). Tenth of the 13 Historical Books of the Old Testament.

Justus (JUHS-tuhs). Surname of Joseph Barsabbas (Acts 1:23).

Kidron (KAI-druhn). Valley along the east side of Jerusalem that joins the Valley of Hinnom and extends 20 miles to the Dead Sea.

Kings (kings). Third and fourth of the 13 Historical Books of the Old Testament.

Kor (also spelled cor) (kor). An indeterminate large weight measure.

Lamb of God (lam uhv god). A title of Jesus to show that he bears the sins of mankind and offers himself as a sacrificial lamb, prefigured by the paschal lamb through whose blood the Israelites were saved from their Egyptian bondage (Jn 1:29).

Lamentations (lam-en-TAY-shuhnz). Third of the 18 Prophetic Books of the Old Testament.

Law (law). Primarily the Ten Commandments that God gave to the chosen people, which were concerned mostly with external obedience. The new law was instituted by Christ and is based on charity (which sums up the Ten Commandments). It requires both internal and external obedience.

Lazarus (LAZ-uhr-uhs). Brother of Martha and Mary (Jn 11:5). He was raised from the dead by Jesus (Jn 11:43ff) and was present at the supper in his honor (Jn 12:2). This is also the name of the poor man in the parable of Lazarus and the rich man who would not assist him (Lk 16:20ff).

Lebanon (LEB-uh-nuhn). Mountainous chain north of Palestine, heavily wooded and known especially for its cedars (Jgs 9:15; Is 35:2).

Levi (LEE-vai). Name of two persons. (1) The son of Jacob and Leah (Gn 29:34), who gave his name to a tribe of Israel (Mal 2:4). (2) The tax collector who became an apostle and is called Matthew (Mt 9:9ff), the eventual author of the first gospel.

Levites (LEE-vaits). Members of the tribe of Levi, who assisted the priests in temple worship. In the parable of the Good Samaritan the Levite failed to help his neighbor (Lk 10:32).

Leviticus (li-VIT-i-kuhs). Third Book of the Pentateuch.

Libya (LIB-ee-uh). Ancient Greek name for northern Africa west of Egypt, which has Cyrene as one of its cities (Acts 2:10).

Lord (lawrd). Originally a title that signified nothing more than "sir." From the 3rd century B.C. onward, the Jews replaced the ineffable name "Yahweh" with "Adonai" (Lord) in reading the Bible. Applied to Jesus by the first Christians, the name "Lord" was thus equivalent to an affirmation of his divinity (Acts 2:36).

Lud (luhd). The name for two separate regions, one in Asia Minor (Is 66:19; probably Lydia) and one in Africa (Jer 46:9; Ez 30:5).

Luke (look). Companion of Paul and author of the third gospel and the Acts of the Apostles.

Lyre (LAI-uhr). A string musical instrument used to praise the Lord (Ps 81:3).

Lysanias (li-SAY-nee-uhs). Tetrarch of Abilene (Lk 3:1), a small region in Lebanon.

Lystra (LIS-truh). A city in Lycaonia (Asia Minor) where Paul and Barnabas were mistaken for Zeus and Hermes (Acts 14:6–18).

Maccabees (MAK-uh-beez). Twelfth and thirteenth of the 13 Historical Books of the Old Testament.

Macedonia (mas-uh-DOH-nee-uh). A Roman province north of Greece in the Balkans that was visited by Paul (1 Thes 1:7).

Magdala (MAG-duh-luh). A town on the northwest shore of the Sea of Galilee, 3 miles north of Tiberias (Mt 15:39), home of Mary Magdalene (Jn 19:25).

Magdalene (MAG-duh-luhn). Alternate surname of Mary of Magdala, who followed the body of Jesus to the grave (Mt 27:61) and was the first to learn of the resurrection (Mt 28:1–8).

Malachi (MAL-uh-kai). Last of the 12 Minor Prophets of the Old Testament.

Malchiah (mal-KAI-uh). A prince who owned the cistern into which Jeremiah was thrown in an assassination attempt. He was rescued by Ebedmelech (Jer 38:6ff).

Malchus (MAL-kuhs). A servant of the high priest whose ear Peter cut off with a sword (Jn 18:10).

Mammon (MAM-uhn). A word derived from the Aramaic mamona, meaning property, both in the New Testament and in rabbinic writings.

Mamre (MAM-ree). A site near Hebron. It was marked off with an ancient oak tree and was probably a sanctuary.

Man (man). In the eyes of the Jews, a being dependent on God for his life. The Christian has two selves within him: the "old self," drawn to evil, made up of body and soul; and the "new self" created by the Holy Spirit, who must triumph over sin (Rom 6:6).

Manna (MAN-uh). Food miraculously supplied by God to the Israelites during their 40 years in the desert (Nu 11:9), a type of the Eucharist—the Bread from heaven (Jn 6:31ff).

Mark (mahrk). Companion of Paul and author of the second gospel.

Martha (MAHR-thuh). Sister of Mary (Lk 10:38) and Lazarus (Jn 11:1).

Mary (MAY-ree). The Virgin, mother of Jesus (Mt 1:18ff; Lk 2:6). Mary was

also the name of the mother of James and Joses (Mt 27:56), who was present at the crucifixion and at the burial of Jesus (Mt 27:61) as well as on the morning of the resurrection (Mt 28:1). She seems to be the same as Mary the wife of Clopas (Jn 19:25). This is also the name of the sister of Martha and Lazarus (Lk 10:38; Jn 11:1) and of the woman from Magdala who was a follower of Jesus (see **Magdalene**).

Massah (MAS-uh). Name given to the site of the rock in Horeb from which Moses drew water for the rebellious Israelites (Ex 17:1–7; Ps 95:8f). The name is coupled with Meribah (Dt 33:8).

Matthan (MATH-an). Grandfather of Joseph, Mary's husband (Mt 1:15).

Matthew (MATH-yoo). One of the twelve apostles identified with Levi, son of Alphaeus, and a tax collector (Mt 9:9; Mk 2:14). He is regarded as the author of the gospel that bears his name.

Matthias (muh-THAI-uhs). The disciple chosen by lot to replace Judas Iscariot (Acts 1:24ff).

Medad (MEE-dad). One who prophesied in the Israelite camp in the wilderness (Nm 11:26ff).

Medes (meedz). Inhabitants of the land of Media, some of whom were in Jerusalem on the day of Pentecost (Acts 2:9).

Melchizedek (mel-KIZ-uh-dek). King of Salem and priest of God who offered bread and wine as a sacrifice in thanksgiving for Abraham's victory (Gn 14:18–20). The Church sees therein the figure of the sacrifice of Jesus, "a priest forever according to the order of Melchizedek" (Ps 110:4; Heb 5:6, 10; 6:20; 7:11, 17).

Meribah (MER-i-buh). Hebrew word signifying "the (place of the) quarreling" that served to designate the same site as Massah (Ex 17:7).

Mesopotamia (mes-uh-puh-TAY-mee-uh). The area between the Tigris and the Euphrates rivers, some of whose inhabitants were in Jerusalem on the day of Pentecost (Acts 2:9). It is Iraq today.

Messiah (muh-SAI-uh). A Hebrew word signifying "one who has been anointed." The kings of Israel were

anointed in the name of God (1 Sm 9:16). The term Messiah later was used to designate a "future king" who would make all things new (Dn 9:25–26). This son of David, expected by the Jewish nation, was the Messiah par excellence (Mk 10:47–48), a term that has been rendered in Greek by Christos. This was a common name that ultimately became a title for Jesus the Savior (Rm 1:1).

Micah (MAI-kuh). Sixth of the 12 Minor Prophets of the Old Testament.

Midian (MID-ee-uhn). Son of Abraham by Keturah (Gn 25:1–6), whose descendants became a tribe of nomads and merchants called Midianites (Nm 31:1–12, 32–34).

Moriah (muh-RAI-uh). The place where Abraham was told to offer up Isaac (Gn 22:2).

Moses (MOH-zis). The leader and lawgiver of the Israelites, who successfully brought them out of Egypt (Ex 12:50) through the desert (Ex 19ff), to the shores of the Jordan. On Mount Sinai he received the law, which contained ethical teaching (Rom 5:12ff).

Mosoch (MOH-sok). An area believed to be in the vicinity of Armenia.

Mount of Olives (mount uhv OL-uhvz). A mountain with three summits east of Jerusalem. Gethsemane is on its lower slope. It is closely associated with the life of Jesus (Mk 11:1; 14:26). See also **Olivet**.

Myrrh (mir). An odorous resin (Mt 2:11).

Naaman (NAY-uh-muhn). A general of the king of Damascus who was healed of his leprosy by Elisha (2 Kgs 5).

Nahshon (NAH-shon). The son of Amminadab (1 Chr 2:10, 11) and ancestor of Jesus (Mt 1:4).

Nahum (NAY-huhm). Seventh of the 12 Minor Prophets of the Old Testament.

Name (naym). Identical with the person it designates. The name of God indicates God himself and all his perfections. "To act in the name" of someone means to participate in the reality (and its power) expressed by this name. A change of vocation often involved receiving a new name (e.g., Peter).

Naphtali (NAF-tuh-lee). One of Jacob's sons (Gn 46:24), who gave his name to one of the twelve tribes (Jos 19:32–39) that later formed part of Galilee.

Nathan (NAY-thuhn). (1) Son of David by Bathsheba (2 Sm 5:13) and an ancestor of Jesus (Lk 3:31). (2) A prophet who dissuaded David from building the temple and promised him a sure succession (2 Sm 7:1ff), and who rebuked him when he sinned (2 Sm 12:1ff).

Nazarene (NAZ-uh-reen). A word derived from Nazareth, the hometown of Christ. He was often called a Nazarene (Mt 2:23). Another form of the name is "Nazorean."

Nazareth (NAZ-uh-rith). A town in low Galilee, which is the hometown of Mary and Joseph, mother and foster father of Jesus (Lk 1:26; 2:4) and where Jesus spent his early life (Mt 2:23).

Nazirite (NAZ-uh-rait). One who is set apart for service of the LORD by a vow. Nazarites were not to cut their hair, nor drink wine, nor partake of any fruit of the vine.

Nazorean (naz-uh-REE-uhn). An alternate form of "Nazarene" (Mt 2:23).

Nehemiah (nee-huh-MAI-uh). Cupbearer of the Persian King Cyrus, who helped to reestablish the Jewish commonwealth after the Babylonian Exile and is the main character of the eighth of the 13 Historical Books of the Old Testament.

Neighbor (NAY-buhr). Jesus declares that one's neighbor is every person, even one belonging to a hostile group (Lk 10:29–37).

Ner (nuhr). The father of Abner, the commander of the army of King Saul of Israel (1 Sm 26:5).

Netherworld (NETH-uhr-wuhrld). The ancient concept of the abode of the dead (in Hebrew: "sheol"), which supposed no activity or lofty emotion among the deceased, who were pictured as surrounded by the darkness of oblivion (Ps 16:10).

Nicanor (nai-KAY-nuhr). One of the seven deacons of the Church at Jerusalem (Acts 6:5).

Nicholas (NIK-uh-luhs). A convert to Judaism from Antioch who became one of the seven deacons of the Church at Jerusalem (Acts 6:5).

Nicodemus (nik-uh-DEE-muhs). Greek name borne by an influential member of the Sanhedrin, who came to Jesus by night and later interceded for him when the plot was hatched that ended in his death (Jn 3:1–10; 7:50f).

Nineveh (NIN-uh-vuh). The later capital of Assyria, the great city on the Upper Tigris, whose inhabitants repented at the preaching of the Prophet Jonah (Jon 3:1ff).

Noah (NOH-uh). Patriarch who with his family was saved in the Ark from the Flood (Gn 6ff).

Nun (nuhn). Father of Joshua (Nm 11:28).

Obadiah (oh-buh-DAI-uh). Fourth of the 12 Minor Prophets of the Old Testament.

Obed (OH-bid). Son of Boaz and Ruth (Ru 4:17) and an ancestor of Jesus (Mt 1:5f).

Olivet (OL-i-vet). Alternative name for the Mount of Olives (Acts 1:12).

Omega (oh-MEG-uh). Last letter of the Greek alphabet. Used with "Alpha," it means the first and the last (Rv 1:8).

Ophir (OH-fuhr). A region on the coast of southern Arabia or eastern Africa—famous for its gold (Ps 45:10).

Pamphylia (pam-FIL-ee-uh). A small Roman province of southern Asia extending 75 miles along the Mediterranean coast and 30 miles inland to the Taurus mountains, some of whose inhabitants were in Jerusalem on the day of Pentecost (Acts 2:10).

Paraclete (PAR-uh-kleet). A word used in the Gospel of John for the Holy Spirit. It could be translated as "comforter," "consoler," "advocate," etc. The paraclete will reveal that which the disciples could not understand (Jn 14:26; 16:13). He is the Spirit of Truth (Jn 14:16).

Parapet (PAR-uh-pet). The railing that one was to build on the edge of all roofs in Israel.

Parmenas (PAHR-muh-nuhs). One of the seven deacons of the Church at Jerusalem (Acts 6:5).

Parthians (PAHR-thee-uhnz). Inhabitants of the Parthian Empire to the east, known today as Iran, some of whom were in Jerusalem on the day of Pentecost (Acts 2:9).

Paschal (PAS-kuhl). An adjective referring to the Passover of the Old Testament and the Passover of the New (i.e., Easter).

Passover (PAS-oh-vuhr). Feast instituted to commemorate the departure from Egypt with the "passing over" of the angel of death and the crossing of the Red Sea (Dt 16:1–8). At this observance (Last Supper) Jesus instituted the Eucharist (Mt 26:26ff).

Patriarchs (PAY-tree-ahrks). Name given to those who founded the Hebrew race and nation. The New Testament applies it to Abraham (Heb 7:4), the sons of Jacob (Acts 7:8, 9), and David (Acts 2:29).

Pentateuch (PENT-uh-took). The first five Books of the Old Testament.

Pentecost (PEN-ti-kost). The Jewish feast, fifty days after Passover, that recalled the giving of the law and offered in thanks the firstfruits of the wheat harvest (Lv 23:15–22). At Pentecost the Holy Spirit came upon the apostles and the others gathered in the Upper Room (Acts 2:1ff), marking the birthday of the Church and inaugurating the Christian feast of Pentecost.

People of God (PEE-puhl uhv god). Term by which Israel is designated throughout the Bible. In its turn, Christianity is also called the People God claims for his own, but it rejects any kind of national particularism (1 Pt 2:9).

Perez (PEE-riz). Son of Judah by Tamar (Gn 28:29) and an ancestor of Jesus (Mt 1:3).

Perga (PURH-guh). A city in Pamphylia (Asia Minor). It was visited by Paul and Barnabas (Acts 13:13f).

Persians (PUHR-zhuhnz). Originally, a Median tribe that settled in Persia, east of the Persian Gulf, whose members are mentioned in 2 Chr 36:20. Scripture also mentions Cyrus the Great who released the captive Jews (Ezr 1:1); Darius, who confirmed the decree of Cyrus (Ezr 6:1), and Artaxerxes (Ezr 4:7; 7:1).

Peter (PEE-tuhr). One of the twelve apostles (Mt 10:2) and author of two of the seven Catholic Letters of the New Testament. His name was Simon, but he was surnamed Cephas (Jn 1:42) or its Greek equivalent Peter. He was made the first head of the Church (later called pope) by Jesus (Mt 16:16ff).

Phanuel (fuh-NYOO-uhl). Father of Anna (Lk 2:36).

Pharaoh (FAR-oh). Title of Egyptian rulers.

Pharisees (FAR-uh-seez). Jewish sect that sought the perfect expression of spiritual life through strict observance of the law and tradition alone. Some of its members were greatly at odds with Jesus (Jn 9:16, 22).

Philemon (fi-LEE-muhn). One of Paul's Letters of the New Testament.

Philip (FIL-ip). Name borne by the apostle from Bethsaida (Jn 1:43f), the deacon (Acts 6:5), the tetrarch, son of Herod the Great and Cleopatra (Lk 3:1), and Herod Philip, son of Herod the Great and Mariamme (Mt 14:3).

Philippi (fi-LIP-ai). City of Macedonia, named after Philip, father of Alexander the Great. It was evangelized by Paul (Acts 16:12ff).

Philippians (Fi-LIP-ee-uhnz). Inhabitants of Philippi to whom Paul wrote one of the Letters of the New Testament.

Phrygia (FRIJ-ee-uh). A province in southwest Asia Minor, where Paul preached on his 2nd and 3rd missionary journeys (Acts 16:6; 18:23), some of whose inhabitants were in Jerusalem on the day of Pentecost (Acts 2:10).

Pilate (PAI-luht). The fifth procurator or governmental representative of Rome in Palestine 26–36 A.D., who condemned Jesus to death (Jn 19:16).

Pisidia (pi-SID-ee-uh). One of the small Roman provinces in southern Asia Minor north of Pamphylia, visited by Paul on his 1st and 2nd missionary journeys (Acts 13:14–50; 14:21–24).

Pontius (PON-shuhs). First name of Pilate (Lk 3:1).

Pontus (PON-tuhs). A large province of northern Asia Minor located along the Black Sea, some of whose inhabitants were in Jerusalem on the day of Pentecost (Acts 2:9).

Poor (poor). Originally, a word with a purely economic and social meaning. Gradually, it took on the meaning of humble, modest, small, the little people often oppressed by the rich and powerful but who remained faithful to God (Am 2:6f). It was in this sense that Jesus said: "Blessed are you who are poor" (Lk 6:20).

Praetorium (pri-TAWR-ee-uhm). The residence of a Roman praetor, or his military headquarters, where he had his guard and held court. The procurators of Judea in the time of Christ had their praetorium at Caesarea, in the palace of Herod the Great (Acts 23:35). Tradition makes the fortress called Antonia the praetorium where Christ was tried (Mk 15:16).

Prochorus (PROK-uh-ruhs). One of the first seven deacons of the Church at Jerusalem (Acts 6:5).

Prophets (PROF-its). Men chosen by God to speak in his name. They were the teachers and guardians of the religion of Israel, at times advisers to kings, defenders of the poor and oppressed, and heralds of the future Messiah and his kingdom.

Proverbs (PROV-uhrbs). Third of the 7 Wisdom Books of the Old Testament.

Psalms (sahmz). Second of the 7 Wisdom Books of the Old Testament.

Put (poot). A region most probably in Africa (Jer 46:9).

Qoheleth (koh-HEL-ith). The name of the author of the Book of Ecclesiastes. The name means "preacher," and this might be a symbolic name. His work is marked by cynicism and yet respect for the fact that the will of God is a mystery.

Quirinius (kwi-RIN-ee-uhs). Roman legate of Syria (Lk 2:2).

Rabbi (RAB-ai). A title for the teachers of the law. It means "my master" (Mt 23:7–11; Jn 1:38) and was often applied to Christ.

Rahab (RAY-hab). A non-Jewish woman who played a large role in the capture of Jericho (Jos 2:1) and became the mother of Boaz, great-grandmother of King David and ancestor of Jesus (Mt 1:5).

Ram (ram). An ancestor of David (Ru 4:19) and of Jesus (Mt 1:4).

Raqa (RAH-kah). An Aramaic word probably meaning "fool," "imbecile," or "blockhead"—a term of abuse (Mt 5:22).

Redemption (ree-DEMP-shuhn). Deliverance procured by payment of a ransom. It refers to the deliverance of the human race from sin, its effects and punishments, by Jesus Christ, who by shedding his blood on the cross paid the price of our salvation (Rom 3:24). It was prefigured by the deliverance of Israel from bondage in Egypt and Babylonia.

Rehoboam (ree-huh-BOH-uhm). Son and successor of King Solomon (1 Kgs 11:43) and ancestor of Jesus (Mt 1:7).

Remnant (REM-nuhnt). An expression used by the prophets designating the survivors of great catastrophes (Gn 7:1f; Is 6:13) who will remain the depositories of the promise (Mi 4:6f) and help in the restoration (Is 37:31f).

God reserves this Remnant for himself to help in the restoration (Isa 37:31). It is they who are and will remain the depositaries of the promise (Mi 4:6–7). In the New Testament, the Church is presented as fulfilling the function of the faithful Remnant and the "Israel according to the flesh" is contrasted with the "Israel of God" which is the Church (Rom 9:27; 1 Cor 10:18; Gal 6:16); and this interpretation follows the teaching of the Old Testament.

Resurrection (res-uhr-REK-shuhn). The resurrection of Jesus, which became the fundamental historical fact, the principal witness of his divinity (1 Cor 15:4, 12). It is also the divine judgment that has ordered the defeat of death and pledges salvation and resurrection to the faithful (Rom 4:25; Col 2:12ff).

Revelation (rev-uh-LAY-shuhn). The only apocalyptic book of the New Testament. It speaks about the need to give witness to one's faith while one awaits the end of time.

River (RIV-uhr). A term that standing alone refers to the Euphrates River, the longest and most important river in Western Asia (Ps 72:8; Zec 9:10).

Romans (ROH-muhnz). One of Paul's Letters of the New Testament.

Rome (rohm). Capital of the Roman Empire, which like Babylon became a symbol of organized paganism and opposition to Christianity. The city also had a small Christian community from the forties onward. Both Peter and Paul were martyred there.

Rufus (ROO-fuhs). Son of Simon of Cyrene and brother of Alexander, mentioned during the way of the cross (Mk 15:21).

Ruth (rooth). A Moabite woman who married an Israelite, was widowed, and returned to Jerusalem with her mother-in-law, and became the ancestor of David and Jesus (Mt 1:5). Also, the last of the three Books that follow the Pentateuch.

Sabbath (SAB-uhth). Seventh day of the week, consecrated to God, on which no work could be performed (Dt 5:12–15). Among Christians, the day after the sabbath gradually became the sabbath or first day in commemoration of the resurrection of Christ—hence "the Lord's day" (Jn 20:19ff; Acts 20:7).

Sadducees (SAD-joo-seez). A religious party of the Jews. They believed in God but rejected the oral traditions of their forefathers and denied the resurrection of human beings and the existence of angels. They opposed Jesus (Mt 22:23ff) and the apostolic Church (Acts 5:17).

Saints (saynts). A common Old Testament term to designate those who belong to God that was applied in the New Testament to those who believed in Christ. It occurs first in Acts 9:13 and is frequent in the writings of Paul.

Salem (SAY-luhm). The city ruled by Melchizedek (Gen 14:18), most probably a name for Jerusalem.

Salmon (SAL-muhn). Father of Boaz (called Salma in 1 Chr 2:11) and ancestor of Jesus (Mt 1:4).

Salome (suh-LOH-mee). One of the women present at the crucifixion of Jesus (Mt 15:40) and at the empty tomb (Mk 16:1).

Salvation (sal-VAY-shuhn). A term referring to the work of God on behalf of his people's deliverance (Ps 33:16f; Is 31:1; Hos 5:13—6:3) and then personal deliverance (Ps 51:14). In the New Tes-

tament it means the work of spiritual deliverance—remission from sin (Lk 17:19) and the liberation from the servitude that sin brings to human beings (Mt 1:21; Lk 1:77; Acts 5:31).

Samaria (suh-MAYR-ee-uh). Capital of the kingdom of Israel after the schism of the ten tribes that was destroyed in 721 B.C. by Sargon (2 Kgs 18:9–12). It was rebuilt by Herod the Great and called Sebaste and Philip preached the gospel there (Acts 8:5–9).

Samaritans (suh-MAYR-uh-tuhnz). Inhabitants of the central region of Palestine between Judea and Galilee who were a mixed race of Israelites and Assyrian colonists, and very hostile to the Jews at the time of Christ. Our Lord passed through their country more than once, and preached and worked miracles among the people. He also spoke well of them (Lk 10:30–37), defended them (Lk 9:51–56), and commanded that the gospel be preached to them.

Samuel (SAM-yoo-uhl). The greatest of the Judges (1 Sm 7:15) and a prophet (1 Sm 9:9) instrumental in instituting the monarchy (1 Sm 9ff). The first two of the 13 Historical Books of the Old Testament are named after him.

Sanhedrin (san-HEE-druhn). Civil and religious council of the Jews, composed of 71 members and presided over by the high priest.

Sapphires (SAf-airz). Precious stones (Is 54:11).

Sarah (SAR-uh). Wife of Abraham who conceived in old age and gave him a son (Isaac) in accord with God's promise (Heb 11:11). Her name was changed by God from Sarai to Sarah (Gn 17:15).

Sarai (SAIR-ai). *See* **Sarah.**

Saraph (SAR-uhf). *See* **Seraph.**

Satan (SAY-tuhn). God's great adversary who seeks to destroy human beings (Mt 13:19, 28). This devil or prince of demons is a spirit completely given up to evil. By dying on the cross Christ crushed his power (Rv 20:1ff).

Saul (sawl). First King of the Israelites around 1020–1000 B.C. (1 Sm 10:17ff). This is also the Hebrew/Aramaic form of the name of the man known as Paul (the Greco/Roman version), who became a great apostle of the Good News to the Gentiles (Acts 13:9).

Scribes (skraibz). Jews devoted to the study of the law (Mt 2:4; 17:10).

Scriptures (SKRIP-chuhrs). The inspired Books of the Old Testament, the work of the Holy Spirit, comprising the law, the prophets, and the writings (Foreword to the Book of Sirach). Christianity added its own writings: the gospels and letters of the New Testament (1 Tm 5:18; 2 Tm 3:16; 2 Pt 3:14–16).

Scythian (SITH-ee-uhn). A member of a nomadic people from central Asia.

Sea (see). A term that when standing alone refers to the Mediterranean Sea (Ps 80:12).

Sea of Galilee (see uhv GAL-uh-lee). A lake only 13 miles long and 8 miles wide, 60 miles north of Jerusalem, subject to sudden violent storms (Mt 8:24). Also called the Sea of Gennesaret (Lk 5:1) and the Sea of Tiberias (Jn 6:1).

Seba (SEE-buh). An unknown territory, possibly in Africa.

Seraph (SER-uhf). One of the choirs of angels who sing, "Holy, holy, holy" before the throne of God (Is 6). It is also a name for a poisonous serpent (Nm 21:8; Dt 8:15) but spelled "saraph" by the Lectionary text.

Servant (SUHR-vuhnt). An expression applied to the people of Israel within the framework of the covenant (Ex 7:16; Pss 69:37; 102:15) and the faithful in general (Ps 34:1). It became a Messianic title as the result of its use by Deutero-Isaiah in the so-called Servant of Yahweh Songs (Is 42:1–9; 49:1–13; 50:4–11; 52:13—53:12) and as such is applied to Jesus (Mt 12:18; Acts 3:13).

Shaphat (SHAY-fat). The father of Elisha the prophet (1 Kgs 19:16).

Sharon (SHAR-uhn). Coastal plain between Joppa and Mount Carmel, a plane proverbial for its fertility, pasture lands, and beauty (Is 35:2).

Shealtiel (shee-AL-tee-uhl). Father of Zerubbabel (Ezr 3:2) and an ancestor of Jesus (Mt 1:12).

Sheba (SHEE-buh). The Kingdom of the Sabeans in southern Arabia, whose people are pictured as traders in precious stones and incense (Is 60:6).

Shebna (SHEB-nuh). Majordomo of King Hezekiah (Is 22:15ff).

Shekel (SHEK-uhl). A measure of precious metal. Each vendor would measure a given shekel against one's own sample shekel.

Shema Israel (shuh-MAH iz-RAY-uhl; -REE; IZ-ruhl). Ancient Jewish confession of faith recited daily by the pious. It is composed of three passages: Dt 6:4–9; 11:12–21; and Nm 15:37–41. The name comes from *Shema Yisrael* ("Hear, O Israel": Dt 6:4), the words with which the confession begins.

Shiloh (SHAI-loh). A sanctuary town in Israel and a site where the ark of the covenant was kept (1 Sm 4).

Shinar (SHAIN-ahr). Plain of Babylonia in which were located Babel, Erech, Accad, and Calneh (Gn 10:10) and where the Tower of Babel was built (Gn 11:1–9).

Shunem (SHOO-nuhm). A place in a very rich section of Palestine (2 Kgs 4:8), north of Jezreel and belonging to the tribe of Issachar (Jos 19:18).

Sidon (SAI-duhn). Phoenician port north of Tyre, on the Mediterranean (Mt 15:21). These two pagan cities served the evangelists as symbols of a corrupt civilization (Lk 10:13–15).

Silas (SAI-luhs). *See* **Silvanus.**

Siloam (sai-LOH-ahm). Pool situated south of the city of Jerusalem to which Jesus adverted in a talk about workmen killed there (Lk 13:4).

Silvanus (sil-VAY-nuhs). Also known as Silas, a Jerusalem Christian sent with Paul to Antioch (Acts 15:22ff) who later accompanied him on his 2nd missionary journey (Acts 15:40) and was imprisoned with him in Philippi (Acts 16:19ff).

Simeon (SIM-ee-uhn). Name of three persons: (1) the old man who received the child Jesus in his arms at the temple (Lk 2:25–35); (2) an influential member of the Christian community at Antioch (Acts 13:1); (3) Peter the apostle, according to his Hebrew name (Acts 15:14). (He is also called Simon.)

Simon (SAI-muhn). Name of several persons, including: (1) the father of Judas Iscariot (Jn 13:2); (2) the prince of the apostles, later called Peter or Simon Peter (Jn 20:1–9); (3) a Pharisee who entertained Jesus (Lk 7:40) and in whose house a woman anointed Jesus' feet.

Sinai (SAI-nai). A peninsula south of the Wilderness of Paran between the Gulf of Aqabah and Suez. Also applied to a wilderness (Ex 19:1), where Israel came after they left Egypt and to the mountain (Ex 19:20) where God gave Moses the law.

Sirach (SAI-ruhk). Last of the seven Wisdom Books of the Old Testament, whose author is Jesus, the son of Sirach (Sir 50:27).

Sodom (SOD-uhm). One of the cities destroyed by God because of their immorality (Gn 19:1ff). It became a symbol for God's judgment upon the sinful.

Solomon (SOL-uh-muhn). Son and successor of David, who was a pious king (1 Kgs 3:5, 7–12) but eventually lost much of the empire David had built up (1 Kgs 11:14ff) and led to discontent in Israel (1 Kgs 11:26ff). Also, an ancestor of Jesus (Mt 1:6).

Solomon's Portico (SOL-uh-mouhnz POR-ti-koh). A protected area in the outer court of the temple (Jn 10:23).

Son of Man (son uhv man). A Messianic title found in the Prophet Daniel (7:13f) and used by Jesus. It expresses Christ's twofold destiny of suffering (Mk 8:31) and of glory (Mk 8:38).

Song of Songs (song uhv songs). Fifth of the 7 Wisdom Books of the Old Testament.

Sosthenes (SOS-thuh-nees). An associate of Paul in the First Letter to the Corinthians (1:1).

Stephen (STEE-vuhn). One of the seven deacons of the Church at Jerusalem (Acts 6:5) and the first martyr for Christ, who—like his Master—prayed for his executioners (Acts 7:60).

Sychar (SAI-kahr). Village of Samaria located near Jacob's well, where Jesus encountered the Samaritan woman (Jn 4:5).

Synagogue (SIN-uh-gog). A place where the Jews gathered on the sabbath to listen to the explanations of the Scriptures. Each locality had one in which Jesus prayed and studied (Lk 4:20).

Syria (SIR-ee-uh). The region between Asia Minor to the north and Palestine to the south, whose chief cities were Damascus and Antioch. A Roman province to which Palestine was subordinated (Lk 2:2).

Talitha Koum (TAHL-uh-thuh koom). An Aramaic phrase meaning "Little girl, I say to you, arise," recorded by Mark 5:41 in the episode of the raising of Jairus's daughter.

Tamar (TAY-mahr). Canaanite woman who bore Perez and Zerah to her father-in-law Judah and became an ancestor of Jesus (Mt 1:3).

Tarshish (TAHR-shish). Phoenician colony in southern Spain, whose name denotes a center of smelting metallic ore (1 Kgs 10:22; Ps 72:10).

Tarsus (TAHR-suhs). Birthplace and early residence of the apostle Paul (Acts 21:39; see also Acts 9:30). It was the capital of the Roman province of Cilicia, and located at the confluence of East and West.

Temple (TEM-puhl). House of worship that was built by Solomon, destroyed and then rebuilt after the Babylonian Exile, and finally destroyed in 70 A.D. by the Romans. The Body of Christ is the new temple built at his resurrection. The Church is the spiritual temple made up of living bricks who are the baptized Christians.

Terebinth (TER-uh-binth). A tree, possibly an oak. Trees, especially ancient trees, were highly visible in a desert area and served as landmarks and shrine sites.

Tetrarch (TE-trahrk). Originally, a ruler of the fourth of a country. In Roman times it was employed merely as a title for a ruler over part of a divided kingdom or a prince below the rank of a king (Mt 14:1).

Thaddeus (THAD-ee-uhs). One of the twelve apostles. In certain texts he is called Lebbaeus. He is identified with Judas (Jude), brother of James "the less" (Mt 10:3).

Theophilus (thee-OF-uh-luhs). The personage to whom Luke addressed both his gospel and the Acts of the Apostles (Lk 1:3; Acts 1:1).

Thessalonians (thes-uh-LOH-nee-uhnz). Two of Paul's earliest Letters written to the people of Thessalonica, capital of the province of Macedonia (Acts 17:1–9).

Thomas (TOM-uhs). One of the twelve apostles, surnamed in Greek Didymus, which means "twin" (Jn 11:16; 20:24).

Tiberius Caesar (tai-BIHR-ee-uhs SEE-zuhr). The successor of Augustus Caesar from 14 to 37 A.D. as emperor of the Roman Empire (Lk 3:1).

Timaeus (tai-MEE-uhs). Father of Bartimaeus (Mk 10:46).

Timon (TAI-muhn). One of the seven deacons of the Church at Jerusalem (Acts 6:5).

Timothy (TIM-uh-thee). Son of a Greek father and a Jewish mother, who was converted by Paul, and became one of his most devoted colleagues. Two of the Letters of the New Testament are addressed to Timothy.

Titus (TAI-tuhs). A Greek convert whom Paul calls his true child in the faith. One of the Letters of the New Testament is addressed to Titus.

Tobit (TOH-bit). Ninth of the 13 Historical Books of the Old Testament.

Trachonitis (trak-uh-NAI-tis). A territory to the east of the Jordan. The eastern portion of Bashan (Lk 3:1).

Tubal (TOO-buhl). This is the name of an individual (Gn 10:2; 1 Chr 1:5) and an area. It was probably a city on the Black Sea.

Twelve, The (twelv, thuh). Proper name used by the evangelists for the twelve apostles (Mt 26:14; Mk 14:10; Lk 22:47; Jn 20:24).

Tyre (TAI-uhr). Phoenician city located on the rocky isle facing the eastern coast of the Mediterranean Sea (Mt 11:21f).

Ur (oor). The ancestral city of Abraham. It is unclear whether it is the city of Ur in Babylon or a city in Turkey (Gn 11:28).

Uriah (yoo-RAI-uh). Bathsheba's husband, whose death David arranged (2 Sm 11:14ff). He is mentioned in the genealogy of Jesus (Mt 1:6).

Uzziah (uh-ZAI-uh). Son and successor of Amaziah as King of Judah (2 Kgs 14:21), and an ancestor of Jesus (Mt 1:8f).

Wadi (WAH-di). An often dry river bed (Gn 26:19). The Wadi of Egypt was one of the boundaries of the Davidic kingdom.

Water Gate (WAW-tuhr gayt). A gate restored by Nehemiah on the east of Jerusalem (Neh 8:1ff).

Wisdom (WIS-duhm). Sixth of the 7 Wisdom Books of the Old Testament.

Yahweh (YAH-weh). The proper personal name of the God of Israel, signifying "I am who I am" (Ex 3:14f). It is commonly explained in reference to God as the absolute and necessary Being. It may be understood of God as the Source of all created beings. Out of reverence for this name, the term Adonai, "my Lord," was later used as a substitute. The word LORD in the *New American Bible* version represents this traditional usage. The word "Jehovah" arose from a false reading of this name as it is written in the current Hebrew text.

Yahweh-yireh (YAH-weh-YIR-ee). A Hebrew expression meaning "The LORD will see," which Abraham used to name the site where God had stopped him from killing his son Isaac (Gn 22:14).

Zacchaeus (za-KEE-uhs). A tax collector who entertained Jesus (Lk 19:1ff).

Zadok (ZAY-dok). One of the chief priests during the reigns of David (2 Sm 8:17) and Solomon (1 Kgs 1:8, 32ff) and also an ancestor of Jesus (Mt 1:14).

Zarephath (ZAR-uh-fath). An Old Testament town remembered chiefly because Elijah resided there during the latter half of the famine caused by the drought (1 Kgs 17:9ff), which was specifically mentioned by Jesus (Lk 4:26).

Zealot (ZEL-uht). Member of a fanatical Jewish party, strongest from 6 to 70 A.D. It sought to overthrow the Roman authority and establish a Jewish theocracy over the earth. Its members resorted to violence and assassination

and provoked the Roman War, which ended with the destruction of Jerusalem in 70 A.D. It seems to have been headed by Judas of Galilee (Acts 5:37). One of Christ's disciples was a member of this party (Lk 6:15; Acts 1:13).

Zebedee (ZEB-uh-dee). Father of the apostles James "the less" and John (Mt 4:21).

Zebulun (ZEB-yuh-luhn). One of the twelve tribes of Israel springing from Zebulun, the son of Jacob and Leah (Gn 30:19f). Christ later carried on his ministry in its regions and thus fulfilled the ancient prophecy of Isaiah (Is 8:23ff; Mt 4:12–16).

Zechariah (zek-uh-RAI-uh). Name of many people, such as: (1) the son and successor of Jeroboam (2 Kgs 14:29); (2) husband of Elizabeth and father of John the Baptist (Lk 1:5ff); (3) the eleventh of the 12 Minor Prophets of the Old Testament.

Zedekiah (zed-uh-KAI-uh). Son of King Josiah, brother of King Jehoiakim, and uncle of King Jeroiachin, he was the last king of Judah (597–587 B.C.). After being warned by the prophet Jeremiah about the consequences of his policy (Jer 34:2ff), he was captured while fleeing from Jerusalem when it fell in 587 B.C. The Babylonians blinded him and carried him off into exile (2 Kgs 25:6ff).

Zephaniah (zef-uh-NAI-uh). Tenth of the 12 Minor Prophets in the Old Testament.

Zerah (ZIR-uh). Son of Judah, who is mentioned in the genealogy of Jesus (Mt 1:3).

Zerubbabel (zuh-RUHB-uh-buhl). Grandson of Jehoiachin (1 Chr 3:19), who returned from Babylon and became governor (Hg 1:1), and an ancestor of Jesus (Mt 1:12).

Zion (ZAI-uhn). Central part of the hill on which the temple of Jerusalem was built. This term is often used to designate Jerusalem as a holy city (Pss 2:6; 132:15; Zec 9:9), the Church of God (Heb 12:22), and the heavenly city (Rv 14:1).

Ziph (zif). A city of Judah, probably in the vicinity of Hebron where David spared Saul's life (1 Sm 26:2ff).

APPENDIX 4: INDEX OF BIBLICAL TEXTS

READINGS

420

RESPONSORIAL PSALMS

RESPONSORIAL CANTICLES

ALLELUIA VERSES AND VERSES BEFORE THE GOSPEL

NOTES AND REFLECTIONS

NOTES AND REFLECTIONS

NOTES AND REFLECTIONS

NOTES AND REFLECTIONS

NOTES AND REFLECTIONS

NOTES AND REFLECTIONS

NOTES AND REFLECTIONS

NOTES AND REFLECTIONS

NOTES AND REFLECTIONS